The Complete Works of
Kālidāsa

The Complete Works of
Kālidāsa

In three volumes

VOLUME 1

Translated
from the original Sanskrit and Prakrit
with an introduction by

CHANDRA RAJAN

SAHITYA AKADEMI

The Complete Works of Kālidāsa Vol. I : Translation in English by Chandra Rajan, Sahitya Akademi, New Delhi (1997) Rs. 350.

First published 1997

Sahitya Akademi
Rabindra Bhavan
35, Ferozeshah Road
New Delhi 110001

Sales Section
Swati, Mandir Marg
New Delhi 110001

Regional Offices
Jeevan Tara Building, 4th Floor
23A/44X, Diamond Harbour Road
Calcutta 700054

172, Mumbai Marathi Grantha Sangrahalaya Marg
Dadar, Bombay 400014

ADA Rangamandira, 109 J.C. Road
Bangalore 560002

Madras Office
Guna Building, Nos. 304-305
Anna Salai, Teynampet
Chennai 600018

ISBN 81-7201-824-X

Rupees : Three Hundred Fifty

Typeset at Vikas Print Communication Services, 3/56 West Punjabi Bagh, New Delhi 110026

Printed by : Nagri Printers, Delhi-110 032.

Contents

VOLUME 1

The Poems

Acknowledgements ix

Abbreviations xi

Key to the Pronunciation of Sanskrit Words xii

Key to Prose Passages in the Translations of the Plays xiii

Foreword—A Note on Texts and Translations xv

General Introduction 1

Poems:

Ṛtusaṃhāram 75

Kumārasaṃbhavam 107

Meghadūtam 291

Notes and References 323

Appendices I Kālidāsa's Dates 363

II Myths 371

III Interpolated stanzas in *Meghadūtam* 379

A Select Bibliography 383

Map 385

Afterword 387

Om Namaḥ Śivāya

(Homage to Śivam, The Good, The Beneficent)

yakṣasvarūpāya jaṭādharāya
pinākahastāya sanātanāya /
divyāya devāya digambarāya tasmai
yakārāya namaḥ śivāya //

[Śaṅkara: *Śivapañcākṣarastotra* (5)]

To That, assuming Form to be adored;
Wearing the *yogi's* topknot
—thick, twisted, matted hair—
Holding the Trident that is Time;
To the Everlasting;
To that wondrous Effulgence
Mantled in Space;
In-forming that mystic syllable—*ya*
To Śivam, The Good, The Beneficent,
Homage!

Acknowledgements

I first wish to thank my husband, Professor Balachandra Rajan, and my daughter, Professor Tilottama Rajan, for the unfailing support and encouragement they have given me in my work. In spite of their teaching and other academic responsibilities and the demands of their own writing, they have both found time to read large portions of the translations in this book. They have given generously also of their time, listening to me talk interminably about Kālidāsa and Sanskrit literature in general—a far cry from their own fields of specialization and interests—offered comments and suggested the possibility of other perspectives. I am indebted to them in a deeper though less tangible way—for the wide-ranging discussions we have had over the years on Literature, Aesthetics, and Art in general. For all of this I am grateful.

I wish to thank the staff of the Inter-library loan section of the Weldon Library, University of Western Ontario for the promptness and efficiency with which they procured out of print texts or xeroxes of these for me.

I wish to express my appreciation of the interest shown by Professor Indranath Choudhuri, Secretary of the Sahitya Akademi, who approached me to make a translation into English verse and prose of all the works of Kālidāsa from the original Sanskrit and Prakrit.

I wish to thank M. Vijayalakshmi, Librarian, Sahitya Akademi Library for her help in procuring xeroxes of texts not available in the Akademi library. She knows her way around her library, locates any book required and hands it with a smile.

I also wish to thank Sri Jithendra Nath of the Sahitya Akademi for the care with which he has prepared this manuscript for printing.

Finally I wish to take this opportunity to remember with affection and respect two persons who are no more. Firstly, my grandfather, Dr P.S. Chandrasekhara Iyer, an eminent physician but more importantly a fine scholar of Sanskrit, who early inculcated a deep love in me for Sanskrit and its great literature and who opened the doors of its rich treasure-house of myth and legend to me in my childhood. Secondly, my first teacher of Sanskrit, Sri Ramasetu Sastrigal, who led me, an ignorant nine-year-old, into the Kālidāsan world, pointing out its varied beauties and laying out the subtleties of the poet's language when we first started our exploration of this fascinating world with the invocation to Śiva-Śakti that opens Kālidāsa's great epic, *Raghuvaṃśam*:

May the Parents of the Universe
Pārvatī and the Supreme Lord
eternally con-joined as Word and Meaning
grant fittest utterance to my thoughts.

New Delhi CHANDRA RAJAN
Asadha Purnima,
12 July 1995 Vikrama 2052

Abbreviations

AUS	Allahabad University Studies
AV	*Atharvaveda*
BM	Bharata Mallika—seventeenth century commentator on *Meghadūtam* (The Cloud Messenger)
BNM	*Bharata-Nāṭya-Mañjarī*
BORI	Bhandarkar Oriental Research Institute, Poona
comm.	commentary
IP	Indian Philosophy
JUB	Journal of the University of Bombay
KS	Kashi Series, Chowkhamba Press, of the *Nāṭyaśāstra*
Kumāra	Kumārasaṃbhavam
Mal.	Mālavikāgnimitram
Mbh.	Mahābhārata
Megh.	Meghadūtam
MNG	*Nāṭyaśāstra*, ed. with tr. by M.N. Ghosh
NS	*Nāṭyaśāstra*
R	Raghuvaṃśam
Ram.	*Rāmāyaṇa*
Ṛtu.	*Ṛtusaṃhāram*
RV	*Ṛgveda*
Śak.	*Abhijñānaśākuntalam; Śakuntalā* for short
ŚB	*Śatapatha Brāhmaṇa*
Skt.	*Sanskrit*
St.	Stanza
v.	Verse
Urvaśī	*Vikramorvaśīyam*

KEY TO THE PRONUNCIATION OF SANSKRIT WORDS

Vowels: The line on top of a vowel indicates that it is long.
a (short) as the u in but
a (long) as the a in far
i (short) as the i in sit
i (long) as the ee in sweet
u (short) as the u in put
u (long) as the oo in cool
ṛ with a dot is a vowel like the i in first or u in further
e is always a long vowel like a in mate
ai as the i in pile
o is always long as the o in pole
ow as the ow in owl

The *visarga*, two vertically lined points ':' is transliterated into roman as an 'ḥ' and sounded like the 'ḥ' in 'loch'; e.g. pramattaḥ, bhartuḥ, Duḥṣanta.

Also note the final 'i' in feminine nouns are long in the nominative case but short in the vocative case; e.g. Vetravatī and Vetravati (when she is addressed by name).

Consonants: k is the same as in English as in kitten
kh is aspirated
g as in goat
gh is aspirated
c is ch as in church or cello
ch is aspirated
j as in jewel
jh is aspirated
ṭ and ḍ are hard when dotted below as in talk and dot
ṭṭ is the aspirated sound
ḍḍ is aspirated
ṇ when dotted is a dental; the tongue has to curl back to touch the palate.
t undotted is a th as in thermal
th is aspirated
d undotted is a soft sound—there is no corresponding English

sound, the Russian 'da' is the closest.
dh is aspirated
p and b are the same as in English
ph and bh are aspirated
The Sanskrit v is an English w

There are 3 sibilants in Sanskrit: S as in song, Ṣ dotted below as in shower and a palatal Ś which is in between, e.g. Śiva.

KEY TO PROSE PASSAGES IN THE PLAY

Lines of prose in the play are referred to using points and plus and minus signs; e.g. 1.20. + 16–18 refers to lines 16-18 after st. 20 in Act 1; 3.36, –2, 3 refers to lines 2 and 3 before st. 36 in Act 3.

Foreword: A Note on Texts and Translations

Kālidāsa's works have unfortunately come down to us not in their original form but in several recensions (divergent versions of a text) current in different regions of the country. The ancestry of the recensions is not clear. But it is evident that after his lifetime, Kālidāsa's poems and plays became subject to alterations, the reasons for which are again not clear. It is not uncommon for this to happen in the history of Sanskrit literature. Many factors would have contributed to the process of the one true text becoming many diverse recensions. The manuscripts of the works, none of them contemporaneous with the author, belong to one or other of the recensions. They display a bewildering variety of readings; the length of the texts themselves as well as the number and order of the verses in them vary; interpolations present a problem. Some of the variants are substantive enough to warrant a somewhat different reading of the text, as in the case of *Abhijñānaśākuntalam* (*Śakuntalā* for short).

The translations in these volumes differ in their textual basis from the great majority of other translations. The texts of both *Meghadūtam* and *Abhijñānaśākuntalam* follow the Eastern Indian (Bengal) recensions to which insufficient attention has been given. Even though the Bengal version is not the one translators most frequently use, the bibliographical arguments for it, and for *Śakuntalā* in particular, are not unequal to those for other texts and, as I shall endeavour to show, there are strong, aesthetic arguments for it. These arguments are rehearsed in the introduction to *The Plays* Volume 2.

I have based my translation of *Kumārasaṃbhavam* on the Nirnaya Sagar edition of the complete poem with Mallinātha's commentary on cantos 1-7, and Sitarama's commentary on cantos 8–17. This edition includes Mallinātha's commentary on canto 8, but places it at the end as a sort of appendix. I have looked carefully at Dr Suryakanta's edition of the complete poem for the Sahitya Akademi and used a few of the variant reading readings that he has listed, mostly those established by Bharata Mallika. It is my great regret that the *Kumārasaṃbhavam* according to Bharata Mallika has not been edited and published, because he is a very sensitive critic and commentator and his comments on a phrase or an image are so often extremely enlightening.

The translation of *Meghadūtam* in this volume is based on the text of the poem on which the early seventeenth-century Bengal scholiast, Bharata Mallika wrote his highly informative and sensitive commentary, Subodhā. I have used the critical edition of this text with commentary, produced by J.B. Chaudhuri. The differences between this critical edition and the critical edition produced by S.K. De for the National Academy of Letters (Sahitya Akademi, New Delhi) are few and minor. The text of the poem established by Mallinātha, the fourteenth-century scholiast from South India, contains a longer version. This text has had wide acceptance and is the one frequently translated. The verses in Mallinātha's text which have not been accepted as genuine by Bharata Mallika (or by De) are placed in Appendix III.

I have used the Nirnaya Sagar Press edition of *Rtusaṃhāram* with Maṇirāma's commentary—a rather perfunctory commentary.

We now come to the matter of translation and the translation of Kālidāsa's texts specifically. Translation is like serving two masters at the same time. Languages do differ widely in their grammatical and syntactical structures and though one hopes to meet the demands of the source and receiving languages in a balanced manner, it is a fact that compromises have to be made one way or the other. We endeavour to provide the best approximation to the original not only within the limitations set by our own abilities but more so within those set by the receiving language.

Sanskrit is a highly inflected language; and it has some distinctive features which indeed constitute some of its strengths; for example, the extensive use of compound words and prefixes, and an array of synonyms with slight nuances of meaning that colour the expression of what is being said. The inflexional structure and the use of compound words give the language a tightly knit compactness which is of importance in poetry; this compactness suffers some dilution in translation. Because Sanskrit is a highly inflected language, word order is not of special importance as it is in English; punctuation is minimal consisting of a vertical stroke (/) to mark the end of the second quarter of a stanza and two vertical strokes (//) that correspond to the period in English. Inversions are frequent, with the predicate often separated from subject and object by long clauses consisting of single compound words, with their sub-units linked alliteratively, not only for euphonic but other poetic effects as well. This lends the language a musical quality difficult to convey in another language. This is especially true in the case of poetry which was and still is chanted or sung and not read silently.

Compound words are also able to project images with immediacy: for example the word, *paruṣapavanavegotkṣiptasaṃśuṣkaparṇāḥ* (Ṛtu.: 1.22) conveys strongly the picture of wild winds and their force and energy: by splitting the compound word into its sub-units we have the following:

paruṣa-pavana-vega-utkṣipta-saṃ-śuṣka-parṇāḥ

violent-winds-by great velocity-hurling-up-shrivelled-leaves

Compound words can also articulate ambivalences (see notes on Megh.).

Puns, proverbs and certain kinds of wordplay especially those dependent on sonic resemblances or identity are almost untranslatable; for example, the phrase *dhanuṣkhaṇḍam ākhaṇḍalasya*, the literal meaning of which is—a fragment of the bow wielded by the fragmentor (breaker)—we need notes to make the point clear. However, this is a difficulty present in all translation; for example, in the following line from Keats: 'Thou *still* unravished bride of quietness', something is bound to get left out in translating it into an Indian language; specifically, one would be hard put to find a single word to convey both senses of the word 'still'.

Kālidāsa's poetry like much of Indian art is stylized. The stylization is not a rhetorical procedure but part of the self-awareness with which the verse shapes itself. The translation therefore, to be faithful, has to somehow contrive to be stylized and readable; to steer clear of a literalness of rendering as well as an identification of readability with contemporaneity. It has been my endeavour throughout this volume of translations to be faithful not simply to what the poetry says (its paraphraseable meaning) but also to how it says what it says. That would be to respect its way of perceiving itself to create artifacts of the imagination. To accomplish this with some degree of success, inversions are unavoidable at places, and also the occasional passive construction which is frequent in Sanskrit. I have used these sparingly.

The translation of the prose in the plays poses its own brand of problems. Kālidāsa uses several dialects (prakrits) current in his day. It is not possible to differentiate between them by style or through diction. Therefore, there is an unavoidable ironing out of the rich variety of speech of that age into one flat prose.

But I have attempted some slight differentiation in another area. There are several levels of speech in the play, depending on the occasion, private or public, and on the relationships of the speakers to one another; and here some differentiation is possible which I have endeavoured to make.

Nature has a life of its own in Indian thought; it enshrines centres of power, radiating holiness, plenitude, beauty. For this reason, I have refrained from using the neuter form of the English pronoun. A hill is therefore a 'he' and a stream is a radiant 'she'.

I have translated only a few of the names of the flora in the Kālidāsan landscape. While there are several kinds of lotuses mentioned, each with its own distinctive name in the original and each beautifully evocative, I have reluctantly used the generic term 'lotus'. I have however retained the Sanskrit names for many other flowers, trees, shrubs and vines mentioned or described, for two reasons. Firstly, English equivalents are not readily available (except botanical terms) and identifications are not always definitive. Secondly the Sanskrit names form part of the poetic effect in certain passages; they frequently sound like the roll call of epic heroes and their weapons.

> Beauty, Genius of Blossom-Time, forsaking
> the *kadamba*, *kuṭaja*, and *kakubha*,
> The *sarja* and the *arjuna*,
> now dwells with the *saptaparṇa*. (Ṛtu: 3.3)

Here, the poet seems to be having some fun at the expense of the epic poets.

On the other hand, I have translated nearly all of the epithets of Indra in *Meghadūtam* as well as those given to Śiva and Pārvatī in *Kumārasaṃbhavam* because the meaning of a particular epithet chosen by the poet has a specific significance in the context. In *Meghadūtam*, I have translated for instance *Śūlapāṇi, Caṇḍeśvara*, (34–6) and *Tryambaka* (60) because they are epithets resonant with mythic and metaphysical meaning in the context.

In *Kumārasaṃbhavam,* Kālidāsa employs several names/epithets for three of the four main characters in the poem: Śiva, Kāma, Himālaya. I have used the specific names for them in the text wherever I felt that there could be a loss of meaning if they were not used. For instance, I have retained *Smara* and translated the epithet as Remembrance or The Lord of Memories. Similarly for Śiva, I have retained or translated the names that the poet employs, such as *Rudra, Pinākī* (The Trident-Armed Lord, or Wielder of the Trident). This is done in order to alert the reader to the rich suggestiveness in Kālidāsa's use of proper names available to him; to make available to the reader the mythic and metaphysical allusions that surround the simple word with an aura of meaning; and to provide the reader with those rich resonances to words similar to the resonances that overtones lend to musical notes when struck or sounded just right. At other places where a name or epithet is not performing a special function, I have used the terms Śiva and Kāma which are most familiar to most readers.

At places I have included an elucidatory word or phrase to avoid an excess of annotation; for instance, I include the word moon, to the translation of *oṣadhīnām adhipasya* (7:1), of the Lord of Plants.

The translations are accompanied by a long introduction, notes and appendices. The introduction suggests ways of looking at the three works in this volume singly and as a group. These are however not exhaustive for want of space. Still, an attempt has been made within a brief compass to relate these works in a meaningful way and trace a pattern of development in the poet's *oeuvre*. The myths that lend an added depth and resonance to a work, especially *Meghadūtam*, are briefly recounted in Appendix II. An in-depth analysis of a verse from *Ṛtusaṃhāram* which is the earliest of Kālidāsa's works, has been included as part of the notes to show how the poet's multilayered imagery functions as an integral part of the structure (note 7).

The notes should be of some help in bridging gaps in communication by explaining the numerous mythological and metaphysical allusions in the poems and the play. They also point to the possibility of multiple readings of a line or passage; in most cases a translation can convey only one of the possible readings.

Because Kālidāsa's works emerge out of a philosophical context (as all great works of art do) and return us to it, some information about religious and metaphysical concepts both Vedic and Śaiva, is unavoidable. It has been kept to a minimum.

The presence of all this background information in no way implies that Kālidāsa cannot be read with pleasure and delight without this explanatory apparatus. The response to great poetry (and poetic drama) is the immediate response to it as poetry. While it is true that the Indian and the European intellectual traditions are different, emerging as they do, each from its own world view and intimately interwoven with it, the two worlds of these traditions ought not to be treated as totally opaque to each other. If an educated Indian is able to read and enjoy the Greek tragedies and Tolstoy in English translations, which is the only way for most of us who have neither Greek nor Russian, we can safely assume that English readers (both within the culture and outside it) who have no Sanskrit can appreciate and enjoy Vyāsa, Vālmīki and Kālidāsa, through translations of their works into English. With numerous hurdles to negotiate in the course of translation, it is a matter of satisfaction that translations can 'carry over' much of the power and beauty of the original. The notes and annotations are simply a means to enable the reader to explore the depths and reaches of Kālidāsa's art and taste its full flavour—*Rasa*.

The translations of the two long poems *Ṛtusaṃhāram* and *Meghadūtam* in this volume first appeared in *Kālidāsa* : *The Loom of Time* by Chandra Rajan (Penguin Classics 1989). They have been revised. The general introduction also appeared in this same book, but it has been revised and expanded.

Kumārasaṃbhavam in this volume has been translated in its entirety, all 17 cantos into English verse.

Introduction

I give power and knowledge to him I love:
I invest him with Holy Power:
I make his a sage, a seer.

(*Ṛgveda* 10:125:5)[1]

I

Kālidāsa's status as the major poet and dramatist in classical Sanskrit literature is unquestioned.

Once, when poets were counted, Kālidāsa occupied the little finger; the ring finger remains unnamed true to its name; for his second has not been found.[2]

That is high praise. Kālidāsa's accomplishment is distinguished not only by the excellence of the individual works, but by the many-sided talent which the whole achievement displays. He is a dramatist, a writer of epic and a lyric poet of extraordinary scope. In his hands the language attained a remarkable flexibility, becoming an instrument capable of sounding many moods and nuances of feeling; a language limpid and flowing, musical, uncluttered by the verbal virtuosities indulged in by many writers who followed him; yet, remaining a language loaded in every rift with the rich ores of the literary and mythical allusiveness of his cultural heritage. By welding different elements to create new genres, his importance as an innovator in the history of Sanskrit literature is clearly established. The brilliant medieval lyric poet, Jayadeva, in praising Kālidāsa as *Kavi-kula-guru* (Master of poets), conveys his recognition of this aspect of the poet's greatness. Bāṇa, the celebrated author of the prose-romance, *Kādambarī*, exclaimed,

Who is not delighted when Kālidāsa's perfect verses spring forth in their sweetness, like honey-filled clusters of flowers?

Thus drawing attention to the exquisite craftsmanship of the poet's verse. For nearly two millennia, Kālidāsa's works have been read with deep appreciation, widely commented upon and lavishly praised. It would be safe to assume that the poet enjoyed success, fame and affluence during his lifetime. We sense no hint of dissatisfaction in his works, no sign of bitterness at not receiving his due recognition. Yet, we do not possess any information about him, his life and the time in which that life unfolded and fulfilled itself. All we are left with are a few legends. The poet has drawn a veil of silence round himself so complete that even his real name is unknown to posterity.

No name is affixed to the poems and the epic; they have come down to us virtually anonymous. What information we possess is derived from references to them by later poets[3] and writers,[4] by the commentaries written on them and from inscriptions.[5] The name is met with only in the plays, where in each prologue, the author styles himself as Kālidāsa. Like others in Sanskrit literature, this name is descriptive: Vyāsa meaning 'the compiler' is the author of the *Mahābhārata*; Vālmīki, 'he who emerged from the anthill (*valmīka*), of the *Rāmāyaṇa*; similarly *Kālidāsa* means the votary or servant of Kālī. *Kālī* is time in the feminine (*kāla* is time); the concept of Time as a creative principle is as old as the Vedas.[6] We can then translate the name Kālidāsa into 'the servant of Time': an intriguing idea.

Kāla and Mahākāla are among the many names given to Śiva, the Absolute; the many names given to godhead are descriptive of its different aspects and functions as seen in the world of phenomena and apprehended by the human consciousness. Formless, Eternal, One, Śiva is pure consciousness, the changeless reality behind the manifold, changing world that is brought into being by his inherent power of *śakti*—cosmic energy. Kālī is one of the many names of Śakti; the names descriptive of the creative power are the feminine forms of the words pertaining to the many aspects and functions of the unitive godhead: Śivānī, Bhavānī, Kālī, Mahākālī derived from Śiva, Bhava, Kāla and Mahākāla define the feminine, creative aspect of the One. In iconography this concept is imaged as *ardhanārīśvara*—the Lord whose one half is woman. Śiva and Śakti are therefore one indivisible Whole.

The natural consequence of the poet's reticence is, that a number of legends have gathered round his name. One of them presents him as a simple, unlettered Brahmin youth of uncommon beauty and grace of manner, who was orphaned at six months and brought up by the driver of an ox-cart. Through devout prayer and worship of the goddess Kālī, he obtained profound learning and the gift of poetry and is said to have assumed the name of Kālidāsa—'the servant of time' or 'the servant of creative power'.

Legends surround the name and fame of many ancient writers. A popular legend speaks of the transformation of the author of the *Rāmāyaṇa* from a cruel highway robber to a great and holy sage. It is said that repenting of his misdeeds, the robber performed severe austerities over a period of time so long that his body was buried in an anthill that formed round it. Emerging from it finally enlightened, he assumed the name Vālmīki. The description of an ascetic in Mārīca's hermitage seems to contain an allusion to this legendary happening (*Śak.*: 7:11). Rather than being dismissed summarily as apocryphal, such legends are better read as metaphors for the divine inspiration that is seen to lie behind poetic composition and as underlining that powerful vision and extraordinary felicity of expression that some poets possess more than others. They are perceived as being born again touched by the divine fire: the new name is assumed to indicate this and identifies their initiation into their calling. The legends surround them with an aura of the miraculous, setting them apart as vehicles of the Holy Power of the creative word, *vāc*.

Some Sanskritists in fixing the poet's dates have theorized that his works contain veiled references to his patron, King Vikramāditya of Ujjayinī with whom Indian tradition associates the poet, and base their identifications of the king accordingly. If this were the case, it would be reasonable to assume that the poet may well have left a few clues about himself, his family and birthplace in his works that we could all then set out happily to discover. But he has not. All this points to something of significance; that it was the poet's deliberate decision to strip his texts of all biographical detail, veiled or otherwise. In its turn, this decision must be seen as indicative of Kālidāsa's attitude to his writing. It suggests that he did not choose to situate it in his individual personality and relate it definitively to his own life and times, but, projected himself as a medium, as a voice. The poet has effaced the authority of his own voice from his texts. It is open to the reader to see this self-effacement from a metaphysical point of view as a transference of authority to a voice beyond Time, to 'the voice of silence'[7] that shaped the universe; or to perceive the texts as situated within time and responsive to cultural shifts in the course of time but not fixed in any specific context. The name Kālidāsa would relate equally to both meanings of the word *Kālī* in the name: creative power and Time.

To look at the first of the possibilities: *vāc*,[8] the *śakti* or inherent power of the Supreme Spirit in the Vedas, speaks through the poet who has constituted himself as her medium. And in doing so, Kālidāsa places himself in the ancient tradition of the vedic poet-seers who saw themselves as speaking the word and uttering the Truth. Looking deep within, into the depths of their consciousness,[9] they saw the light that never was on sea or land and expressed the vision they discovered there 'for all ages to come'.[10] The word reveals the unseen through the seen,[11] using the language of metaphor and links the transcendent with the transient. The poet, *kavi* (from which the word *kāvya* for poetry is derived), establishes communion between the two worlds, between men and gods.[12]

The second possibility is particularly useful in the interpretation of Kālidāsa's plays by enabling the reader to adopt readings other than or in addition to the strictly historical one that places them in the framework of the poet's milieu and the poetics that were current in his age. There is more in a great work of art than can be compassed in any single mode of interpretation that sets out to explore its significances.

A classic does not simply belong to its own time. The very definition of a classic implies the recognition that it speaks to all ages, despite the complex ways in which it relates to and reflects the specific circumstances of the world in which it originated. A classic work must carry within itself the potentialities for relevance to future generations of readers in different cultural contexts. The very lack of biographical detail, the self-effacement of the author, frees his texts from a specific context with its own social and literary codes. Drama which is the most socially-oriented of literary forms comes across with immediacy to audiences, even when their responses are shaped and ordered by social and literary codes different from those in which it was embedded. While placing *Abhijñānaśākuntalam* in a particular set of poetics is no doubt useful and interesting as providing a historical *reading*, it is more illuminating and rewarding to see the play's accomplishment as lying in the manner in which it escapes the constraints of those poetics even as it acknowledges them.

II

Kālidāsa's dates have not been established conclusively. Three dates have been put forward, none of them even remotely exact, and spanning centuries:

(i) The second century BC, during the period of the Śunga Empire, which held power roughly from 184 BC to 78 BC over most of northern and central India up to the Narmada river; Kālidāsa is claimed to have been the court-poet of Agnimitra who ruled at Ujjayinī, the second and western capital of the empire, as his father's viceroy. He is the hero of Kālidāsa's first play, *Mālavikāgnimitram*, a romance with some historical basis.

(ii) The first century BC, in the reign of the celebrated Vikramāditya of story and legend who ruled at Ujjayinī and is believed to have founded the Vikrama era (still used) in 57 BC to commemorate his victory over the Śaka invaders of Malwa. A long and persistent Indian tradition associates Kālidāsa with this monarch making him Vikramāditya's court poet.

(iii) The fourth-fifth centuries AD during the period of the Gupta Empire, in the reign of Chandragupta II who assumed the title of Vikramāditya (the Sun of Valour), after he had completely overthrown Śaka power in Western India.

These dates are discussed briefly in Appendix I.

It is only too obvious that Kālidāsa's birthplace is not known for certain. Various regions in the country have laid claim to the honour of being the poet's place of birth. It is clear though from reading his works that the greater part of his life must have been spent in Malwa (ancient Avanti); and that in the deepest sense, Ujjayinī, of which he writes with such affection and pride, was the poet's own city. 'Indeed, you would have lived in vain', says the *yakṣa* to the rain cloud, admonishing it not to miss the chance of a visit:

to Ujjayinī glowing in splendour
like a brilliant piece of Paradise
come down to earth with traces of merits
of dwellers in Paradise returning,
the fruit of their good deeds almost spent.

(*Meghadūtam* [The Cloud Messenger. st. 32])

The first and third poems in this volume reveal an intimate knowledge of the region of the Vindhya mountains. The poet describes the topography of the Vindhyas and the Malwa region with a loving exactitude as if the landscape lay on the palm of his hand. Malwa, in central India (now part of Madhya Pradesh), watered by many rivers and streams with glades and pleasure-gardens on their banks, dotted with groves and meadows and woodlands stretching along the slopes of the hills, its holy spots and long low hills containing caves overgrown with bushes,[13] stir the poet's imagination and evoke in us the beauty that once was. It may well be that the poet belonged to this region and that Ujjayinī was his place of birth.

Ujjayinī was one of the great cities of ancient India with a continuous history of centuries as the capital of powerful kingdoms such as few cities possessed; it was during most of its history a cultural and commercial centre. Among its many names were, Viśālā, the wide and gracious city; Puṣkaraṇdini, the city of flowers; Mahākālapurī, the city of Mahākāla (Śiva). Lying at the junction of the two great trade routes of ancient India, the east-west and north-south routes with their network of branches Ujjayinī grew wealthy and prosperous. The trade-routes connected the imperial capital of Pāṭalīputra (Patna) at the confluence of the Gaṅgā[14] and the Sona, to various regions within the country; to the Arabian Sea ports such as Broach and Pātāla that carried the extensive overseas trade to Alexandria and Rome; and to the caravan routes extending west through the Kabul valley to the Mediterranean. Ujjayinī was the emporium of its time. The city was long a centre of learning and intellectual activity; an observatory had been built fairly early in its history and the prime meridian passed through the city, making Ujjayinī the Greenwich of ancient India. It was one of the earliest centres of importance for Buddhism, some of Buddha's first disciples belonging to Ujjayinī. Jainism was well established. Judging from the great antiquity and sanctity of the Mahākāla shrine, it is evident that the worship of Śiva was predominant.

Ujjayinī's splendour and opulence are reflected in Kālidāsa's writings. Its mansions and groves, its palaces and pleasure-gardens are described in vivid detail in *Meghadūtam* and *Ṛtusaṃhāram* in this volume. The glowing descriptions of the palaces and gardens in the dream-city of Alakā in *Meghadūtam* (The Cloud Messenger), as well as those of King Duḥṣanta in *Abhijñānaśākuntalam*, who is a monarch of the mythic past, might have been drawn from those that made Ujjayinī splendid and beautiful in the poet's own times. But it is also likely that the poet was drawing on his literary reminiscences of the epics; some of the details of his descriptions e.g. of the *yakṣa's* mansion and gardens in Alakā and of the Vindhyan landscapes in *Ṛtusaṃhāram* are self-consciously allusive but with the jewelled perfection that is all the poet's own.

> 'And Maya built in the Assembly Hall, a lotus pool peerless in beauty paved with priceless gems and studded with pearl-drops; therein bloomed lotuses with leaves of beryl and stalks of gems; a flight of steps led down to brimming waters translucent in all seasons, stirred by lotus-scented breezes; abounding in many kinds of water-birds, turtles and fishes . . . . Surrounding the Hall were thick groves, beautiful, dark-blue, providing cool shade with many kinds of great trees ever blooming, redolent of flower-fragrances; and dotted all around with pools of blue waters haunted by wild geese, teals and red geese.' (*Mbh*: 2:3:23–26).

There are also verbal echoes of passages from the *Rāmāyaṇa*, describing the palaces and pleasure-gardens in Rāvaṇa's capital Laṅkā.[15] However, Kālidāsa celebrates the glory of Ujjayinī not only for its beauty and wealth, but also for its sanctity, because it is a place of hierophany. It is one of the twelve hierophanic spots in the country, where Śiva, the Absolute, descended into Time and Space to abide as a terrestrial presence for the 'salvation of the godly.'

Such a city, wealthy and cosmopolitan, possessing a rich culture and a cultivated audience belonging to a leisured class, and with a splendid court and merchant-guilds to provide patronage for the arts, would have been the ideal centre for the flowering of drama. Legends speak of the brilliant court of King Vikramāditya, learned, wise and generous, patron of poets and scholars. Some of the great dramas are laid in Ujjayinī; others build their plots round the life of the beautiful princess, Vāsavadattā of Ujjayinī, daughter of the ruler of Avanti in the time of Buddha.

Though it cannot be stated with any certainty, Sanskrit drama probably developed in Ujjayinī under the patronage of the kings and merchant princes of that region. There is an interesting piece of information in Bāṇa's *Harṣacaritam* (Life of Harṣa)[16] where he mentions that Sumitra, the son of Agnimitra, who took great delight in drama, was attacked 'in the midst of actors', by one Mitradeva and had his head 'shorn off with a scimitar as if it were a lotus-stalk'. Sumitra is called Vasumitra in Kālidāsa's first play *Mālavikāgnimitram* and is the fourth Śunga emperor of the first century BC at which time it is highly probably that the capital had been shifted from Pāṭalīputra in the east to Ujjayinī. We can imagine that an emperor who was an enthusiastic patron of drama might have been present at a rehearsal or might even have been trying out a role himself. Kālidāsa's play, *Mālavikāgnimitram* opens with a scene in the theatre attached to the palace, where the king and queen are watching a dance performance by the heroine,

Mālavikā, complete with music and other accompaniments. The theatre with its easily accessible costumes and props would certainly have been a most convenient place to plan and effect an assassination of a monarch who would otherwise have been heavily guarded.

This little anecdote in Bāṇa's work provides a possible date for the classical drama as we have it now. Fragments of plays written on palm leaves in the Kushan script, discovered in Turfan, Central Asia, and attributed to Aśvaghoṣa, the Buddhist philosopher and poet, show that the form of classical drama was well established by that time. Aśvaghoṣa's dates have been fixed in the period of the first century BC to the first century AD. The relative chronology of Aśvaghoṣa and Kālidāsa is disputed; but it is not unlikely that Kālidāsa might be earlier than Aśvaghoṣa.

III

The origins of drama are shrouded in antiquity. Space does not permit a detailed discussion of the problem but some of the influences that directed its evolution might be outlined briefly. Three avenues can be explored: the Vedas, the epics and the dance.

The *Nāṭyaśāstra* (The Treatise on Drama) of Bharata, the oldest surviving text of the theory of drama and dramatics, claims a divine origin for itself. It styles itself as a fifth Veda, accessible to all including those who were precluded from the study of the four Vedas[17], such as women and Śūdras; and sets out to instruct through pleasure. Brahmā the creator took elements out of the existing four Vedas to create this new fifth Veda known as Nāṭya-Veda. Among its aims set out in the first chapter are: to represent the ways of the world both good and bad; to give good advice and provide enlightenment through entertainment; to bring peace of mind to those afflicted with the ills of the world and its many problems. Drama represents a generalized view of the world and the actions of persons divested of particularities of character; it does not deal with individuals and their specific situation and emotions. The chief goal of drama is to produce *rasa*, the aesthetic emotion, evoked by the appropriate mood built cumulatively through not only words, but also by mime and gesture, music and dance, costume and jewellery. *Rasa* is not raw emotion but emotion depersonalized, divested of all the accidents of circumstance; it is emotion represented, distilled by art. Sanskrit drama is therefore a blend of many elements: verse and prose, dance, music and spectacle. The *Nāṭyaśāstra* treats poetry, music and dance as one art. The words *naṭa* (actor, dancer, mime), *nāṭya* (dancing, dramatic art) and *nāṭaka* (play) all derive from one root, 'naṭ' to act or represent.

The *Nāṭyaśāstra* is obviously either a compilation of texts that existed prior to it in one form or another, or a systematic arrangement and organization of a body of floating theories and practices. In its present form it might well be later than Kālidāsa, depending on which century we choose to place the poet in. It is possible that the author of the *Nāṭyaśāstra* sat down to compose his treatise with Kālidāsa's plays before him in much the same manner as Aristotle did with the plays of Sophocles in view. It seems more plausible that a critic and theorist would draw upon the work of a great writer to formulate his theories; the reverse view that a creative writer of the genius and accomplishment of Kālidāsa would write according to the book, is less tenable.

Though we might be grappling with uncertainties because there is no concrete evidence to draw a clear line of descent from one to the other, the origins of drama could be traced back to the Vedas. In the *Ṛgveda* we find a number of poems with dramatic elements in them: dialogues such as the lively debate between Saramā, the hound of heaven and the Panis[18]—traders or demons of darkness—over wealth or tribute, where promises of friendship and veiled threats of hostilities are traded; the dialogue between Urvaśī, a celestial nymph and the mythic king Purūravas,[19] which is the distant source of Kālidāsa's second play, *Vikramorvaśīyam* (*Urvaśī Won by Valour*); monologues like the declamation of *vāc* proclaiming her role in the creation of the universe[20], soliloquies like Vasiṣṭha's,[21] a cry of despair rising out of a profound sense of alienation from the divine presence. In some of the poems in this group there are three or more voices speaking; and a few contain the germ of a story or a cryptic reference to an event, that could develop into a plot in the hands of a great dramatist—this is what did happen to the Urvaśī-Purūravas dialogue when Kālidāsa fleshed out the bare bones of the legend (or myth) into a delightful, lyrical play.

The Vedic hymns were chanted and sung by several voices and the presence of a refrain[22] in some suggests a choral element. The rituals themselves of the great sacrifices—and there were many of them extending over days and even longer periods—have a dramatic character to them because the complex round or ceremonies that accompanied the chanting contains an element of dramatic representation. The rituals are a re-enactment of cosmic events; re-enactment is the essence of the Vedic sacrifice (*yajña*). It is plausible that the priests officiating at the sacrifices played the roles of gods (*devas*) and seers (*sādhyās*) in re-enacting the cosmic events. There is mention in Vedic literature of maidens, beautifully dressed and jewelled, singing and dancing and circling the sacred altars with jars of holy water in their hands. A chariot race is mentioned as well as a contest between a fair Vaiśya and a dark Śūdra for the possession of a round white skin symbolizing the sun (Light). These imply a certain amount of action that must have accompanied the chanting of the sacred verses and the performance of the rituals; a notion of conflict or contest is also implied—an essential element in drama.

It is suggested that the Urvaśī-Purūravas poem was a 'staged dialogue . . . a dramatic substitute for what had originally been the sacrifice of a male in a fertility rite after a sacred ritual wedding'[23] and that the theme of separated lovers derives from this. But the theme of separation and reunion of lovers also belongs to folk and fairy tale. However, the first part of the suggestion points to the possibility that vegetation and fertility cults of the ancient world are among the contributing factors in the evolution of classical drama. It is interesting to note in this connection that the medieval and modern religious drama relating to Kṛṣṇa's nativity and exploits and culminating in the slaying of the cruel Kaṃsa by Kṛṣṇa displays a ritual aspect that connects it to ancient vegetation cults. *The Binding of Bāli* and *Kaṃsa's Slaying* are two plays referred to in the literature of the second century BC; it appears that in the staging of these early religious plays the colours of black and red have been used symbolically in the make-up of the actors to represent dark Winter and bright Summer.[24]

The *mudras* (*hastas*) or hand-gestures used and the stances adopted during the performance of Vedic rituals (that continue in use even now), were incorporated later into classical drama. Often, the stage-directions in a play indicate miming, and call for a specific *mudra*, as for instance, in *Śak.* 6:3, the *kapota-hastaka*, the dove-shaped hand-gesture, that conveys adoration or supplication, where the hands are folded together with the palms slightly hollowed and not touching but with the tips of the fingers and the base touching, so as to form the shape of a dove. However, *mudras* and stances are not only part of the ceremonies accompanying vedic liturgy but also of priestly rituals in temples; for instance, the waving of lights before the deity goes through an intricate sequence of movements. They also belong to the grammar and vocabulary of the dance, which is closely associated with temple-worship. Further *nāṭya* is closely associated with Śiva who is imaged in stone and metal as Naṭarājā the Lord of Dance.

The *Nāṭyaśāstra* assumes the close association of Śiva with the performing arts. For Bharata, in his dialogue with Brahmā, the Creator, speaks of having witnessed the dance of Śiva (Nīlakaṇṭha—the blue-throated god), 'full of feeling' and expressive of the sentiments of love (*śṛṅgāra*), conveyed through graceful sequences of movement and gesture.[25] Further, Śiva highly pleased with the performance of the two plays, *The Churning of the Ocean* and *The Burning of the Triple-City* (*Amṛtamanthana* and *Tripura dāha* or *Tripura Vijaya*)—the latter play is referred to in *Meghadūtam*(58)—composed by Brahmā himself and performed by Bharata and his troupe on the Himālayas against the natural scenery of its 'beautiful caves and waterfalls'[26] instructs his disciple Taṇḍu to teach Bharata certain dance-sequences that formed part of the 'preliminaries'[27] in the staging of a play. This statement in the *NS* suggests the coming together of two traditions in the performing arts or the influence of one upon the other.

The 'preliminaries' (*pūrva-raṅga*) consist of a series of religious ceremonies with prayers and offerings of flowers to the deities, all performed with specific gestures and sequences of movements to the accompaniment of music. It serves the dual purpose of framing drama in a religious setting and of providing the audience with some entertainment. Sanskrit drama is secular but there is a religious and ritual dimension to it; the association with Śiva also provides the quality of prayer to what is basically secular drama, as evidenced by the invocation at the beginning and the benediction or *bharata-vākya,* the stanza spoken by the actor at the end of a play.

Bharata is obviously an assumed name. The Bharatas were originally the rhapsodes or bards[28] of the powerful Bharata tribe celebrated in the *Ṛgveda.* A bardic ancestry is therefore implied and pre-supposed in the name. The word came later to signify an actor. The bardic tradition of the epics had a strong influence on the development of drama. In the *Mahābhārata*, bards recite the story of the Great War and events that led up to it, to Janamejaya, the great-grandson of Arjuna, the foremost warrior in the war. And the recital takes place at the performance of a great sacrifice. The story of Rāma and Śitā is recited by their sons Kuśa and Lava (Kuśi-lava)[29] at their father's court before they are recognized and acknowledged. Recitations of stories may have taken the form of several voices delivering different parts of the narrative or of speaking the parts of the different characters and accompanying their recitals with appropriate gestures and facial expressions. Recitations of the epics continued to be popular forms of entertainment (and instruction) for centuries and have continued right to this day in temples and village squares.[30] The epics stand solidly behind classical literature in both drama and the long poem (*mahākāvya*). The plots of several plays and poems are taken from them.

Dancing figures found at Mohenjo-Daro,[31] point to the antiquity of the dance as an art-form in India. The flexion of the torso of the male dancer, and the stance, the pert look and the hint of a smile worn by the little metal statuette of a dancing girl, her right arm on her hip, her left arm loaded with bracelets, legs slightly bent at the knees, resemble stances and facial expressions that are still part of the language of the classical dance. And the dance is an art-form that blends the lyrical and narrative modes, conveying them through mime and gesture articulated within the metrical pattern of the foot work. The dance also provides the elements of ritual and stylization to drama.

It would appear then that many of the elements of drama were already in place at a very early time—perhaps by the middle of the first millenium BC, at the time of Pāṇini, the great grammarian who was also a poet. With various traditions converging at this time, the literary tradition of the Vedas and epics, the popular and folk play traditions centering perhaps round vegetation rites and festivals such as sowing and harvesting, the ritual drama and the dance with its story-line, it was inevitable that drama as we understand it should have been evolving into its final form.

The man and the moment[32] are the two pre-requisites for the emergence of any particular art-form, literary or other. Various influences come together at some *moment*; all that is needed is the *man* to seize the moment. Kālidāsa mentions his predecessors, Bhāsa, Rāmila, Saumilla, Kaviputra and others in the prologue to *Mālavikāgnimitram.* While we do not know which man of genius welded disparate elements to write the first play, we can be sure that in Kālidāsa's hands drama reached a high peak of achievement.

The *Nāṭyaśāstra* is a compendious treatise on practically all the literary aspects of drama and all matters relating to the theatre, from the construction of the playhouse or *nāṭyamaṇḍapa* to audience-response.

Chapter 2 of the text gives us a general idea of the ancient Sanskrit theatre but we cannot claim to have a clear and accurate picture of it in all its details, because some passages are not very clear in their meaning and certain technical terms are variously interpreted by scholars.

> The *nāṭyamaṇḍapa* (playhouse) should be designed in the shape of a mountain cave, have two ground-levels, small windows, and be free from gusts of wind (drafts), so that the voices of the actors and singers as well as the sound of the musical instruments will be resonant.
>
> (*Nāṭyaśāstra*: 2:80-82)

The 'shape of a mountain cave' is an interesting detail, because not only does it reveal an awareness of the acoustical properties of structures but it also suggests that originally shows and spectacles and even plays might have been presented in cave-theatres.

The playhouse was built of close-set bricks of fine quality, on level ground and faced east. The walls were plastered and then whitewashed; the inner walls were covered with beautiful paintings of sinuous, meandering vines and of men and women enjoying themselves. It is clear that Bharata intended the playhouse to be not merely a place of entertainment but one with aesthetic appeal. Carved figures of elephants, tigers and snakes and statues (on pedestals?) were required to be placed at different spots in the theatre. Architectural features and details were both functional and decorative: mouldings and supports in decorative woodwork are mentioned; ornamental turrets, balconies, railings, roundels and pedestals, niches, brackets, lattices, ornamental windows (*gavākṣa:* shaped liked the eye of a cow) that were mechanically operated are some of the details of interior decoration mentioned.[33] Pillars are described as raised at different levels and beautifully carved with figures of women by the side of trees;[34] these remind us of the carvings and sculptured figures of *yakṣis* and *vṛkṣakas* (tree-divinities) at Bharhut and Sāñci and Mathura.

The text mentions three shapes of playhouses; oblong, square, triangular, and some verses suggest that a type of thrust-stage might have been in use. Three sizes are also mentioned. But Bharata strongly recommends that the medium-sized playhouse of 96 feet by 48 feet is the most suitable, because: 'in a larger playhouse, the voice will not carry far; it will lose its quality of tone and become weak and indistinct'; and due to its large size the subtle play of expressions on the face that are the means to convey the emotions and produce the *rasas* will not be seen clearly by the spectators sitting towards the back (*NS:* 2: 28–30).

The playhouse was divided into two equal halves, the auditorium and the stage with the greenroom behind it, each 48 feet by 48 feet, if we take the medium-sized playhouse as the model. The auditorium had seats of brick and wood arranged in rising tiers 'like a staircase'.

The stage was raised 27 inches off the floor of the auditorium and demarcated into the front stage which was the acting area for the most part and the back stage where the musicians and drummers were seated. Jewels and precious gems were placed underneath the stage during the building of the playhouse according to prescriptions based on their auspiciousness. A wall with two doors, one for the entry and the other for the exit of actors, separated the stage from the greenroom. A curtain of rich material hung before the doors; off-stage effects might have been produced either in the space behind the curtain or in the greenroom itself: e.g., Hamsavatī's song and the bards' praise-songs in Act 5 of *Abhijñānaśākuntalam*; the mystic voice in Act 4 that announces to sage Kaṇva that his daughter is pregnant with Duṣhanta's son.

There was little or no scenery, and a minimum of props made of light materials were used. Language, therefore, became very important as in the Elizabethan theatre; the imagery painted the scenes and much was left to the imagination of the spectator. We see instances of this use of language in Act I of *Abhijñānaśākuntalam*, where the King as soon as he enters describes the fleeing deer and a little later he describes in detail the outskirts of the hermitage (1:13, 14).

Sanskrit drama clearly reveals its dance-origins; miming is often indicated by the stage-directions. Dance is very much a part of it; the whole of the fourth act in *Vikramorvaśīyam* in the Bengal recension, comprises song and dance interspersed with snatches of prose as the King wanders around demented. Even where there is no formal dancing as such, it is clear that Sanskrit drama leans heavily on dance-technique: the stances adopted by the various characters, their gestures, facial expressions, their very gait and style of walking, belong to the grammar and vocabulary of the dance. There is little that is naturalistic about the dramatic art of the Sanskrit theatre.

Dramatic performances were usually held on special occasions; coronations and other royal events, great weddings, religious festivals and fairs. Private theatres, beautifully decorated, would have existed in the royal palace, mansions of nobles and merchants and perhaps in guild halls. The audience would have been select, comprising the few and fit. Open-air performances are also known, which were probably staged in front of temples or in their quadrangles, with large, mixed audiences. There might have been open-air theatres also. Bhavabhūti's play *Mālati-Mādhava* was performed for the festival of Kāla-priya-nātha (Śiva). But we do not know whether it was staged in an open-air theatre or in the temple-square.

Women played the female roles. Bharata is mentioned as putting it to Brahmā that drama could not be presented successfully without actresses and Brahmā, seeing the point made, created *apsaras* (celestial nymphs) for this purpose. But we find that in *Mālati-Mādhava* the director (*sūtradhāra*) and his assistant take on female roles.

Certain stage-directions are conventional: 'enter with a toss of the curtain' indicates hurry, excitement, agitation; 'walk around' and 'turn around' indicate changes of location.

Costuming, jewellery and hair-styles were important, serving as the means of ethnic, regional and hierarchical signification; they also represented emotional states: for instance, 'Enter the King *costumed* as suffering from remorse' in *Śak.*: 6:5, and 'Enter Sakuntalā with her hair done in a single braid' to signify the grief of a woman separated from her husband (7:21).

Colour was used symbolically, both in the costumes and the make-up. Faces may have been painted, as is still done in the Kathakali and Chhau dance-forms. Four main colours, blue, red, yellow, black and four combinations of these, grey, gold, green and pink, appear to have been in use; other colours are also mentioned as blends of these.

Masks may have also been in use. The use of masks that rightly belongs to ritual drama, is significant, because the mask covers and transforms. It signifies the depersonalization of the actor and his transformation into a fictive character. The actor steps into the role assigned to him the moment the mask or make-up and the costume are put on, to *become* the character. All these external trappings of a character immediately convey a great deal about the play and the story to the least educated and unsophisticated among the audience.

Stylization in speech and acting, the symbolic use of colour, the use of masks (made up of paint and also of materials) and of dance and miming, all serve to distance the play-world of drama and separate it from the everyday world. The classical drama of India uses Prakrits or regional dialects as well as Sanskrit, which is spoken by Brahmins, kings and high officials. Women (even queens), children and the court-jester (*vidūṣaka*) speak Prakrit; low characters like the fishermen and policemen in Act 6 of *Abhijñānaśākuntalam* also speak in dialect. This provides Sanskrit plays with a rich variety in speech, but it is not possible to make the differentiation between the classical language and the dialects and between the dialects themselves in translation.

To what extent classical drama was a form of popular entertainment is hard to say. The relatively small size of the playhouse, whose seating capacity could hardly have exceeded 400, makes the Sanskrit theatre an intimate one with a small, select audience. The open-air theatres would have drawn a much larger and mixed audience but nothing definite can be said on this point.

IV

Turning to lyric poetry, the line of descent seems somewhat clearer than in drama. The *Ṛgveda* contains a few true lyrics of which *Night*[35] (*Rātri*) and The *Forest-Spirit*[36] (*Araṇyāni*) are notable. The hymns to Dawn (*Uṣas*) and the lovely marriage hymn, *Suryā's Bridal*,[37] are lyrical in tone and the *Atharvaveda* contains the beautiful *Ode to Earth*[38] (*Pṛthivī-sūkta*).

Kālidāsa's poetry forms a kind of watershed in the vast terrain of classical literature and his finest poem, *Meghadūtam*, has a special place, standing as it does at the end of a long tradition of the narrative-dramatic poetry of the first millennium BC and at the head of a new tradition of lyric poetry.[39] His earlier poem, the epic, *Raghuvaṃśam*, brings to a close the great epic-saga tradition of the *Rāmāyaṇa* and the *Mahābhārata* with its emphasis on action, its exalted and heroic theme, its alternating narrative and dramatic styles and its story-within-story structure. But it also differs from that tradition. The poet places his own unique stamp on this new epic. *Raghu's Dynasty* has the exalted theme; the rise and fall of empire, the lives and exploits of heroes, chiefly of Raghu who is portrayed as the ideal blend of a conquering warrior and a just and compassionate king. It lays out the ideal of kingship and holds the mirror up to princes. But it is more in the nature of a chronicle; character is not pitted against character; there is no play of opposing forces. Built on righteousness and the heroic valour of warrior-kings, the dynasty goes through a series of rulers of little note and no achievement and comes to an ignoble end with the reign of the last ruler, Agnivarṇa, a hedonist with no ideals, unmindful of his glorious heritage and the interests of his subjects (he puts his foot out of the window of the royal balcony of audience for his subjects to pay homage to) and a dissolute monarch who spends his brief life in a whirl of dissipation until it peters out in the silence of death. Secretly consigning his body to the flames, the council of ministers carry on having consecrated the pregnant queen and placed her on the throne. The last stanzas of cannot 19 are filled with a quiet bitterness and the epic ends abruptly, incomplete and inconclusive.

The *Mahābhārata* and the *Rāmāyaṇa* have lyrical passages interspersed in the narrative; however, these are not integral but peripheral concerns in the main thrust of the work. *Meghadūtam* (and to a lesser extent *Ṛtusaṃhāram*) announces a new poetic movement; a lyrical mode lying emphasis on exhibiting subtle emotional nuances rather than weaving the story-line. The imagination plays on the surface of the drama as the mind turns inward; it does not engage itself with the clash of external events of feuds and wars and the intricacies of power struggles that lead up to them as the epics do; action is internalized. *Śṛṅgāra* (Love) becomes the dominant emotional mode and the single stanza comes into its own to possess its autonomy. Though the stanzas are units in a long poem, each stanza is exquisitely crafted round one image, one feeling, one instant of experience.

The poet has left us seven works: three long lyrical poems, three plays and an incomplete epic. Their chronology is uncertain.

Poems	*Ṛtusaṃhāram*	The Gathering of the Seasons
	Kumārasaṃbhavam	The Birth of Kumāra *or* The Birth of the Son
	Meghadūtam	The Cloud Messenger
Plays	*Mālavikāgnimitram*	Mālavikā and Agnimitra
	Vikramōrvaśīyam	Urvaśī Won by Valour
	Abhijñānasākuntalam	The Recognition of Śakuntalā
Epic	*Raghuvaṃśam*	Raghu's Dynasty

Ṛtusaṃhāram is an early effort, perhaps the poet's first that looks forward to the greater work to come; but it is by no means to be read as an apprentice effort. It is an accomplished poem, brilliant in parts. What strikes the reader immediately is the extraordinary particularity with which the world of nature is observed in all its variousness in the changing seasons: parched under the burning sun and devastating drought, revived and renewed in the rains with brilliant colours splashed all around; mellow in autumns's golden plenitude; shivering and pale under the wintry moon's icy glitter. Each season leaves on the landscape its impress of beauty caught in the glowing imagery.

The poem is both naturalistic and stylized. What the poet's eye notes with such loving precision is expressed in highly stylized imagery and diction that anticipate the more sophisticated and richly-textured poetry of *Meghadūtam* and the intricate harmonies of *Śakuntalā*. The vision deepens and more ambivalences complicate the structure and meaning of the later works; but the keenness of observation of nature and the rich detail with which it is rendered is not excelled in any of them.

The poem is not simply a description of nature; it is an interweaving of the beauty of nature and woman, with the emotional response to both.

> Dotting the woodlands are charming glades besides streams
> haunted by timorous gazelles easily alarmed
> —tremulous eyes like deep-blue water lilies enchanting—
> and the heart is twisted with sudden longing. (2:9)

An interesting point to note here and in other places in the poem, e.g. 6.:18, is the direct address to the beloved in the second half of the stanza; the speaker turns from the scene they are both watching, to her, to *tell* her of nature's beauty that images her own. It is in the nature of an 'aside', a comment bringing together the beloved and the gazelle, both shy and timid and possessing liquid, lustrous eyes, and the blue lily trembling in the pool; all three objects compared have one thing in common, the tremulous petal-eyes.

Whereas the beauty of nature magically heightens the loveliness of woman, transforming her into an enchantress, she in turn serves as an ornament for it. Beautifully dressed and jewelled, she provides the colour, glow and fragrance absent from nature when the cool seasons (cantos 4 and 5) etch the landscape in muted tones. Nature and woman complement each other, each enhancing the other's charm.

Analogies are drawn constantly between the natural and human worlds; men who have to travel far from home are desolated,

> Seeing the glow of the beloved's dark eyes
> in the blue-lotuses;
> hearing the tones of her gold girdle bells
> in the love-mad murmur of wild geese;
> recalling the rich red of her lower lip
> in the *Bandhūka's* flame-clusters . . . . (3:24)

The two worlds interact. The flower-scented breezes and the enchanting twilights jewelled by moon and stars kindle passion in man; the breezes *consort* with lotuses and wipe away their tears of dew drops; clouds lean over to kiss the hills. The season steps in to deck lovely women with the prettiest and freshest flowers as a lover does; and the wild forest-fire leaps up, 'smitten with longing,' to clasp the greenery of the woodlands in a passionate and consuming embrace. The winter of separation makes the young girl and the slender vine grow pale and wither. Man and nature together celebrate a joyous festival of love and grieve together in sorrow. In Indian thought, a sharp line is not drawn between the worlds of man and nature. The universe is one ordered *Whole* of which man is a part. Imbued with the Spirit that is transcendent and immanent, the same life-giving essence that is in man, circulates in every part of it.[40] The propelling force therefore in Kālidāsa's poetry, is to see nature, not as a setting for man and a backdrop to the human drama, but to perceive it as possessing a life of its own and as related to the human world in many complex ways.

Both woman and nature with its teeming energies are the vehicles that carry the procreative energies of *Śakti,* Śiva's inherent power. When the poet says,

> Conferring the radiance of the moon
> on the faces of lovely women,
> the entrancing tones of wild geese
> on their gem-filled anklets,
> the *Bandhūka's* vibrant redness
> on their luscious lower lip,
> the splendour of bountiful Autumn
> is now departing—to who knows where! (3:25)

he is not indulging in a mere flight of poetic fancy; the philosophical assumptions of his culture are behind it. In *Ṛtusaṃhāram* woman and nature borrow each other's attributes when they are not competing in a friendly manner; in *Meghadūtam* woman and nature are one, the identification is complete; the landscape *is* the beloved.

Śṛṅgāra, Love, in its many aspects is a perennial theme of lyrical poetry. Love secure and fulfilled, or thwarted, betrayed, angry and jealous, and above all, love in separation, are all given glowing or poignant expression in Kālidāsa's poetry. In *Meghadūtam*, these various moods that love displays itself in, are delineated in single stanzas, each like a miniature painting (26, 30, 31, 41, 42, and 43). The two poems in this volume, *Meghadūtam* and *Ṛtusaṃhāram*, each treats of love in its two conventional aspects, love-in-union, and love-in-separation, though the latter is much more than just a love-poem. However, this does not in any way make the two contemporary; in fact they mark the beginning and the end of Kālidāsa's poetic career. *The Seasons* celebrates the fulfillment of love with hardly a trace of anguish; *The Cloud Messenger* is a poem of longing and separation. *Śakuntalā*, having delineated love's ecstasy and fulfillment as well as its anguish in the separation that follows the anger and bitterness of its cruel betrayal, finally gathers it all in the closing scene in an epiphanic moment of recognition, restoration and reunion. It also adds something that is not present in the other two works—the child, token of love and symbol of continuity of the family and survival of the self.

Young in heart, as yet untroubled by the weight of thought of the later work and untouched by the pensive note present in *Meghadūtam*, *The Seasons* is the exuberant response of the poet in love with the world in all its beauty; and in love with love itself. Where *Meghadūtam* is haunted by the loneliness of the human heart, even in the midst of the world's loveliness, *Ṛtusaṃhāram* breathes an air of pure joy. Longing—and the word occurs again and again—has lost its ache because the beloved is close at hand, seated next to the speaker of the poem. The ardent expression of love's longing and the restlessness it rouses is in fact the response of the lover to nature's beauty and the beauty of the beloved mirroring and evoking each other. Coming at the end of the stanza it is phrased to suggest an invitation to love.

> Glancing at the amaranth's blossoming sprays
> glowing in exquisite loveliness just-revealed
> —loveliness that rightly belongs to the beloved's face—
> how can a responsive heart not flutter in pain
> stung by proud Love's flying arrows, my love? (6:18)

There is an element of hyperbole in this young lover's statements; an extravagance of emotion and gesture is displayed from time to time. We see it again in st. 20, where he indulges in a flamboyant gesture of despair to convince the beloved that he is destroyed and consumed, to die again and again for love of her.

The patterning of the poem is interesting and intricate, the complexity of which has not been noticed before. The poem has been treated mostly as showing a keen observation of nature expressed in vivid descriptions. A canto is given to each season and the moods it creates in the natural and human worlds. Each canto is a self-contained unit, opening with the traditional announcement of theme and closing with a benediction. The title, *Ṛtusaṃhāram*, or *Gathering of the Seasons*, unifies the poem. The titles that Kālidāsa gives to his works hold a significance that unfolds in the course of the work.

The new year begins with Spring around the vernal equinox. But the poem begins with Summer so as to end with Spring; an auspicious ending, for Spring is renewal. The old year is dead and the advent of Spring is welcomed with song and dance and religious ceremonies. In ancient India this was known as the *Spring Festival* or *The Festival of Love* and it was celebrated with uninhibited revelry in a carnival atmosphere.[41] New plays were written and staged as part of the festivities. The prologue to Kālidāsa's first play *Mālavikā and Agnimitra* mentions it as the new play presented at the Spring Festival. We know from literary references that works were commissioned for special occasions: a royal wedding or the birth of an heir to the throne, a royal victory or possibly celebrations in great houses. It is likely that *Ṛtusaṃhāram (The Seasons)* was just such an 'occasional poem', composed for and presented at the Spring Festival, in which case it is eminently fitting that it should end with Spring and bring the celebrations to a memorable close. The closing stanza is a prayer to the god of Love, the presiding deity naturally of the festivities, attended by his companion Spring, asking him to bestow his blessings on the beloved in the poem, and on the audience.

The opening stanzas of Summer serve as a framework for the poem, visualizing a pair of lovers, seated perhaps on a balcony or terrace, as pictured in miniature paintings centuries later. (It is important to note that the love the poet describes so ardently in such glowing terms is married love) This parallel should not come as a surprise because miniatures were often painted either to illustrate love-poetry or were inspired by it. Once the scene is set, the refrain is dropped so as not to constitute an intrusive element in the flow of the poem which then moves out of the small world of the lovers into the large world outside: to the woodlands and fields and cities, and into the worlds of other lovers. But the poem always comes back to where it started, to the pair of lovers and the audience. In the closing stanza the speaker sums up the beauties and virtues of the season and calls down blessings on the audience and the beloved. The movement is circular. The form of each canto and the poem as a whole is also circular, circles wheeling within a circle imaging the circling year into which the seasons are *gathered*. As Time is cyclic in Indian thought, it is rewarding to see the poem and *read* it as a celebration of Time itself in its endless circling procession of nights and days, of seasons, of worlds born, dissolved and born again until the end of time. The rhythms of the human and natural worlds image the cosmic rhythms presided over by Mahākāla.[42] the terrestrial presence of Śiva enshrined in Ujjayinī, the poet's own city.

The word *saṃhāram* (gathering in, or collection) in the title of the poem has a specific metaphysical meaning, of universal dissolution when all creation is *drawn in* at the end of time into Śiva, its ground and source. The mystery of Śiva and his presence is never far from any of Kālidāsa's works. In them the poet is revealed as a devotee of Śiva and Devī (Śakti). This does not imply however that the poet is sectarian and narrow in his religious views. Śiva is the poet's chosen form for the adoration and worship of divinity (*iṣṭa-devatā*). Hindu praxis recognizes the propensity of the human mind *to image*, and provides for it in the concept of the *iṣṭa-devatā*; a form iconic or aniconic, a mental image or sound visualized, as in the word *Om* (*Omkāranātha* is one of Śiva's names), is chosen as the object for rites of worship and as the focus for that single-minded meditation upon the transcendent, which is the first step in the path of enlightenment (*jñāna*) and release (*mokṣa*). The form chosen is one that the devotee (or his *guru*) perceives as eminently suited to his spiritual temperament and needs.

The invocations in the plays and the epic are made to this unitive godhead, *Śiva-Śakti*: in *Śakuntalā* and *Mālavikā and Agnimitra* to Śiva's eight-fold form perceptible to human consciousness; in *Urvaśī Won by Valour*, to Śiva as the Primal Being spoken of in the Upaniṣads; and in the epic the indivisible Whole is invoked as the *Word. Kumārasaṃbhavam* (*The Birth of Kumāra*) is all about Śiva, the *yogi* and ascetic, and about the sacred marriage of Śiva and Umā[43] (Śakti), which in Saiva mythology and metaphysics initiates the process of creation. *Meghadūtam* (*The Cloud Messenger*) reverberates with Śiva's presence.

As the chronology of Kālidāsa's works is uncertain, it is only the sense of a developing pattern in the poet's *oeuvre* that places them in a certain, tentative order. That *Mālavikā and Agnimitra* is an early play and followed *Ṛtusaṃhāram* (*The Seasons*) is fairly certain. It was probably followed by *Vikramorvaśīyam*, then the incomplete epic *Raghu's Dynasty* and *The Birth of Kumāra*, also incomplete. *The Cloud Messenger* and *Śakuntalā* are clearly the last works of the poet. In these, Kālidāsa's vision has mellowed and deepened and the language responds like a finely-tuned instrument to every touch. The unerring choice of *the word* that expresses perfectly and precisely the intended nuance of meaning,[44] and that *oneness* of language and thought that the poet prays for in the invocation to the epic, are fully realized in these two works.

V

The narrative poems *Kumārasaṃbhavam* (*Kumāra* for short) and *Raghu-vaṃśam* are defined in Sanskrit Poetics by the general term *mahākāvya,* 'the great poem'. The latter work will however be referred to in the introduction as an epic.

The two poems are different in theme, tone and structure. The epic is an eloquent statement of the imperial theme in all its glory, of the rise and expansion of the divinely descended solar dynasty of kings and its inevitable decay and fall. The vast sweep of the epic embraces in area all the land between the Oxus in Central Asia and the Kaveri in southern India. In time, the epic compasses both pre-and-proto history coming almost down to the threshold of history itself. Vālmīki's great epic, the *Rāmāyaṇa*, is encapsulated in the poem with Rāma's birth placed at midpoint in the narrative in canto ten as befitting a hierophany. But in the kind of themes it chooses to articulate in such splendour the epic restricts itself to this world and its concerns; to earthly achievements and earthly joys and sorrows except for a brief excursion at the beginning by Dilīpa, the founder of the dynasty into Indra's world of eternal light (*svarga*). The epic is celebratory in tone.

Kumāra on the other hand situates itself in mythic time in a mythic world. The poem is based on the story of a hierogamy as ancient as can be; the story of the sacred marriage of Śiva and Pārvatī can only be taken as the relation of a primal event that happens at the beginning. Since the *Śivapurāṇa* which follows the outlines of the story in the poem very closely, is a late work, the source of the story of the sacred marriage has to be sought in the rich, age-old oral literature of the country. With this story, the poem weaves another ancient story of the war of the *deva* and *asura*, god and anti-god or immortals and titans. This again is a tale that tells of another primal event, the search for the elixir of immortality, *Amṛta*, the churning of the ocean to gain it (see Appendix II) and the enmity of *deva* and *asura* that rose because the latter were deprived of the *amṛta* though they had laboured hard at the churning.

The characters in *Kumāra* are all divine and semidivine and the action is placed in a world between earth and heaven which partakes of the nature, qualities and even the landscape of both worlds. This world is the realm of Himālaya, characterized in the poem as 'divine regions' (*devabhūmayaḥ*, 5:45). It is peopled by seers and sages, by *apsaras, kinnara-kinnarī, vanadevatāḥ* and so on (nymphs, fauns, dryads, sylvan goddesses) and also by hunters and forest dwellers who roam with their wives and sweethearts. This world is the temporal abode of the Absolute, Śiva and the birth place of his *Śakti*, Pārvatī and also of the holy Gaṅgā seated in the tangles of the matted hair of the great *yogi*, Śiva. But it is also haunted by lions and elephants and by soft-eyed does and flamboyant peacocks. The idea of this dual nature of the divine ground that is Himālaya's kingdom is reified in the person of Himālaya himself, who has a twofold nature: animate and inanimate, moving and rooted firmly, a mountain that is the firm support of the earth yet a being of 'indwelling divinity' (*devatāmā,* I:1) as befitting the role of parent of the Mother of the Universe. Himālaya plunges deep into the ocean depths but his lofty peaks thrust up into the skies, aspiring to worlds beyond. The delineation of Himālaya is the finest in characterization in the poem. The twofold nature of this *persona* is created and sustained through the effective use of language. Words such as lofty, firm, upright, and vast, endowed with strength and substance are employed in their physical and spiritual-ethical meanings. To illustrate: in 3:76, the closing stanza, we have a striking image:

> . . . The Mountain
> strode along on his way back his body
> lengthening out from great speed . . . .

This is the kind of perception that someone travelling in a line parallel to a long range of mountains might have especially if he or she were going in a moving vehicle. And again in 6:50:

> The Mountain *rose up* at a distance
> carrying his offerings . . . .

Kumāra is a poem of uneven accomplishment. The poem begins on an exalted note and in canto 2 it reaches sublime heights conveying abstruse metaphysical concepts in noble verse. Canto 3 balances the worlds of the ascetic and the erotic beautifully, juxtaposing springtime spreading through the penance groves setting them ablaze with passion (3: 23–39) with the *yoga* of Śiva who sits at its heart in profound self contemplation. Opposing ideals are set against each other. The erotic is contained by being placed in a context of discipline and self restraint. The verse displays the delicacy and refinement of feeling that Kālidāsa invariably brings to the delineation of *śṛṅgāra*, the mode of love, which is seen here operating in the world of nature and not in the human world. The canto closes on the note of rejection of one of these two opposing principles and is balanced symmetrically by the last stanza in canto 5 where the rejection is changed to acceptance. Many years appear to pass between cantos 3 and 5 and in that period of time Pārvatī has become the great *yogini*, the appropriate counterpart to the great *yogi*, Śiva. She is in essence now Sati who abandoned her body in the fires of *yoga* (*Kumāra* I.21) The closing stanza of canto 5 is one of acceptance of woman and the principle of love.

Kumāra is in an ultimate sense the articulation in poetry of a metaphysical concept; the concept of the descent of The Timeless into Time-and-Space; of the One, ungendered, into duality as Śiva and Śakti, represented iconographically as *ardhanārīśvara* (the lord whose half is feminine); of the mystery of Being-Becoming (*Bhava-Bhavānī*). The myth of the hierogamy contains the metaphysical concept that has to be translated into metaphor to come alive. And the poem self-consciously introduces a metaphysical element into its poetry by the use of such terms as *akṣara* (imperishable, 3:50); self-born (*ātmayonī,* 3:70); the World's Refuge (*jagatśaraṇya,*5:76); *Viśvamūrti* (the World's Form or universal form); the World's Self (*viśvātmā*, 6:I). And the blend of the mythic, and the metaphysical with story and legend is accomplished effectively in the first five cantos. It fails however in canto eight where the attempt to speak of the mystic union of Siva and Śakti in narrative poetry is nothing short of a total fiasco. The mystery dissolves and vanishes into the thin air of disappointment. The union of the divine with itself can only be suggested, not stated; and definitely not be spelled out in explicit detail as it is in canto 8.

This criticism has perforce to apply also to cantos 6 and 7 to a lesser degree. Having distanced itself from the mundane world with its largely trivial preoccupations by the choice of the theme and its location in mythic time in a mythic world shot through with metaphysical colours, the poem now permits the intrusion of that selfsame world into the narrative. There is a tonal shift and a change in characterization after canto 5. In the narrative structure, this shift might be placed precisely at 7:51; where Śiva descends on to the surface of Himālaya's realm, the poem makes its descent into the mundane world. The defining image pointing to the tonal shift is of Śiva referred to as blue-throated like rain clouds by the epithet *ghananīlakaṇṭha* with all the mythic associations of this term resonating, descending from mythic time and space (*svabāṇacihnāt mārgāt*, marked by the path of his own arrow) on to the earth's surface (*bhūpṛṣṭhaṃ*, literally the earth's back), from the firmament where *once* in 'the backward abyss of time', his deadly arrow flew to punish transgression of the Law (*ṛta*). The allusion in this image is to two myths: the destruction of Tripurā, the triple cities of gold, silver and iron of the *daitya-dānavas*, ancient rivals of the *devas*; and the myth of Brahmā who pursued his own daughter in lust (see n, 7:16).

The poem shifts in tone at this point; the characterization changes; the world is foregrounded. Umā, the bride, Śiva, the bridegroom as the sages describe them in 6:82, have a fabulous marriage like any wealthy human couple and go on to engage in amorous pleasures, though the wedding is performed in the celestial city of Oṣadhiprastha and the lovemaking takes place in that intermediate world in pools where golden lotuses blow and groves of paradisal trees abound. The hierogamy loses its aura of sacrality. Too much anthropomorphization has killed the sense of mystery which should always surround primal events in their telling. The marriage of Śiva and Śakti is in the poem too much of the earth, earthy.

The characterization changes with the shift in tone and treatment of the theme. Himālaya and Mena are like ordinary householders. Himālaya becomes a courtier; Mena a worried mother at first who becomes delighted to see the way in which her daughter is 'enjoyed' by the bridegroom (8:12). The aura of divinity is lost. If the poem had ended with canto 5 it would have been more accomplished aesthetically and more satisfying as a work.

The poem exists as a complete poem of seventeen, long cantos beginning with the birth of Pārvatī and ending with the slaying of Tāraka by Kumāra, regarded as the son of Pārvatī and Śiva. However, a strong school of opinion holds that only the first eight cantos are Kalidasa's and that the latter half of the poem, cantos 9-17 are by some other poet.

The poem was edited for the prestigious Nirnaya Sagar Press in its totality, as a complete poem of seventeen cantos. The Sahitya Akademi published it in 1962 (reprinted 1982) also as a poem of seventeen cantos. Dr. Surya Kanta edited it. Pandit Devadhar has edited and translated the poem as well as a poem of seventeen cantos. In this volume, the present translator has rendered all seventeen cantos of the poem into English verse making no distinction in treatment between the authentic eight cantos and the unauthentic later cantos, assuming that it is all authentically Kālidāsa's but without dismissing the possibility that it might be the work of more than one poet. Multiple authorship of many texts in Sanskrit is not unknown or rare. The two great epics, The *Mahābhārata* and the *Rāmāyaṇa* are excellent examples of multiple authorship. Though the phrase itself is not used, we have happily accepted the fact.

Kumārasaṃbhavam is textually a problematic work. It is not easy to determine and decide that only the first eight cantos are authentic, i.e., composed by Kālidāsa and that only these ought to be considered and discussed as a text, and translated for study and critical evaluation.

Without going into the merits of the arguments that might be adduced by the proponent of the 8-canto school, some brief comments could be made on the text of *Kumārasaṃbhavam*.

The poem could be looked at in three ways: as a complete poem of seventeen cantos with single or multiple authorship; as a poem of eight cantos, complete in itself; or as an unfinished poem, a 'fragment', if we take the position that the later cantos are unauthentic. A 'fragment' is a legitimate art-form. There might be any number of reasons why the work was not 'finished' in the accepted conventional sense of the term.

To look at the poem 'then as unfinished, (as Sri Aurobindo does), a 'fragment', the poem might be looked at from the perspective of the title: titles are important as providing clues to understanding, and Kālidāsa's titles are very suggestive as has been noted earlier in this introduction. Kumārasaṃbhavam signifies an event; the manifestation of a hierophany. Literally taken, the title means the birth or origin of the son. Now, if we look at the narrative of the poem carefully, we note that the last verse of canto 5 is important because it holds the promise of marriage and therefore of offspring. Similarly, the close of canto 7 holds the same promise even more definitely, because the hierogamy of Śiva-Pārvatī has taken place. Brahmā's promise in canto 2 is nearing fulfilment. The poem could very well have ended with either canto 5 or canto 7. The close of canto 8 cannot make any special claim to be a proper and formal ending that would give meaning to the title. There is no sign of any offspring at the end of canto 8. The divine couple spend a hundred years and more in lovemaking with no thought of the defeated and dispirited immortals waiting at the gate for the arrival of a son who would lead them to victory against Tāraka.

A significant point that ought to be borne in mind in the context is that *kumāra*, the son is self-begotten of Śiva. His birth is miraculous as it should rightly be. It is extra-ordinary as the birth of great heroes are. In metaphysical terms it might be appropriate to regard *kumāra* as the emanation of Śiva. The poet articulates this idea beautifully in *Meghadūtam*,

> . . . for he is the blazing energy, sun-surpassing,
> that the Wearer of the Crescent Moon placed
> in the Divine Fire's mouth to protect Indra's hosts.
>
> *Megh*. 45:4-6.

The idea expressed so pregnantly in a striking image in the above-quoted lines from *Meghadūtam*, is elaborated in cantos 9, 10, the first two unauthentic cantos.

The complete poem of seventeen cantos meanders on in a leisurely manner detailing various events. It is not that the authentic Kālidāsan cantos 6-8 are not given to some prolixity. As suggested already, some of the writing in these three cantos are tired, uninspired and coarse (8). Cantos 9-11 describe the three stages of gestation of Śiva's emanation, Kumāra: first within Agni, the Divine Fire; second, in Gaṅgā's waters. One ought to remember that Gaṅgā also born of Himālaya is Śiva's consort and regarded with intense jealousy by Gaurī (see *Megh*. 50); then taken in by the Kṛttikas, the Pleiades into their wombs when they bathe in the river's holy waters. Unable to bear the burning heat of the foetus, they throw it back into Gaṅgā's waters, who pushes it into a clump of reeds on the bank. Śiva's emanation, *kumāra* is born in this spot. In their wanderings Pārvatī chances upon the newborn babe blazing in splendour and accepts him as her own son. All this time, the *devas* have been waiting patiently, miserable, for the eagerly expected event that is to bring them deliverance from Tāraka. Finally the child who had grown into immeasurable strength and prowess in a few days is consecrated as commander of the armies of the *devas* (*devasenā*). Now follows the description of the opposing armies, their fierce encounter, the wavering fortunes of battle and finally the slaying of Tāraka by Kumāra employing not conventional weapons but a special, sanctified, powerful missile, a *śakti*.

The nine cantos of the 'sequel' are uneven in writing. However this criticism does apply in some measure to the authentic cantos of the poem as well, cantos 6, 7, 8. Parts of the sequel are impressive in conception and articulation. Cantos 14, 16 and 17 stand out as highly dramatic narrative verse, with vivid descriptions. In canto 14, the narrative moves swiftly and inexorably like mighty armies marching in splendid panoply, banners flying, drums and conches sounding, warriors and their mounts marching *en masse,* phalanx after phalanx in order. The verse reflects the colour and excitement of battle.

The final two cantos form a highly dramatic, and impressive piece of writing, vivid in their descriptions of the horrors of war, of the blood and violence often glossed over because the glory of valour and heroism are foregrounded. The writing is exciting but at the same time a tragic streak runs right through the narrative, such that the reader is compelled to sense the pity of it all, of the waste of human potential for worthless aims, greed and ambition, even injustice in this case, because the story of Tāraka is a story of injustice done to a noble and great ruler and his queen, both pious. He takes his revenge. The story like many other Puranic stories of *deva* and *dānava* is one-sided. The *devas* are not perfect set against the *dānavas* who are painted as beings of unmitigated evil. The *devas* are flawed beings too. And Kālidāsa is not unaware of this fact as is clear from our reading of 3:3-9.

The material that the poet has at hand, on which he works to create the poem, is intractable. It is an uneasy mix of the several components in the poem, the mythic, the metaphysical and the story-element. This last element probably comes out of the rich, age-old oral tradition of the country.

Whatever the 'intention' of an author might have been, a work can only be considered on the basis of its accomplishment. A work of art does not and it need not proceed on lines that the author might have originally planned. Often the work of art proceeds on its own impetus taking a direction that might not have been part of the original, intended plan. There are many intangibles in the process of literary creation. The creative imagination often makes choices changing, rejecting, as it works on the mass of material which it is shaping into a work of art.

There is a fascination for a critical reader in following the poetic imagination even when it appears to be wayward. And unfinished works have a charm. The unpredictability makes a work open-ended, problematic; it teases the reader into thought. This is seen at work in the epic.

Formally *Raghuvaṃśam* is a finished poem. But in aesthetic terms it is not. It is open-ended in much the same way as *Meghadūtam* is. The term open-ended is used advisedly. In a real sense the great solar dynasty collapses suddenly. When the last monarch, Agnivarṇa burns himself out in wild dissipation and is secretly burned on the funeral pyre in the palace gardens with no pomp, no ceremonial mourning and all the other trappings of royalty as one might expect, the royal priest and ministers place the sorrowing widowed queen consort 'who bears within her womb a child, as the earth bears a handful of seeds to sprout in time', on the lion throne and consecrate her as the ruler. She rules 'her husband's kingdom' in undisputed sway (*avyāhatājña*) 'with the aid of the hereditary ministers', while the subjects wait in eager expectation for the birth of her child.

Many questions rise inevitably in the reader's mind as they do in the reading of *Meghadūtam* (see intro. section VIII). The lines referred to above which come at the end of canto 19 suggest that the queen ruled as regent for the unborn heir. Did she continue on the throne? Was the child born in proper time? Was it a son? The epic chooses not to provide any answers. Again, as in *Meghadūtam* it offers only hope as consolation but no certainties. The use of the word *ākāṅkṣā* at this juncture is significant. To quote the relevant phrase: . . . *prasavasamayākāṅkṣiṇīnām prajānāṃ* (while the subjects waited in eager expectation of the time of birth . . .).

VI

The two works, *Meghadūtam* and *Śakuntalā,* which I have placed last in order in the poet's *oeuvre*, have certain features in common: they move in several worlds and touch upon different planes of consciousness; the poetic vision they project is similar and they share a pensive and reflective tone; a fairy tale element is present in both.

In the poem, *Meghadūtam,* three worlds are laid out. At the world's summit on holy Kailāsa, instinct with Śiva's divine presence, is Alakā, the earthly paradise. Here below, is the world of nature and human experience, and in between the elemental world of the rain cloud which mediates between the natural and divine worlds. The rain cloud belongs to both the natural world and the divine order that sustains it.

Alakā is a world created by our dreams and desires where time stands still and whose ways are untrodden by the unimaginative; where 'sensual music' fills the nights to overflowing under the moonlight (*Megh*. 66, 68). No other work of the poet reveals more clearly the blend of the erotic and spiritual that characterizes Śiva-mythology and is reflected in Kālidāsa's work; a mystic feeling for the transcendental combines with a sensuous feeling for beauty in woman and nature to give his poetry its distinctive quality.

The action of the play *Śakuntalā* moves out of the green world of nature, set apart and centering round the heroine who is presented as the lady of nature, into the gilded world of Duḥṣanta's palace and pleasure-gardens, and finds its resolution in yet another world—a higher world that is inaccessible to ordinary mortals and which partakes of the quality of timelessness because it is presided over by Mārīca and Aditi, whose origins *are* before the world ever *was*; a world that is the creation of art to be held against the insistent, pushing realities and pressures of the actual world.

The movement out of the green world is accomplished with much reluctance on the heroine's part. When she disappears from view behind a line of great forest trees, the green world, magical, vanishes too. I use the word 'magical' advisedly because a magico-sacral aura surrounds the deer that 'lures' Duḥṣanta into the depths of the forest. The blackbuck is a sacred animal in the Vedas. The image in 1:6 of Pinākī (Śiva) is resonant with mythical allusiveness. The myth alluded to refers to the destruction of the sacrifice of the gods by Śiva who was enraged at being denied his share in it. The sacrifice (*yajña*), out of fear of Śiva's arrow, flew up into the sky in the form of a deer; Śiva aiming his arrow at the fleeing deer, decapitated it and its head became the star *Mṛga-Śiras* (Deer's head).

When Śakuntalā leaves the hermitage and the green world vanishes, what remains is 'an empty desert', for she is the lady of nature. Attempts made in Act 6 to restore this world and all the 'happenings' of the initial meeting of Duḥṣanta and Śakunatalā that led to their love and union, fail. The re-enactment of the events turns into a 'mirage'. The image of the mirage (6:17) ought to be linked with that of 'the empty desert'. The representation of that magical world in all its details, the blossoming trees and vines, 'the full-flowing' river, the mating deer and pairs of geese on the river-bank, rendered with dead accuracy by the amateur painter and praised by a pair of art-critics belonging obviously to the school of realism, remains just that—lifeless. The illusion that Duḥṣanta strives to transform into the living presence of the beloved whom he spurned is shattered by Māḍhavya's caustic wit to which nothing is sacred.

No overt comment is made about the relative merits of these several worlds, nor is a stark contrast drawn between one and the other, for it is not characteristic of Kālidāsa's poetic vision to see experience in simple black-and-white terms.

Different planes of consciousness are touched upon in these two works: dream—awakening; delusion and loss of memory; disorientation, where the mind whirls around unfocussed (*bhrama*); recollection and re-cognition. Interesting observations are made about a state of mind where recollection stands on the pre-conscious threshold, inhibited from stepping over the thin line drawn by the conscious mind acting as censor for whatever reason, to produce uneasiness and perplexity, until some incontrovertible, tangible fact breaks the barrier down. We refer to such passages as the following: the beloved, distraught, forgetting the melody no sooner had she composed it (*Megh.* 85), hovering uncertain 'between waking and dreaming/a day-lily on a cloudy day neither open nor shut', and nervously pushing back her tangled braid off her cheek (*Megh.*: 90,91). In *Śakuntalā* at the opening of Act 5 we see Duḥṣanta is disturbed; not knowing why, his mind is filled with restlessness, as 'a sadness ineffable' falls like a shadow over it. The stage-direction at this point requires the actor to portray a state of bewilderment, of disorientation, *paryākula* (5:9). And at the end of the act the king gives expression to the nagging doubts that cloud his mind in brooding uncertainty.

In both works, at certain points, the line between the real and the imagined or visionary worlds is hazy. In the play, in the portrait-episode in Act 6, the real and the imagined fuse. It needs the caustic comment of the realist, Māḍhavya, to break them apart and demarcate them into separate areas. To him, the line between the real and the illusory (not the imagined) is hard and clear and on its further side lies madness, to which the king is perilously close, as he, Māḍhavya, views the situation.

This is especially true in *Meghadūtam.* Perceptions of reality and illusion fuse as the actual world and the imagined worlds are interfused. The poem, cast in the form of dream vision teases us into thought, into asking what the real theme of the poem is. Is it only the exteriorization of a *yakṣa's* dream of love and longing? Or is it also the realization in language of the poet's vision of Beauty (that is also truth) which he seeks and sees everywhere, but only in fragments, not in that perfect *wholeness* which he seeks.

> But alas! o cruel one! I see not
> your whole *likeness* anywhere in any one thing (*Megh.*103)

It is the poet's passionate cry that the *whole* is cruelly denied to him even as a *likeness*, an image, a reflection. Is the poet not anguishing over the barriers that confront human vision and limit the imagination?

VII

Meghadūtam is a many-layered poem of great complexity and it will be my endeavour to unravel some of this complexity and point to the several levels of discourse that operate in it shaping an intricate pattern of meaning.

The poem's sources probably lie embedded in an extensive body of popular tales, much of which has been lost.[45] The legend of the *yakṣa* who was banished under a curse for neglecting the duties entrusted to him by his overlord, Kubera, might have been familiar to the poet's audience. But we do not know this for a fact.

The old Sanskrit commentaries provide the barest outline of the legend in two versions that vary slightly in detail. In one version, the *yakṣa* is put in charge of Kubera's beautiful groves and gardens, especially the sacred pool of golden lotuses, the holy lake Mānasa. But while he is away from his post of warder for a long time, the celestial elephant Airāvata comes in one day, ravages the gardens and rooting around in the lake, as elephants tend to do, destroys the golden lotuses. This incident comes into the poem in st. 64 as one of the *yakṣa's* many memories. In the other version, he is entrusted with the duty of gathering fresh lotuses from this same holy pool at dawn and bringing them to Kubera to offer in worship to Śiva (see sts. 7 and 73). Reluctant to leave his wife's side so early in the morning, the *yakṣa* once picks the buds late in the evening and keeps them ready for the following morning's worship. When Kubera takes the flowers up to offer to the Lord, a bee that had been trapped in one of the shut buds flies out and bites his finger. That morning happens to be a specially sacred one, the morning of the Awakening of Viṣṇu—*Hari-Prabodhinī*—after the long *yoganidrā* (sleep) of four months (110), which makes the *yakṣa's* dereliction of duty more serious. The poem does not rehearse this story; it plunges straight into the heart of the matter, the central situation where the *yakṣa* fallen from greatness, is seen pining on a far hilltop, separated from his beloved.

Yakṣas and *yakṣīs* are ancient divinities belonging to the cults and cultures of the oldest inhabitants of the land. Envisaged as centres of powers in nature out of which flowed all the rich blessings of life, they were personified and worshipped as deities of groves and waters that they guarded (*see Megh.* n.1). Temples as well as small village shrines were built for their worship (*Megh.*: 25). Divinities of the sacred grove and indwelling spirits of the great forest trees are invoked in the play to bless Śakuntalā on the eve of her departure for her royal husband's home; they bestow rich gifts on her and pronounce their blessings for her safe and pleasant journey (*Śak.*: 4:7, 13). In *Meghadūtam*, tree-goddesses are described as sharing the grief of the speaker (106).

As forces of nature associated with life and fertility and guardians of sacred groves and pools, *yakṣas* and *yakṣīs* would have probably figured in folk and fairy tales. In the *Mahābhārata* saga, which is a vast amalgam of popular tales, folk and fairy tales and legends, there are episodes where the Pāṇḍava heroes encounter *yakṣas* guarding pools, one of which relates to Kubera's pool of golden lotuses. Men of great stature, power and valour, and women of uncommon beauty and grace met by the heroes of epics and romances are often asked with admiring wonder if they are beings of divine origin: *yakṣas, gandharvas, apsaras*.

Apsaras, 'born of the Waters'— the waters of creation (see note 8), are, like *yakṣa-yakṣīs*, associated with life and fertility and seen as beneficent powers. In the earliest mention of Śakuntalā in Vedic literature, she is described as an *apsara* who conceived and bore the great Bharata at a place called Nāḍapit.[46] In the epic, which is the direct source for the play, Śakuntalā is not an *apsara* herself but the daughter of one and she is presented as such in the play. Kālidāsa does not let us forget that the heroine is not wholly of this mortal world of ours. She belongs to two worlds, sharing the qualities of her parents who belonged to two different worlds, invested with nature's beauty and spontaneous creative energies as well as its holiness from Menakā, her mother and inheriting the ability for ascetic control from her father Viśvāmitra that makes her a striking presence in the last act though she speaks only a few words.

Abandoned at birth, Śakuntalā is looked after by birds (*śakunta*) that encircle her protectively so that she remains unharmed until the sage Kaṇva finds her and names her Śakuntalā, because she was cared for first by birds. She is portrayed as a child of nature, or the lady of nature, kin to all forms of life in the sacred grove. Says Śārṅgarava, hearing the cuckoo's song:

> Kin to her during her woodland sojourn
> the trees now give her leave to go (*Śak.*: 4.12)

This aspect of Śakuntalā's personality ought to be kept in mind. She brings to the king something of significance that is lacking in his life. Duḥṣanta's childlessness, referred to indirectly in Act 1 in the blessings pronounced by the anchorite, and emphasized in Act 2, is a metaphor for barrenness of more than one sort. I might venture to characterize it as spiritual barrenness. Duḥṣanta is led by the deer into Śakuntalā's world, the green world of nature possessing plenitude, fertility, beauty and grace and holiness. Later, he is led into yet another world, the golden world of Mārīca and Aditi which appears to be the world of nature *perfected*. Duḥṣanta's narrow and enclosed world of the gilded court, circumscribed by the round of royal ceremonies and pleasures, is thus expanded by virtue of his encounter with Śakuntalā, who is of this world, and yet not wholly of this world.

Fairy-tale elements are present in the poem as well as the play. The sacred pool of golden lotuses guarded by a Genius with specific instructions to follow; the failure to carry them out, the curse and consequent loss of love, status and superhuman powers are characteristic of folklore and fairy tale. The frame story of the lost *Bṛhat-Kathā*[47] as retold in the extant *Katha-sarit-sāgara* (The Ocean of Story-streams) is one such, where the speaker, an attendant of Śiva, is banished from the Divine Presence for wrongdoing and cursed to fall into the human condition. Release from the curse and restoration is promised at the expiry of a term after certain conditions have been fulfilled.

In the play, to the curse-fall-restoration motif certain other elements are added: the loss and discovery of the child and heir to the throne, which is interwoven with the loss and recovery of the token of identity, and a pattern of dream-illusion and forgetfulness-recognition.

Folk and fairy tale contain irrational elements; they are far from being realistic and are frequently amoral in the attitudes they display. The curses in them are prime examples of this irrationality, for the punishment meted out is invariably far in excess of the wrongdoing; often punishment strikes sudden and swift even in the case of an error committed unwittingly.

These factors should be kept in mind in our approach to and our interpretation of the events in the poem and the play—the *yakṣa's* exile, Durvāsa's curse and Śakuntalā's repudiation by the forgetful Duḥṣanta. The proneness to indulge in strictly realistic, moralistic responses, seen often in critical evaluations of our literature ought to be played down and contained in an overall view which takes into account the several elements from different cultural-literary sources that come together to shape the world of a play or a poem.

The curse itself does not lend itself to any simple explanation. It represents a whole complex of ideas, one of which would be to perceive it as the exteriorization of a state of mind where some exclusive and obsessive preoccupation results in a psychological imbalance. This is the simplistic view held by the sage Durvāsa, who is himself obsessed with a sense of his own holiness and ascetic powers. Some critics adopt an ethical view. Tagore speaks of Śakuntalā's 'Fall'[48] and her redemption through penitence, terms that belong to another intellectual tradition, the Judaeo-Christian; S.K. De[49] describes the curse of Durvāsa as playing 'the part of a stern but beneficent providence.' He interprets the Kālidāsan vision as purely moralistic, which it is not. But a curse is also a metaphor for the arbitrariness of life; it points to that inexplicable, even absurd element that is of the very essence of life and which is not only beyond explanations and justifications, but beyond all comprehension. Wherever a curse operates, the human failing is trivial compared to the enormity of suffering entailed. It concretizes that troubling question which faces every human being at one time or another. Why did this happen? Why does it have to be so? The curse also shapes the answer to that question in the form of the uncertain certitude with which man has to shore up his crumbling faith in order to survive; call it Fate or *karma* or 'the absurd' or simple acceptance—This is how things are; this is life. Śakuntalā herself blames her actions in a former life for her unhappiness in the present: the *yakṣa's* response is acceptance, with the faith that things have to change for the better. Kālidāsa does not preach; he does not moralize. He shows us life as it is in all its beauty and splendour, as well as its inexplicable vagaries, which bring misfortunes deservedly or undeservedly. It is significant that the poet does not underline the *yakṣa's* wrongdoing in the poem. The poem does not describe it; it merely speaks of the curse as a consequence of 'neglect of a *special* charge', a failure to perform the duties belonging to *one's* own office; the phrases *underlined* are the two meanings of the phrase *svādhikāra-pramādaḥ*. (The phrase in the text—*svādhikārāt-pramattaḥ*—is the adjectival form.) In both versions of the legend provided in the old commentaries, the duties assigned to the *yakṣa* appear to be a privilege and an honour bestowed on him and his failure to carry them out seems to indicate that he was insufficiently sensible of the high regard and esteem in which he was held by Kubera, his overlord. The golden lotuses are one of Kubera's 'nine treasures'—the sacred pool itself is one of the 'treasures' carefully guarded; among Kubera's many attendant-lords, it is our erring *yakṣa* who is *chosen* to bring fresh lotuses each dawn to offer to the Supreme (Śiva). In this connection it is interesting to note the comment made by Duḥṣanta when he conveys his own awareness of the esteem in which Indra held him and which spurs him to do 'momentous deeds' (*Śak.*: 7:4). The neglect of duty under the stress of an obsessive love (or passion) that bears within itself the seeds of its own unhappiness and leads to near-tragic consequences seems to have engaged the profound concern of the poet. We see him returning repeatedly to a consideration of it in varying situations to explore it in slightly different ways: in *Meghadūtam (The Cloud Messenger)*, in *Abhijñānaśākuntalam (Śakuntalā)* and in *Vikramorvaśīyam* (*Urvaśī Won by Valour*). He touches upon it lightly in the epic.

In the poem, the reason for the curse is not explicitly stated, but we infer from the form it takes—separation from the beloved—that it was related to the *yakṣa's* passionate love for her. The words used in the poem to characterize the *yakṣa* are significant: *kāmī* (passionate), *kāmārta* (sick with passion); one who whispered in her ear words of no special import, only to touch her cheek with his lips (102). A curse usually deprives the person of the object that was responsible, directly or indirectly for his or her wrong-doing. But in *Śakuntalā*, Durvāsa's curse neatly phrases the failure of duty (wrongdoing in his eyes), in balanced clauses. The punishment is far in excess of the negligence of which Śakuntalā was guilty: there were extenuating circumstances in her case. What makes the *yakṣa's* dereliction of duty more serious is that it happened on a specially sacred day known as The Awakening of Viṣṇu—*Hari-Prabodhinī* (110). However, the point that is subtly made in the play is, that Śakuntalā was also not sufficiently appreciative of the esteem in which her father held her and which prompted him to *entrust her* rather than one of his pupils with the important duties of welcoming guests and offering them hospitality during his absence from the Hermitage (1:12+2.3). The word used in the text means 'put in charge' or 'appointed to'. Anasūyā has to remind her more than once of her obligations to perform the duties of hospitality and in fact, it is she and not Śakuntalā who actually performs them when the king arrives at the Hermitage as a guest. A traditional interpretation would treat the disregard to appointed duties in both the cases of the *yakṣa* and Śakuntalā as a betrayal of trust.

In the other play, *Vikramorvaśīyam* (*Urvaśī Wom by Valour*), a double curse is seen operating, both called down on Urvaśī on account of the errors she commits when she is disoriented by her obsessive passion for the king. The initial curse exiles her from heaven but out of pity, it is commuted to a limited period on earth as the wife of the king whom she loves so passionately. To celestial beings, life on earth as a mortal is tantamount to a dire punishment. But here the poet balances the loss against the gain—the loss to Urvaśī of her great status in heaven and the bliss of a paradisal way of life against fulfilment on earth of her love for the king. The second curse takes effect as a consequence of the first when Urvaśī whose love for the king is intolerantly possessive, is seized by jealousy and rushing blindly in anger into the sacred grove of Kumāra, forbidden to women, is at once transformed into a vine. The king himself dotes so much on Urvaśī that leaving the governing of his kingdom to his ministers, he passes his life in a round of pleasures with her, valuing what he describes as 'desirable servitude'[50] to her more than the glory he gained through his conquering prowess. And when he loses her he is plunged into madness, because the centre of his world is no more. The spring of his life that kept it going is broken.

In the epic,[51] Aja, is devastated by the untimely and sudden death of his queen, Indumatī, whom he loved to distraction. Drowned in inconsolable grief he cannot come to terms with it despite the wise counsel of the Royal Preceptor, the sage Vasiṣṭha and he barely manages to survive to carry on the government till his son grows up to shoulder the yoke of sovereignty, at which point Aja abandons his body to rejoin his wife in the other world.

The exile-theme is found in both the *Mahābhārata* and the *Rāmāyaṇa* but considering how frequently the motif of a curse-exile-penance following the breaking of a command occurs in Sanskrit literature—the Purāṇas or old chronicles have many such examples and the Purāṇas contain a great deal of folk-lore and fairy-tale—I would hazard the guess that it was a motif deeply embedded in the popular imagination and used in different ways in the floating body of popular tales. But the parallel with Rāma's exile is noteworthy if only because the poet refers to it so pointedly in the opening stanza. The *yakṣa* spends his exile in Rāmagiri.

VIII

Meghadūtam is a *dūta-kāvyaṃ* or messenger-poem, the first of its kind, giving rise to a spate of imitations over the centuries.[52] To call it a *dūta-kāvyaṃ* is only to place it in a definable genre. The poem is much more than just a messenger-poem, as I shall try to indicate later on in the introduction.

The *Nāṭyaśāstra*[53] lists the *dūtī* or female messenger amongst the *dramatis personae*, as a class of characters. The device is therefore well known in literature. The *Ṛgveda,* the earliest Indian text mentions one.[54] However, while noting that in the *Ṛgveda,* the *devas* send Saramā, the hound of heaven as a messenger to the Pāṇis to negotiate what would now be described as a trade deal and a very one-sided one, and that in the *Mahābhārata*[55] a golden swan carries love-messages between Nala and Damayantī, it must be stressed that these parallels have little relevance in the serious consideration of our poem. In the land where the beast-fable had it origin, the idea of using a non-human messenger must have been a very old one. It was probably the most commonly used device in story-telling and story-telling was indeed a very ancient art in India. More to the point is the parallel with Hanumān's journey from another hill not far Rāmagiri, taking Rāma's message and his signet-ring to Sītā sorrowing in distant Laṅkā. The poet himself draws attention to Hanumān's meeting with Sītā in stanza 99. Further, in this Rāmāyaṇa[56] episode, there is some description of the landscape and the events that happen during Hanumān's aerial flight, whereas, in the Nala-Damayantī story in the *Mahābhārata*, the bird-messenger is a mere mechanical device. It is not central and integral as the cloud-messenger is in our poem.

Further, the similarities between *Meghadūtam* and the *Rāmāyaṇa* which some Sanskrit commentators point out, can be more fruitfully viewed from another stand-point, as indicative of a fundamental factor—the poem's filiation. Kālidāsa places himself firmly in the *kāvya* tradition which begins with the *Rāmāyaṇa*. The continuity of literary tradition is proclaimed here as it is in his other works. But a great writer uses his literary inheritance in many different ways, often relating himself to it by differences rather than by similarities. Kālidāsa's poem is one of a kind, owing little to what went before and leaving nothing for what came after, having exhausted all the possibilities of the form.

In ancient cultures, non-human forms of life, birds, beasts and even trees were believed to possess superhuman abilities and powers, to have a special kind of wisdom and bear a special relationship to sacred forces.[57] Such beliefs were part of the thought of the early Paleolithic culture of the Eurasian landmass. But to cast a rain cloud, an inanimate, elemental thing (as the poet himself reminds us in st. 5) as a messenger, is to have made a literary choice of extraordinary imaginative power and poetic sensibility. The poet dismisses the *yakṣa*, it is true, at st. 5, with a cavalier gesture, as one love-sick, pining on a hilltop, clouded in mind and unable to discriminate between intelligent and inanimate forms of life. A double purpose is served by this. The light-hearted, almost flippant gesture of dismissal is made by the poet to distance himself from his fictive creation; and the authorial voice is no longer heard after this point. This is significant because in the absence of the authorial voice, we are given the option of a *reading* that is not strictly bound to the frame of reference provided by the poet's contemporary world and are therefore able to pursue lines of interpretation and understandings of the poem which are not defined by the norms and ideals of its culture. But it is necessary to point out that an interpretation conforming to the values of that world could and ought to be held in tension with any other adopted. Any work of art of sufficient depth does contain within itself hints of self-questioning. While it reflects its own time and landscape, it often adopts a stance that can only be defined as questioning, if not critical. A great writer does not passively accept the social mores and moral values of his world in their totality, though he may not push his implicit questioning of these to a position of articulate dissent. More about this later when assessing where and how the weight of the poetry falls. Secondly, the seeming lack of discrimination in the speaker of the poem makes the poem what it is; and the cloud, an elemental thing blended of the four elements (as all forms of life are in ancient cosmogony), becomes not only a unifying symbol in the poem, but transformed by poetic power, as a central character—the *yakṣa's* 'other self'. There is a deliberate irony here which makes the conception of the cloud's role in the poem unique.

Meghadūtam (*The Cloud Messenger*) is more than a poem of longing and separation with glowing descriptions of nature. Myth and legend, dream-vision and literary reminiscences are blended with topographical and conversational[58] dimensions to give a love-poem depth and a multilayered texture. Further, the lover-beloved (*nāyaka-nāyikā*) framework of the dramatic tradition in which the poem can be seen as placed in its own times is raised to another level where it is the landscape that figures as the beloved of the cloud-lover that is itself the *alter ego* of the real lover—the speaker in the poem. The natural and physical characteristics of a rain cloud as well as its mythic associations (which we shall come to presently) are brought into play during its long course over a vast stretch of land, and constantly and consistently related through some of the most richly textured imagery in the poet's work to legendary and semi-historical places and personages. Many of these places are holy spots of pilgrimage; places of atonement and purification associated with persons guilty of wrongdoing of one kind or another. The poem is a totally new genre in the lyric mode.

We realize at the end when we have completed our *reading* of the poem that the relationships between the human and natural worlds which are explored in the way they are and the objectives set out in the poem could only have been undertaken and articulated so effectively by making a rain cloud the messenger. The appropriateness of the choice is clear when we trace the distant source for the kinship of cloud and hill which functions as a key metaphor. A Vedic text[59] tells of the myth of the ancient winged mountains, first-born of the Creator, that flew around creating hazards in mid-air, until Indra, sustainer and protector of the universe, severed their wings and fixed them into the earth like pegs; the severed wings floated free transformed into 'thunder clouds'.

> Hence, they ever float over mountains; this is their origin.

The poet is able to make use of this mythic association of cloud and mountain to set up a relationship between them and by extension between the cloud and the landscape, which is a crucial one in the poem. Behind this specific and organic relationship lies the general and symbolic one of the marriage of heaven and earth on which the well-being of the world depends. In st. 19, a lover-beloved relationship is implied between earth and her cloud-lover; the cloud as we note in st. 6 is the *power* of Indra, lord of *svarga*, the Realm of light, and of the Immortals.

The cloud is introduced at the opening of the poem by the key-phrase, 'embracing the crest of the hill'. What was once sundered and placed in two separate planes, aerial and terrestrial, is united. This parallels the situation of the lovers in the poem and their spatial separation. Alakā, the dream-city where the beloved lives, is the abode high up in the Himalayas, of *yakṣas*, semi-divine beings who move freely in the air and through space like the cloud. The hilltop of Rāma's Hill, on the other hand, is of the earth, earthy, where the lover, shorn of all his powers, is fixed, earth-bound. He is unable to move freely, like the primeval mountains that had also transgressed the cosmic law *Ṛta* that relates and binds all forms of being in a harmonious pattern of behaviour so that order in the universe may be maintained. The separation and reunion of cloud and hill is a metaphor for the *yakṣa's* own parting from his beloved and the reunion which he so keenly longs for and finds vicariously in the coming together of cloud with hill and stream. Human love and union (for all practical purposes the *yakṣa* and the beloved are human) are placed in the larger frame of the cosmic union of heaven and earth. This is one among many metaphors that builds the totality of meaning of this multi-layered poem; and it constitutes the initial step in the shaping of the central role of the cloud. A silent cloud which at first glance seemed to be no more than a captive audience to a love-sick *yakṣa*, turns out on closer scrutiny to be an actor playing a unique role and fulfilling a number of functions that are instrumental in realizing the objectives that the poem has set out for itself. But before the cloud can accomplish all this, it has to be endowed with a special status above and beyond what the bare vedic myth has provided. It has to be invested with the powers and responsibilities that are part of that status.

Cast right at the beginning in the role of a lover, of hill (2, 27) and stream (26, 30, 31, 42, 43) and of the whole landscape (19, 25), the cloud is invested with qualities moral and physical, through a series of images and comparisons that serve to magnify and glorify it. But first, a personality is created for it round a few phrases from Puranic accounts of *Origins*. The *Purāṇas*[60] not only provide descriptions of the origins and genealogies of gods, anti-gods and demons, of kings, seers and sages, but also of inanimate forms like rivers, mountains and *clouds*. The *Puṣkarāvartaka* clouds in the poem (6) are described as 'possessing deep resonant voices and the power to assume various shapes at will', as 'brimful of water, raining down beneficial rains', and as appearing as agents of destruction at the end of an epoch to preside over the dissolution of the universe. Thus they are envisaged as participating in the creative-destructive cycle of the cosmic process, being finally subsumed in the primordial *waters* in which the creative principle lies hid, resting, until it is time to recreate the universe. Our cloud is born of this lofty lineage. It is the instrument of Indra, lord of heaven and bountiful giver of riches. A cluster of images delineate the cloud as the fertilizing force in the worlds of Nature and Man; trees and shrubs burst into luxuriant bloom, (25, 27, 28); cranes and wild geese rejoice at its arrival knowing that it is mating time and form its retinue as it moves north majestically to Kailāsa and lake Mānasa which is also the breeding place for the birds (9, 11). The onset of rains is that magical time in a tropical country, of the greening of the earth after the burning summer and devastating drought; of hope springing up in the hearts of grieving women waiting anxiously for the return of their husbands who have to travel to far places on business of various kinds (8, 10, 98). The rainy season in Indian literature is like springtime and all that it suggests in western literature. But it is also the time of unendurable anguish for those separated from their loved ones, as the *yakṣa* and his beloved are.

As the poem progresses, the rain cloud, nobly-descended, as we have seen, is gradually elevated in status through the attribution of qualities and virtues enumerated as pertaining to the character of a hero; splendour and grace, courage and compassion, poise, steadfastness of purpose, self-respect that will not tolerate an insult, high breeding, courtesy, gentle speech, charm and beauty of form. It is to be presumed that the *yakṣa* invests the cloud with these qualities and virtues that rightly belong to himself as a hero, a hero of the *udātta* type in Indian Poetics.

By various comparisons with deities in the pantheon—Balarāma, Kṛṣṇa, Viṣṇu—the cloud is touched by the light of divinity and is provided with its own epithets, as all forms of divinity possess and ought to possess: *jala-da* and *jala-dhara* (giver and bearer of water), *jīmūta*, (containing the precious water that sustains life). It is addressed as brother and friend, a refuge; and implored for help in distress. The cloud assumes different shapes to perform its several functions as a benefactor to nature and man; as a lover, desirable, welcomed by the rivers; as a stern judge who punishes the presumption of the *Śarabhas* puffed up with vanity and in the form of Viṣṇu's dark-blue foot extended that curbed the arrogance of Bali. Balarāma, was not only a form of divinity, being the elder brother of Kṛṣṇa and a part of the Supreme incarnated on earth, but also a cult-hero, as is clear from the epither Plough-Bearer; a cult-hero who harnessed the waters of the river Jumna for irrigation, to benefit his people and therefore a benefactor of humanity. He was also a personage guilty of wrongdoing like the *yakṣa* who atoned for it as he did through the instrumentality of the cloud (as we shall see later). Thus this particular comparison serves more than one purpose.

The cloud's other awesome aspect as described in the *Purāṇas* is also brought in at various points in the poem. As it sweeps along the sky, soaring up like the uprooted peak of a great mountain, it displays its size and power. It hurls down thunder and hail like missiles to scatter the *Śarabhas* (56) and break their overblown pride. In the *Mahākāla* passage (34-38) which constitutes a high point in the poem, the cloud takes on the aura of divinity by virtue of its resemblance to the blue-black throat of Śiva and is therefore viewed with awe and admiration by the celestial attendants of the Lord. The image suggests that the cloud is part of the supreme; and a little later it *does* become a part of the divine, merging into the 'forest of uplifted arms' of the god who *dances* the universe into existence. At this point the cloud attains its apotheosis, performing the role of the drum in the Cosmic Dance. The imagery in this passage should be carefully noted; there is an undertone of subdued violence. A wild energy is conveyed in images that combine power and beauty which is of the essence of the Śaiva conception of creation. The tremendous power of cosmic energy, *Śakti*, flows into time and space, shaped by the guiding principle, *Śiva*, into the pattern of dance. The images of the dark forest of uplifted arms and the blood-red glow of dawn and sunset (the word *sandhya*[64]—evening—signifies both dawn and sundown), splashing a tropical sky and reflected on the dark cloud thundering, point to both the dawn of creation and its destruction, at the beginning and at the end of Time. And the cloud-drum image occurs again (58) in connection with the destruction of the triple-city. *Tripurā* or the triple-city symbolizes the triple darkness of ignorance, evil and illusion and is linked with the demonic elephant (38), which in myth, was the illusory form created by the heretic sages to attack manifest deity (Śiva). Śiva's cosmic dance is a continuing re-enactment[62] of cosmic events and the places on earth where they occur are cosmic centres for millions of devotees. The shrine of Mahākāla is one such; it is also an important stop on the journey of the cloud which is a pilgrimage for the *yakṣa* as we shall see presently.

That the cloud does the bidding of a higher power in helping to sustain the world and preserve order is made clear by several of these comparisons which serve to set it up as a foil to the hero (*nāyakā*) of the poem, the *yakṣa*; in fact it is presented as an *ideal*, which the hero does not appear to be. The cloud is a wanderer-at-will (*kāma-cārī*), moving freely as a benefactor to nature and man; it assumes whatever shape it *wills* (*kāmarūpī*) because it is the instrument of a higher will. The *yakṣa* on the other hand, is subjected 'to an alien will' (8), because he is self-willed and his will is directed by obsessive passion to the exclusion of other duties and responsibilities; he is described as *kāmī* and *kāmārta*, passion-ridden and sickened by passion. In the traditional framework of meaning, the cloud is a dharmic hero and the *yakṣa* has swerved from the path of *dharma*.

The *yakṣa,* shorn of his powers, the eight *siddhis*, which all semi-divine beings and perfected seers possessed, is confined in the human existential condition and tied by the terms of the curse to his place of expiation, Rāma's Hill. The only action he is left with is purely verbal which takes the form of a long lyrical monologue, and action by proxy which can only be undertaken by the cloud: '. . . his way barred by an adverse decree'

'. . . . . .
he, gone beyond range of your hearing
not seen by your eyes, speaks
through my mouth. . . .'(102)

is the preamble of the *yakṣa's* message to his wife. The cloud is already perfect in the role of lover to the landscape; it now has to take on another role, that of the lover in the poem, the hero, and become his 'other self'. To effect this, the landscape has to be identified with the beloved—*kāntā.* And this is what the poem does next.

The beloved, the third person in the poem, is the unseen lady, seen only through the eyes of her husband and occasionally overheard, but whose presence is dominant and pervasive in the poem. The *yakṣa* sees her everywhere.

In the *śyāma*-vine I see your slender limbs;
your glance in the gazelle's startled eye;
the cool radiance of the moon in your face,
your tresses in the peacock's luxuriant train:
your eyebrow's graceful curve in the stream's small waves:
but alas! O cruel one, I see not
your whole likeness anywhere in any one thing. (103)

He hears the tones of her voice, seductive, loving, half-inviting, half-reluctant in Vetravatī's waters purling along her banks with 'knitted eyebrows of tremulous wavelets'. Wherever he turns he sees her only; every detail in the landscape is but a small part of her. Only the whole landscape can hold out the possibility of yielding that 'whole likeness' which he complains of being cruelly denied.

The natural world and the human world both participate in the divine. They both share in the cosmic creative energy, *śakti*. And in so far as they are vehicles for this cosmic energy, they reflect each other. The creative forces in Nature and in Woman both flow from the same source and reservoir. There is an interchangeability, then, of the roles of Nature and Woman; symbolically each part, each limb of the feminine form has its corresponding form in nature. This is already made clear in *Ṛtusaṃhāram* (see section V of introduction).

In the great reliefs of Bharhut and Sanchi, the sculptor has seen this vision of an all embracing cosmic energy manifesting itself in the beauty of form of nature and woman. The teeming energies of nature blossom in flower and tree; the sensuous form of *yakṣīs* and *vṛkṣikas* (tree-spirits) twine round blossoming vines and trees, clasping them.

The imagery invests the landscape with a personality. When the *yakṣa* tells the cloud of the river Gambhīrā with her clear waters, 'a tranquil pool of consciousness', and 'those dazzling upward leaps of glittering fishes bright as water lilies', which are her welcoming glances, what he is seeing and talking about is not the landscape, but the beloved. In Kālidāsa's poetry landscapes are specific, yet symbolic. As the poet caresses the landscape with his languages, it takes on the form and identity of the beloved in the *yakṣa's* imagination. On reaching Vidiśā, says the speaker to the cloud:

> . . . you shall at once obtain
> the unalloyed fulfilment of a lover's desire
> tasting Vetravatī's sweet waters, as a lover his beloved's lips,
> with sonorous thunder passing along her banks
> as she flows with knitted brows of tremulous wavelets. (26)

and on meeting Nirvindhyā:

> wearing a girdle strung of chiming bells
> —a row of water-birds plashing on her undulating waves—
> weaving her serpentine course with charming unsteady gait
> to reveal eddies forming her navel
> —such coy gestures are women's first statements of love. (30)

the speaker tells the cloud:

> be sure to be filled with love's fine flavour. (30)

and again in another tone of voice, the speaker remembering the sorrow of the beloved, envies the cloud the happiness he himself cannot have:

Crossing that river, O fortunate love!
Yours will be the happy task to induce Sindhu
visibly grieving at your absence,
her waters shrunk to a thin braid and pale
with the paleness of dry leaves
fallen from trees rooted on her banks,
to cast off the sorrow withering her. (31)

The rivers are the *nāyikas* (heroines) listed in the *Nāṭyaśāstra*,[63] and they express the many moods of the beloved that the *yakṣa* knew so well during their brief life together: feigning anger and displeasure, coy, playing hard to get, proud and noble (*gambhīrā*) but loving.

The cloud as the *yakṣa's* proxy and alter ego and the landscape as the substitute for the beloved are consolations which the poem constructs for the speaker but which can only be offered to him as the poem progresses. We begin inevitably in a world without consolations, with nothing to hold on to: the *yakṣa* has only the agonizing sense of the loss of every thing of value in his life and the haunting memory of 'her' who had to be left behind 'unsupported' (*abalā*). The word *a-balā*, without strength, does not imply weakness but the absence of 'supportive-ness'; the centre of a woman's world was the husband and children and the beloved is left without either.

The poem begins on a note of sorrow and despair; the passionate cry, '. . . banished/from wife and kinsman by divine decree, I entreat you'(6) rings out, pointed by a sharp sense of alienation brought about by the violation of hierarchical order. A world is fractured.

There are certain poetic qualities that are difficult to convey in a translation without some explanation. The first stanza conveys so much and with such economy, through suggestion, allusion and by its cadences that an analysis of the four lines is necessary to give some idea of the dense texture and feel of the original poetry.

kaścit kāntā-viraha-guruṇa svādhikārāt-pramattaḥ
śāpenāstam-gamita-mahimā varṣa-bhogyeṇa bhartuḥ
yakṣaś cakre janaka-tanayā-snāna-puṇyodakeṣu
snigdha-chāya-taruṣu vasatiṃ rāma-giryāśrameṣu.

Sanskrit metres are quantitative; short syllables are short and long syllables have double the duration (*mātrā*) of the short. In addition, conjunct consonants and consonants that immediately precede them are counted as *long*: e.g., both the consonants in the very first word *kaś-cit*, are counted as long. The compound words are hyphenated for readers who do not have any Sanskrit to read more easily; in the original it runs as follows: *kaścitkāntāvirahaguruṇa svādhikārātpramattaḥ* . . . . The metre used is the stately *mandākrānta*, which is defined as appropriate for love-poetry. Each line is 17-syllabled with a pause after the tenth. The lines have a measured cadence in an intricate pattern of 3-syllable units:---, -uu, uuu, --u, -u-, -- (-is long and u is short). The compound words in the first line move heavily, as if the weight of sorrow bears down on each syllable: *kā ntā -vi ra ha gu-ru ṇa, svā dhi kā rāt pra ma ttaḥ*; they do not come tripping on the tongue. Taking the second line apart to show how the metrical pattern 'suggests' (*dhvani*), setting the tone and mood: *śāpena* (by the curse) *astam-gamita mahimā* (gone or *set*, the glory); here the two words are combined by rules of euphony to become—'*sā pe nā stam ga mi ta ma hi mā*', and we have four long syllables suggesting how time drags on, followed by five short ones, to show how quickly the glory has gone—*gamita*—then a long syllable and a pause (there is almost an echo of a sigh here because a quick breath has to be taken before continuing with the line). Again, the second half of the line has 6 long syllables '*varṣa-bhogye-na-bharṭuḥ*' and the harshness of the '*r*', '*s*' and aspirated '*b*' suggests the unendurable harshness of the separation; '*bhogya*'—what is *eaten* or *enjoyed*—is *sorrow*; the word *bhartuḥ* (the lord's) from '*bhartā*', one who 'bears, protects, sustains', implies a certain feudal relationship of lord and vassal, with rights and obligations on *both* sides. The second word of the first line—'heedless of duty'—is balanced against the second word in the third line—'waters hallowed by Janaka's daughter's baths' suggesting firstly that the *yakṣa's* disregard of a command and neglect of his duty is to be seen in contrast to the perfect fulfilment of duty by Sītā; and secondly that the holy waters will purify the erring *yakṣa*. It is in the rightness of things that the *yakṣa's* transgression be expiated by penance in the place where Rāma and Sītā spent part of their exile following dharmic ideals while carrying out the parental command after voluntarily renouncing the kingdom. The word '*varṣa*' in line 2 has the double meaning of 'a year', and 'a sacred spot'; the time and place of the curse are thus set out by one word. The first image in the poem, of the setting sun (line 2) conveys the sense of the loss of powers as well as their restoration at the end of a specific period—a year, just as the sun's glory is restored the next day, at dawn. There is hope for the separated *yakṣa-yakṣī*.

The *mandākrānta* with its long line and intricate metrical pattern serves the poet's purpose well. The long line is able to present a scene or a moment of experience in significant detail within its compass. For example, the first line in st. 30 is one long compound word made up of seven units each describing one detail in the scene being viewed:

vīcikṣobhastanitavihagaśreṇikāncīguṇāyāh

vīci—kṣobha—stanita—vihaga—śreṇi—kāncī—guṇāyāh
wavelets—agitated—sounding—birds—rows—pearl—girdle-strings

The compound word takes in the scene as the eye sees it and expresses it with striking immediacy: the river (metaphor for the beloved), its girdle formed by white water-birds splashing and calling as they sway on the wavelets (an element of turbulence is indicated by the word *kṣobha*), gliding along like a woman wearing a girdle edged with tinkling little gold bells evokes a poignant memory of the beloved.

The intricate patterning of alliterative syllables provides the verse with a formal structure that serves to contain the emotion which is intense at times, the emotion which threatens to disrupt the tone and structure of the poem. The emotion is contained within the strict metrical pattern and the stanzas attain to a sculptured, contemplative beauty, of the kind displayed in the superb art of Bharhut and Sanci.

The highly self-conscious manner in which the language of the poem shapes itself also contributes to this containment; st. 101 is a good example; I quote the first two lines of the text:

aṅgenāṅgam pratanu tanunā gāḍhataptena taptam
sāśrenāśru-drutam aviratotkaṇṭham utkaṇṭhitena

aṅgena-aṅgam pra-tanu tanuna gāḍha-taptena taptam
śāsrena-aśru-drutam avirata-utkaṇṭham utkaṇṭhitena
(The second set of lines are split for easy reading.)

the repetition of the pairs of words *aṅga, tanu, tapta, aśru* and *utkaṇṭha*, one in the instrumental—*aṅgena, taptena* etc. referring to the *yakṣa* and the other in the accusative *aṅgam, taptam* etc. to the beloved is a self-conscious play on those words which imposes a certain formality of structure to contain the stark emotion. This is possible only in a highly inflected language. The beauty of *Art* is shaped by the subtle use of *artifice*.

But to sustain this difficult metre over a hundred odd stanzas in a long poem with such depth of feeling and thought and with such superb skill is a brilliant *tour de force*.

A tone of uncertainty marks the opening of the poem. '*A certain yakṣa*' passed *some* months on a hilltop (this is particularized to provide the allusion to the *Rāmāyaṇa*), separated from his beloved wife. He is given no name, because he is Everyman; he is any man suddenly and unexpectedly parted from his newly-wed wife[64] whom he loves *passionately*. (The poem uses the word *kāmī* and *kāmārta,* passion-ridden to describe him; later a distinction is made between passion or craving, and love, in st. 112). The nature of the *yakṣa's* transgression is not specified either. That he violated his lord's command is taken as sufficient reason for punishment. What matters is the conception of *dharma* as inviolable, not the precise form the violation takes in any given situation.

It is not sufficient to translate the word *dharma* into English by one word: The Law, duty, right action, virtue, moral and social order, the inherent property of a thing. All these several meanings are included in the concept.

Dharma (derived from the root, *dhṛ* 'to support'), is the reflection of *Ṛta*, the Cosmic Law on which universal order depends. As such, it is a co-ordinating concept in a world-view where all these meanings are brought together and the ethical, religious and social life of man is integrated. It is the base and support of the existential condition, the frame on which all relationships are woven. By breaking the command of Kubera, his overlord, the *yakṣa* who is his vassal upsets the delicate balance of the network of relationships and endangers *order*.

The beloved has no name either; naming bestows identity and the characters in the poem are name-less. Even though there are dramatic elements in *Meghadūtam,* there is no attempt at characterization. No story is provided; the narrative is slender, contained in the first five stanzas; the nature of the wrongdoing remains unspecified. All this unspecificity is deliberate and there is a deep poetic logic behind it, indicating that the concerns of the poet which direct the main thrust of the poem lie elsewhere—in the journey and its significance.

Rāma's Hill and Alakā are the two halves of the fractured world we spoke of. The wrongdoing that caused the world of the *yakṣa* and his beloved to break apart has to be expiated; the fractured world has to be made whole through penance, through suffering. This can only be effected through the instrumentality of the cloud, which as we have seen has been held up as portraying dharmic ideals and carrying them out; which has also been presented as constituting the *yakṣa's* 'other self'. The journey is a bridge that connects the two halves. But we have to note that the poem offers us only the hope of restoration; the end is deferred.

In the texts established by the old commentators like Mallinātha and others, the poem is divided into two parts, *Pūrva* and *Uttara Megham*, the former comprising the journey, stanzas 1-65 and the latter, the Alakā-part, st. 68-115. Many printed editions still observe this division which shows an implicit recognition on the part of the old commentators, of the structural and tonal differences between the two parts. But the poem is a unified whole, revealing an inner, organic unity effected by the presence of the cloud and the continuity of the journey.

Rāmagiri in the Vindhyas and Alakā on the Kailāsa mountain are not simply two points on the map of India; and the journey from one geographical point to the other is not simply the path traversed by a passing rain cloud during the monsoon. It is also an inner journey, through an interior landscape contoured by literary reminiscences and peopled by bitter-sweet memories. Rāma's Hill and Alakā are the beginning and end of this *journey* too. At one level of discourse, the poem feeds on memories and in turn feeds them until the whole landscape, inner and outer, is meshed in a network of memories. The cloud's journey through the actual physical landscape stretching between the two mountain ranges, both sacred to Śiva and Śakti (Pārvatī or Śakti is known as Vindhyāvāsini—one who resides in the Vindhyas) functions as a metaphor for the inner journey. For through reverie or dream-vision—the waking dream of st 106, the *yakṣa* travels every step of the way with his 'other self'; he travels back to Alakā, to his home and his beloved. The intense longing which is pointedly described in st. 3 as 'brooding' with all grief bottled up inside—antar-bāṣpaḥ—(tears welling within and checked) and the imagined return are verbalized. Sorrow that is shared is lightened and becomes easier to bear, says Priyaṃvadā, in the play (*Śak.* 3: 12.+3). At another level, the speaker treads the path of pilgrimage, which is the path of purification.

Two kinds of *tīrthas* (fords), sacred bathing places on rivers, streams and pools, like Apsara Pool, holy Saci's Pool and Indra's Landing mentioned in Act 5 of Śakuntalā, are described in the *Mahābhārata*[64a]: those that are accessible and those that are inaccessible. Both are places of pilgrimage that bestow spiritual merit and lead to *mokṣa* (release from the world); 'one should go in thought' to the latter. On account of the curse, all the holy spots that the cloud and we meet during the journey are inaccessible to the *yakṣa*. The actual start of the pilgrimage for the *yakṣa* and the cloud, his alter ego, is Mahākāla, heading north to Kailāsa, both places being sacred to Śiva and Devī and hallowed by their temporal presence. The north, in cosmography, is the place of light and life and the south, as the abode of Yama, god of Death, is the place of darkness and death.

The inner and outer journeys have a parallel movement as they pass through their respective landscapes and are related by the literary reminiscences that the poem draws heavily on. The inner journey progresses through memories re-lived vicariously through the cloud-landscape relationship and passes from the recognition of wrongdoing in the form of violation of order, to an understanding hammered out of the mind's dialogue with itself. The recognition however of wrongdoing and the violation of hierarchical order is not made explicit at any point. It is implicit in the manner in which the cloud is portrayed and held up as an *ideal*. The awakening in nature under the beneficent touch of the rain-bearing cloud is also suggestive of *renewal* which implies restoration and a new life.

Those images in the poem that serve to magnify and glorify the raincloud are also images bodying forth the ideas of transgression, punishment and penance followed by purification. Balarāma, for instance to whom the cloud is compared, resorts to the holy waters of the Sarasvatī to expiate his sin of Brahmanicide; Bali who is subdued by the ever-extending triple stride of Viṣṇu, to which the cloud is also compared, is a case of overweening pride as the story-tellers of the Purāṇas see him. In all these examples, the cloud is asked to pause over these spots where the events of the myths and legends occurred and offer worship as a devotee on behalf of the *yakṣa*, though it is itself not guilty of any form of transgression.

The acts of penance and purification are emphasized. The cloud is promised a pure inner being even if its exterior remains dark, even as Balarāma and Bali were purified. It is constantly praised as a benefactor, intent on service to others, especially the weak and helpless and those struck by adversity, and linked to other hallowed personages who were also benefactors in the past such as Gaṅgā, the celestial river that descended to the mundane world, not only to provide salvation to the sinful sons of Sagara, but also to become the greatest benefactor to the people of India. She came down to earth as the result of the arduous penance of Bhagīratha who wished to save the souls of his sinful ancestors. Images of salvation are interspersed in the description of the landscape, even where there is no wrongdoing involved: for instance, in the Mahākāla passage, which we have already noted and again at the peak still known as Śiva's sacred Foot (57) on the way to Kailāsa, where the cloud is promised the eternal station of the Lord's attendants (*śiva-pādam*). As the cloud is the alter-ego of the speaker, it is reasonable to conclude that these acts of adoration and worship lead the *yakṣa* from a fallen state upwards to a state of blessedness.

Much of the imagery surrounding the cloud, either through comparison, identification or association, as when the cloud is asked to *transform* himself into a flower-cloud and rain blossoms that have been freshened and sanctified by being sprinkled with the waters of the heavenly Gaṅgā (that is before her descent into this world) on Skanda, who is the emanation of Śiva's effulgence to battle against the dark forces and save the world, serves the purpose of providing a way to redress the alienation from the divine. We should refer this back to the *yakṣa*, for the cloud is itself sinless and dedicated to the happiness of others, not its own. This is brought out most clearly in stanza 60, where a sharp contrast is drawn between the self-abnegating cloud which is welcomed as a guest by Kailāsa and Rāvaṇa who is punished for his sublime egotism. Rāvaṇa wished to uproot the peak of Kailāsa and carry it to his palace with Śiva and Devī on it, so as to have the sacred presence of the Primal Parents always with him and for himself alone.

This geographical part of the poem as Wilson terms it,[65] is therefore a pilgrimage, for the cloud, as it is to millions of Indians; more so, it is a pilgrimage for the speaker of the poem, the *yakṣa*. Mental worship and adoration, mental ablutions and offerings to the divine (*mānasa pūja*), with offerings made mentally in the form of words, when circumstances did not permit of their actual performance, and the 'going in thought' on a pilgrimage when it was not physically possible to undertake one, is very much a part of Hindu thought and praxis. An example of this is seen in the poem itself when at the beginning the *yakṣa* welcomes raincloud with a few wild flowers (*kuṭaja*) and affectionate words.

In v. 109, the *yakṣa* says something of great significance, having, it appears, to have come to a conclusion after 'reflecting' deeply, '*bahu vigaṇayan*' is the pertinent phrase in line 1 of this verse. *Bahu*, many times; *vigaṇayan* having pondered over something or having carefully deliberated.

But no more of me; reflecting deeply
I bear up drawing on my own inner strength.
You too, lady most blessed,
should resist falling into utter dejection.
Whom does happiness always attend?
Or misery always befall?
Man's state on earth like the rim of a wheel
goes down and comes up again.

I interpret this verse as conveying a sense of the speaker having attained to some measure of wisdom. I suggest that the poet intends us to read it this way. In support of this suggestion I might point out that the tone of the poem and with it the tone of the speaker's words, changes sharply from this point on, to lead to the benediction (*bharatavākya*), which is instinct with peace, 'all passion spent'. Peace enters the mind when the inner being is purified in the fire of *tapasyā* (penance, penitence, contemplation—the Sanskrit word cannot be translated by a single English word). The *yakṣa's* words constitute more than a statement of resignation by a man shoring up his grief. It ought to be read as a positive utterance of understanding, even of faith.

As the tone of the poem changes, we sense that the speaker has extricated himself from that brooding passion of sorrow for his fate and the fate of his beloved, the sorrow that we saw pouring out in rising anguish (sts. 82–92), reaching a peak of intensity (sts. 101–8), until it is reined in, in the first half of st. 109. In this stanza, a measure of objectivity is revealed in the generalization phrased in the second half. We get a sense that the *yakṣa's* mind is no longer clouded as it was when we first met him (5). He is now able to provide consolation to his 'second self' left behind in Alakā, 'unsupported'. It goes further. The objectivity gained is sufficient to enable him to express the wish for general happiness which is characteristic of the *bharatavākya* spoken at the close of all literary works in Sanskrit.

Several poems in the *Rgveda* end with a prayer addressed to the deity invoked in the poem to grant blessings; the speaker, or seer of the poem presumably acts as the spokesperson for the congregation and therefore the community as a whole. I venture to suggest that the tradition of speaking the *bharatavākya* derives from this. At which point in the evolution of *mahākāvyas* (long poems) and dramas, this became established as a convention is perhaps not easy to determine. But even if the convention *had* become established by Kālidāsa's time, we ought not to overlook the fact that a great poet *uses* conventions to serve his own purposes. The *bharatavākyas* in *Meghadūtam* as well as *Śakuntalā* seem to have a special significance.

In *Meghadūtam,* the last stanza marks a point of *return*. Like the wheel (a water-wheel, known also as Persian wheel), the poem comes full circle to close on a note of quiet acceptance and a subdued feeling of hope. The pronoun 'you' includes the audience and the world-at-large with the cloud; the speaker also includes himself, because the cloud is his alter-ego. As he wishes the cloud 'greater glory' in all the lands it would roam over, we notice that the phrase harks back to the opening of the poem where the *yakṣa* is presented to us as fallen from *great glory* (*astam-gamita-mahimā*). To reiterate the point made earlier, the stark emotion of st. 101 and the poignancy of utterance of the next six stanzas is toned down in st. 109, leading to a quiet acceptance and subdued feeling of hope.

Both Rāma's Hill and Alakā are sacred spots; but to the *yakṣa*, the former is a place of suffering and torment, a place of deprivation. To semi-divine beings like *yakṣas* and *apsaras* (celestial nymphs), being earth-bound and leading the life of a mortal is a torment. The *yakṣa's* anguish is amply apparent, verbalized at great length. So great is it that the word for hermitage, in line 3 of the opening stanza is put in the plural, suggesting that he moved around restlessly from one hermitage to the other in the region seeking peace and tranquillity. There is irony here. It underlines the contradiction between a hermitage which is a place of passion-free tranquillity, and the tormented soul of the passion-driven lover. Alakā on the other hand, is a place of joy, love and plentitude where there are no change of seasons, for all flowers bloom at all times (67). In our mundane and flawed world, the *kadamba* blooms at the first rains, the *lodhra* and jasmine (*kunda*) in winter, the *kurabaka* in spring and the *śirīṣa* in summer. Not so in Alakā which is not burned by the sun but illuminated by the radiance of the moon on Śiva's forehead. It is the Earthly Paradise. That is the *yakṣa's* simplistic way of looking at things, clouded as his mind is by passion and anguish. He is unable to come to grips with the present and his mind dwells forever in the past that he has lost and which he idealizes. We hear dimly the authorial voice that pointed this out before it retired into silence at the beginning of the poem. In reality Alakā is not simply a hedonist's paradise; there is sorrow there and a human heart grieving in anguished separation.

The beloved, with her husband in exile and having no child, lives or what is truer, *exists* in a world that holds no real meaning for her. Eschewing all entertainment and all personal adornments—fine clothes, jewels, flowers, fragrances—she has no thought other than her husband's safe return. The imagery used to describe the beloved and her situation is one of privation and deprivation, of disorientation, of fading and waning and wasting away, cut off from life's deepest springs. She is compared to a day-lily on a cloudy day, uncertain whether to open or to close, a lotus deprived of sunshine or blighted by hoar frost, the waning moon in its very last phase, a sliver, before it is swallowed up by darkness. The lotus-sun is a key image in Sanskrit literature, and here the sun is the husband (79). A whole set of stanzas, sixteen to be exact, from 81 to 96, is devoted to the description of the beloved, grief-struck and leading the life of a woman parted from her husband (*proṣita-bhartṛkā*).[66] In *Śakuntalā*, one stage-direction and a stanza suffice to describe the heroine sorrowing in separation. This is accounted for mainly by the difference in treatment of the idea in the lyric and the dramatic modes.

Alakā is therefore a place where life's fullness is not truly realized in its totality; something is lacking. It is a place of innocence. And Rāma's Hill is more than a place of deprivation and torment as the *yakṣa* perceives it to be. Framed as it is in the opening stanza in an epic allusion, it can and ought to be seen as a place of penitence and purification. Sanctified by Rāma's enduring presence (12), by his steadfast adherence to duty and by Sītā's purity and constancy (the beloved is compared to her in st. 10, 99), it is a place of *experience*, where love is tried and tested, corresponding to Mārīca's Hermitage in the play of *Śakuntalā* (Act 7). We might add that not only love but strength of character is tried and tested too, as it is in *Śakuntalā*. One of the prime virtues of a hero is resilience and the courage to endure. In a certain kind of ethic, suffering and penance (*tapasyā*), is a part of learning and growing up; sometimes it is the only way to gain that maturity which is at bottom the ability to see life steadily and as a whole. A harsh ethic but not exclusively Indian in conception. The speaker of the poem, as we saw earlier, attains to some measure of understanding that is more than resignation or sheer acceptance of the inevitable. For acceptance of the situation is already in place at the very beginning of the poem; 'the wrath of the Lord of Treasures' and the resulting banishment have been accepted as the 'divine decree'. This is one view which we shall typify as the ethical-hierarchic that might be adopted in interpreting the poem. But as indicated earlier, it is not the only possible approach; it compasses only part of the poem's meaning and the vision it embodies. The poem itself directs the reader into making another set of responses.

There are two worlds in the poem and the poem moves constantly between these two worlds of the mythic and epic past and the speaker's present. But the two worlds are continuous and one phases into the other without the sharp break made in *Śakuntalā* at the close of Act 4 in the play, between the 'green world' and the gilded. Alakā is a presence in the distant background in the first section (which I shall label as the Mahākāla section), clinging to Kailāsa's slopes besides the holy Mānasa lake, and the beloved's presence is pervasive (7, 8, 10, 11). The splendour of Ujjayinī is reflected in the Alakā-world; the same flowers bloom, but in a different, more perfect setting. But the Mahākāla and Alakā sections differ in mood and tone. The former is celebratory in tone, joyous and reverential. Beginning on an elegiac note the poem swings into a joyous celebration of love and the beauty of nature blossoming under the beneficent influence of the rain cloud. The effect of the poetry is to create the impression that the curse and the exile provide the opportunity for this celebration. The poet uses it for this purpose. There is an expansion of consciousness for the reader as several landscapes unfold before him. Each stop on the cloud's journey and the speaker's pilgrimage is related to some memorable event in the past. Sometimes a poignant memory, intensely personal, of the speaker is evoked; st. 51 is a beautiful example. The amber coloured eyes of Revati, Balarāma's beloved wife, reflected in the wine, evoke memories of the *yakṣa's* own beloved wife as she sat with him drinking the wine that reflected the colour of *her* eyes. And this poignant memory is interwoven with the literary memories of the fratricidal war of the *Mahābhārata* saga and all the wrongdoing that was part of it, and of Balarāma's own transgression purified by the waters of the river most celebrated in the Vedas, the holy Sarasvatī on whose banks the ancient civilization first arose.

It has been suggested that some personal experience of the poet underlies the longing and the grief of parting that the poem voices so eloquently. But one has to be careful in bringing a writer's biography into his work, especially with one so reticent and self-effacing as Kālidāsa. It is misleading to treat literature as a transcript of life as it is actually lived.

The *yakṣa* when we first meet him, is shorn of his powers and earth-bound like one of us mortals; he is humanized to elicit our sympathy more fully. But his 'other self' (and we with it), soars, floats in air, roams freely in space as he did in his pre-lapsarian state, providing a double-perspective of the world: one close and detailed, the human perspective, that sees the beads of sweat collecting on the temples of the flower-gatherers and the bee hovering over a swaying spray of white jasmine; the other a panoramic view of the whole landscape in a larger and all-inclusive perspective, of the earth itself like a beautiful woman, wearing the broad river with its white waters gleaming like a single strand of pearls. We have an over-view not only of the planet we live on, but get to see vast spaces where the colossal elephants that guard the quarters roam, and the laughter of the Primal One towers up into space as eternal snows gather from the beginning of Time. The experience provided by even a cursory reading of the poem is an explosion of the imagination bodied forth in bold conceits such as the one here of Śiva's tumultuous laughter and the striking conceits occurring earlier (19, 42, 48, 52, 62). With a careful *reading*, we find ourselves exploring the poem's ever-expanding world of meanings, as images open up whole vistas extending back into time (38, 45); or for example in the play of several ideas in the image of Gaṅgā on Śiva's head. In this image we are not only taken back into mythic time when Gaṅgā descended on earth from her celestial path, but taste the delicious sense of humour in the rivalry that is part of the relationship of the sisters whom myth makes co-wives—Gaṅgā and Gaurī—the one proud and exultant having found a permanent place on the head of the Supreme, the other angry and jealous. (Sitting on someone's head is a colloquial way in many Indian languages of expressing the domination of a much-spoilt person over another)

The two views are not mutually exclusive, for there is an ambivalence at the heart of the poem. An ideal—a dharmic ideal—is set up; but the radiance of the love of the *yakṣa* and his beloved glows so strongly in the poem that the beauty of the poetry dulls the edge of whatever wrongdoing it was on the part of the *yakṣa* that brought such dire and swift punishment. Further, the nature of the transgression not only remains unspecified but it is not stressed and underlined. The quiet acceptance by the lovers of the pain of separation of such an intense love induces the feeling in the reader that such love has to have a place in the accepted scheme of things. The two views should be held in tension against each other.

The celebratory tone of the first part of the poem continues into the Alakā section which begins on a paradisal note and continues in that mood till st. 80, at which point the elegiac tone with which the poem began takes over, making doubts surface about the poem's conclusion. Does it have a 'happy ending'? As we contemplate the poem as a whole, we are filled with doubts and misgivings. Will the cloud reach its destination in time? Will it reach it at all? Will the beloved be still there to receive it and the message? The weight of woe carried by the poetry in the Alakā section is too overwhelming to be ignored. *There* she sits as he pictures her in his grief, in the midst of Alakā's loveliness, a 'young girl', sorrowing, 'alone, speaking little', 'the Creator's master-work'.

> How beautiful, if sorrow had not made[67]
> Sorrow more beautiful than Beauty's self.

We should not forget that the beloved is a young girl of sixteen years-*bālā*—Kālidāsa uses this word again in the play in referring to Śakuntalā (3:2). These two heroines are in the first flush of youth and experience love for the first time in all its freshness and ardour; it is a love that takes over their whole beings as an all-enveloping experience embracing every moment of their young lives. In the play, this feeling of the heroine's youth is strengthened by the use of the word *mugdha*—innocent and inexperienced (1:24; 2:3). And then tragedy strikes, unexpectedly. A strong sense of the pity of it all is inescapable.

A series of stanzas, each single one picturing the grieving beloved in vivid detail like a miniature painting (82–92), carefully delineates her in gradual decline: pale and wasted, distraught and disoriented, unmindful of her personal appearance, praying for the husband's return with no thought but of him. She is presented as desolated, at death's door:

> Seeming like the last sliver
> of the waning moon on the eastern horizon. (88)

before it is swallowed up in the total darkness of the new moon. This stanza harks back to the *yakṣa's* fears for the beloved at the opening of the poem (4). Will she survive? The poet, by stopping short of the last two stages of grief—withdrawal and death, of the ten mentioned in the *NS*[68] leaves the outcome uncertain. However, this image is itself ambivalent, because the disappearance of the moon is only *apparent*. The moon waxes in *time* and is restored to its glory.

This description of the beloved is by no means a conventional picture of a wife mourning the absence of her husband.[69] It might have become conventional later and it probably did and classical dance continues to portray the grieving heroine (*proṣita-bhartṛkā*) in this stylized and conventional manner. However, Kālidāsa's poetry conveys the beloved's emotions of love and anguish in such a manner as to make the reader *feel*, not simply that this was the way she felt and acted but that there is *no other way* she could have, the images are so totally infused with the emotion they embody. And this serves as a prime example of the point made earlier in the introduction with reference to drama and to Śakuntalā, that Kālidāsa's accomplishment lies in the manner in which his poetry escapes the constraints of the poetics of his time even while it acknowledges those poetics, if indeed there existed a *poetics* at that time that directed his genius.[70]

The elegiac tone of the poem continues to make doubts surface repeatedly in the mind of the reader. Will the cloud reach its destination in time? Will it reach at all? The cloud has already been characterized as inanimate, 'blended of mists and light, winds and water' (5) that could be dissipated anytime into its constituent elements. Its life is enmeshed in the life of all things in nature, animate and inanimate. Will it get lost in the clear waters of the river Gaṃbhīrā, lost in love for her? (42, 43). We are also reminded more than once, that it suffers from a proclivity for delay and for loitering around when it should be steadily going north on its way to Alakā (24, 28, 40). It has to be asked not to pause too long dallying on the hill where *kadamba* groves burst into bloom at its touch and peacocks welcome it with joy and not to spend too much time on terraces watching pretty girls. At one point, we encounter the suggestion that the cloud may have melted into the presence of Mahākalā (Śiva as Great Time), and at another that its devotion is to be rewarded by obtaining the eternal station (*śiva-padam*) of the *gaṇas* or attendants who stand round the Supreme in their allotted places (57). The poet has carefully placed such sign-posts here and there on the path of the cloud to alert the reader to the possibility that mishaps may occur on the way; that the journey might not have a 'happy ending' and more, that it might not have an ending at all. The outcome is uncertain.

This is not to stack the cards against a happy ending, but to draw attention to the strategy of the poem, to the manner in which it deploys the imagery and lays out several possibilities of viewing the poem that results in a fuller understanding of its meaning. There are other images in the poem that prefigure the reunion of the parted lovers and a happy outcome. The authorial voice does not dictate any view as preferable, having erased itself from the text right at the beginning. We see the beloved placed beside the jasmine that is revived by a fresh shower of rain drops (97); like Sītā she lifts her face up to hear the 'glad tidings', 'her heart opening like a flower in eager expectation' (99). Two significant images argue for a happy ending: one we have already noted as ambivalent—the image of the last sliver of the waning moon on the eastern horizon; also ambivalent is the other image of the Persian wheel which comes up, returning like the rising sun (109). It symbolizes the year, which is the period of the curse. But the wheel *re-turns*; ever-turning, endless, it is a symbol of *time*. Waning and waxing, the turning wheel, everything is part of the *Play of Time* (Mahākāla) presented on the cosmic stage in the dance-drama referred to in st. 58.

Further, the beliefs that formed part of the ethos in the poet's own time ought not to be overlooked. Penance, purity of love and constancy found their own rewards. The beloved and the speaker in the poem suffered and richly deserved the reward of reunion and the restoration of their original happy state. The touching belief that the chastity of a loving and loyal wife had the power to overcome all obstacles and accomplish her heart's desire, which was none other than her husband's well being and happiness, and her own, the two being identical, would have directed the responses of audience and reader in the past. Did not Sāvitrī encounter Death, conquer it and restore her dead husband to life? But the comparison with Sītā is of doubtful value on this point, because though Sītā was restored to her husband and to her rightful position as queen at Ayodhya, she did not 'live happily ever after' with Rāma.

In the poem the journey has no end because we do not know what *happened* at the end; we are not told. The poem is open-ended, leaving us with the hope that the lovers will be re-united; no more than that. And while there *is* hope, hope is but a 'slender thread'. Otherwise, we move in an area of suppositions: that the cloud could and did reach its destination and delivered its message of hope; that the beloved survived to receive it; and that the speaker was able to return to her at the end of the curse. The cloud, an elemental thing, bound by the laws of nature, makes its annual, recurrent journey, endlessly. We are sure of only one thing, that the journey continues, 'ever keeping to the north', which is the place of life and light and of the temporal presence of Śiva with his Śakti. The effect that the totality of meaning of the poem's structure and language sets out to create and succeeds in doing *is*, that the end is not important, the going is; and the *going* is an exploration. It is an ongoing exploration; it was for the poet in his *oeuvre*, and it is for the reader.

IX

The poem deploys its resources on a large scale. The canvas is the vast stretch of land from the Vindhyas to the Himālayas, crisscrossed by great rivers and innumerable streams, dotted by sacred fords and places of pilgrimage associated with myth, legend and hierophany. From a solitary hermitage the poem moves out into vast spaces and into different planes of consciousness. The landscape unfolds gradually as the speaker desribes it *introspectively* in sorrow and the *recollected* emotion of joy; it is presented from several points of view. The lonely 'voice' sounds in the background while the foreground is filled with the busy hum of great cities and the myriad sounds of nature celebrating the advent of the season of love and renewal ushered in by the rain cloud.

The cloud sweeps along, brimming with life-giving water the thin trickles of rivers, thin as the single braids of grieving women looking out anxiously for their husband's return; driving women of pleasure to their midnight trysts in an exuberance of passion; making the landscape bloom, and renewing the earth. As the poem's canvas expands in range and sweep, the rain cloud gains in physical magnitude and attains an extraordinary status. It is transfigured by the light of divinity into something strange and unfamiliar, into something marvellous. Having gathered on its long course the sacral aura of the hallowed places it has passed through and paused over—Mahākāla, Skanda's Hill, the holy rivers and their sources—it finally arrives, sanctified, fit to enter the holiest of places, Kailāsa, temporal abode of the Supreme. And it arrives like an honoured guest, prefiguring the speaker's own return home.

The landscape is drawn in a definite pattern to form a backdrop. Starting at a point on a remote and lonely hilltop where the speaker of the poem is visualized as seated watching a rain cloud curling round the crest of the hill, the canvas expands in range and sweep until it is *drawn in* to a point on another remote and lonely hilltop—a gem-studded pleasure-hill—opposite the casement where the beloved is presented, restless and anguished. As the landscape starts to expand from a small space and then narrows down to another small space, the rain cloud goes through a corresponding process of magnification followed by a diminution and descent, scaled down to the ordinary and familiar. It settles down on the jewelled crest of a miniature hill, transformed to the size of an elephant cub, small enough for the beloved to feel comfortable with.

Within this large and inclusive pattern of symmetry several minor symmetries are fitted in carefully. We see the obvious symmetries immediately, the two hilltops with the lonely figures on them and all that vast space of land in between, symbolizing spatially the love-in-separation of lover and beloved in the *nāyaka-nāyakī* tradition. Then we note the less obvious: she is the 'second self', the moon shorn of its glory to his sun whose lustre is dimmed, the fading lotus that waits for his 'ray-fingers' to wipe off its dew-tears and make it bloom again. The *yakṣa's* armlet slipping off his 'wasted forearm' parallels the beloved divesting herself of all ornaments, casting them aside and lying pale and emaciated (2,92). He wakes up suddenly out of a 'waking dream', cooled by Himālayan breezes scented by the fragrance of her body, imagining he was holding her in his arms; she is woken up out of a dream in which she fancies she was in his arms, by the breeze cooled by fresh rain drops and scented by the jasmines (106, 96). Coming out of his reverie, he sees a rain cloud on the hill, resembling a playful elephant; and she sees a small elephant cub on the jewelled pleasure-hill outside her window. Words, phrases and images echo one another and form links. Many such verbal and other symmetries provide the detail that shapes the world of the poem.

At the close of the poem we become sharply aware that we are still on Rāmagiri and the rain cloud is still clinging to the crest of the hill. Nothing seems to have changed—or has it? The voice is still echoing within us. The poem has come back to where it started; its form is circular, as in *Ṛtusaṃhāram*. But we have travelled far and wide in space and time. Time takes several forms in this poem: the past, present and future; the mythic, epic and cosmic; days, seasons, the year and aeons. The beloved counts days out laying a flower for each day that has gone by and reckons the hours by her sleepless anguish. The period of the curse is a year, one revolution of the sun; the symbol for this in the poem is the *water-wheel* (109). The remaining period of separation is four months or one season, the season of the rains, when Viṣṇu is immersed in contemplation. (The year was originally divided into three seasons of four months each). Time is measured out by the steps of temple dancers, reflecting the great dance of creation. Time stands still in Alakā where the seasons do not change and all flowers bloom at all times and the *yakṣas* who live in a world of order experience only love and happiness. We have seen that uncertain time in the future when the parted lovers hope to enjoy on nights bright with the autumn moon, all the pleasures imagined during the long separation. We have even glimpsed Time, beyond aeons, at its very beginning, when the Dance began; when Śiva's laughter started to pile up into the eternal snows of the Lord of Mountains and Viṣṇu's triple-stride measured out the Universe. We return finally to our short span of time in the theatre or the temple at Mahākāla, to the time it took for the poem to be chanted, initially perhaps by the poet himself. And we have not moved except in our imagination.

X

Kālidāsa's first play, *Mālavikāgnimitram* (*Mālavikā* for short) is a drama of romance and palace intrigue with a slender historical basis. The other two plays, *Vikramorvśīyam* (*Urvaśī Won by Valour, Urvaśī* for short) and *Abhijñānaśākuntalam* (*Śakuntalā* for short) use material for their plots from ancient texts; the *Ṛgveda*, the *Śatapatha Brāhmaṇa* and the *Mahābhārata* which the poet and dramatist changes, shaping it skillfully to convey his own vision of life and its problems.

In *Mālavikā*, the poet invents his plot basing it on the life of the historical monarch, Agnimitra, the second Sunga emperor of the second century

BC (see genealogical table in Appendix I). The play is very cleverly constructed.

The action is placed in the small enclosed world of the royal court of Agnimitra who is at the time ruling at Vidiśā, the western capital of the Śunga empire, as his father Puṣyamitra's viceroy. Puṣyamitra's court is at the main imperial capital of Pāṭaliputra in the east, the traditional capital of the great empires of the first millennium BC: the Magadha, Maurya and Śunga empires. The play enacts the love-story of the king and Mālavikā who has taken sanctuary with the Queen Consort, Dhāriṇī, but who is in reality a princess fallen on hard times. There are the usual obstacles to the fulfilment of love but finally everything turns out happily with wedding bells ringing and the queen reconciled to the painful state of having a younger rival in her husband's affections.

But though the action is located in the palace and the private royal gardens, Kālidāsa places the drama in the larger world of politics, war and the power game outside the charming, enclosed, private world of romance, love and pleasure. The palace intrigue, light-hearted, is paralelled, though not foregrounded but kept in the background by the political intrigue that is deadly serious, threatening the peace and security of the empire on its southern frontiers. And there is trouble on the north-western frontiers as well from the invasions of the Indo-Greek rulers ensconced in the regions on the far side of the river Sindhu and based in Gāndhāra. Mālavikā is the link to the world of war and power politics in the Narmada valley where two kings, subordinate to the Śunga emperors are fighting for control of the valley; one the brother of Mālavikā and the other a cousin. Queen Dhāriṇī's son and the heir-apparent to the empire, Vasumitra is the link to the outside world of the Indo-Greek menace, a distant legacy of the invasion of Alexander of Macedon in the third century BC. The plot of the drama is very intricately woven.

The next play, *Vikramorvaśīyam* or *Urvaśī*, is a very different play. It goes back far into mythic time when gods and heroes walked together and were comrades in arms in mythic wars of *devas* and *daitya-dānavas*, (or immortals and titans) like the war in *Kumārasaṃbhavam.* The hero Purūravas is a mythic monarch, divinely descended, the grandson of the moon; the heroine is a celestial, Urvaśī, one of the principal dancers in Indra's court in *svarga.* The action is however placed in the mortal world, in the royal palace and pleasure gardens of the king. Again there are problems. The course of true love does not run smoothly but it is much easier than in the previous play. But the most significant difference of this play from the other two is in its structure. The fourth act is unique to this play in all Sanskrit drama, for it is a blend of dance, music and speech with only one character on stage, the king himself, mad as a hatter, having lost his loved Urvaśī, who suddenly vanished in the grove they had entered to engage in love-sport. This act performs an important role in the structure and vision of the play, exploring the nature of passionate obsession leading the lover to the very verge of madness; exploring states of consciousness that are para-normal. The poet explores such states of consciousness but somewhat differently in *Śakuntalā* as well as the following paragraphs will reveal. [Detailed analyses of both *Mālavikā* and *Urvaśī* are provided in the introduction to volume 2: Plays; studies of place and position of the queens in the polygamous set-up in palaces and the roles of the two jesters in the two plays are also provided there.]

We now proceed to an exploration of the many aspects and problems of the most important play of Kālidāsa's, *Abhijñānaśākuntalam*.

The play *Śakuntalā* is a beautiful blend of romance and fairy tale with elements of comedy. In the last sections of the *Śatapatha Brāhmaṇa* that are devoted wholly to a description of the rituals of the Horse-Sacrifice (*Aśva-medha Yajña*), where the names of some of the kings who performed them are mentioned, we come across this line: 'In Nāḍapit, the *apsara* Śakuntalā conceived (bore), Bharata.' This is the earliest literary reference to Śakuntalā and her son (the little boy Sarvadamana in the play) who performed many horse-sacrifices on the banks of the river Yamuna after he had conquered the world, thus fulfilling the prophecy of the mystic personage, Mārīca, in the play (7:33). Nāḍapit is glossed by the commentator[71] as Kaṇva's hermitage. But that identification has obviously been made on the basis of the Śakuntalā-Duḥṣanta story in the *Mahābhārata*,[72] where, however, the name Nāḍapit does *not* occur. The original story of Śakuntalā referred to in the *SB* is lost to us; we have only a very long and earthy version of it in the epic (*Mbh.*: 1: chs. 62–69). It must be our guess then, that Nāḍapit was some place of enchant-ment, a pool of *apsaras* perhaps, where strange things could happen and mortals meet and fall in love with celestial nymphs.

With the very first lines of the play we are transported to a world of enchantment. A handsome, young king, out hunting, is lured far out into 'another world'; and the inevitable happens. The song of the actress (*naṭi*) has already lured the waiting audience into this world. Music is used skil-fully to make this transition. A point to note here is that the word used for the fleet deer that has drawn King Duḥṣanta far way, is *sāraṅga*' which is also the name of a *rāga* or musical mode. The *rāga, sāraṅga*, is defined as one that through the 'attractive arrangement of notes, *colours* the mind of the hearer.' (*Raṅga* signifies colour, paint and also the stage.) Music projects the appropriate mood.

The play is located in the mythic past in a world where mortals still moved with gods; the human and divine intermingled. In this world, the gods were not distant but friends of heroes like Duḥṣanta who participated with them to keep order in the universe. By removing the action of the play into the world of the past, distant in time, a poetic and dramatic purpose is served; it inhibits a realistic approach to the play. It clearly marks the line that separates the fictive world of the play from our everyday world. In the Sanskrit text the two words '*Atha*' (now) and '*Iti*' (thus) at the beginning and end of a play enclose it as it were; lirerally, it would read as follows: *Now* begins the play, entitled *Abhijñānaśākuntalam;* and *thus* ends the play, etc.

The play-world thus created contains another world—the world of the deep and dark forests near the river Mālinī, the 'green world' into which we are lured by the deer and meet Śakuntalā, the child of Nature who as noted earlier on, is also envisaged as the guardian deity of the woodland.

As already noted, *apsaras*—born of the *Waters* i.e. the creative waters where life originated—are powers of nature, associated with fertility and plenitude as *yakṣa-yakṣīs* are. In the ancient myth of the Churning of the Ocean by gods and anti-gods to obtain ambrosia, the cup of Immortality, the *apsaras* rose out of the waters, together with many other wondrous things, including Beauty (Śrī) herself (see under Myths-Appendix II).

In the vedic myth referred to, Śakuntalā is an *apsara* and the daughter of one in the epic tale which is the immediate source of the play. This is an aspect of her origin that is important to keep in mind, because in the play she is seen as the Lady of Nature, one who lives in the 'green world', into whom has flowed 'the beauty born of murmuring sound'; she possesses the beauty of nature as well as its holiness. In her, 'nature' and 'nurture' blend without being in opposition to each other; for her 'green world' is also an *āśrama*, a hermitage, a *tapovana*, or penance-grove, where tranquillity prevails ordered by discipline. She is an 'ornament' of the Hermitage (an image out of the gilded world of the royal court), as well as a creature of the woodlands; both phrases are the king's. Not only are a number of flower-images other than the conventional one of the lotus-petalled eyes and slender vine-like arms used to describe her, but she is also seen as a flower—the jasmine. She and the jasmine are constantly brought together (as the beloved is also in *Meghadūtam*); they are sisters, born of the same mother—nature. Can this flower, this 'sensitive plant' survive in the 'other world'—the glittering gilded world of the Paurava monarch? It cannot, it seems; Śakuntalā herself poses this question: 'Rent from my dear father's lap like the sapling of the sandal tree uprooted from the side of the Malaya mountain, how can I survive ever in an alien soil!' (4:22.-2,3). This image of the sandalwood tree will recur in a later, very significant context in Act 7, to which we shall refer presently. Act 5 is clear proof that she is trampled on, stripped and mutilated (figuratively) and is at the point of death, when she is rapt from the astonished gaze of the beholders and carried away by a shaft of light (5.33b.). In this connection it is very important to note two facts made clear in the play. Firstly, Śakuntalā is never seen as actually living in the gilded world of the court and be a part of it; the fact is only talked about in various ways by different people at different times; but it is not part of the play. She is never brought into direct contact with the Queen, or the Queen-mother or any of the ladies of Duḥṣanta's palace, as the heroine of the other play *Urvaśī Won by Valour*, who is also as *apsara*, is. Śakuntalā is a heroine different from the others: Mālavikā and

Urvaśī, the noble Dhāriṇi[73] and Auśinari,[74] Sudakṣinā and Indumatī.[75] She is special, in a class by herself with the beloved (the *yakṣī*) of the poem *The Cloud Messenger*.

Secondly, the benediction is not spoken in this play in the world of the court, in the king's world. It is spoken in a world beyond this, which is the *perfected* world of the Primal Parents, Mārīca and Aditi. There is talk certainly of a return to this world. But the play comes to its end in Mārīca's Hermitage, on Hēmakūṭa (Kailāsa) which mortals cannot reach. 'But mortals cannot come to these regions on their own, noble lady.' (7:20.+1). Before the king can enter this world he has to be purified. First he proves his worth by battling the forces of darkness and disorder that threaten the order of the universe. For this he has to be roused from the state of utter despondency into which he had fallen weighed down by an overwhelming sense of guilt. He had become disoriented, nerveless and had swooned away (6:28). It is significant that it is deep concern for someone very near him, Māḍhavya, that pulls him out of this depression, this lack of will to live. Duḥṣanta's path to Mārīca's Hermitage and the finding of what has been lost is essentially similar to that of the *yakṣa's* in the poem, though they are framed differently because of the differences in the two literary modes—drama and lyric. The images of sanctity and purification are repeated: Viṣṇu's triple-stride, Gaṅgā's celestial stream, the sacred pool of golden lotuses.

The whole of Act 7 is placed in the world of Mārīca's Hermitage, where the 'highest penances are wrought' in the penance groves of the Perfected Seers; it is a world which ascetics perform severest austerities to attain. Here Mārīca (the luminous) born of the Self-Existent Light, himself performs penance with his consort, Aditi. The last stage-direction that brings the play to a close is *Exit all*; no distinction is made between the characters belonging to the Hermitage and the mortals who have to descend to Duḥṣanta's capital.

In *Vikramoravaśīyam*, whose theme is also the marriage of a mortal, King Purūravas, descended from the moon, to a celestial nymph and their parting and re-union, the benediction is spoken on earth, at the king's court after Nārada who has come down to earth with a message of goodwill from Indra, has consecrated the little prince Āyus (from whom Duḥṣanta is directly descended) as the Heir-Apparent.

Another significant point to note in the last stanza of *Śakuntalā* (the benediction) is the tone and quality of the final words of the poet and dramatist:

> May the Self-Existent Lord who unites in Himself
> the Dark and the Light,
> Whose Infinite power pervades the Universe
> annihilate forever the round of my births. (7:35)

Nīla-lohita is the epithet used of Śiva; *Nīla*, suggesting the dark-blue of the poison the Lord swallowed at the Beginning to save the newly-created world, and *lohita* (*rohita* is variant), the brightness of Gaurī or Śakti. The dyads and triads in Indian thought are richly multivalent and their meanings and symbolism can be endlessly explored and defined; day-night; light-dark; beauty-power; end-endless and so on. The tendency of the human mind is to see the world as constituted of categories of polarities; the bent of the Indian mind leads it to see these as *balanced*, and to attempt to reconcile them in a *oneness* in which the opposites are perceived as aspects of one and the same. The duality is reconciled in the trinity, as in the classic Trimūrti, the three-aspected image of Śiva at Elephanta near Bombay. Mārīca is described as the offspring of the *Self-Existent Energy* (7:27); this should be read in juxtaposition with the benediction.

There is one further point to consider in relation to the benediction. *The Recognition of Śakuntalā* is Kālidāsa's last work and the words spoken last are therefore eminently fitting as the final utterance of the great poet and dramatist; it is his farewell to his work; and to the world in an ultimate sense. Kālidāsa has arrived at that point in his life and career where 'every third thought' is of the other shore. But the words have a deeper poetic significance in the dramatic structure of the play. The two worlds of the play, the green world of the woods and the gilded world of the Royal Court, are too far apart (as we shall see presently), and the reconciliation, re-union and *restoration* cannot be celebrated in either of them. Whereas the two worlds in the poem, *The Cloud Messenger* are continuous and even interfused, there is a sharp break made in the play between the two worlds at the close of Act 4. Therefore that moment of epiphany has to happen elsewhere, in another world which I shall call the golden world of the Imagination, a phrase suggested by the world Hemakūṭa used for Mt. Kailāsa which we know from the poem, *The Cloud Messenger,* to be the temporal abode of the Supreme and hence the holiest of places on earth. It is not the initial world of enchantment we stepped into, the green world of the deep and dark forests; it is as we saw earlier, a place coveted by ascetics who perform the severest penance to gain it; it is the place where the highest forms of penance are wrought in the penance groves of the Perfected Seers and filled by the luminous presence of the Primal Parents of the universe. Here, in this golden world,

> common bird or petal
> And all complexities of mire . . . .

are miraculously transformed into the 'glory of changeless metal', into 'the artifice of eternity'.

The difference in tone and character of the two worlds—the initial green world and this golden world which is the *artifice* of eternity—is seen clearly in the kind of imagery that shapes them. (The two worlds of Acts 1 and 7 reflect each other in many respects, as we shall see). The world of Act 1 is the world of *nature*, with flowers blooming, honey-bees hovering over them, of green foliage and tender young shoots and buds being prised open, of clear waters flowing in channels to lave the roots of trees and the fresh cool spray of Mālinī's snow-fed waters wafted by the breeze. The colour-words present in the descriptions are those of the fresh colours of the woodlands and of budding youth. In Act 7, on the other hand, the colour-words are drawn mostly from a world of gold and gems and jewels (but of an elemental world, and not words describing the glitter of the Royal Court): the *golden sheen* of the waters, the glitter of rain drops, the gleam of the flickering lightning and the liquid gold of the mountain itself reflecting the red and gold of sunsets. Here, the lotuses are golden as in Alakā; the places of meditation are not green meadows where deer roam or the roots of trees under the green shade of leafy trees, but jewelled caves with celestial nymphs, gorgeously dressed and jewelled and seductive, walking about. It is a world of austere beauty, luminous with the light of spirit; it is not a world of Nature, spontaneous, informed by instinct, but of nature *perfected* by restraint and discipline. In the last act, time past, present and future are brought together in Mārīca's blessings, to be contained within the golden round of Time; the word in the text, *yugaśata-parivartanaiḥ* is literally 'the revolutions of hundreds of epochs' (aeons) (7:34).

Certain prophecies are made in this golden world about the future, after Duḥṣanta's time. The interest in this act is focussed on the little prince, the future Bharata (Bearer of the earth) who is to inherit the future. Mārīca's prophecies (7.33, 33.–1) echo the incorporeal voice of the Mystic Fire that has already spoken (4:4). The little boy, flanked by two hermit women is the centre of the last Act, as Śakuntalā, his mother, accompanied by her two friends, is of the first. The two acts reflect each other in many respects. The scene where the King, after dismounting from the chariot, is about to enter the grove of Mārīca's Hermitage and has his first glimpse of his son, is a replica of the scene of Act 1 where also the King, dismounting from his chariot at the fringes of the grove of Kaṇva's Hermitage, enters and sees the boy's mother for the first time. The *finding* of the lost son and heir precedes and leads to the *recognition* of the mother. An interesting parallel is provided in the last scene of Shakespeare's *The Winter's Tale*.

Words are keys to open doors for the imagination on its journey of exploration into the fictive world. The title—*Abhijñānaśākuntalam*—underlines the central issue in the play. Śakuntalā is *recognized* by virtue of a *token* of love, not by love itself. In the absence of concrete, tangible 'proof of love' and marriage, she is lost; she is nothing. Again, there is an interesting parallel with Shakespeare. In *Othello*, proof of the heroine's chastity and love is demanded. Desdemona's chastity hangs on a handkerchief; Śakuntalā's on a ring. Both heroines are blissfully unaware of the importance of the *token*. To them love is its own proof and a witness to their chastity. It is in Acts 5 and 6 that Kālidāsa probes most deeply into the heart of his society's accepted norms and values. He makes Miśrakeśī ask a highly significant question (6:13.+10-11): '. . . does a love like this need a token of recognition? How can this be?'

The probing is accompanied by another equally significant question—the question of *knowing*, which is related to the *recognition* of Śakuntalā at the close of the play. How does one know? Is 'the truest *inner prompting*, its own unassailable authority' to the noble and virtuous? This is the way of knowing that the King claims for himself; but the claim is subjected to ironic scrutiny and found to be not well-founded.

What is *knowing*? The king at first knew Śakuntalā carnally, as an object; and frankly as an object of pleasure. She is a flower to smell, a gem to hold and an ornament to wear. She is hardly a person to him. It is only at the close of the play that he sees her as a person and *knows* her truly. Something has to be added to *his view of her* to make him see her as a 'person' of intrinsic beauty and not merely a beautiful object. In *Meghadūtam* the idea of outward lustre being the *semblance* of inner glow (of powers) is introduced in the opening stanza. Priyaṃvada (Act 4: lines 119–10) is able to correlate outer beauty with the inner. But Duḥṣanta seems to be unable to do this until the long separation and grief at losing Śakuntalā and his son and an intense sense of guilt, give him eyes to see deeply. When Śakuntalā stands before him, pale with suffering, the flesh mortified to let the spirit glow forth, the King truly *sees* her and knows her 'Aha! Here is the Lady Śakuntalā; it is *she*:

> Dressed in dusky garments,
> her face fined thin. . . . (7:21)

It almost appears as if her exquisite beauty had been a barrier to his understanding of her. All he saw then was the glow of passion and youth and beauty which he described in images of blooming flowers and tender shoots. Initially, Duḥṣanta had known Śakuntalā only carnally; she was an object of pleasure to be enjoyed. The imagery of Acts 1 and 3 convey this quite clearly. He is the 'bee circling at day break over the 'jasmine's cup'. Even while he is setting himself up as the noble and self-restrained man shying away from the touch of another man's wife, his appreciative eye, the trained eye of a connoisseur of feminine beauty sees the sweetness beneath the enveloping veil, 'barely-revealed', as she stands 'like a bud/not burst into bloom . . . / a tender sprout among yellowing leaves'.

The play examines accepted ideals and the relation of what *seems*, to what *is*, of *semblance* to truth, through the comments of Māḍhavya and by means of ironies built into the structure and language of the play. A fine example of the ironies that convey a critical point of view is in Act 1. Duḥṣanta is passing himself off as the Paurava monarch's Minister for Religious Affairs, visiting the penance-groves that are specified as Groves of Righteousness (*Dharma-Araṇya*), to see that they are free of impediments to the performance of all sacred rites. Yet, by ceaselessly hunting and creating terror and confusion in the woods, he is responsible for the wild tusker 'crazed with fear' charging into the sacred grove like the 'very embodiment of hindrance to penance.' Recklessly charging towards Kaṇva's Hermitage chasing a blackbuck, he stops short of killing the sacred animal only when an anchorite stands barring his way. Again, there is unconscious irony in Duḥṣanta's words, when he admonishes the little boy teasing a lion cub in Mārīca's Hermitage and describes him as 'the young of a black serpent that spoils / for other creatures the pleasant sanctuary / that is the fragrant sandal tree' (7.18). In this image, Duḥṣanta is the black serpent which initially trespassed into the sanctuary (Kaṇva's hermitage); the sandal tree should be linked with Śakuntalā's description of herself as 'the sapling of the sandal' rent from the side of the Malaya mountain—its sanctuary (4.21.+8–10). When this image is seen in the context of the trial-scene in Act 5 and placed beside the images the king uses to characterize Śakuntalā's conduct—the turbulent river sullying its own 'crystal stream' and uprooting the trees growing on its banks and the cuckoo stealthily creeping into another's nest and leaving its offspring there—the irony is devastating.

The whole of Act 5 is disturbing, full of ironies; questioning is implicit in its tone from beginning to end. The question of truth-speaking and dissimulation is raised; wearing the mantle of virtue while practising deception is characterized as the art that princes are taught. A reference to manuals on statecrafts such as Kauṭilya's *Arthaśāstra* may be seen here. But Kālidāsa alerts the reader to another view. A king who gains or inherits sovereignty has to keep it, guard it presumably, by whatever means are deemed necessary. What then is the ideal of kingship? And more important, what does the word *rājā-ṛṣi*, royal sage, mean? How is a king a sage? Is the word a mere 'praise-word' as the young hermit says in unconscious irony? A public image as different from or opposed to a private image? The play raises many questions but by no means in a strident manner. Further, Kālidāsa does not leave us without an idea of what a royal sage could be. In the verses spoken by the two young hermits who see the king for the first time, we have a sketch of a monarch who is a great warrior and a good ruler, a complete king or royal sage (2:15, 16). Dilīpa, the founder of the illustrious solar dynasty in Kālidāsa's epic, *Raghuvaṃśam*, is this ideal monarch, a royal sage. But is Duḥṣanta one? Verse 15, is interesting on account of its use of certain words in their double meanings; *āśrama*[76] is a hermitage and also one of the four stages in a man's life; *yoga* is contemplation, but it also means 'through' or 'by means of'; *vaśin* is one who has his senses (passions) under perfect control, and a king who has his subjects under perfect control; that is to say the kingdom is well-ruled. Each of the two meanings refers to one of the two parts of the compound word, *rājā* (ruler) and *ṛṣi* (sage). It strikes us as something of an etymological exercise, true to the letter; the young hermit who is also a student in displaying his knowledge. But I leave it to the reader to judge whether it is true to the spirit.

The play subjects not only the ideal of kingship but also the character of Duḥṣanta as king and man to an ironic scrutiny. In the process, Duḥṣanta's personality is seen as far more complex and interesting than it would be if we were to perceive him as the ideal hero (*dhīrodātta nāyaka*) of the ancient texts on drama, and as a *rājā-ṛṣi*. He is presented as the great king he undoubtedly was in the popular imagination fed on story and legend. His personal appearance is described in images that convey majesty and strength as well as uncommon beauty and grace of manner. His frame is likened to that of a magnificent tusker roaming the mountains and as being spare and instinct with energy; his beauty of face and form dazzle like a priceless gem cut and polished by the exquisite art of a master craftman. Even the rather cantankerous Śārṅgarava grudgingly admits that the kingdom is well-ruled. A number of images glorify him as a godlike hero; the very first image compares him to Śiva himself. But we have to keep in mind that the *sārathi* (charioteer) who makes this comparison is also a bard and bards are given to praising highly the monarch they serve. However, an ironic point of view is adopted to show this great king as more human and fallible and less godlike and ideal. A 'public image' of Duḥṣanta is built up by the 'praise-words' of hermits and bards alike; the latter are the public relations officers in the bureaucracies of the past. But, there is the 'private image' of the king too, the face other than the 'royal face' that we see from our privileged position as readers and audience. We see this when the king is in the company of his friend and close companion, Māḍhavya, who is probably a childhood companion of Duḥṣanta's, judging from his words in Act 2: 'Māḍhavya, my friend, you have always been accepted as a son by our mother'. It is also sharply revealed in the many 'asides' given to the king in the play, mostly, in acts 1 and 3, as he watches Śakuntalā from where he is concealed behind bushes and thickets of vines. The two together, the 'asides' and the familiar and relaxed conversion with Māḍhavya, complete the characterization which cannot be accomplished in all its fulness by the ceremonious verse alone used to project the royal and public image. Often the 'two faces' are dialoguing, commenting on each other through carefully arranged juxtapositions as in Act 2.

Another device used to project the two images of the king is symbolic gesture. Act 1 furnishes a striking examples of how symbolic gesture is manipulated to achieve several ends. In entering the sage Kaṇva's penance groves, after some distance, Duḥṣanta dismounts, takes off the regalia, his crown and jewels, and hands them over with his bow and arrows to the charioteer. This gesture (and I suspect that on the stage, it would have been done deliberately and elaborately like a ritual by the actor), is symbolic in two ways: it represents the reverence the king feels in the sacred grove and all that it stands for and for the great sage who presides over it; it also signifies the act of 'putting off' of the royal image. The 'public image' of a king is a *mask* which he puts on like an actor putting on theatrical make-up and the costume to suit the role he is about to play. It goes with the regalia and the pomp and panoply which serve to impress and dazzle the world and through that to control it. Duḥṣanta now enters the hermitage simply dressed, like an ordinary person, a visitor. Further, in putting off his 'royal face', Duḥṣanta is released from certain expectations and inhibitions on the part of others as well as his own. He enters another world, far removed from the court and its pressures in more senses than one—Śakuntalā's world. Śakuntalā does not see him in his awesome majesty and splendour. She and her friends see Duḥṣanta simply as a noble from the court, an officer of the king which is how he introduces himself. And we too begin to see him, not as the great monarch bearing the heavy burden of his dynasty's fame and surrounded by the aura of Puru's idealism and exemplary conduct, but as just a young and handsome courtier, well-spoken, with an eye for pretty girls. The effect of the 'unmasking' is to put Śakuntatā's friends at ease; and a lively conversation ensues. However, this too is a mask, for Duḥṣanta *is* the king only pretending that he is not the king. Priyaṃvadā and Anasūyā soon see through his threadbare disguise and the mask is quietly dropped, though the girls play along and keep up the pretence. But the action has already been initiated; Śakuntalā has fallen deeply in love and the plot must now move under its own impetus.

A good deal of good-humoured irony is also pointed at the ascetics in the Hermitage; those 'hermits rich in holiness' who have blazing energy hidden deep within like sun crystals that can suddenly kindle into flames if provoked, are in fact as tame as the deer they love and care for. It is an outsider, Durvāsā, who blazes into a furious passion at being disregarded, and the object of his fury is a guileless and innocent young girl. The ideal of asceticism is being questioned here and a contrast drawn a few lines later between Durvāsā, self-important and arrogant, and Kaṇva. The patriarch Kaṇva is the ideal of a sage put forward, self-restrained and noble, gentle and warm and understanding.

Ascetic claims are also subjected to ironic scrutiny in Act 5. Kaṇva's disciples do not come off very well. Śārṅgarava is an angry man, arrogant and tactless; we can see him develop into a Durvāsa in time. We are surprised to see that he does not convey the message of Kaṇva (his *guru*) to the king in the sage's own words. Śāradvata, is a cold, harsh and uncharitable ascetic, somewhat obsessed by the idea of cleanliness. Neither seems to exemplify the popular idea of ascetics and of ascetic ideals. In contrast, the high priest for whom Śārṅgarava and Śāradvata show some contempt is the only one in the trial-scene who makes a kind and humane gesture towards the suffering

Śakuntalā. And it is he who sees the miracle—Śakuntalā transported to another world.

Foreshadowing as a device is used a great deal in the play and skilfully. Śakuntalā's adverse fate is mentioned right at the beginning. (The sign given to Kaṇva at the cave of fire at Prabhāsa strikes one, however, as being cryptic.) Hints of future events are strewn around in the conversation of Śakuntalā and her friends. But the most important examples are in Act 5. The theme of failing memory, 'wakeful one moment / shrouded in darkness the next' and 'the dying flame', in the chamberlain's speech have subtle overtones. Then comes the song of betrayed love sung in the background and we see the strange effect it has on Duḥṣanta. Music makes a portent more ominous.

> O, you honey-pilfering bee!
> Greedy as ever for fresh honey!
> once, you lovingly kissed
> the mango's fresh spray of flowers—
> and forgotten her? So quickly? (5:8)

This little scene takes us back to the beginning of the play, to the first little scene where Duḥṣanta stands concealed behind the trees watching, envying the bee hovering round Śakūntala's face (*bhṛṇga* and *madhukara* are both terms signifying a bee, but the former term also mean a libertine). The word *madhukara* (honey-foraging thief) used at that point is also used in the song which Queen Haṃsavatī is singing at the opening of Act 5. Sanskrit is a language rich in synonyms and the different roots from which words are formed account for subtle nuances in meaning. The question that comes to the mind in this! What is in store for Śakuntalā?

We, the audience do not know that the signet ring that Śakuntalā was given by the king is lost. And Kālidāsa's audience would not have known it either because the Ring and the Curse linked to it are not part of the Śakuntalā-Duḥṣanta story in the *Mahābhārata* that his audience would undoubtedly have been familiar with.

We already know about the king's many amorous adventures and his proneness to philandering, from his conversation with Māḍhavya in Act 2:

> King : Until you see her, you will continue to hold forth like this.
> Māḍhavya : If that is so she must indeed be a miracle of loveliness, to arouse such breathless admiration in *you*.

Māḍhavya's remark immediately before this exchange of comments about the king's jaded appetite seeking fresh interests (2: 9.+1–3) is reinforced by the second line of Haṃsavatī's song. What is different however, is the streak of callousness pointing the king's comment on Haṃsavatī's song. 'Yes, I once loved her deeply . . .' . a callousness that turns into cruelty in the trial-scene that follows immediately.

Śakuntalā a young girl—*bālā* the word that the king refers to her by, is a girl of sixteen—is out of the sheltered hermitage where she has grown up, her father's 'life-breath', for the very first time when she stands trial in the enclosure surrounding the Fire Sanctuary. The king's words to her so barbed with venom are unworthy of a great king who is the protector of the sacred groves in the kingdom, where she has grown up. An example of the insults Duḥṣanta flings at Śakuntalā is the comparison he makes of her with the cuckoo that flies away abandoning its offspring in the nest of another bird. The reference is not only to her mother Menakā, one of the *apsaras* (beings who fly in the air) abandoning her child, Śakuntalā, but to Śakuntalā herself, who according to Duḥṣanta, is passing off her offspring by another man as his child. When Duḥṣanta first met Śakuntalā, he found the strange circumstances of her birth an added attraction; she was the 'lightning's splendour', not of this earth. But that was in another world; it was Śakuntalā's, not his. In the world of the court, which she had characterized as 'alien soil' on which, like the sapling of the sandal tree rent from the parent mountain, she would not survive, Śakuntalā is unimaginably humiliated. Stripped of dignity and modesty, unveiled in public, an outrage in that society (as it is still in some societies), every word she speaks is twisted into a lie. Finally, she stands alone, abandoned by all. Such isolation is of the essence of a tragic situation in life. The play is poised on the edge of tragedy from which it must now be retrieved.

A point that should be noted is, that Śakuntalā is on trial in a very special place. It is not the king's hall of justice, where in other circumstances, the fisherman might have stood trial for having a valuable ring, the royal signet ring, in his possession. It is the 'raised enclosure of the Mystic Fire'—*Agni*, which witnesses men's deeds and words—which the king himself has selected as the place 'proper to receive ascetics'. The Mystic Fire has already announced Śakuntalā's marriage to Duḥṣanta to Kaṇva, and prophecied the greatness of the son to be born of this union. The marriage is therefore a sanctified one.

Kaṇva is a revered sage, a *kulapati*, or head of a community of ascetics and the king has expressed his profound veneration for the sage in whom holy power (Brahmā) is vested as a result of his 'immense penance'. His people would have shared this view. Yet, his regard for the sage carries little weight in Duḥṣanta's assessment of the situation at this juncture. It has no influence on his manner and conduct or the way he judges the sage's daughter. This might partly be the consequence of the manner in which the two disciples, especially Śārṅgarava, handle the situation. By putting the marriage of Śakuntalā to the king on a quasi-legal instead of a sanctified basis, as one would expect an ascetic to do, and by introducing public opinion as a factor into the situation, Śārṅgarava foregrounds the question of *proof* in the mind of someone responding defensively as the king does. Doubts about the legality of the marriage and the legitimacy of the unborn child would inevitably surface in the minds of the ministers, the court and the people. And these doubts have necessarily to form part of the king's reasoning as he faces an unexpected and difficult problem. (In the epic story, Duḥṣanta clearly states these doubts as the reason for his repudiating Śakuntalā in the Hall of Assembly.) He poses a question to Śārṅgarava to which a clear answer cannot be given. The alternatives are, as Duḥṣanta puts it, the desertion of a legally wed wife or adultery (or what seems to him to be adultery). Which is the lesser evil, he asks, since both are forbidden by the law and regarded as heinous sins. Śāṅgarava has no answer. It is a problem which the audience might have pondered over. Insensibly, the sanctuary of the Mystic Fire, (*Agni-śaraṇa*) has been transformed into a court of law. Śakuntalā stands no chance of winning her case because she cannot produce the only concrete evidence of a secretly contracted marriage, the royal signet ring given to her by Duḥṣanta. She is lost. In the last moments of her hour of sorrow and tribulation, when she flings her arms up to the indifferent skies and invites death as her last resort, a flash of light appears and carries her away. Śakuntalā vanishes, never to be seen again in this world. The reconciliation and reunion of Śakuntalā and Duḥṣanta takes place in another world, the 'golden world' of the Primal Pair. The resolution of the plot is effected in this mythical world; therefore, one way of *reading* the play is to see it as having a fictive ending. By introducing the device of a *deus et machina*, the situation is saved, temporarily; the tragedy is averted, but the tragic tone remains.

The story of Śakuntalā and Duḥṣanta in the *Mahābhārata* is the main source for the play. In it, Śakuntalā is portrayed as a fiery and spirited girl who fights tenaciously for her son's rights. She literally reads the Law to the king and when she finds him obdurate, gives him such a tongue lashing that we practically see him squirming on his jewelled throne and wishing he were elsewhere. The story as the epic tells it in the swinging narrative style, is powerful though rough hewn. It reflects the epic tone and the way of life of the heroic age. But to Kālidāsa, it provides the bare bones of a story which he has shaped into an intricate plot structure to produce a deeply moving play that probes and asks questions. Kālidāsa has drastically changed his sources to convey his own vision of life and his view of certain problems which seem to have deeply concerned him. The epic story has only two characters, Śakuntalā and Duḥṣanta, with Kaṇva making a brief appearance. In the play, the conception of the two main characters are totally different. Kaṇva is an important figure and we have all the minor characters which are the dramatist's creations, for which there is not even a hint in the epic story. Kālidāsa has also introduced the curse and the king's loss of memory, and the ring as the token of recognition. The story of the ring might have been part of some old tale, folk or fairy tale, which is lost. The epic story has a happy ending. An incorporeal voice heard by everyone in the Hall of Assembly testifies to the truth of Śakuntalā's words and accepted as proof of marriage and the legitimacy of the son.

I venture to suggest that the characterization of the hero and heroine and the general mood of the play might be influenced by the old, lost tale of *apsara* Śakuntalā, of which only a tantalizing hint remains embedded in the vedic text referred to earlier. Śakuntalā's close association with nature, her kinship with tree-divinities (*yakṣīs*) and the reference to her as the 'guardian deity' of the Hermitage, point to this. The terms in which Duḥṣanta talks of his meeting with her 'Was it a dream? a magical vision? . . ' and the frequent use of the word *moha* (and *sam-moha*) which has several meanings—wonder, illusion or delusion—to mention a few in this context, also point in this direction.

Other meanings of *moha* are: bewilderment, perplexity, the inability to discriminate. It is a state of mind hovering between different planes of consciousness, where the real and the imagined are interfused as in the portrait-episode in Act 6, which the pragmatist Māḍhavya would characterize as being on the verge of madness. In fact it is one of the last stages in the progress of the malady in an unhappy lover which leads to death, as laid down in Bharata's *Nāṭyaśāstra*. The delusion under which the king labours is brought on by the curse, ostensibly. The operation of the curse is described in images of veiling darkness, blindness and drunkenness with its unsettling consequences. We might single out as an example the comparison with a man who sees but does not *recognize* the object, who then infers its appearance and disappearance from traces (or a token) left behind (7.31). The curse and the manner in which it operates is related to the problem of recognition. It should therefore not be treated as is often done, simply as a device to gloss over the unpleasant side of Duḥṣanta's nature—his proneness to philandering, the streak of callousness in him verging on cruelty, his self-indulgence—or to exonerate him from the blame of harshly repudiating Śakuntalā and in so doing showing disrespect to a great sage. That might very well be one of the purposes of the curse. Kālidāsa's audience would have been as mixed as any audience at any time anywhere; and their responses would have varied, as in the case of audiences now. To see the image of a great monarch, a hero of the celebrated Puru dynasty which held a special place in story and therefore in the popular imagination, tarnished by ignoble behaviour without cause, was (and is still with some) bound to have been emotionally difficult to accept. To strip a people of cherished myths is not to be lightly undertaken. But as the curse can be seen and interpreted in more than one way, it ought to be considered as the means which Kālidāsa uses to explore different states of consciousness and to probe beneath the surface of Duḥṣanta's personality.

While the loss of the ring and the loss of memory resulting from the curse, provides the necessary complication in the plot structure, there is something else to which Kālidāsa alerts us. He directs us to question the whole idea of furnishing tangible proof for all those things in life we take on trust: love, constancy, fidelity. In Act 6 while the king and Māḍhavya discuss the circumstances in which the ring has been lost, Miśrakeśī makes a significant observation: 'Does a love like this need a token of recognition? How can that be?' I would take it that she refers to the love of both Śakuntalā and the king at this point. There are many instances in the literature of the world where this question needs to be asked: in the *Rāmāyaṇa* when Sītā is asked to prove her chastity by undergoing the ordeal of fire a second time to allay the suspicions of the public; in Shakespeare's *Othello* and *King Lear* where proof of fidelity and of filial love is demanded, with tragic consequences. Śakuntalā is placed in a situation where she is unable to furnish proof of her marriage to the king who has in the meantime forgotten her. The royal signet ring which is the mark of authority and used to stamp documents to validate them (perhaps to stamp objects too, to prove the *legitimacy of ownership*) has gained an added importance and status; Śakuntalā is recognized or not recognized by virtue of its presence or its absence. As the play progresses, this ring, an inanimate thing—'a mindless thing' as the king describes it, becomes a *character* in the drama and plays a *role*. Its fall and loss go hand in hand with the fall of Śakuntalā's fortunes and the loss of memory of the king and his fall into delusion and 'deep dejection'; its finding brings awakening and pain. The theme of *knowing* and recognition hinges on the presence or absence of the ring.

XI

The *vidūṣaka* or jester in Sanskrit drama is the friend and close companion of the hero. The *vidūṣaka*, Māḍhavya in *Śakuntalā* is taken as both representative of this class of characters and yet not typical, and discussed. Incidental observations about the *vidūṣaka*-character in Kālidāsa's other two plays are made as part of the discussion, but detailed analyses of the other two (in *Mālavikā* and *Vikramorvaśīyam*) will be found in the introduction to volume II in the series. He performs two functions which are related to the two meanings contained in the word: a figure of fun who excites laughter by his odd appearance and manner, and his witty speech; and a 'detractor' or critic who deflates everyone around him through the exercise of a sharp and often caustic wit.

An ill-favoured hunchback, Māḍhavya, the *vidūṣaka* in the play *Śakuntalā* is the butt of ridicule for the world which in turn is the target of his wit. And this includes him; for Māḍhavya can laugh at himself. For example, at the opening of Act 2, we hear him talking to the king about the bent reed growing by the river bank, buffeted by the force of the current and tottering 'to and fro with the grace of a hunchback's gait'. Māḍhavya's wry laughter is not without an element of pathos, a hallmark of most clowns and jesters who play the fool.

A relationship of deep affection exists between king and jester. It is reflected even in the tone of their conversation which has the easy familiarity of two friends who have grown up together from childhood. Māḍhavya often addresses the king, in private, as *vayasya*—dear friend, (literally 'one of the same age'). The king is able to put off his regalia and his public image, remove himself from the splendour and pressures of the court and relax in Māḍhavya's company and be himself as he can with no one else.

As the friend and confidant of the king, Māḍhavya is a privileged person and this fact taken together with his capacity to laugh at himself, makes him something of an ironic commentator in the play. His wit is no respecter of persons; even the Queen receives her share of his barbed comments and the king himself is not exempt. There are several examples in Act 2 where Māḍhavya slips in some pointed criticism of the king, under the guise of affectionate banter. On entering, he first treats the audience to the sorry tale of his aching joints. His body is battered, galloping all day over rough paths following the king whose lust for the chase seems to be boundless. (Hunting is regarded as one of the eight vices that princes are warned against in manuals on ethics). He misses the good life: good food, rest, sleep and 'sweet dumplings', needless to say. This is Māḍhavya's *mask*; using it, he plays his role true to form, pretending to be slow on the uptake, but sharp and astute as he slips in his ironic comments smoothly and adroitly. He stands like a broken reed, supporting himself on his stick and when the king asks 'And what has paralyzed your limbs?' Knowing full well what Māḍhavya's ploy is likely to be, the latter seizes the cue he has been waiting for. (King and jester understand each other well.)

Māḍhavya: A fine thing to ask; do you hit me in the eye—and then ask why it is watering?

King: My dear friend, I do not follow; make your meaning clear.

Māḍhavya: If the bent reed by the river totters to and fro with the grace of a hunchback's gait, does it do so on its own . . . hm . . . or, is the force of the current the cause?

King: Why, in that case, the force of the current is the cause.

Māḍhavya: Yes, as you are, in mine.

King: And how is that?

Māḍhavya (as if angry): Go on, you abandon the affairs of the kingdom . . . .

This is how he puts it to the king. He, Māḍhavya, the hunchback, is only an insignificant reed growing beside the river tottering and perhaps his well being is not that important. (We have to link this with what the king says towards the end of the act, that he is like a river which has to divide to go round a rock—an obstacle). But, the affairs of the kingdom are a different matter; and the king is neglecting them to lead the primitive life of foresters, chasing wild animals (and a girl), unmindful of his duties. However, Māḍhavya does not push the point too far; after all Duḥṣanta is the king and kings could suddenly turn against the best of friends if provoked. But he has made his point to the king and to the audience, and lets it rest there. A little later in the act he makes an oblique reference to the same point, when he tells the General, Bhadrasena that the king is 'recovering his true nature' and ask the General to fan the king's lust for the chase, but to go to hell himself.

Again, as he is leaving, rather put out, the king stops him to ask for help in 'a matter that will not cause you the least bit of exertion'. Māḍhavya knows what the matter is but he pretends not to and asks rather ingenuously 'Like tasting sweet dumplings, perhaps?'

Māḍhavya's witty comments effectively deflate the king whenever the latter makes self-serving statements or holds forth on the theme of Śakuntalā's charms. When the jester remarks drily that there was little point in attempting to meet Śakuntalā once more since she was the daughter of a sage and therefore beyond the king's reach, Duḥṣanta retorts with a flourish: 'You are a dull fellow, Māḍhavya. Has Duḥṣanta's heart ever been drawn to a forbidden object?' and proceeds to explain Śakuntalā's real parentage, to which Māḍhavya's tart comment is: 'Oho! That's how it is, eh? Like one whose palate jaded by enjoying delicate candies made of the sweetest dates, hankers after a taste of the sour tamarind, you too, Sir, sated with the pleasures of the royal apartments . . . are consumed with a passion for this hermit-maiden.' Māḍhavya deflates the king's craving for beautiful women by placing it on the same level as his own for sweet dumplings and candied dates; and further, sets against Duḥṣanta's phrase describing Śakuntalā as 'the flower of the fragrant jasmine', his own of 'the sour tamarind'. Again, to the king's rapturous outburst regarding Śakuntalā's shy responses that concludes with:

> 'Love neither shone radiant nor was it concealed',

Māḍhavya's quick retort is:

> 'What, Sir, did you then expect her to leap into your arms as soon as she set eyes on your Honour?'

and again,

> 'Go quickly, Sir, and rescue her before she falls into the hands of some forest-dwelling hermit with greasy head and hair plastered down with ingudi oil.'

Māḍhavya provides the element of wit and humour so necessary to offset the element of romance in the play. His sharp comments serve as the tart tamarind to the cloying sweetness of Duḥṣanta's declamation on love, its raptures and its pain. They also bring an ironic and critical perspective into a court where there is considerable adulation of the king; for Māḍhavya serves as a foil to the court bards, whose duties are to compose and sing hymns of praise to the reigning monarch. His refreshing wit blows in some fresh air into the hothouse atmosphere of the court.

Though Māḍhavya shoots off his witty barbs at the king whenever an opportunity presents itself, he is a loyal and true friend, supportive and not given to flattery. But this relationship of king and jester has to come to an end before the play proceeds to its conclusions. At the end of Act 6, Māḍhavya is dismissed, not casually, or with disdain, but affectionately and with honour. He is entrusted with an important assignment, to inform the Chief Minister, Piśuna, about the momentous mission the king is setting out on and the circumstances leading up to it, and to instruct the minister to carry on the government in the meantime. Māḍhavya accepts the royal command and leaves with quiet dignity. We never see him again; for he is no longer needed as the king's companion, to amuse and divert him. His witty comments, his homely wisdom spiced with time-worn proverbs containing sound practical sense are not needed either; not where Duhṣanta is headed for. And Māḍhavya has no place in that 'other world' in the mythic world of Act 7: neither in the vanguard of Indra's battles against the dark forces nor in the 'golden world' of the Primal Pair, Mārīca and Aditi.

Duhṣanta is no longer the king he was. He has grown in understanding and has learnt compassion and caring for others. This is implied in the ruling he makes, which almost sounds like the setting up of a legal precedent, that the estate of the wealthy merchant who died in a shipwreck should not be confiscated by the state, but be inherited by his unborn child. This ruling has an extension in the form of a royal proclamation, that the king would be a friend and kinsman to all his subjects who follow the right path. Duhṣanta had to experience the grief of childlessness himself and realize the dangers to an heirless kingdom before he is able to understand and feel for his subjects. He seems to have grown in another way too. After a long spell of penitential grief, he has gained the capacity to know and value true love, which is a matter of more than the delight of the eye and of pleasure. When he meets Śakuntalā again in Mārīca's hermitage, he *sees* her knowing her true worth; it is recognition, or *abhijñānam*, the highly suggestive word which forms the first part of the compound word that is the title of the play—*Abhijñānaśākuntalam*. The carnal knowledge he had of Śakuntalā which had carried him to dizzying heights of rapture only to plunge him into deep despair under the weight of an overwhelming guilt, is transformed. Māḍhavya has no place in this changed world.

Initially, Māḍhavya has no place in the 'green world' situated within deep forests. With the kind of opinion he expressed regarding ascetics as longbeards, with greasy heads and hair plastered down with ingudi oil, he cannot possibly feel at ease in Mārīca's hermitage. In fact he would have been miserable in the 'golden world'. The jester has his feet firmly planted on the earth; we cannot imagine him sitting at the feet of Mārīca and Aditi, hymning their praises. In this connection Māḍhavya's words to Duhṣanta when he is released by Mātali at the close of Act 6, are significant: 'He was about to slay me as if I were a *sacrificial beast*, and here . . . you welcome him. . . .' The denouement towards which the play is now leading, demands that Māḍhavya be *sacrificed*.

The *vidūṣaka* or jester of Sanskrit drama, belongs essentially to the world of the court, especially to the world of jealousies and intrigue of the royal harem. Apart from the aged chamberlain, he is the only male permitted entry into the inner and private apartments of the palace. This is the *vidūṣaka's* world where he practises his cleverness, his talent for manipulation to bring the hero's many love affairs to a successful conclusion and to placate the other wives (or queens) or trick them into accepting the latest object of the hero's affections as co-wife or queen, as the case may be. However, Māḍhavya is not the typical *vidūṣaka*; he is hardly involved in intrigue. As Śakuntalā is a different kind of heroine, Māḍhavya is a different kind of jester and king's companion. The heroine and the jester never meet in this play. With exquisite poetic tact, Kālidāsa keeps them and their worlds apart. Māḍhavya, as we noted earlier, never enters the 'green world'; he stands on its fringes complaining about his aching joints. At the end of Act 2, he is shunted off to the capital, ostensibly to take the king's place as a surrogate son in the Queen Mother's rites to ensure the succession. (That Duḥṣanta is childless is made quite clear at the play's beginning). He is absent in Act 3, where Duḥṣanta courts Śakuntalā and their *gāndharva* marriage takes place. In the trial scene in Act 5, Māḍhavya is again not present when the ascetics and Gautamī arrive with Śakuntalā: he has been despatched immediately before this to pacify Queen Haṃsavatī, smarting under Duḥṣanta's neglect of her, the reason being that it would have been fatal to the plot to have had Māḍhavya around at that point. In the two earlier plays of Kālidāsa, the *vidūṣaka* is thrown into close contact with the heroine (*nāyikā*). But all Māḍhavya knows about Śakuntalā is what the king tells him; he hears a great deal about her from Duḥṣanta; he sees her in a portrait done by Duḥṣanta. Śakuntalā is presented to the jester only through the eyes of the hero—*nāyaka.* And unlike the jesters in the other two plays, Māḍhavya is bored by the whole matter of Śakuntalā.

No one from the court comes into close contact with the heroine of this play; in fact no one belonging to the court gains entry into her world—'the green world'. The king's retinue and companions only mill around its periphery, creating terror and confusion. And they leave with the jester at the close of Act 2, when he departs in state in the role of the king's younger brother—the heir apparent. When the play begins to gather all the threads—the *sūtradhāra,* the director-producer is the one who holds all the threads in his hands—and wind to its conclusion, the true heir-apparent, Śakuntalā's son, Sarvadamana, is in place, acknowledged as son and heir by the king.

In these and in many onther respect, some of which have been discussed or touched upon, this play is totally different in tone, treatment of character and issues, from Kālidāsa's other plays. The moral and poetic vision that structure *Abhijñānaśākuntalam*, is unique as it is in *Meghadūtam* and it is somewhat similar. This seems to suggest that they were written at about the same time and were the poet's last works. There is a gentle melancholy under the surface in both works, even in the happiest moments, an under current of regret at the passing of the first flush of happiness of a newly-wed pair of lovers. In *Meghadūtam*, when the lovers are reunited, if ever they are, we sense that their love would be a chastened one; in st. 112, the poem draws a contrast between *bhoga* or sensual ejoyment and *prema* or deep affection; between passion and love. This contrast is more fully articulated in the play. At the end, the glow of youthful and exuberant love and happiness of the first and third acts of the play has faded into the common light of duty: the focus and interest shifts to the son born of those first moments of intense passion. The last stanzas of the poem are coloured by a certain tentativeness of statement, and a hope for the reunion of the *yakṣa* and his beloved wife. In the play, the long period of penance for Śakuntalā and repentance for Duḥṣanta end in a reconciliation based on mutual respect and trust that brings some measure of happiness for both by finding a common ground in the child and his future.

There are moments of overhanging gloom, even darkness in *Abhijñānaśākuntalam.* There are moments too of bitter irony accompanied by flashes of pure good humour. But the play, though it has had its tragic moments closes on a note of serenity, expressing the poet's vision of peace and harmony in a world where order has been restored. The little prince Sarvadamana—All-Tamer—will grow up and be known as Bharata, he who bears, protects and sustains the world. It is after him that the country is called Bhāratavarṣa (modern Bhārata or India), the land of the Bhāratas who are the people of India.

All those born in this land before Bharata,
All those born after, are called after his name. (*Mbh.* I. 69. 49)

Ṛtusaṃhāram
(The Gathering of the Seasons)

A Poem in Six Cantos

Ṛtusaṃhāram

Canto 1: Summer

1

The sun blazing fiercely,
the moon longed for eagerly,
deep waters inviting
to plunge in continually,
days drawing to a close in quiet beauty,
the tide of desire running low:
    scorching Summer is now here, my love.

2

Night's indigo-masses rent by the moon,
wondrous mansions built on water,
cooled by fountains; various gems
cool to the touch; liquid sandal;
the world seeks relief in these
    in Summer's scorching heat, my love.

3

Palace-terraces perfumed, luring the senses,
wine trembling beneath the beloved's breath,
sweet melodies on finely-tuned lutes:
lovers enjoy these passion-kindling things
    at midnight in Summer, my love.

4

Curving hips, their beauty enhanced
by fine silks and jewelled belts;[1]
sandal-scented breasts caressed by necklaces of pearls,

fragrant tresses bathed in perfumed water:
with these women soothe their lovers
    in burning Summer, my love.

5

Swaying hips; soles tinted deep rose;
anklets with tinkling bells
imitating at each step the cry of the wild goose:
    men's hearts are churned by desire.

6

Breasts rubbed smooth with liquid sandal,
crowned by strings of pearls lustrous as dewdrops,
hips encircled by golden belts—
    whose heart will not yearn restless?

7

High-breasted women in the flush of youth,
limbs shining with beads of sweat, throw off
heavy garments and put on thin stoles
    right for the season to cover their breasts.

8

The breeze of moist sandal-scented fans,
the touch of flower-garlands on the beloved's breast,
the lute's exquisite murmuring sound:
    these now awaken sleeping Love.

9

Gazing all night longingly
on the faces of lovely women sleeping happy
on terraces of sparkling white mansions,
the moon pales[2] at dawn struck by guilty shame.

10

Hearts burning in the fire of separation,
men far from home can scarcely bear to see
the swirling clouds of dust tossed up
from the earth burnt by the sun's fierce heat.

11

Antelopes suffering from Summer's savage heat,
race with parched throats[3] towards the distant sky
the colour of smooth-blended collyrium, thinking:
—'there's water there in another forest.'

12

As enchanting twilights jewelled by the moon
instantly kindle desire in pleasure-seekers' minds,
so do the graceful movements, subtle smiles
and wayward glances of amorous women.

13

In an agony of pain from the sun's fierce rays,
scorched by dust on his path, a snake with drooping hood
creeps on his tortuous course, repeatedly hissing,
to find shelter under a peacock's shade.

14

The king of beasts suffering intense thirst, pants
with wide open jaws, lolling tongue, quivering mane;
powerless to attack he does not kill
elephants though they are not beyond his reach.

15

Dry-throated, foaming at the mouth,
maddened by the sun's sizzling rays,
tuskers in an agony of growing thirst,
seeking water, do not fear even the lion.

16

Peacocks, exhausted by the flame-rays of the sun
blazing like numerous sacrificial fires,
lack the will to strike at the hooded snake
thrusting its head under their circle of plumes.

17

By the hot sun tormented a herd of wild boars
rooting with the round tips of their long snouts
in the caked mud of ponds with swamp-grass overgrown,
appear as if descending deep into the earth.

18

Burning under the sun's fiery wreath of rays,
a frog leaps up from the muddy pond
to sit under the parasol hood
of a deadly cobra that is thirsty and tired.

19

A whole host of fragile lotus plants uprooted,
fish lying dead, sarus cranes[4] flown away in fear,
the lake is one thick mass of mire, pounded
by a packed elephant-herd pushing and shoving.

20

A cobra overcome by thirst darts his forked tongue out
to lick the breeze; the iridescence of his crest-jewel
flashes struck by brilliant sunbeams; burning
from Summer's heat and his own fiery poison
he does not attack the assemblage of frogs.

21

A herd of female buffaloes frenzied by thirst
emerges from the hill's caves, heads lifted up
sniffing for water, spittle overflowing from cavernous jaws
and frothing round their lips, pink tongues hanging out.

22

A raging forest fire burns tender shoots to a cinder;
cruel winds hurl shrivelled leaves high up with impetuous force;
all around waters shrink to the bottom in the sizzling heat;
O what a scene of horror the woodland's outskirts present!

23

Birds sit panting on trees shorn of leaves;
lean monkeys troop into caves overgrown with bushes;
wild bulls roam around looking for water;
elephant cubs diligently draw up water from a well.

24

Relentlessly driven by the force of violent winds,
the fire, brilliant as the vermilion petals
of the mallow rose unfolding,
speeds in every direction, smitten with longing to clasp
the tops of trees, bushes and creepers, and burns the earth.

25

Springing up at the skirts of the woodland,
the fire's glare tires the creatures of the woodland;
it blazes in the glens fanned by the winds,
crackles and bursts through dry bamboo thickets
and spreads in the grass, waxing each moment.

26

Incited by the winds, the wild fire roams
all around the woodland, seeming to assume
multiple forms in the bright silk-cotton groves;
it glitters, burnished gold, in the hollows of trees
and springs up tall trees, to branches whose leaves are singed.

27

With their bodies burning in the fire's fierce heat,
elephants, wild bulls, lions, lay aside their enmity,
and come quickly out of grasslands scorched by fire, together,
like friends, to rest on the river's wide, sandy banks.

28

O lady, whose singing flows so sweet
in the night over moonlit terraces,
may Summer waited upon by lovely women,
when pools are strewn thick with lotuses
and the air scented by pāṭala[5] flowers,
when waters are pleasant to laze in
and garlands of pearls cool with their touch,
pass in greatest delight and ease for you.

Canto 2: Rains

1

With streaming clouds trumpeting like haughty tuskers,
with lightning-banners and drum beats of thunder claps,
in towering majesty, the season of rains
welcome to lovers, now comes like a king, my love.

2

Overcast on all sides with dense rain clouds, the sky
displays the deep glow of blue-lotus petals,
dark in places like heaped collyrium, smooth-blended,
glowing elsewhere like the breasts of a woman with child.

3

Implored by cātakas[6] tormented by great thirst,
and hanging low weighed down by large loads of water,
massed clouds advance slowly, pouring many-streamed rain:
and the sound of their thunder is sweet to the ear.

4

Hurling thunderbolts that crash down to strike terror,
bending bows strung with lightning-streaks, letting loose
fierce, sharp-shooting showers—cruel arrows fine-honed—
clouds, relentless, wound the hearts of men far from home.

5

The Earth covered by tender shoots of grass
brilliant as emeralds shivering into points of light,
by up-springing kandalī[7] leaf-buds and by ladybirds,
dazzles like a woman decked in gems, green and red.

6

A bevy of peacocks that sound ever-delightful,
eagerly watching out for this festive moment,

caught up in a flurry of billing and fondling,
now begin to dance, gorgeous plumage spread out wide.

7

Rivers swollen by a mass of turbid waters
rush with impetuous haste towards the seas,
felling trees all around on their banks
like unchaste women driven by passion-filled fancies.

8

Adorned with piles of tender tips of lush green grass
lying scattered, fallen from the jaws of browsing does,
and beautiful with burgeoning trees,
Vindhya's groves now captivate the onlooker's heart.

9

Dotting the woodlands are charming glades by streams,
haunted by timorous gazelles easily alarmed
—tremulous eyes like blue water lilies, enchanting—
and the heart is twisted with sudden longing.

10

Clouds loudly roar again and again:
nights are pitch-dark:
only the lightning's flashes light the way:
even so, amorous women driven by passion
are on their way to midnight trysts.

11

Clouds burst with terrifying peals of thunder;
lightnings flash. Women shrinking in fear
cling closely in bed to their loved husbands,
though these men are guilty philanderers.

12

Teardrops from eyes lovely as blue lotuses
rain down on soft lips red as ripe berries:

wives of men who travel far are desolate,
and toss aside their jewels, flowers, fragrances.

13

Thick with insects, dust and bits of grass,
a dirty-grey in colour, headed downward,
rain water snakes slowly on its tortuous way,
watched anxiously by a brood of nervous frogs.

14

Bees forsake pools where lotuses have shed their petals;
sweetly humming, the fools thirsting for honey
swarm round circlets on the plumes of dancing peacocks,
in the hope they are fresh-blossoming blue lotuses.

15

Infuriated by the thunder of the first rain clouds,
wild elephants trumpet again and again:
their temples spotless as bright blue-lilies are drenched
by the flow of rut with bees swarming over them.

16

Inlaid on all sides with sparkling waterfalls,
teeming with peacocks commencing their dance,
rocks kissed by low-hanging, rain-filled clouds—
the mountains kindle unbearable longing.

17

Blowing through groves of kadaṃba[8] and sarja[9]
and ketakī[10] and arjuna,[11] shaking the trees,
scented by the fragrance of their flowers,
consorting with clouds and cooled by rain drops—
whom do these breezes not fill with longing?

18

Hair cascading down to the hips,
fragrant flowers nestling behind the ears,
pearl strings fondling the breasts,

wine perfuming the breath—
women set the hearts of their lovers on fire.

19

Gleaming with rainbows,
filigreed with the lightning's glitter,
life-giving clouds, pendent, packed with water—
and women dazzling in gem-set earrings
and belts festooned with bells—
both work together to steal
the hearts of men journeying abroad.

20

Women twine round their coiled hair
wreaths woven of fresh kadaṃba flowers,
kesara buds[12] and ketakī fronds,
and place the arjuna's blossoming sprays
as pendants over the ears,
arranging them in many pleasing shapes.

21

With gorgeous mane of hair flower-scented
and limbs rubbed smooth with liquid sandal
and cream of black aloes,
hearing the thunder's voice
in the early hours of the night,
women slip at once away
from the apartments of their elders,
and quickly enter their own bed-chambers.

22

Lofty clouds deep-blue like blue-lotus petals,
stooping low, rain-laden, shot through with rainbow gleams,
move imperceptibly, waved on by gentle winds:
they seem to carry away the hearts of women,
grief-stricken, parted from husbands who travel far.

23

The first fresh showers break the drought,
the woodland seems to thrill with joy
as kadaṃbas burst into bloom;
it laughs displaying the ketakī's bright leaf-buds
and dances; trees sway gesturing with wind-swept branches.

24

This season of massed rain clouds arranges
chaplets of bakula blossoms twined with buds of mālatī,[13]
yuthikā[14] and other fresh-blooming flowers
on the heads of young wives as a fond husband would,
and fresh kadamba sprays to fall over their ears.

25

Women adorn their beautiful breasts with nets of pearls,
and drape pale delicate silks round their shapely curving hips;
the fine line of down above the navel rises up
to meet the cool tingling touch of fresh raindrops:
how charming are the folds that furrow their waists!

26

Perfumed by the ketakī's pollen-dust and
cooled by the fine spray of fresh raindrops,
the wind that instructs in dance
the trees bowed by loads of flowers
ravishes the hearts of men sojourning abroad.

27

'This noble mountain is our firm support
when we are bent double carrying loads of water'
thinking thus, rain clouds bow low to offer their gift of showers
and gladden Vindhya's hills grievously scorched
by the savaging flames of Summer's fierce forest fires.

28

A source of fascination to amorous women,
the constant friend to trees, shrubs and creepers,
the very life and breath of all living beings—
May this season of rains rich in these benedictions
fully grant all desires accordant with your well-being.

Canto 3: Autumn

1

Robed in pale silk plumes of kāśa blooms,[15]
full-blown lotuses her beautiful face,
the calls of rapturous wild geese
the music of her anklet bells,
ripening grain, lightly bending, her lissome form:
Autumn has now arrived, enchanting as a bride.

2

The earth is bright with kāśa blossoms,
nights with the cool rays of the moon;
streams are lively with flocks of wild geese
and pools are strewn with lotuses;
groves are lovely with flower-laden trees
and gardens white with fragrant jasmines.

3

Prettily girdled by glittering minnows darting about,
garlanded by rows of white birds on the margins,
with broad curving flanks of sandy banks,
rivers glide softly like young women rapt in love.

4

Squeezed dry of rain, a host of clouds
palest silver like delicate sea-shells,
float free in places, waved back and forth
by brisk winds with the utmost ease:
the sky appears like a great king
fanned by a hundred fleecy chowries.[16]

5

The sky glows, a mass of glossy collyrium,
the earth dusted by bandhūka[17] pollen
is the colour of dawn;

mellow golden are river banks
and fields with ripening corn:
whose heart in the days of youth will not be seized with longing?

6

Its topmost twigs are tangled by a gentle breeze;
sprays of blossoms rise out of delicate leaf-crowns:
bees are whirling drunk on honey trickling down:
whose mind is not ripped by the beauty of this kovidāra tree?[18]

7

Splendidly jewelled by numberless star-clusters,
Night wraps herself in moonlight's shining robe
when the moon her face struggles free of obscuring clouds.
Day by day, she grows like a young girl
stepping gracefully into proud womanhood.[19]

8

Ringing with mournful belltones of wild geese,
waters dyed rose-red by lotus pollen
and ruffled by circling ripples where teals plunge in,
banks noisy with black ducks and sarus cranes jostling,
streams all around bring delight to watchers.

9

The moon, the eye's delight,
captivates all hearts with aureoles bright:
Bringer of Joy, showering beams cool as snowflakes,
it consumes the limbs of women
pierced by the poisoned arrows
of separation from their husbands.

10

A breeze sets the bending ears of corn swinging,
great trees bowed down by masses of flowers dancing,
pools thick with blossoming lotuses quivering;
and violently unsettles soft young minds.

11

The breathtaking beauty of rippling lakes
breathed on by a passing wind at daybreak,
where lotus and lily glow brilliantly
and pairs of love-drunk wild geese float entrancing,
suddenly grips the heart with longing.

12

Lost is Indra's bow in the bowels of the clouds;
lightning, the sky's banner, quivers no more;
egrets no longer beat the air with their wings;
peacocks do not watch the sky with upturned faces.

13

The dance-display ended, Love deserts the peacocks
to attend the honey-sweet concert of wild geese;
Beauty, Genius of Blossom-Time, forsaking
the kadaṃba, kuṭaja[20] and kakubha,
the sarja and aśoka,[21] now dwells in the sapta-parṇa.[22]

14

Redolent of the fragrance of śephālika[23] blossoms,
resonant with bird-song in undisturbed quietness,
groves with lotus-eyed gazelles wandering in the glades
kindle restless longing in everyone's heart.

15

Playfully tossing lotuses, pink, white and red,
deliciously cooled moving fondly among them,
wiping away the dewdrops edging their petals
the breeze at daybreak rocks the heart with wild longing.

16

People rejoice to see the village-bounds
crowded with large herds of cows lying undisturbed,
where ripe grain lies spread in heaps on threshing floors
and the air rings with cries of wild geese and sarus cranes.

17

The gait of wild geese surpass the rare charm of women's steps,
full-blown lotuses the radiance of their moon-bright faces;
blue water lilies rival the lustre of passion-glowing eyes,
delicate wavelets the play of their eyebrows graceful.

18

Śyāmā[24] creepers curving with tender flower-filled twigs
usurp the brilliance of women's jewel-loaded arms;
fresh jasmines peeping through vibrant aśoka flowers
rival the sparkle of smiles brilliant as moonlight.

19

Young women fill with a wealth of jasmine buds
their thick midnight-blue hair curling at the ends;
they place varied blue-lotuses
behind ears decked with fine gold earrings.

20

Globed breasts adorned with pearls sandal-misted,
wide curving hips with girdles strung with bells,
precious anklets making music on their lotus feet,
lit with happiness deep within
women now enhance their beauty.

21

A cloudless sky inlaid with the moon and countless stars
wears the exquisite beauty of lakes glowing
with the sheen of emeralds, and strewn with moon-lotuses,
wide open; and a regal swan floats serene.[25]

22

Autumn skies are enchanting, star-sprinkled,
lit by a clear-rayed moon; serenely beautiful
are the directions of space, free of thronging rain clouds:
the earth is dry; waters sparkling clear;
breezes consorting with lotuses blow cool.

23

Wakened by the morning beams, the day-lotus
now expands to look like a lovely maiden's face;
but the moon-lotus droops with the setting moon
like the smiles of women whose husbands are far from home.

24

Seeing the glow of the beloved's dark eyes
in the blue-lotus,
hearing the tones of the golden bells of her jewelled belt
in the love-mad murmur of wild geese,
recalling the rich red of her lower lip
in the bandhūka's flame-clusters,
travellers, their thoughts whirling, lament.

25

Conferring the radiance of the moon
on the faces of women,
the melodious tones of wild geese
on their gem-filled anklets,
the bandhūka-bloom's vibrant redness
on their luscious lower lips,
the splendour of bountiful Autumn
is now departing, to who knows where!

26

Full-blown lotuses, pale-pink, her face,
deep-blue lilies unfolding, her dark eyes,
fresh white kāśa blooms, her bright robe,
glowing with the brilliance of moon-lotuses,
may this Autumn, like your beloved
lost in love for you,
fully grant your heart's highest happiness.

Canto 4: The Season of Frosts

1

The sudden burst of the barley's young shoots
shows delightful; lodhras[26] are in full bloom;
paddy golden ripe; lotuses all withered:
thick-falling dews usher this season of frosts.

2

Pearl-garlands pale, misted with liquid sandal,
lustrous as dew drops or jasmines or the moon,
do not enhance with their elegance
the orb-like breasts of graceful women.

3

Delicate bodices do not tenderly touch
the swelling breasts of young women moving
with exquisite grace;
fine new silks do not cling to their curving hips;
bracelets and armlets do not clasp their arms.

4

Women in their pride of beauty and youth
do not adorn their hips with gold girdles, gem-studded,
or their lotus-feet reflecting the glow of lotuses
with anklets that sound the bell-tones of wild geese.

5

Women now prepare for love's festival,
perfuming their hair with black-aloe smoke,
tracing leafy lines on their lotus-faces,
and rubbing their bodies with white-aloe salve.

6

With faces pale and drawn from love's weariness,
young women whose lips smart from love-bites

are afraid to laugh out loud
even when a happy occasion arises.

7

Seeming sensible of the sensuous beauty
of women's breasts, sad to see them pressed so hard,
the frosty season cries out at dawn, letting fall
dew drops that cling to the tips of blades of grass.

8

Fields richly covered with ripening rice,
where charming does roam in herds
are sonorous with the calls of demoiselle cranes.
Ah! What restlessness they arouse!

9

Where the chill waters of lakes shimmer,
blue lotuses open wide in beauty;
mallards court in wild excitement:
all hearts are transported with boundless delight.

10

Languishing blanched in the chilling frost,
ever-shivering in the blowing wind,
like a sprightly girl parted from her love,
the priyaṅgu[27] now grows pale, my love.

11

Mouths redolent of the fragrance of flower-wine,
limbs perfumed from mingled breaths—
men and women sleep, twined in one another's arms,
blended in the sweet poetry of love.

12

Sharp imprint of love-bites on bruised lips,
the lover's nail-inscriptions[28] on breasts—

these clearly reveal the passionate enjoyment,
relentless, of women in the first flush of youth.

13

A certain young woman, mirror in hand,
decorates her radiant lotus-face, basking
in the gentle warmth of the mild morning sun
and gazes with interest, pouting, at the love-bites
her beloved left when he drank his fill
of the nectar of her lower lip.

14

Yet another, her body, limp
from toiling at passion's intense play,
her lotus-eyes painfully red
from the long night's long vigil,
—richly-flowing mane of hair waving
wildly over weary, drooping shoulders—
falls asleep,
warmed by a tender sun's gentle rays.

15

Other young women whose willowy frames
sway a little
bearing the burden of high, swelling breasts,
remove from foreheads framed by hair,
midnight-blue like dense rain clouds
the faded chaplets worn at night
—the exquisite fragrance quite lost,
once enjoyed—and dress their hair again.

16

Another, with curving eyes, and
dark hair flowing down in playful curves,
the charm of her lower lip restored, radiant,
looks down at her body enjoyed by her lover,
notes carefully the nail-marks
and then glowing with joy, puts on her bodice.

17

Toiling long hours at love's passionate sport,
other lovely young women o'ercome with fatigue,
have their slender, languid bodies massaged with oils:
—the chilly air makes their breasts and thighs tingle.

18

May this season of glittering frosts, delightful
by virtue of its many excellences
that enthralls the hearts of women;
when the village-bournes are brimful
of bountiful harvests of golden grain;
when the dew falls thick
and the air is sweet with the curlew's notes,
fully grant you all happiness.

Canto 5: Winter

1

Stacks of ripe rice and sugar-cane cover the earth:
the air rings with the hidden calls of curlews:
love grows exuberant: Dear to lovely women,
winter is now here; hear now, my love.

2

People close their windows tight, light fires,
keep warm in the sun and wear heavy garments:
men find the company of youthful women
pleasing at this time of the year.

3

Neither cream of sandalwood chilled by moonbeams
nor breezes cool with falling dew, nor terraces
of mansions bright with the autumnal moon,
delight the mind at this time of the year.

4

Cold, cold, with heavy dews falling thick,
and colder yet with the moonbeams' icy glitter,
lit with ethereal beauty by wan stars,
these nights give no comfort or joy to people.

5

Wives eager for love, their lotus-faces
fragrant with flower-wine, enter their bed-chambers
aromatic with the incense of black aloes,[29]
taking betel-rolls and garlands and hot perfumes.

6

Women whose husbands continue unfaithful
though bitterly chided again and again,

note them flustered, visibly shaken by guilt:
yet, yearning to be loved, they overlook these wrongs.

7

Enjoyed long through the long night in love-play
unceasing by their lusty young husbands
in an excess of passion, driving,
unrelenting, women just stepped into youth
move at the close of night slowly,
reeling, wrung-out, with aching thighs.

8

With breasts held tight by pretty bodices,
thighs alluringly veiled by richly-dyed silks,
and flowers nestling in their hair, women serve
as adornments for this wintry season.

9

Lovers enjoying the warmth of budding youth,
pressed hard against breasts glowing golden,
saffron-rubbed, of lively women gleaming sensuous,
sleep, having put to flight the cold.

10

Young women in gay abandon drink at night
with their fond husbands, the choicest wine,
most delicious, exhilarating,
heightening passion to its pitch:
the lilies floating in the wine
tremble deliciously under their fragrant breath.

11

At dawn, when the rush of passion is spent,
one young woman whose tips of breasts are tight
from her husband's embrace, carefully views
her body fully enjoyed by him
and laughing gaily, she goes from the bed-chamber
to the living-apartments of the house.

12

Another loving wife leaves her bed at dawn:
elegant and graceful, slender-waisted,
with deep navel and ample hips;
the splendid mane of hair with curling ends
flowing loose, the wreath of flowers slipping down.

13

With faces radiant as golden lotuses
and long, liquid eyes; with lustrous red lips
and hair playing enamoured round their shoulders,
women shine in their homes these frosty mornings,
bearing the semblance of the goddess of beauty.

14

Young women burdened by their ample loins,
and drooping a little at the waist,
wearied bearing their own breasts, move very slowly:
quickly casting off garments worn at night
for love's sweet rites,
they put on others suited to the day.

15

Staring at the curves of their breasts covered by nail marks,
touching gingerly the tender sprout of the lower lip
bruised by love-bites, young women rejoice to see
these coveted signs of love's fulfilment,
and decorate their faces as the sun rises.

16

This wintry season that abounds with sweet rice,
and sugar-cane,
and mounds of dark palm-sugar dainties:
when Love waxes proud
and love's sport is at fever-pitch;
when the anguish is intense of parted lovers:
May this season be to you ever auspicious.

Canto 6: Spring

1

Sprays of full-blown mango blossoms—his sharp arrows,
honey-bees in rows—the humming bowstring:
Warrior-Spring set to break the hearts
of Love's devotees, is now approaching, my love.

2

Trees put forth flowers, waters abound in lotuses,
women's thoughts turn to love; the air is sweetly scented:
mornings are pleasant and days delightful:
all things are more alluring in springtime, my love.

3

The waters of pools, gem-studded girdles,
the moon's brilliance, women proud of their beauty,
mango trees bowing low with blossoms: on each
Spring pours its profusion of grace and bounty.

4

Fine woven silks dyed scarlet with mallow juice
swathe round hips; delicate silks saffron-dyed,
shining pale gold, veil the perfect orbs of breasts:
women now dress with light-hearted elegance.

5

Fresh karṇikāras[30] nestle at their ears,
Aśoka blooms and fragrant full-blown jasmines
dapple trembling blue-black curls—they gain brilliance
when chosen to enhance the sensuous beauty of women.

6

Garlands of pearls moist with cream of liquid sandalwood
caress the breasts; armlets and bracelets clasp the arms,
and girdles with golden bells embrace the hips
of lovely, love-tormented women.

7

Lines of petal and leaf are delicately traced
on the golden-lotus faces of graceful women;
beautiful, like pearls set in between gems,
amid the traceries spread beads of sweat.

8

Women whose limbs unknot and become limp
under the nagging ache of love, take heart
reviving from the nearness of the husbands they love;
they are now filled solely with impatient longing.

9

The Bodiless One[31] makes women thin and pale
languid from desire, to stretch and yawn greatly
again and again; breathless and flustered
from the excitement of their own loveliness.

10

Without form, Love now shapes himself many ways:
in women's roving, wine-heavy eyes,
in their pale cheeks and in their hard breasts,
in their sunken middle, in their plump buttocks.

11

Love has now made the limbs of beautiful women
bewitching from languor, sleep-induced;
their speech somewhat slurred, drowsy from wine; their glances
awry from the arch play of arching eyebrows.

12

Young women languid with intense desire,
cream their fair breasts with sandalwood paste
blended well with turmeric and saffron,
musk and fragrant priyaṅgu seed.

13

Struck by spring fever, to cool their bodies,
people quickly put off heavy garments
and wear thin ones instead, dyed red with lac-juice,
and perfumed by the incense of black aloes.

14

Drunk on the honey of mango blossoms,
the koel rapturously kisses his mate:
the bee, too, humming among the lotuses,
whispers sweet flatteries to his sweet love.

15

The hearts of women throb with deep yearning
watching mango trees swaying in the breeze
with low-hanging sprigs of coppery-red shoots,
and branches showing off their blossoming loveliness.

16

Gazing on aśoka trees putting forth tender shoots
and covered down to the roots in a profusion of buds
coral-red and rich copper,
the hearts of maidens budding into youth
fill with ineffable sadness.[32]

17

Tender leaf-shoots on young atimukta[33] creepers
bend and wave in a gentle breeze, their lovely blossoms
ardently kissed by intoxicated honey bees:
intently watching, lovers experience sudden longing.

18

Glancing at the amaranth's blossoming sprays
glowing in exquisite loveliness, just-revealed,
—loveliness that rightly belongs to the beloved's face—
how can a sensitive heart not flutter in pain
stung by proud Love's flying arrows, my love?

19

All around kiṃśuka[34] groves blaze fiery red;
trees swaying in the breeze bend low flower-laden;
instantly transformed by Spring, the earth glows
like a radiant young bride in her red silk robe.

20

Lost already to beautiful girls,
are not young men's hearts pounded to bits
by kiṃśuka blossoms bright as parrots' beaks?
Are they not already burnt
by the golden campa's brilliant blooms?
And now, the cuckoo with its honey-sweet notes
sounds their death knell!

21

The liquid notes, indistinct, of koels enraptured,
the exulting hum of honey bees, intoxicated,
make the hearts of even decorous and bashful brides,
highbred, of noble houses, greatly perturbed.

22

Gently frolicking with the mango's flowering branches
carrying the koel's cooing, far, in all directions,
the balmy breeze, dew-free, blows most gracious,
captivating all our hearts now in springtime.

23

Enchanting pleasure gardens resplendent with jasmines
sparkling as the playful laughter of lovely women
can entice even a saint's heart serene and passion-free;
Can young hearts turbid with passion remain unmoved?

24

With belts of golden bells dangling at their waists,
strings of pearls clinging to their breasts,
slender women, soft and yielding from the flames of love,

accompanied by the sweet symphony
of bees and cuckoos in honied spring
ravish the hearts of men.

25

People thrill with joy gazing at hillsides
richly decorated with flowering trees;
rocky hilltops inlaid with lace of alpine flowers,
valleys overflowing with raptures of joyous koels.

26

Seeing the mango trees in full bloom, the traveller,
desolate, parted from his beloved wife,
closes his eyes, grieves, sheds tears,
covers his nose with one hand and cries aloud.

27

The hum of madly excited honey bees,
the cuckoo's sweet melodies, blossoming mango trees;
golden campa gaily festooned with flowers—
with these sharp arrows, the month of flowers, rakes
the proud hearts of noble women
and Love's flames kindle and blaze.

28

His choicest arrow—the lovely spray of mango flowers:
his bow—prettily-curved kiṃśuka blooms:
the bowstring—rows of honey bees:
the royal white umbrella, spotless—the moon:
his proud elephant—the balmy southern breeze:
cuckoos his bards:
May bodiless Love, world-conqueror, joined by Spring
grant you all happiness, evermore.

Kumārasaṃbhavam

Kumārasaṃbhavam

Canto 1

1

There in the north[1] is[2] The Monarch of Mountains,
Himālaya[3] named, of divinity indwelling;[4]
plunging into the great oceans, east and west
he stands, a rod taking the Earth's whole measure.

2

Choosing him as the calf[5] and Meru,[6]
skilled herdsmen as the milker, all the mountains
by Pṛthu[7] guided, milked the sustaining earth
of her brilliant gems and precious medicinal herbs.[8]

3

The snows barely rob him of his magnificence,
who is the inexhaustible source of priceless gems;
a single flaw is lost in a mass of merits,
like the moon's dark spot in his[9] myriad rays of light.

4

He bears on his peaks ores of rich colours
whose splendours cast on swirls of rain clouds seem
sunsets glowing outside their time enhancing
the seductive adornments of apsaras.[10]

5

Siddhās[11] having enjoyed on the lower peaks
the shade of clouds girdling his middle slopes
now resort harassed by outbursts of rain,
to his high peaks perpetually sunlit.[12]

6

There, kirātās[13] not seeing the paw marks washed clear
of blood by rivulets of melting snows
yet find trails of lions that have struck tuskers down,
by pearls[14] dropped from the interstices of their claws.

7

Letters pricked out on barks of birch trees,
with liquid mineral dyes, and red as the spots[15]
on full grown elephants, serve to convey
messages of love of lovely woodland nymphs.

8

That mountain fills the hollow bamboo-stems
with breezes he exhales through his cave-mouths
as if wishing to accompany with flutes,
note by note, the high, clear melodies of the fauns.

9

There, the mountain slopes are redolent
of the aromatic resins oozing
from the trunks of cedars bruised by elephants
rubbing their temples to ease their itching;

10

While herbs that glow luminous at night
light up the interiors of cave-dwellings
and serve as oil-less lamps for the love-play
of forest-dwellers and their loving women.

11

There, though their feet are frost-bitten walking
on the mountain's icy paths, lissom dryads
burdened by the weight of full hips and breasts
do not abandon their easy, languid gait.

12

The mountain protects the owl-like darkness
lurking in his caves afraid of the sun;
indeed, the lofty-souled unfailingly treat
suppliants, noble or base, as their own kin.

13

Bushy-tailed does flick their tails glowing like moonbeams,
to and fro, cutting arcs of beauty in the air;
by waving these royal chowries[16] over the mountain,
they make his title of 'Mountain-King' ring true.

14

Rainclouds hanging down by fortunate chance
over the round openings of cave dwellings,
serve as concealing screens for the sweethearts of fauns
overcome by shame as they are disrobed.

15

There, hunters on the mountain stalking deer enjoy
the breezes that repeatedly shake the cedars,
tousle peacocks' plumes and waft the fine spray
of Bhāgīrathī's[17] cascading waters.

16

And once the seven holy sages[18] have gathered
lotuses growing there in high mountain lakes,
the sun circling below awakens the buds
left behind, slanting his rays upwards.

17

The Creator gave him lordship over mountains,
and a share in the Sacrifice,[19] knowing him to be
the source[20] of sacrificial materials; and for having
the strength to support the supporting Earth.

18

Mindful of his duty to preserve the lineage,
He, Meru's kinsman, with due sacraments,
married Menā, mind-born daughter of the Fathers,[21]
his equal, honoured even by holy sages.

19

As they began engaging in the rites of love
appropriate to their beauty and powers, in due course
the bride of the Earth-Supporter, invested
with the fresh loveliness of radiant youth, conceived.

20

She gave birth to Maināka[22] who acquired a Nāga-bride[23]
and the Ocean's lasting friendship, so that he never knew
the pain of thunderbolts Vṛtra's[24] Foe hurled enraged
to sever the wings of the wandering mountains.[24b]

21

Then, Śiva's former consort, the faithful Satī,[25]
Dakṣa's[26] daughter, driven by her father's insults
to abandon her body through yogic power[27]
now resorted to the Mountain Queen to be born again.

22

The Lord of Mountains generated that Blessed One[28]
on Menā disciplined in the mind's holiness,
as indomitable energy[29] flawlessly directed
into consummate statecraft begets complete fruition.

23

The skies were clear in all directions
the day she was born; the winds were free of dust;
conches sounded in space; flowers showered from the sky;
all embodied beings rejoiced, sentient and insentient alike.

24

As the land round Vidura hills[30] is radiant with lustre
sprayed from the veins of gems laid open by the sound
of fresh thunder, so, the mother holding her daughter
shone brilliant within a circle of scintillating light.

25

Risen like the crescent moon's faint streak, as the waxing moon
adds digit after digit of radiance hidden within,
the daughter assumed day by day singular beauties
that possessed the tremulous lustre of pearls.[31]

26

The darling of her kin, she was lovingly honoured
with the patronymic, Pārvatī, Daughter of the Mountain;
only later did the lovely girl get the name Umā—*u-mā*!
Ah! Do not, her mother's words forbidding her, her hard penance.

27

Though blessed with many children,[32] the Mountain-King
was never sated by the sight of this child of his.
With the endless show of flowers in spring, circling bees
are specially drawn to the mango's buds.

28

As a lamp by an intensely brilliant flame,
as the highest part of the triple-world[33] by the Triple-pathed river[34]
as the wise through the use of perfected speech,
so he, through her, became more hallowed and glorious.

29

Entering into the very spirit of childhood
that is the passion for play, she amused herself
often in the midst of her friends with balls and dolls
and altars of sand she raised on Mandākinī's[35] banks.

30

As flights of geese to Gaṅgā's streams in autumn,
as intrinsic glowing to sovereign herbs at night,
so did learning gained in earlier lives and firmly retained,
appear on its own at the time of her instruction.

31

Past childhood, she came of age, when youth itself
is nature's adornment for the slender form,
intoxicating, though not by wine;
an arrow more potent than Love's flower-arrows.[36]

32

Like a painting taking shaping under the brush;
like a lotus unfolding under the touch of the sun;
her form moulded in exquisite symmetry
in its fresh fullness of youth, was enchanting.

33

As the glitter of her shapely nails poured out
a profusion of rich redness, it seemed her feet
invested the earth they trod on with the opulence
of glowing lotuses moving on land.[36b]

34

Was she whose shoulders bent slightly forwards[37]
instructed in her lilting gait so graceful
by regal swans[38] who in turn were eager to learn
the sweet tones of her chiming[39] anklets, perhaps?

35

Having formed her lovely thighs, rounded, even,
and just right,[40] the Creator must have made
a great effort gathering the exquisite graces
required to fashion the rest of her limbs.

36

The trunks of lordly elephants have too rough a skin;
plantain-stems are ever chill to the touch;
even though they have forms of full, flowing curves,
they are hardly fit comparisons[41] for her thighs.

37

The beauty of the region graced by the jewelled belt[42]
of this faultless lady may best be inferred knowing
that The Lord of The Mountain would in the end place it
on his lap, to which no other woman could aspire.

38

A fine line of new down stepping over the knot
of her garment to enter her deep navel[43]
seemed a ray of light flashing from the deep-blue gem
at the centre of her jewelled belt.

39

The young girl bore three delicate creases of skin
on her slender waist narrowed at the middle
like an altar; as if fresh youth had formed
a flight of steps for Love himself to climb.

40

She with eyes like deep-blue water lilies,
had full rounded breasts, pale gold, with dark tips, pressed
so closely against each other, not even
a fine lotus-fibre could pass between them.

41

More delicate even than the delicate
Śirīṣa[44] flower were her arms, I guess, since Love,
the dolphin-bannered god though destroyed by Śiva
yet made them the bonds round the neck of the lord.

42

Her throat arching tapered over her high breasts
and the necklace of pearls that encircled it,
borrowing from each other their several splendours
became both the adorned and the adornment.

43

Lakṣmī, fickle goddess of Beauty and Wealth enjoys not
the riches of the lotus when she visits the moon;
nor possess the moon's glory when she dwells in the lotus;
but by resorting to Umā's face, she gains a twofold delight.

44

Were a flower to be placed on a young leaf-bud,
or a pearl set in bright coral, only then
could it compare with the sparkling smile
that played round the burnished redness of her lips.

45

When she with the courteous speech of those nobly-born
conversed in tones of fine spun nectar, she shamed
even the koels that sounded harsh to the ear
like the strings of an ill-tuned lute.

46

Not unlike blue lotuses trembling in a fresh wind
were her tremulous glances; did that lady
of the long, liquid eyes borrow them from the pretty does,
or did the pretty does borrow their glances from her?

47

Seeing the glowing crescents of her eyebrows
deeply curving as if pencilled in glossy collyrium
and so expressive in movement, Bodiless Love[45]
lost all pride in the curving beauty of his own bow.

48

If animals were endowed with a sense of shame
it is certain the chamari-deer[46] viewing well
that gorgeous mane of hair of the mountain king's daughter
would have their fondness for their fine tails grow cold.

49

In his eagerness to see all beauty in a single form,
what efforts must the Maker of the Universe have expended,
assembling all things[47] that serve as similes
and fixing each in its proper place to form her!

50

Once, it is said, Nārada,[48] Wanderer-at-will
looking at the young girl by her father's side,
declared that she would become Śiva's sole bride,
and through love half His body appropriate.

51

Therefore, though she was in the pride of youth, the father
entertained no thought of another bridegroom for her.
For no luminous thing other than the holy fire
is worthy of oblations hallowed by prayer.

52

Yet The Mountain could not offer his daughter,
unasked, in marriage to the Lord of lords.
From fear of refusal of his suit, a virtuous man
takes no action even in matters close to his heart.

53

Since this lady with bright teeth gave up her body,
filled with wrath against Dakṣa[48a] in her former life,
The Lord of Beings gave up all attachments
and from that time on lived without a wife.

54

Mantled in the elephant hide,[49] with senses restrained,
He sat in tapas on a shoulder of the Snowy Range,
where Gaṅgā's current moistened the cedars and the odour
of musk and the music of kinnaras flowed all around.

55

With tassels of Nameru-flowers[50] at their ears,
wearing garments of birch-bark soft to the touch,
painted with pigments of mineral ores, the gaṇas[51]
sat on rocks laced with streaks of fragrant resin.

56

His humped bull[52] tore up with his hooves masses of solid ice,
and chafing at the sound of the roaring of lions
set up a deep thunderous bellowing
watched by great mountain bulls shaking with terror.

57

There the Lord known in eight Forms,[53] consecrating the Fire
—itself a form of Him—kindled with sacrificial wood,[54]
practised penance out of some inscrutable desire of His own
—Himself the Giver of the fruits of all penance.

58

The Mountain-Lord having adored Him who is adored
by the Dwellers in Light,[55] Him beyond all adoration,[56]
with an offering[57] worthy of a guest,[58] directed his daughter,
self-restrained, to serve Him with her two companions.

59

The Lord was pleased not to refuse her service
even though she came in the way of contemplation;
they only are firm-minded who remain
undistracted in the face of temptation.

60

She gathered flowers for His daily worship;
she cleared the altar with dedicated care;
she brought water for the prescribed rites
and the sacred kuśa grass;
She, of resplendent hair attended
day after day on the Mountain-dwelling Lord;
all her weariness was overcome
by the moonbeams streaming from His head.

Thus ends Canto one entitled *Umotpattiḥ* (*The Birth of Umā*), in the long poem *Kumārasaṃbhavam* composed by the illustrious Kālidāsa.

Canto 2

1

At that time the Dwellers in Light
harassed greatly by the great Tāraka[1]
went to the Abode of the Self-Existent[2]
with the mighty Indra[3] at their head.

2

Then, before them whose faces were wan
and lustreless, Brahmā appeared
like the brilliant star[4] at daybreak
over lakes where lotuses still slept.

3

Then bowing down to Him
Who is the Support of All,
Who faces all directions,
they hymned the Lord of the Word with words fit

4

'Lord, we adore You in Your Three Forms:
who before creation was in essence
Whole, Absolute: spinning Your Self out
into the Triple-Strand, You then became manifold.

5

Unborn One! the Holy Chants sing
this world of things that move and those that move not,
as the flower of that potent seed
You once into the waters[5] cast.

6

Proclaiming Your Greatness
through Three Aspects, though One and Absolute,
You have become the Cause
of worlds created, sustained, dissolved.

7

You split Your Self into two forms
male and female, desiring to create.
The seers declare these the Father and the Mother
of creation when it flows into being.

8

Separated into Day and Night
by Your own measure of Time,
Your waking and Your sleeping are the rise
and dissolution of all things.

9

Womb of the world, born of no womb:
the World's End, without end Yourself:
the World's beginning, without a beginning:
of the World the unruled Ruler.

10

By Your Self You know yourself:
of Your own Self You create Yourself:
by Your own power supernal
You dissolve wholly into Your Self.

11

Flowing, You are solid where atoms join:
gross, yet subtle: light yet heavy:
manifest, yet not manifest: Your Will
irresistible is bodied forth by miraculous powers.

12

Whose Primal Utterance is the sacred *Om*:
that is uttered using three tones:
whose rite is Sacrifice: whose fruit is Heaven:
You are the Origin of those Vedas.

13

They speak of You as Nature, unrolling
the play of human endeavour:
they also know You as Supreme Soul,
viewing Nature, aloof, unconcerned.

14

Father of the most ancient Fathers:
Light beyond all Forces of Light:
Higher than even the Highest:
Creator of Creating Forces.

15

You alone are Sacrifice and Sacrificer:
Eater, and what is eaten: Eternal,
Knower and known:
Contemplator and the goal of Contemplation.'

16

The Creator heard their praises
going straight to the heart, truthful:
Inclined graciously towards them
He replied to the Dwellers in Light.

17

The words of that Primal Seer
flowing fourfold
uttered by the four mouths
accomplished their desired aim.

18

'Welcome to you, long-armed warriors,
rich in heroic valour, who have held
by your own divine power your sovereignties
several, and are now gathered here together.

19

How is it that your faces
do not wear their onetime splendour
but appear like bright stars
obscured by heavy mists?

20

This thunderbolt held by Vṛtra's Slayer[6]
does not glitter with its rainbow hues:
with its flames quenched, its Glory
appears as if tarnished.

21

And why is this noose in Varuṇa's[7] hand
from whose just coils no enemy can recoil
hanging abject like a hooded snake
impotent, bound by a compelling spell?

22

Kubera's[8] arm, bare of the fearful mace
resembles a tree with a broken bough:
His looks bespeak the sorrow of defeat
that festers like a dart within his mind.

23

And Yama,[9] the lustre of authority
of his invincible sceptre dimmed,
idly traces marks on the ground with it
as if it were a mere firebrand's burned-out stub.

24

How have all these sons of Aditi[10]
cooled, lost their blaze of splendour
and become mere painted pictures
that any one can stare at with impunity?

25

As waters blocked by a dam back up
forming eddies, so these Storm Winds
recoiling bewildered, make it evident
their power has been broken.

26

Even the horns of the moons on the twisted topknots
of the Rudras[11] point downwards;
their menacing challenges are stilled:
their bent bows speak of some crushing defeat.

27

Have you all been hurled
by the strength of mightier foes
from the ancient pre-eminence you had gained,
as general rules are overthrown by exceptions?

28

Speak plainly then, my children:
assembling here, what do you ask of me?
Only the creation of the worlds rests with me:
to you is entrusted their protection.'

29

Then Indra, with his thousand eyes
brilliant as a host of lotuses
stirring in a gentle breeze, turning
towards the Preceptor,[12] urged him on.

30

He, the Lord of Speech, who with his two eyes
was Indra's Eye, more serviceable
than a thousand eyes, spoke, with folded hands,
thus, to the Creator on the lotus-throne.

31

'Mighty Effulgence! It is as You have spoken:
our great stations are seized by our foes:
But how can this not be known to You
Who within every form of being dwells?

32

Puffed up with pride from a boon acquired from You,
a great asura,[13] Tāraka named
has arisen like a blazing meteor,
calamitous to all the worlds.

33

Over his city, the Sun diffuses
only those rays that suffice
to awaken the lotuses
that fill his lovely long lakes.

34

The Moon waits on him continually
with its many changing forms
all together, save one, the crescent
set as a jewel on Śiva's matted hair.

35

Fearing to be punished for stealing the flowers,
the Wind refrains from roaming in his gardens.
When close to him, it blows gentle
as the breeze from a palmyra fan.

36

Foregoing their orderly procession,
the Seasons serve as his gardeners;
diligent, with no thought but to amass
a wealth of flowers year round for him.

37

The Lord of Rivers[14] can barely wait
for the rare gems deep within his waters
to grow into the perfection
of a fitting tribute for him.

38

And at night the great earth-serpents
wait on him, led by Vāsukī, their king;
the dazzling ray-plumes of the gems of their hoods
make them serve as his lamps everlasting.

39

Even Indra, eager to gain his goodwill,
makes himself agreeable, repeatedly sending
by the hands of messengers, gifts
of precious jewels offered by the wish-granting trees.

40

Though honoured thus he still afflicts
the three wide worlds: the wicked are controlled
only by returning wrong for wrong done;
never by showing any kindness.

41

The trees in the groves of Nandana,[15] whose
delicate blossoms are picked tenderly
by the wives of the Immortals,
now first know the pain of being cut and felled.

42

He is fanned while asleep by chowries
sprayed with the tears showered by celestial maidens
abducted by him, who raise breezes
light as their own sweet light breath.

43

Uprooting Meru's[16] peaks trodden only
by the hooves of the Sun's tawny coursers,
he has had fashioned miniature hills,
in his palaces for his pleasures.

44

In holy Mandākinī,[17] only the waters
darkened by the rut of the elephants that guard
the sky's quarters remain: his pleasure-lakes
are now the home of the golden lotus beds.[18]

45

The celestials no longer enjoy
the delight of exploring the worlds:
deserted are the paths of the aerial chariots
from fear of sudden assaults by him.

46

The oblations offered by the priests
in the sacrifices duly begun
are snatched away[19] by him, versed in magic,
even from the Fire's mouth; while we watch helpless.

47

He has borne away that gem of horses,
the noble Ucchaiśravas[20]
—the Glory incarnate of Indra
earned over the ages.

48

All the remedies we tried out
against this Oppressor are beaten back,
even as the most potent healing herbs are
in an extremity of sickness.

49

Viṣṇu's discus, on which hung our hopes
of victory, shot up a ray of fire
glancing off him; and then seemed
to hang as an ornament round his neck.

50

His elephants, having vanquished Airāvata,[21]
now practise butting in play
against the banks of swirling
dark blue diluvial clouds.[22]

51

Therefore, Supreme Lord, we desire
a leader be created for his end;
even as seekers of release from the world
desire right action to cut the Karmic bonds.[23]

52

Placing that Protector in the vanguard
of the celestial armies, Indra,
Breaker of Mountains, will free from the enemy
the Glory of Victory and bring her back.'

53

When he had ended his speech
the Self-Existent uttered words
far surpassing the blessedness
of the fall of rain after thunder.

54

'This wish of yours is sure to be fulfilled:
you need to be patient for a while:
But, I shall not Myself engage
in the act of creation for its fulfilment.

55

From here the son of Diti[24] obtained his glory:
he is not to be destroyed from here:
It is not proper to cut down a tree
reared by yourself, even if it turns out poisonous.

56

This alone he craved for, long ago:
and this I promised him: his penance
so great, its power could burn the worlds,
I calmed by granting of this boon.

57

Who can withstand that great warrior
when he is ready and girt for war,
except a portion of the spilled seed
of the Blue-Throated Lord[25] with bright tawny hair?

58

That Shining One, He alone is the Highest Light,
abiding steadfast beyond the Darkness.
The magnificence of His power lies
far beyond Viṣṇu's comprehension and mine.

59

As a magnet draws iron to itself,
so would Umā's beauty draw Śiva's mind,
now steadfast in unruffled meditation.
You should all strive to accomplish this.

60

Only two forms can carry
the energies of the Two:
Śiva's seed by her; and mine
by one of His Forms, The Waters.

61

That Self[26] of the Dark-Throated Lord,
leading your armies, will loosen the braids[27]
of celestial women held captive,
by a magnificent display of majesty and power.'

62

Having thus addressed the Wise Ones,[28]
The Source of The World[29] vanished from sight.
The Shining Ones returned to the World of Light
certain in their minds of what ought to be done.

63

Deciding then on Kāma[30] as the means
fittest in accomplishing their object,
Indra flew in thought towards him
with a speed doubled by his eagerness.

64

Then, the bow with its ends curved beautiful
as the eyebrows of graceful women,
slung over his neck bearing
the imprint of Rati's[31] bracelets;
and his arrows of mango buds placed
in the hands of his companion, Spring,
the God of the Flower-Bow,[32] with folded hands,
waited upon the God of a Hundred Sacrifices.[33]

Thus ends Canto two entitled *The Manifestation of Brahmā,* in the long poem *Kumārasaṃbhavam* composed by the illustrious Kālidāsa.

Canto 3

1

All at once the thousand eyes of The Munificent Lord[1]
turning away from the thirty three gods[2] alighted on Kāma.
Fickle is the regard masters have for servants as a rule,
directed by the use they have in mind for them.

2

Offering him a place beside his own high seat,
The Lord of Riches[3] said: 'Come, be seated'.
In courteous acceptance of his Lord's high favour,
Kāma bowed his head, and started to speak in private.

3

'You who know the true essence of all beings,[4]
command what you wish to have done in the worlds.[5]
I desire to have your command enhance further
the favour you have shown in remembering me.

4

Who, aspiring to your seat[6] has roused your ire
by his performance of penances formidable?
He shall be brought at once within the range
of this bow of mine, its arrow fixed and ready.

5

Who, fearful of the pain of rebirth seeks to walk
the road to liberation[7] against your express wishes?
Let him live long, fettered by the coy side glances shot
by the gracefully arching eyebrow of a lovely woman.

6

Which of your foes, even one taught the good life[8] by Uśanas,[9]
should I like a great river flooding its banks
harass in his reach for riches and righteousness,
employing my secret agent, passion? Tell me.

7

Which shapely lady having entered your inconstant heart
by her loveliness, remains chaste beyond your reach,
causing you pain; whom you yearn to have, of her own free will
twining her arms round your neck forsaking all shame?

8

Who, quick to anger, marking your ardour cooling
has spurned you though fallen at her feet, O, passionate lover?
I shall bend her frame into burning contrition
seeking solace on a bed of tender, young leaves.

9

Calm yourself, O, great hero! Let your thunderbolt rest.
With his arms drained of power by my arrows, let him,
whichever foe of the gods he is, quail
before even a woman's lower lip quivering in anger.

10

By your grace, and with Spring as my sole ally,
though I am armed only with flowers, I shall break
even Hara's[10] steadfastness, armed with the pināka.[11]
What are other bowmen to me?

11

The Crusher of Foes[12] now removed one foot off his broad thigh
and let it rest on the footstool now honoured by its touch.
He addressed Kāma who had proclaimed his own power
to accomplish the purpose contemplated.

12

All this is well within your power, my friend.
Two weapons I have; my thunderbolt and your honoured self,
The bolt is blunted by the might of ascetic powers,
but you go everywhere and succeed.

13

I know your power; therefore I entrust you,
my equal, with a momentous mission.
Marking his power to support the earth, Kṛṣṇa chose Śeṣa[13]
to support his own cosmic form.[14]

14

By proclaiming your arrow's power to reach The Bull-Emblemed
God,[15]
you have almost assented to the mission. Know then:
Those Who Share The Sacrifice,[16] faced by powerful foes
wish at this moment for this very service of you.

15

For these devas want a general born of Bhava's[17] seed
to lead them to victory. And He,
born of Brahma[18] in Brahma centred,
may be mastered by a single arrow of yours.

16

Strive to make the self-restrained lord[19] look with love
upon Himālaya's daughter sanctified by prayer.
She alone among women is the fitting ground
for His impregnating force: thus has the Self-Born declared.

17

The daughter of the king of Mountains
at her father's bidding attends upon the Eternal,[20]
engaged in penance on the mountain heights:
this have I heard from my informants, the apsaras.[21]

18

Pray go, accomplish the divine mission;
its goal hangs upon yet another goal
that now awaits you, its first cause, as seed
awaits water before it begins to sprout.

19

Fortunate are you that the arrow's flight against him
who holds the promise of victory for The Immortals
is yours alone. A deed so unique that none other can do
is the glory of men, though it remains unknown.

20

These suppliants are The Immortals;
the task concerns the three worlds;
and for your bow not too hurtful a task.
Ah! How enviable your powers!'

21

Spring, your constant comrade, O, Mind-Churner,
would doubtless go as your ally, unasked;
for who would dream of telling the wind:
"Pray go, fan the flames of the Sacrificial Fire".[22]

22

Saying: 'So be it', Kāma received his lord's command
on his head as if it were the remnants of flowers
offered to divinities, and prepared to leave.
Then, Indra passed along his limbs,[23] a hand
roughened by stroking his mount, Airāvata.[24]

23

With Spring, his friend, dear to him, and Rati[25]
his beloved, filled with misgivings, Kāma set out
for The Eternal's [26] Himālayan retreat, resolved
to fulfil his mission even at the cost of his body.

24

Hostile to the profound meditation of hermits[27]
self-controlled who observed silence, Spring unfolded
in that forest assuming his true form
that was the pride of him Who is the Spring of Desire.[28]

25

As the hot-rayed sun violating the fixed order
progressed to the quarter guarded by Kubera,[29]
the southern quarter[30] breathed out fragrant breezes
like the sighs of a loving wife for her absent lord.

26

At once the aśoka[31] put forth sprays of flowers
and tender leaves budding straight from the trunk,[32]
not waiting for the touch of a lovely woman's foot[33]
adorned with tinkling anklet bells to bloom.

27

The moment he finished forming the arrow
of mango flowers and feathered it with lovely, fresh leaves,
Spring inscribed[34] on it in the shape of bees
the letters forming the name of the mind-born god.[35]

28

The karṇikāra[36] though flaunting its gorgeous colour
makes the mind regretful that it lacks fragrance.
As a rule, the Creator is averse to bestowing
the entirety of excellence on any one thing.

29

Palāśa[37] buds not yet fully open,
an intense red and curved like the new moon
appeared at once, like nail marks[38] on the forest glades
tenderly uniting with their lover, Spring.

30

The Genius of springtime showed on her forehead
the prettily drawn beauty mark of tiny dots of lampblack
that were bees clinging to the tilaka flowers;[39]
and her lips that were the tender mango shoots[40]
glowed with the delicate tints of dawn's first light.

31

The deer, their sight blurred by pollen-dust
fallen from flower-sprays of priyāla trees,
ran upwind in wild excitement through forest glades
filled with murmurous sounds of dry leaves falling.

32

Having feasted on mango-sprouts, the male cuckoo
sang ever so sweetly with an impassioned[41] throat
that his song itself became Love's eloquent command
empowered to break the honour of noble ladies.

33

With the passing of frosts, the lips of woodland nymphs[42]
glowed undulled by protective salves;[43] their complexion
had a pale brilliance; rising sweat ran all over
the charming floral designs[44] painted on their cheeks and breasts.

34

Ascetics, dwellers in the forests of The World's Pillar[45]
marked Spring's untimely unfolding and strove mightily
to master the urges stirring within their hearts,
managing somehow to remain masters of themselves.

35

When Madana,[46] holding his flower-strung bow
arrived in those regions with Rati by his side,
all living beings paired, filled with love beyond measure
to display amorous passion through their actions.

36

The bee attending upon his beloved
sipped honey from the same flower-chalice as her;
and the black buck scratched the doe with his horn
as she closed her eyes in pleasure at his touch.

37

Overflowing with love, the cow-elephant offered her mate
a mouthful of water scented by lotus-pollen.
The bird nicknamed chariot-form[47] courted his wife
with the gift of a lotus-stalk he had half eaten.

38

Between songs, the faun[48] kissed his beloved's face,
on which beads of sweat gathering from exertion[49]
somewhat marred the florals painted on it; whose eyes
rolled a little with seductive charm flower-wine gave them.

39

With breasts of full-blossomed clusters of flowers,
with trembling lips of leaf-buds a tender red,
vines, brides of trees, closely clasped their bridegrooms
with bonds of pliant arms of twining stems.

40

Though He heard the apsaras singing at this hour,
Hara[50] remained absorbed in meditation.
Obstacles never arise strong enough to break
the concentration of those who are masters of themselves.

41

Resting his golden staff of office on his left forearm,
Nandī,[51] on guard at the entrance to the bower of vines,
then placed a fore-finger on his lips to warn
the gaṇas[52] to be on their best behaviour.

42

At his command the entire forest froze,
transfixed; a painted scene it was:
trees motionless, bees still, birds silent,
animals quiet, at ease, without roaming.

43

Avoiding Nandī's eye as a traveller would
the sight of Venus[53] at the start of a journey,
Kāma entered that glade where The Lord of Beings meditated,
screened on all sides by a tangle of Nameru branches.

44

Kāma, the destruction of whose body
was imminent, now saw[54] The Triple-Eyed Lord[55]
seated in meditation on a dais
of cedar wood[56] covered with a tiger skin.[57]

45

Erect[58] and motionless, sitting cross-legged,
a cloth wound about the loins, reaching to the knees,
shoulders bowed, the two hands lying on His lap,
palms facing up, seeming a full-blown lotus;

46

a mass of matted hair swept up, tied with a snake,
a double string of rudrākṣa[59] beads hanging from His ear,
a black buck skin knotted round Him, its sheen
enhanced by the dark-blue glow[60] of His neck;

47

His eyes fixed steadily on the tip of the nose,
their light-beams downward-pointing, the pupils still,
smouldering beneath unflickering fringes of thick lashes
under eyebrows that had lost interest in play;

48

like a raincloud containing a pent-up downpour,
like a lake unruffled by rising waves,
like a flame in a windless place unwavering
because the vital breaths within remained motionless;

49

with shoots of light[61] bursting forth out of the opening[62]
in the crown of His head, seeking a way out
through the empty sockets in the Brahmā-skull,[63]
and putting to shame the moon's glory
that streamed from His forehead[64] with a grace
more delicate than that of lotus fibres;

50

mooring the mind[65] mastered by intense contemplation
in the heart's core,[66] its course of action turned away
from the nine portals[67] of the body, He
whom the seers know as The Imperishable
appeared viewing His self within Himself.[68]

51

Observing The Triple-Eyed Lord[69] in this pose,
unapproachable even in thought,
Kāma[70] stood close by; and did not mark his bow and arrow
slipping from his hand whose grip was loosening from panic.

52

The Daughter of The Ruler of Unmoving Beings[71]
then appeared[72] followed by a pair of sylvan goddesses,
seeming by the beauty of her form, to revive
his dwindling courage, now near extinction;

53

wearing for jewels the flowers of spring:
Aśoka blossoms that put rubies in the shade,
Karṇikāra sprays that stole the sheen of gold,
Sindhūvara buds that replaced necklaces of pearls;

54

leaning a little forwards from the fulness of her breasts,
her garment the hue of the young, morning sun;[73]
like a budding vine sauntering, gently curving
with round, full-blossoming clusters of flowers;

55

holding in place time and time again the garland
strung of kesara flowers slipping off her hips,
it seemed Kāma had hung it there, a second string
to his bow, knowing that to be its proper place—

56

warding off continually with her play-lotus
the bee hovering around her lower lip
that resembled a ripe biṃba fruit, its thirst
roused by her fragrant breath while her glances
tremulous kept roving in alarm.

57

Viewing her, of faultless beauty in every limb
that put Rati's loveliness to shame,
the flower-arrowed god felt hopeful once more
of success in his mission involving
The Spear-Armed Lord[74] who had conquered His senses.

58

And Umā neared the entrance to Śiva's grove,
her future lord, just as He who had perceived
The Eternal Light[75] in the heart's core that was the sign
of The Highest Self, came out of His contemplation.

59

Gradually letting the vital breaths pent-up within
flow freely, The Lord slackened His compact yogic stance,
even as The Lord of Snakes[76] strained his utmost to bear
on the crests of his unfurled hoods, the earth under Him.

60

Nandī bowed to The Lord and then announced
The Daughter of The Mountains come to attend on Him;
and ushered her in given permission to enter
by his lord's mere flicker of an eyebrow.

61

Her two friends bowed low and scattered at the feet
of The Three-Eyed Lord,[77] a heap of flowers blended
with bits of tender leaves they had gathered with their own hands
after the passing of the season of dews.

62

Umā bowed so low to Him Whose banner Bore A Bull,[78]
that the tender, young leaf shoot at her ear slipped and fell;
and the fresh karṇikāra flowers glowing
in the blue-blackness of her hair slid down.

63

Bhava,[79] The Origin, simply uttered the truth,
greeting her with the words:
'Obtain a husband who will not love another':
for never in this world do utterances of the great
entertain a meaning contrary to what is said.

64

Sensing the moment opportune for his arrow,
Kāma like the moth inexorably seeking the flame,
stood taking aim at Hara[80] with Umā close by,
and plucking his bowstring again and again.

65

Gaurī,[81] her hand glowing a burnished[82] rose,
proffered the great ascetic, Lord of The Hills,
a string of prayer beads made from seeds of blue lotuses
blooming in the Mandākinī,[83] and dried by the sun's rays.

66

The instant The Triple-Eyed Lord out of affection
for His worshippers reached out to accept her gift,
the god of the flower-bow fixed on his bow
his unerring arrow named 'Fascination';[84]

67

and so, Hara, His firmness a trifle ruffled
like the sea at moonrise lightly rippling,
directed His glances to Umā's face,
its lower lip ripe as a biṃba fruit;

68

while she too, The Daughter of The Mountain,
betraying her emotion by her limbs thrilling
almost like the sudden blooming of kadaṃba buds,[85]
stood turning her face aside that appeared
with the eyes lowered even more charming.

69

Then, The Triple-Eyed Lord through the power of His will
once again reined in firmly His restive senses.
Wishing to discover the cause of the mental disquiet
He cast His eyes around in all directions.

70

The god born of the self[86] He saw, clenched fist
at the corner of the right eye,[87] shoulders hunched,
the left foot drawn back, tensed and curving inwards,[88]
the lovely bow bent in a circle ready to strike;

71

His anger swelling at the affront to His penances,
His face with knitted eyebrows too terrible to gaze upon;
and a blazing fire with leaping flames
sprang suddenly from His third eye.

72

'Control your anger, O, Lord! Control your anger':
even as these words of The Flashing Divinities[89]
sounded in the skies, that Fire born of Bhava's eye
had left of Madana[90] merely his ashes.

73

Her senses numb from sharp, overwhelming shock,
Rati swooned, which seemed more a favour done to her,
since she became unconscious, unaware
for a while of her husband's destruction.

74

As lightning's bolt shivers the Lord of The Forest,[91]
so, The Great Ascetic, Lord of Beings[92]
having swiftly crushed him, the impediment
to penance, vanished with His band of ghosts and imps,
wishing to avoid the presence of women.

75

And The Daughter of The Mountain realizing
how fruitless was her most noble[93] father's fondest wish,
and the lovely grace of her form as well;
being ashamed beyond all reason that it happened
in the presence of her companions, turned homewards
with utmost difficulty, desolated.

76

Instantly picking up in his arms
his daughter, her eyes like shut buds,
a maiden most to be pitied
terrified by Rudra's fury,[94]
The mountain strode along on his way back
his body lengthening out from great speed,
resembling the celestial elephant, Airāvata,
bearing a lotus clinging to his tusk.

Thus ends Canto three entitled *The Burning of Kāma,* in the long poem *Kumārasaṃbhavam* by the illustrious Kālidāsa.

Canto 4

1

Held fast, helpless, in the deep swoon's total grip,
Kāma's wife was now awakened by Fate
instructing[1] her how to endure the anguish
intolerable, of one newly-widowed.

2

Awakening from her world-dissolving[2] swoon,
Rati looked around intently for her beloved lord,
with wide open eyes, not knowing he was for ever lost
to the sight of those unsated eyes of hers.

3

'Ah! Lord of my life! Are you alive?' addressing him thus,
she rose, seeing on the ground before her,
a man's form that was merely the ashes
left behind by the fire of Hara's anger.

4

Once more fiercely ravaged by anguish
she bitterly grieved; with hair streaming wild,
she rolled on the ground, covering her breasts with dust,
as if compelling the earth to share her grief.

5

'Your body so passion-rousing by its splendour
that it served as the standard of comparison
for impassioned lovers, now lies reduced to such a state!
Yet I do not fall apart; hard-hearted indeed are women!

6

Where have you fled, in a moment shattering our love,
throwing me aside, whose very life hangs upon you,

as a flood of water bursting its bounds flees,
leaving the lotus behind?

7

Never have you done a thing to displease me;
never have I acted against your wishes.
Why for no reason then do you not grant me,
Rati, grieving for you, a sight of yourself?

8

Ah! Lord of Memories![3] Do you remember the times
I bound you with my jewelled belt, because
you addressed me by another's name?
And I struck you with the lotuses adorning my ears
so that their pollen falling into your eyes, made them smart?

9

And those words that you spoke: "You live in my heart",
only to please me; I now know you were lying then.
For if it were not an empty compliment,
how could you lie there bodiless, and Rati go unscathed?

10

I shall take the road that you are even now setting forth on,
a new traveller to the world beyond.
But this world is being cheated by Fate, is it not?
Because the happiness of beings with bodies, rests on you.

11

When on city streets mantled in night's thick blackness,
women in love walk terrified by the sound of thunder,
who else but you, sweet love, can guide them
safely to the homes of their lovers?[4]

12

Young women proud of their beauty would roll their reddened eyes;
and stumble over every word they speak.

But now that you are no more, this intoxication
that they display would be sheer mockery, would it not?

13

Knowing that your beauty has become the theme for a tale,
your dear friend, the moon, when he is no longer on the wane,
would grieve to let go of his thinness, because,
O, Bodiless One, his rising would be in vain.

14

Say, for whose arrows will they now be employed?
These fresh mango blossoms rising
from delicate russet and green stalks, their presence
revealed by the male koel's melodious calls?[5]

15

This row of bees that you have employed
many a time as a string for your bow,
seems now to be mourning along with me,
humming in plaintive murmurs over my great sorrow.

16

Taking your captivating form again,
the moment you rise, appoint the hen-koel
whose skill in sweet talk[6] is inborn,
in her office of messenger of pleasures.

17

Those close embraces accompanied by shivers of pleasure,
those ecstatic rites of love so many,
pleaded for with bowed head when we were alone—
remembering them, O, Lord of Memories, I find no peace.

18

These flowers of spring, O, Master of Love's Pleasures,
with which you yourself adorned my limbs,

are still here on my body; but your body
so beautiful is nowhere to be seen.

19

While the rites of adornment were not yet completed,
you were remembered by those unfeeling Immortals.
Come to me; finish colouring this other foot of mine,
the left one, with the lākṣa's bright redness.

20

So long as you are not lured by the practised wiles
of Women of Pleasure in the World of Light,
I shall be in your arms once again, my love,
    following the path of the moth.

21

Though I shall follow you, my beloved lord,
the censure will still cling to my name forever,
that bereft of Madana, Rati lived,
    if only for a moment.

22

In what way can I arrange the last adornments[7]
for you, who have vanished into the other world
in a way most uncommon, and beyond all reason,
losing life and limbs at one and the same instant?

23

I remember you full of smiles, conversing with Spring
and glancing out of the corner of an eye[8]
as you straightened an arrow,
while your bow lay resting on your lap.

24

Where, O, where is Spring, your companion close to your heart,
who fashioned your bow of flowers?

He too has not gone, has he, the way his bosom friend went,
sent by the fierce wrath of The Wielder of the Pināka?[9]

25

Struck to the heart by these woeful words of lament
as if with poisoned darts, Spring then appeared,
manifesting himself to Rati
desolated by sorrow, to console her.

26

Seeing him, she wept, overwhelmed by grief,
beating her bosom to make her breasts one mass of pain.
Sorrow pours forth as if the floodgates had opened,
only in the presence of your own kinsfolk.

27

She spoke to him in anguish: 'Vasanta,[10] look;
see what is left here of your bosom friend! Just this!
Fine particles of ash, like a dove's feathers
variegated; scattered by the wind!

28

Ah! Lord of Memories! Show yourself this instant;
for Spring waits yearning to see you.
The love of man, unstable towards a wife,
never wavers towards his friend; that is certain.

29

Was it not with him at your side that the writ
of your bow strung with lotus-fibres
and fitted with tender flowers for arrows
runs throughout this universe of gods and titans?

30

Gone is your friend, never to return;
like a lamp's flame put out by the wind;

and I its wick; see me, gloomed[11] by swirls
of calamity's smoke, insupportable.

31

By destroying Kāma and sparing me,
Fate has done only half the slaughter.
Will the vine not fall when its unfailing support,
the tree, lies shattered by an elephant?

32

Taking the next step now, do your friend the service needed;
give me who am helpless, unsupported,
to the fire that is the escape from this world,
and help me to reach my husband's side.

33

Moonlight departs with the moon;
lightning vanishes with rain clouds;
even things that lack consciousness show
that women go the way their husbands went.

34

Colouring my breasts solely with these ashes
of the beautiful body of my beloved,
I shall lay my body on the fire
as on a bed of tender young leaves.

35

Many a time have you come to our aid,
O, gracious friend, in arranging a couch of flowers;
now lose no time in preparing the funeral pyre
that I beg for now with folded hands.

36

Once I am offered to the fire, pray urge the south wind
to fan the flames briskly and make it blaze;

for you know only too well that the Lord of Memories
cannot bear to be without me even for a moment.

37

Having done that give the two of us
a single offering of water in the cup of your palm,
and that friend of yours shall drink with me
that water undivided in the world beyond.

38

And listen, O, Mādhava,[12] in the memorial rites
for the Lord of Memories, offer a spray
of fragrant mango blossom with trembling young leaves;
for your friend was fond of the mango's flowers.'

39

As Rati stood resolved to cast off her body,
a voice spoke from the skies, like the first shower of rain
taking pity on a glittering minnow
darting distressed in a pool drying away.

40

'Wife of The Flower-armed god! Not for long
will your husband remain beyond your reach.
Listen and know what act of his led to his burning
like a moth in the flame from Śiva's eye.

41

The Lord of Beings once felt his senses
stir with desire for his own daughter.[13]
Restraining those unnatural urges, he cursed
Kāma, who now enjoys the fruit of his own act.

42

When Hara looks with favour on Pārvatī for her penances,
and leads her round the sacred fire, then,

having gained his own happiness,
he shall restore his form to The Lord of Memories.

43

Entreated by Dharma,[14] the Creator then
uttered these words, thus setting a term to Kāma's curse.
Sages self-restrained and rain-bearing clouds
are sources of both lightning, and the life-giving rain.

44

Therefore preserve this body, O, gracious lady!
For the reunion with your beloved lord.
The river whose waters are drunk by the sun
is at summer's end filled once again with fresh flow of water.'

45

In this way, some incorporeal being relaxed
Rati's firm resolve to die. And the friend of The Flower-armed god,
implicitly trusting in that voice,
consoled Rati with words pleasing and well-chosen.

46

As the moon's crescent by day, pale as dust
from the loss of rays awaits the night,
so too, the bride of the God of Passion waited,
thin with grief, for the end of adversity.

Thus ends Canto four entitled *Rati's Lament,* in the long poem *Kumārasaṃbhavam* by the illustrious Kālidāsa.

Canto 5

1

Seeing Kāma burned to ashes before her very eyes
by the Trident-Armed Lord, and her hopes lying shattered
Pārvatī cursed within her heart her beauty;
for beauty's fruit is the gaining of the beloved.

2

She yearned to make her beauty yield its fruit
through penance performed in profound meditation.[1]
How else was she to win the love foretold,[2]
    and a consort such as He?

3

When she heard that her daughter, her whole being centred
on The Lord of the Mountain,[3] was bent on penance,
Menā pressed her to her bosom and with earnest words
strove to turn her away from a life of harsh ascetic vows.

4

'In our home are deities to fulfil your desires.
How harsh, my child, is penance! And this body of yours,
how delicate! The śirīṣa blossom
can bear the weight of a bee; not of a bird!'

5

Though she exhorted her daughter in this manner,
Menā was powerless to deter her from her firm resolve.
Who indeed can turn back water steadily headed downward?
Or a mind relentlessly pursuing what it desires above all?

6

This girl of steadfast mind once requested
through a close friend, her father who knew well her heart's desire,

to let her lead a life of austerities
in the forest, until they bore fruit.

7

Pleased with the sense of purpose so worthy of her,
her father most exalted gave his consent;
and Gaurī[4] resorted to a peak peopled by peacocks
that later, called by her name gained fame in the world.

8

That girl of inflexible resolve removed the necklace of pearls
whose swaying strings rubbed the cream of sandalwood off her breasts
and tied on a bark garment tawny as dawn, held at bay
by upthrusting breasts from touching her limbs.

9

Her face with matted hair[5] piled high in a topknot
was no less charming than it was, framed by well-dressed tresses.
The lotus close-embraced by spreading duckweed
is no less radiant than it is with rows of clinging bees.

10

The rough touch of the triple-stringed muñja waistband she wore
as a sign of her vows made the hairs on her limbs bristle.
Worn for the very first time now, it turned red
the tender region once graced by the jewelled belt.

11

Turned away from the lower lip drained of colour,
and from the ball[6] tinged by unguents applied to her breasts,
Umā made her hand, its fingers pricked plucking
sharp-bladed kuśa grass, the lover of akṣa beads.[7]

12

She who felt pain even from the touch of flowers falling from her hair
as she turned on her magnificent bed of white sandalwood,

now sat on the bare ground ritually sanctified
and slept with her head pillowed on a slender vine-like arm.

13

Observing strict vows, she left two things in trust
in two places to be reclaimed later:[8]
her movements of curving grace with slender vines
and those tremulous glances of hers with the does.

14

She nurtured the saplings herself, tireless,
pouring water from jars shaped like breasts;
even the young god[9] reared in a secret place
would not deprive these her first-born of a mother's love.

15

Coaxed by wild grain she held in her cupped hands,
gazelles grew to repose such implicit trust in her
that she would measure her eyes playfully
against theirs while her friends watched.

16

Eager to see her clad in bark after ritual baths,
reciting the sacred chants, offering oblations
into the Holy Fire, even sages came there.
Age does not count in those grown mature in spirit.

17

The penance grove itself became a hallowed place;
beasts mutually hostile in Nature forgot their enmities;
trees offered guests all the fruit they desired;
sacred fires were lit in newly-built huts of leaves.

18

When it occurred to her that the desired fruit
could not be had through penances already practised,

she strove to perform penance even more rigorous
with no thought of her body's tenderness.

19

The girl who grew weary even playing with a ball
immersed herself in the silence of ascetics.
Indeed, her body must have been made of golden lotuses,
delicate by nature yet holding strength at the core.

20

In summer's burning heat, the young girl, slim-waisted,
smiling brightly, sat in the middle of four blazing fires.
Having overcome the sun's eye-dazzling splendour,
she looked him straight in the eye.

21

Deeply burned by the rays of the sun,
her face, bronzed, wore the lustre of the lotus.
Only at the long corners of her eyes faint shadows
were creeping in by slow degrees.

22

Only with water dripping down on its own, unsought,
and with nectar-filled rays of the Lord of Stars,
would she break her ritual fast. Thus, her means of subsistence
were indeed no different from that of trees.

23

Relentlessly burned by two forms of blazing energy,
one that moved in space, the other fed by kindling on earth,
then sprinkled by the first fresh shower at summer's close,
both she and the earth exhaled steamy mists that rose upwards.

24

The first raindrops stood an instant on her eyelashes;
then striking the lower lip, broke, to fall on the heights of her breasts,

slid down the three delicate folds on her belly
and after a long time slowly reached her navel.

25

Silent witnesses to her harsh penances,
the nights watched with wide open eyes of lightning gleams,
as she lay on a stone slab, homeless, unsheltered
in the unceasing, wind-driven downpours of rain.

26

Single-minded, she passed the bitter nights of pauṣa,[10]
standing in water while winds blew the endless sleet around;
and she felt pity for a pair of cakravākas close by,
parted and calling out plaintively to each other.

27

With her lotus-fragrant face, its lower lip lovely
as a tremulous petal, she restored in the night
the beauty of a lotus to the waters that had lost
the glory of lotuses destroyed by frost.

28

Living only on leaves that had fallen on their own
is truly penance of severity stretched to the limit;
that too she spurned; hence those versed in ancient chronicles
spoke of the sweet-spoken girl as aparṇā: The Lady With No Leaves.

29

As her frame, tender as lotus filaments, wasted away
practising day and night such austerities and more,
she left totally in the shade the austerities
of ascetics with tough, hardened frames.

30

Now, a man with matted hair, clad in black buck skin,
carrying a palāśa staff, entered the penance grove.

Blazing with the splendour of Holy Power,[11] bold in speech,
He seemed the embodiment of disciplined, young manhood.

31

Quick to welcome guests, Pārvatī walked towards him,
honouring him with reverent ceremony.
Those with tranquil minds act with utmost respect
towards illustrious persons though they may be equals.

32

Having accepted the courtesies duly offered,
and rested for a moment merely for the sake of form,
the ascetic looked at Umā with steady eyes
and observing all due proprieties, began speaking:

33

Are wood and kuśa grass for the holy rites within easy reach?
And waters for ritual baths as well?
Do you practise penances well within your powers?
For the body is the prime means to do good works.

34

Those tender leaf-buds on shrubs you watered coaxing them
into burgeoning, are they still vibrant,
and vying with the colour of your lower lip
that has for long forgotten the rich redness of lip paint?

35

Do you indulge the fawns that out of affection
confidently take kuśa grass from your hands,
flaunting their tremulous glancing eyes that bear a resemblance
to your eyes, Lady With Lotus Petal Eyes?

36

Now listen, Daughter of The Mountain, the saying
that beauty leads not to vicious ways is not proven false;

for your conduct itself stands, Lady of Noble Mien,
a model for even ascetics to follow.

37

The Upholder of The Earth, with his entire race
has not been sanctified as much by Gaṅgā's celestial waters
falling flecked with her laughter of blossoms
offered by the Seven Sages, as by your unblemished acts.

38

Lady of Pure Thought, it flashes upon my mind,
seeing your conduct, that of the three aims of life,[12]
Righteousness is preeminent, since you have embraced
that and that alone, emptying your mind of Profit and Pleasure.

39

You ought not to regard me as a mere stranger
honoured by you with special hospitality,
My Lady of Curving Grace. The wise declare that seven words[13]
exchanged between the good form a friendly bond.

40

Prompted by the curiosity natural to the Twice-Born,
I therefore make bold to impose on your forbearance,
Lady Whose Wealth is Penance, wishing to ask you something;
and if it be no secret, pray answer my question.

41

Born of the lineage of the Primal Creator, Brahmā,
the beauty of the Triple-World risen in your form,
in the bloom of youth, not having to seek the happiness
that wealth and status confer, tell me, what other fruit can penance offer?

42

Granted that unendurable mishaps might drive
proud, sensitive women to such a course of action,

my mind driven on to deliberation's path,
Lissom Lady, fails to see this to be your case.

43

Your beauty cannot possibly be subject to sorrow;
nor can there be lack of honour in your parental home;
you face no stranger's dishonouring touch; for who dares stretch his hand
towards the rays of the cobra's crest-jewel,
O, Lady of Beautiful Eyebrows!

44

What makes you throw aside ornaments in your youth
to put on the bark garment that lends distinction to age?
Tell me, does the night that steps out at dusk
gemmed with moon and stars, long for the tawny dawn?

45

If it is for the World of Eternal Light[14] that you yearn,
vain is penance; your father's domain is itself divine ground.
If for a husband you seek, cease your penance right now.
A priceless gem is sought after; it does not go seeking.

46

Ah! A sigh, breathed out with such burning ardour!
It tells it all; yet, my mind is still plunged into doubt.
Is there a man you'd deign to woo? Hard to believe.
If so, how could a man you woo be hard to get?

47

Strange indeed! That young man you yearn for! How hard-hearted!
To see those strands of matted hair tawny as the tips of ripening rice,
dangling distraught on your cheeks bare for so long
of the lotus nestling at your ear! And still remain aloof!

48

Seeing you pale as the sliver of the crescent moon by day,
the parts of your body once graced by jewels now burned by the sun,
thin beyond measure from harsh ascetic vows,
what man of feeling would not feel his heart twisting with pain?

49

Of one thing I am certain; the man you love must be deluded
by pride in his own beauty, for long has he refrained
from making his face the target of the winsome glances
of these eyes with their curving lashes.

50

Ah! Gaurī! How long will you go on with these penances?
I too have accumulated power through penance
in this, the first stage of my life. Take half of it
to obtain the husband you desire. I wish to know him well.

51

Thus addressed by the brāhmaṇa who had divined her inmost thought,
Pārvatī could not speak of her heart's desire.
But her eyes bare of lustrous collyrium turned
to look at her companion standing beside her.

52

Her companion then spoke to the worthy celibate:
'Listen carefully, if you are curious to know
why my friend here makes her body a vehicle for penance
like someone using a lotus as a parasol.

53

Disdaining great Indra and all the others,
the resplendent lords of the four quarters, this proud lady,
knowing her worth, wants as husband the pināka-Armed Lord,
Who by vanquishing Love, proved that Beauty could not win Him.

54

Formerly, the sharp arrow of Love, the Flower-Armed god,
missing Śiva, the Triple-City's Foe,[15] its target;
and hurled back by the unendurable, mystic sound, hoom,
plunged deep into her heart, even though Love's Form had been shattered.

55

From then on, the young girl racked by love, the fringe of curls
discoloured by the cooling sandalwood balm on her forehead,
failed to find relief even while resting on heaped snows
spread on the floors of her father's mansion.

56

While singing in the woodlands with kinnara princesses,
her companions, many a time would she make them weep
to hear her voice choked with tears, the words stumbling out,
whenever songs celebrating pināki's deeds were sung.

57

When her eyes closed at last in sleep for a moment
in the third watch of the night, all on a sudden she would wake up,
crying out to the empty air: "Ah! Blue-Throated Lord![16]
Where are you going!" And wind her arms round an imagined neck.

58

And in secret, this artless girl would upbraid the picture
she had drawn with her own hands of the Moon-Crested Lord,
saying: "Seers speak of You as All-Pervading.
How then can you not know of this poor girl's love for you?"

59

When she had searched hard for some other way of winning
for her husband the Lord of the Universe, and found none,
with her father's consent and us in attendance,
she came to this penance grove to undertake penance.

60

These trees, witness to her penance, planted
by our dear friend herself are seen bearing fruit;
yet, her hopes, grounded in the Moon-Crested Lord,
show no sign of even sprouting.

61

I wonder when, He, so ardently desired, so hard to get,
will look graciously upon our friend whom we her friends
watch with tears wasting away in penance, as the god of rains looks
on the furrowed field blighted from the withholding of his favour.'

62

As Umā's true feelings were thus revealed by the friend
who knew her inmost thoughts, that handsome stranger
bound to celibacy till death, simply asked her:
'My lady, is this in earnest, or in jest?', showing no emotion.

63

Then, the Daughter of the Mountain, holding a string of crystal beads,
her fingers curling round it in the shape of a bud,
with the greatest of efforts spoke the words
she had been turning over in her mind for some time.

64

'Best of men learned in the Vedas! What you have just heard, that is so.
This humble person is eager to leap to that highest of places;
this penance the means to attain it; perhaps mistakenly so.
Nothing is beyond the reach of wishes.'

65

The young celibate responded thus: 'Ah! That Great Lord!
Do I not know him well? And yet, you keep striving to have him.
Considering the delight he takes in all things inauspicious,
I cannot find it in me to approve this pursuit of yours.

66

Lady so keen on the pursuit of so worthless an object!
When Śiva first takes this hand of yours, the auspicious thread
of marriage twined round your wrist, how can it bear to be grasped
by his hand encircled by a winding-snake-bracelet?

67

Now you just consider carefully for yourself
whether these two things can ever go together—
bridal silks with a lovely woven design of wild geese,
and an elephant hide moist, dripping with blood.[16b]

68

Who indeed, even an enemy, would consider it right
that your feet used to walking on flower-strewn floors
in pillared halls, should leave their red lac-stained prints
on burning grounds strewn with human hair?

69

What could be more incongruous, tell me, than the sight
of ashes of funeral pyres that cover the chest
of the Three-Eyed Lord finding a foothold with such ease
on these twin breasts of yours creamed with pale-gold sandalwood paste?

70

And yet another cause for mortification awaits you
when you who are accustomed to riding a stately elephant,
are seen sitting astride after your wedding on an ancient bull,
watched by a host of noblemen with mocking smiles.

71

The longing for union with the Trident-Armed Lord has brought
two objects into derision, deserving of pity:
the glowing digit of the many-faceted moon, and you,
the eye-delighting autumnal moonlight of the world.

72

Form deformed by oddly-placed eyes; parentage unknown;
the extent of riches displayed by his wearing space:
of all the virtues looked for in a bridegroom, Fawn-Eyed lady,
is a single one to be seen in the Three-Eyed Lord?

73

So pray turn your mind away from such a perverse liking.
What a distance between one of his kind, and you blessed with
auspicious marks!
The godly do not honour the stake in the burning grounds
with Vedic rites offered to the sacrificial post.'

74

While the brāhmaṇa was giving vent to his adverse comments,
Umā looked askance at him out of the red corners of her eyes,
her tendril-like eyebrows now twisting into a frown,
her quivering lower lip clearly displaying her anger.

75

And she said to him: 'From the way you speak to me of Śiva,
it is quite plain that you do not know Him as He truly is.
The mediocre cavil at the way of life of the great
because it is not common in the world, nor understood.

76

Things auspicious are sought after to gain wealth and power,
or to avert calamities. What desires has He
who is the World's Refuge? What need has the Holy One
for such desires that strike at the inner life?

77

Possessing nothing, He is the source of all possessions.
Lord of the Three Worlds, He resorts to the world of the dead.
Awesome is His form, yet He is declared The Beneficent.
None knows the Wielder of the pināka as He truly is.

78

Whether it glows with jewels, or has hooded snakes coiled round it,
whether it is clad in silks, or wrapped in an elephant hide,
whether it has the moon, or a skull, for a crest jewel,
His Form, that is the World's Form, is beyond all imaginings.

79

There can be no doubt that the ashes[17] of funeral pyres
are sanctified by the touch of His body. Therefore,
ashes falling from His limbs during the expressive movements
of His dancing, mark the foreheads of Dwellers in the Empyrean.

80

At His feet who lacks riches and rides a bull, Indra
whose mount is the stately elephant of the East in musth,
bows his diademed head low tinging the Lord's toes red
with the pollen of full-blown mandāra blossoms.

81

You degenerate man! Raring to speak ill of the Lord!
You have said one thing right about Him.
How can the origins be known of Him the seers declare
the Cause of Brahmā, the Self-Born Creator Himself?

82

Enough of this contest of words. Let Him be
what you have heard Him to be, entirely that, and nothing else.
But my heart, filled with love is centred in Him.
She who has made up her mind pays no heed to slander.

83

Dear friend! Pray stop this prating boy from speaking further.
The way his lower lip quivers, it seems he wants to say more.
Not only speaking ill of the great but listening to it
makes a person guilty of wrongdoing.

84

Or better still; let me leave.' With these words the young girl
started to walk away, her bark garment slipping off her breasts.
And the Lord whose banner was blazoned with the emblem of the
Lord of Bulls
assumed His own form, and smiling, swept her into His arms.

85

Trembling, she looked at Him,
her sylphlike figure moist with sweat,
the raised foot poised in air
about to step forward;
The Daughter of the Mountain King
like a river wavering
when she meets a hill blocking her course,
neither moved, nor stayed.

86

'My lady of curving grace,
Won by your penances, from this moment,
I am your slave.'
As the Moon-Crested Lord spoke these words,
Umā instantly felt the weariness
of her penances flowing away.
The weariness of great efforts
refreshes by yielding fruit.

Thus ends Canto five entitled *Tapahphalodayaḥ (The Fruit of Penance)*, in the long poem *Kumārasaṃbhavam* by the illustrious Kālidāsa.

Canto 6

1

Then Gaurī secretly instructed her friend to say
to The Universal Spirit Incarnate:
'The Lord of the Mountains will give me in marriage;
    let his authority be duly recognized.'

2

As her friend conveyed the message,
Pārvatī remained secure in love, lit within,
like a branch of a mango given voice
by the cuckoo awaits the coming of Spring.

3

Acquiescing with these words: 'so be it',
and reluctantly relinquishing Umā,
The Chastiser of Remembrance summoned
the Seven Luminous Sages by remembering[1] them.

4

Possessing the wealth that is penance,
illumining the skies with the brilliance of their aureoles,
with Arundhatī[2] accompanying them,
the sages appeared at once before the Lord:

5

having bathed in Gaṅgā's celestial waves
strewn with blossoms of mandāra[3] trees on her banks,
where the waters are scented by the rut
of the elephants guarding the directions of space;

6

wearing their sacred threads of pearls,
their garments of golden bark;
holding their prayer beads of gems;

and looking as if the Trees of Paradise[4]
had taken to the wandering ascetic's life;

7

and being looked up to by the Sun himself
of a thousand rays, bowing low in respect,
holding his horses below their sphere of light
while dipping his banner in their honour.

8

They who had rested on the Great Boar's[5] tusk,
together with Earth clinging to it with her vine-like arms
as they were lifted out of the Deep
at the Cataclysmic Dissolution of the Universe,

9

these sages were extolled as Primal Creators
by those who knew how it was in the Beginning,
because they carried forward after Brahmā
the process of primary creation that remained undone;

10

and though they enjoyed the fruits of penances done
in earlier lives of ineffable purity, lives
that had now attained perfection, yet remained
still true to the ascetic way of life.

11

In their midst, Arundhatī, the faithful wife,
her eyes fixed on the feet of her husband,
shone with splendour as if embodying
to perfection the success of their penances.

12

The lord looked on her and on the sages
with equal reverence. The virtuous honour

right conduct alone; and view distinctions
of woman and man with indifference.

13

When Śiva looked at Arundhatī,
His wish to have a wife grew stronger.
A virtuous wife is the prime condition
for a life of rites and ceremonies.

14

Even as the call of the righteous life
made Śiva take a step towards Pārvatī,
Kāma's heart still fearful from his wrongdoing
in the past breathed again to beat with hope.

15

Then the sages who had a profound knowledge
of the Veda in its entirety;
now worshipped as one, the Parent of the World;
and thrilling with joy, they spoke these words.

16

'All that profound study of the Vedas;
all the oblations offered with due rites;
all the penances undertaken and done;
all of this bears its ripe fruit for us this day.

17

Since You, who oversees this universe,
has raised and set us up in Your mind's space
—a space beyond the ken and farthest reach
of the rushing chariots of our minds[6]—

18

And as he in whose mind you dwell is most blessed,
blest above all others blessed, how much more blest

is he who is in Your mind, Lord,
You who are the source of Holy Creative Power[7]?

19

It is true we preside over a world
higher than that of the sun and of the moon;[8]
but by remembering us this day
Your grace has raised us far higher than them.

20

Honoured by You in this manner,
most highly do we esteem ourselves.
The respect of the noblest and best validates
as a rule, one's faith in one's own virtues.

21

But, Lord with many splendours for eyes,[9]
where is the need to make known to you
our happiness at being remembered by You
who dwells deep within all beings?

22

We see Your Form before our eyes;
but what You truly are, we do not know.
Be gracious to us, Lord; make Yourself known to us.
You are not within the range of understanding.

23

Which of your Forms is this before us now?
That which makes this universe emerge manifest?
Or, that by which You maintain it?
Or again, that which draws All within itself?

24

But, Effulgent One, let it stand, this question,
soaring, reaching for the inscrutable truth.

Called to mind, here we stand, in Your presence.
Command us. Tell us what we are to do.'

25

With the brilliant gleam of His teeth
enhancing the delicate glow
of the moon set on His topknot,
the Supreme Lord then addressed the sages.

26

'None of my activities are done
to serve myself. You know that well.
That this is how I am, is clearly shown,
is it not, by the Eight Forms[10] I assume?

27

As lightning-charged clouds are looked up to
by cātakas[11] suffering from thirst, so I,
being what I am, am entreated
by the gods harassed by foes, to beget a son.

28

Therefore I desire to have Pārvatī
to engender myself in her
as the sacrificer the sacred wood
in order to generate the Holy Fire.

29

I request you on my behalf
to ask Himālaya for her hand.
Alliances arranged by the godly
will never suffer reversals.

30

Know this too, that I am not unmindful
of the great honour of kinship with him,

so lofty and noble, so upright and firm,
who bears the entire weight of the earth.

31

You do not require to be instructed as to how
he ought to be asked for his daughter's hand.
The wise teach right conduct based on precepts
laid down by Your Honours themselves.

32

And Arundhatī most revered would I hope
play her part in the arrangements.
Matrons as a rule possess the knowledge
and experience required in such matters.

33

So, set out for Oṣadhiprastha,
capital city of Himālaya;
and success be yours. We shall meet again
at this place near the Mahākośī Falls.'

34

When He, foremost of yogis, was moved
by the urge to marry, the sages sprung
from the Creator, no longer felt
any shame for having taken wives.

35

Then, the group of seven sages, saying;
'Very well', set out on their mission.
And the Glorious Lord, Śiva, also left
for the appointed meeting place.

36

Those highest of sages then leapt up
into the sky dark blue as a sword,

and with the swiftness of thought arrived
at the city of Oṣadhiprastha:

37

the city that seemed to be Alakā itself,
treasury of riches, transplanted,
and peopled by an overflow pouring into it
out of the World of Eternal Light;

38

captivating even in its defences,
possessing walls built of enormous gemstones
and ramparts lit by luminous herbs,
encircled by the moat of Gaṅgā's streams;

39

where elephants had no fear of lions
and horses were of celestial breed;
whose townsmen were yakṣas and kinnaras,
and its women sylvan goddesses;

40

where the sound of drums could be told apart
from the echoing thunder of clouds clinging
to lofty mansions only by the measured beat
of hands and feet accompanying it;

41

where the glory of silken banners fluttering
at the gates of mansions was created
without the efforts of the townsfolk
by wish-granting trees with their tremulous foliage;[12]

42

where at night the reflections of stars
on flights of steps in mansions of crystal

took on the beauty of flowers or pearls
scattered with a lavish hand;

43

where women going to meet their lovers
even on nights when skies are overcast,
see their way by the light of glowing herbs,
barely noticing the blinding darkness;

44

where youth is the last stage of life and Kāma
the Flower-Armed god the sole cause of pain,
and sleep when exhausted by lovemaking,
the only loss of consciousness;

45

where lovers gladly welcomed the displeasure
of women who knit their eyebrows making
threatening gestures with graceful fingers
while their lips trembled in jealous anger;

46

whose outer groves were the fragrant forests
of the Gandhamādana Mountains,
where vidyādharas on the road sleep in the shade
of the paradisal tree, santānaka.

47

When they saw Himālaya's city,
the divine sages believed themselves deluded
in having performed acts of virtue
to gain the World of Eternal Light.

48

While the guards at the gates watched, looking up,
the sages flew down to The Mountain's palace

with such speed that their masses of matted tawny hair
stood out motionless like painted flames.

49

As the sages alighted in a line
descending in due order of age
from the sky, they shone like so many suns
reflected in water in a row.

50

The Mountain rose up at a distance
carrying his offerings to honour
the sages most worshipful, bending the earth
under his steps informed with immense power.

51

Lofty, with the great cedars of his arms
and lips of copper-coloured minerals,
his chest of rocks by nature formed,
unmistakably Himālaya he was.

52

Having received them with due courtesies,
he led the way escorting in,
those sages of pure actions,
into the exclusive Inner Palace.[13]

53

Seating himself, the Lord of Mountains
joined his palms in respect and addressed
those exalted sages seated
already on seats made of cane.

54

'Like showers without a trace of cloud,
like fruit without any flowers,

appears to me this seeing of you
so unexpectedly obtained.

55

Through your gracious favour, I now feel
like one who was ignorant turned wise;
like one made of iron become golden;
like one transported from Earth to the World of Eternal Light.

56

From this day on, all living beings
shall resort to me to be purified.
The spot visited by those worthy of reverence
is indeed named a place of pilgrimage.

57

O, Best of Twice-Born Ones![14] I know myself
to have become hallowed by two things:
the waters of Gaṅgā falling on my head,
and the water that has washed your feet.

58

I feel both forms of my two-fold frame touched
by your grace, each in a different way;
that which moves, ready to serve you,
that which is unmoving bearing the marks of your feet.

59

Though they might extend to the ends of space,
yet, my limbs are unable to contain
the growing joy spreading through them, risen
from the grace your revered selves have shown me.

60

Not only is the darkness within my caves
dispelled by the seeing of you blazing with light,
but that darkness lying deep inside me,
deeper than the dark passions[15] is dissolved as well.

61

I do not see what it is that you would need;
and if there is, how can you not obtain it?
Hence, I think your revered selves have set out
to come here solely to make me hallowed.

62

Be that as it may, be gracious enough
to command me to do what you will.
In the matter of serving their masters,
servants regard a command as a favour.

63

Here we are; we ourselves, our wife; and this,
our daughter, the life of the family.
Tell us; which one of us would be of service to you?
All else, our material treasures have no worth.'

64

Thus spoke Himālaya: and it seemed
that he was saying it all a second time
as his words echoed coming rolling
out of the mouths of his caves.

65

Then the sages urged Aṅgirasa,[16]
the best among them who could articulate
beautifully what needed saying, to speak.
And he addressed the Earth's Support.

66

'All that you have just spoken
is more than becoming in you.
The sublime loftiness of your mind
equals that of your towering peaks.

67

They speak true who say of you that you are
The All-Pervading Power[17] in immovable form.
The core of your beings is the support
for all moving things, and for those rooted.

68

How could the World-Snake[18] bear the Earth
on his hoods tender as lotus filaments,
unless you gave him the support needed,
even from the very bottom of the Deep?

69

In an unbroken, unsullied flow
that the Ocean's waves cannot hold back,
the streams of your glories and of your rivers
purify the worlds with their holiness.

70

As Gaṅgā is celebrated for her birth
at the foot of the Supreme Being,[19] so too
is she similarly celebrated
for her second birth on your head lifted high.

71

The vastness of Hari sweeping through the worlds
filling all space, upwards, downwards, cross-wise
prevailed once, when he was bent on taking three strides;[20]
but in you, vastness is of the very essence.

72

With your place assured among The Immortals,
the Sharers of the Sacrifice,
you have rendered insignificant
Meru's lofty peak formed all of gold.

73

Placing all the unbending hardness
in yourself, in your immovable form,
your moving form now bends low
in adoration of the virtuous.

74

Hear now the purpose of our coming,
a purpose that touches you most.
By proffering advice in your own best interests,
we too are sharers of your good fortune.

75

He who possesses the Eight Perfections,[21]
He who wears the half-moon, He who is known
as the Highest Lord, a title so high
to which no one else can lay a claim;

76

He who drives this universe entire by means
of His Eight Forms such as Earth and the others,
working in harmony with their linked powers
like horses drawing a chariot on its course;

77

He whom yogis seek after, the Indwelling Self
resting deep within the inner space;[22]
whose abode the seers declare as the place
with no fear of the cycle of births and re-births;

78

He, Śiva, the Source of Peace Himself,
witness to all actions done in the world;
He, The Granter of Boons, craves the boon[23]
of your daughter's hand through the words we speak.

79

Like yoking its meaning to a word,
it is most fitting that you marry your daughter to Him.
What cause can a parent have for regret
once he gives a girl to a virtuous husband?

80

May all these forms of being, those that move
and those that stay rooted in one place,
look upon your daughter as their mother.
The Lord is the Father of the Universe.

81

And may all the gods after bowing low
to the Blue-Necked Lord, then make her feet glow
with the lustrous rays shooting forth
from the gems on their diadems.

82

Umā, the bride; You, the Giver of the Bride;
Śiva, the bridegroom; we here, asking for her hand
on the groom's behalf: what a perfect equation
to frame the exaltation of your race!

83

Worshipping none but worshipped by all;
lauded in songs by all and lauding none;
to Him, Parent of the Universe, be the parent
joined in kinship through your daughter.'

84

While the divine sage was speaking these words,
Pārvatī, at her father's side with her head
lowered to the ground, counted the petals
of the toy-lotus[24] she held in her hand.

85

Although his wish had gained its perfect fulfilment,
The Mountain looked towards Menā, his wife.
As a rule, the wife is the eyes to the husband
in the matter of a daughter's marriage.

86

And Menā approved of it all happening
as her husband had so dearly wished for.
Wives who are devoted to their husbands never
act contrary to their husband's wishes.

87

When the sage had finished, Himālaya
having deliberated how best to reply, thought:
'This is the fitting reply' He drew his daughter
adorned in auspicious fashion to him and said:

88

'Come, my darling, you have been chosen as alms[25]
by Śiva, the World's Self; the Seven Sages
ask for your hand; I have gained the fruit
of marriage which is the householder's Sacrifice.'

89

With these words to his daughter,
the Earth-Supporter next addressed the sages:
'Here, the bride of the Three-Eyed Lord
bows down to you, reverend sirs.'

90

Commending the eloquent words of The Mountain,
words that had made their wishes come true,
the sages glorified Aṃbikā[26]
with their benediction that was soon to bear fruit.

91

As Umā's golden earrings were slipping down
in her eagerness to make a deep bow,
Arundhatī folded the young girl
overcome by shyness, in her arms;

92

and then she allayed the mother's grief whose face
was wet with tears as she ached with love
for her daughter, by rehearsing the virtues
of the bridegroom who had no other wife.

93

Asked by Śiva's new kinsman to set
the wedding date that very moment,
the bark-clad sages settled
on three days from then; and they departed.

94

After taking leave of Himālaya,
the sages came once again to the Spear-Armed Lord
to inform Him of the success of their mission;
given leave to depart, they flew up into the sky.

95

Even the Lord of Beings, eager to unite in love
with the Mountain's daughter, found it hard to pass those days.
When such emotions touch even The Omnipresent
how can others enthralled by the senses, stay unruffled?

Thus ends Canto six entitled *Umā's Betrothal (Umāpradānaḥ),* in the long poem *Kumārasaṃbhavam* by the illustrious Kālidāsa.

Canto 7

1

On the auspicious day when the moon, Lord of Plants,
waxing, moved into the seventh house,[1] Himālaya
with his kinsmen gathered round him, performed the initial rites
in the ceremony of marriage of his daughter.

2

As groups of matrons of the city, out of affection
became engrossed in getting ready in every house,
auspicious articles for the marriage rites, the city
and the palace of the Mountain appeared to become
    a single home and family.

3

Flowers of Santānaka[2] strewn on the Royal Highway,
rows of flags of the silks of China flying high,
golden arches blazing with dazzling splendour, the city
gleamed like the world of Eternal Light transplanted on earth.

4

Though the children they had were many, Umā alone
who was soon to be given away in marriage
became to her parents their very life's breath,
as if seen after long parting, or returned raised from the dead.

5

She moved from one embrace to another, as a benediction
was pronounced in turn, and jewel after jewel was gifted.
The affections of the Mountain's family though distributed
among the kin now went forth to her as to a single home.

6

At the hour sacred to the sun,[3] when the hare-marked moon entered
the twelfth mansion to unite with uttarāphālguni,[4]

those of her kinswomen who had husbands living and sons,
commenced the ritual of anointing her body.

7

She made more beautiful the musk-scented cloth that she wore
for the ritual of anointing with oil, its beauty
enhanced further by green dūrva shoots and white mustard seed
ornamenting it, and the arrow[5] she held in her hand.

8

The touch of the new ceremonial arrow, consecrated,
made the young girl glow like the new moon's pale crescent
brightening at the close of the dark fortnight
when the radiant ray-finger of the sun enkindles it.[6]

9

Dusted with lodhra powder to remove the oil from her skin
tinged gold by the partly dry paste of sandalwood,
the women wrapped around her a cloth right for being bathed,
and led Umā to a four-pillared sunken bath.

10

Its floor paved with slabs of lapis lazuli
was inlaid in intricate patterns of pearls.
There they bathed Umā, pouring water from jars of gold,
while pipes sounded auspicious music.

11

Bright, flawlessly pure after her ritual bath,
and dressed in fresh wedding garments, she shone
like the rich earth gleaming rain-sprinkled
and mantled in full-blown kāśa blossoms.

12

Chaste women winding their arms round Umā
then led her to a seat under a canopy
raised on four jewelled pillars, at the midpoint of which
was the altar where the Sacred Fire was kindled.

13

Seating that slender girl facing east, the women
delayed for some time, sitting before her,
the adornments ready beside them, their eyes
charmed by the vision of beauty in its pristine state.

14

Her gorgeous mass of hair dried by the smoke of incense
had flowers folded within it and tied by a woman
with a string of pale yellow madhūka blossoms
and green dūrva shoots into a charming chignon.

15

They smoothed cream of white aloe all over her body
and drew on it designs in yellow and gold pigments.[7]
And she glowed in beauty surpassing Triple-Streamed Gaṅgā
gleaming with sandy banks dotted with cakravāka birds.

16

Framed in charming curls, the splendour of her face
outshone the glory of a lotus with bees clinging,
or of the moon's bright orb fringed by wisps of clouds,
so that all talk of comparisons was cut short as vain.

17

The barley shoot placed at her ear held all eyes captive
and appeared to greatest advantage against her cheek,
translucent from the lodhra's bracing lotion
enhancing the brilliant pale gold gorocana.

18

The lower lip of that girl so exquisitely formed,
a line dividing it in the middle, its redness heightened
by a touch of beeswax, and pulsing expectant
of the fruit of its charm soon to come—Ah! How indescribable!

19

When a friend having tinted her feet with lākṣa juice
and blessed her, said laughing: 'With this foot
may you touch the moon on your lord's head,'
without a word, Umā struck her with a garland.

20

Seeing as her eyes were exquisitely lovely
as the petals of some fine blue lotus, the women
adorning Umā applied the collyrium
not to enhance their brilliance, but only
because it was an auspicious mark to put on the bride.

21

Like a vine burgeoning with blossoms,
like the night when stars are rising,
like a stream on which cakravākas are gliding,
she gleamed wondrous as they adorned her with jewels.

22

And gazing at herself so gorgeous in the mirror's oval,
Umā of long eyes, stilled, could hardly wait
for Śiva's arrival. To be seen by her beloved
is a woman's reward for adorning herself, is it not?

23

Picking up the moist paste of auspicious ores,
yellow and red with her fingers, the mother,
Menā, raised her daughter's face adorned by a pair
of fine ivory ear ornaments.

24

And somehow she managed to mark Umā's forehead
with the symbolic bridal mark that gave shape
to the wish that had first risen in her mind
and then grown and swelled with her daughter's swelling breasts.

25

With her sight blurred by welling tears, Menā then fastened
the ritual bracelet of woven wool on the bride's wrist,
but at the wrong place so that it had then to be adjusted
by the nurse to occupy its rightful place.

26

Holding in her hands a new mirror, and invested
in fine new silks, Umā wore the measureless glory
of the foam-mantled shores of the primal Milky Ocean,[8]
or the autumnal night holding the full moon.

27

The mother, knowing what rites had to be performed,
instructed her daughter, the family's joy and support,
to bow to the household divinities duly worshipped
and then in due order at the feet of virtuous women.

28

Umā, bending low to them was blessed in turn by each one
with the words: 'May you have your husband's undivided love'.
She however left her loving kinswomen's blessings far behind
when she appropriated half[9] of the Lord's own body.

29

The Mountain, urbane and skilled in protocol having left
nothing befitting his wealth and his wishes undone,
then sat in his Hall of Audience attended by his kinsmen,
awaiting the arrival of the Bull-Bannered Lord.

30

Meanwhile, on Kailāsa, Kubera's peak, the Seven Mothers,
devout, set before Śiva, Chastiser of the Cities,
adornments befitting His marriage—a marriage
the likes of which had never been witnessed before.

31

Out of regard for them, the Lord of the Universe,
merely touched that wealth of auspicious adornments;
for the very same articles He had on His person,
were now transformed into adornments fit for a bridegroom.

32

Mere ashes became the fragrant powder of white aloe;
the skull itself gained the splendour of a brilliant crest;
His mantle of elephant-hide became a fine silk garment
with designs painted on its borders in yellow.

33

The eye set in the middle of His forehead,
and ensconced within it the fiery pupil
tawny as a flame, served as the golden tilaka,
the auspicious mark of marriage; and looked fine indeed.

34

Only the bodies of the serpent-lords twined round his person
changed in shape to ornaments adorning the proper parts;
their hoods in which were embedded lustrous gems
still remained gleaming, unchanged.

35

Why would Śiva need a diadem for His hair already
illuminated continually by the moon that sheds
his brilliance even by day, undiminished
    by the dark spot on his orb, because he is a crescent?

36

He, the sole source of all that is wondrous,
having created the finest in costuming,
now looked at His own image in a sword
held up by an attendant standing beside Him.

37

Holding on to Nandī's arm, Śiva mounted the bull,
magnificent, resembling Mount Kailāsa, on whose broad back
a tiger skin was spread, and who out of devotion
crouched down to diminish his enormous bulk; and Śiva set out.

38

Circles of light flashing—rings of golden stamens—
from earrings swinging to the motion of their chariots,
lighting up their faces, The Mothers following Śiva
seemed to turn the sky into a pool of lotuses.

39

And behind the Mothers who were glowing with the brilliance of burnished gold
shone the Dark Goddess, Kāli, adorned with gleaming skulls
that looked like a flight of cranes against blue-black clouds
throwing out flashes of branched lightning far ahead.

40

The gaṇas who went before the Spear-Armed Lord then raised high
the tumultuous sound of auspicious pipes that flooded
the high domes of their aerial chariots, announcing
to the Immortals that it was time to join the procession.

41

The sun of a thousand rays held above Śiva,
a new umbrella made by the Divine Artificer, Tvaṣtra,
whose silken fringe hanging just above His head made Him
appear as if Gaṅgā were falling down on His hair.

42

Then, Gaṅgā and Yamunā both assumed appropriate shapes
and served the Luminous Lord, waving chowries over Him
that seemed flights of wild geese alighting on themselves
though they had for the time being ceased to be flowing rivers.

43

The First of Creators,[10] and that First Person,[11] beloved of Śrī,
appeared in person before Śiva; with the words
'Victory be yours', they made His glory blaze more brightly
as oblations poured into the Fire make it blaze higher.

44

A single Form divided Itself three ways, equally,
without distinction of first and last: Śiva above Viṣṇu.
or Viṣṇu above Him; Brahmā might stand above these Two,
at times; or the Two might be the First Creators.

45

The World-Guardians headed by oft-invoked Indra, laying aside
marks of wealth and sovereignty, and unostentatiously garbed,
signalled Nandī to grant them the favour of seeing the Lord:
announced by him, each by name, they then bowed low with palms
joined.

46

Śiva greeted the Lotus-Born with a nod of the head;
Viṣṇu with a word or two; Vṛtra-Slaying Indra[12] with a smile;
and the rest of the celestials without exception
He welcomed each according to his status, with a mere glance.

47

The Seven Sages spoke the benediction before Him,
preceded by the customary cheer of victory.[13] Smiling, Śiva said:
'In this Sacrifice that is the rite of marriage now laid out
in readiness, I have already appointed you the officiants'.

48

As the celestial musicians led by Viśvāvasu,
all accomplished players on the lute, gloriously sang
The Lay of Tripura,[14] the Lord beyond the dark power of change,[15]
who wears a digit of the moon on His head, traversed the skies.

49

And with swinging gait His mount bore Him across the sky
to the tune of tinkling little golden bells, goring the clouds,
tossing his horns time and again as if he were shaking off
the mud clinging to them from butting the banks of rivers in play.

50

As if he were drawn by the golden reins of Śiva's glances
flying far ahead of him, Nandī arrived in no time
at that city protected by the King of Mountains,
which had never come under enemy attack.

51

While the townsfolk looked up in wondering curiosity,
the Luminous Lord with neck blue-black as rain clouds,
descended from the path marked by His one-time mount,[16]
on to the level ground in the outskirts of the city.

52

The Monarch of the Mountains rejoicing at the coming
of Śiva, advanced to receive Him, with his kinsmen bearing
rich gifts and mounted on an array of elephants,
as if with his own slopes covered with trees bursting into bloom.

53

The two parties, Immortals and Earth-Supporters
came together at the city gates wide open,
like two floods breaking through a single dyke,
and the tumult spread far out into the distance.

54

As Śiva who is adored by the three worlds bowed to him,
Himālaya, the Earth-Supporter, was embarrassed,
unaware that his own head had already been lowered
before the supreme glory of the Lord.

55

With the beauty of his countenance enhanced by happiness
Himālaya led the way, conducting his son-in-law
into the heart of his opulent capital
which had its streets strewn ankle-deep with flowers.

56

During that hour, the beautiful women of the city
appeared all along the rows of great mansions, gripped
by a consuming desire to gaze upon the Supreme Lord;
and leaving off all other pursuits, acted as follows:

57

a certain woman hurrying to the round casement window
did not remember to bind her luxuriant mass of hair
flowing loose with its wreath of flowers slipping down,
even though she was holding it in her hands;

58

pulling away her foot still wet with red lākṣa juice
from the hand of the maid holding it, another woman
giving up the slow, languorous gait, hastened, drawing
a line of red footprints up to the lattice window;

59

yet another woman having pencilled her right eye
with rich, glossy collyrium, cheated the other of its share
as she hurried just as she was, straight to the window,
carrying the little collyrium rod in her hand;

60

failing to tie the loosening knot of her lower garment,
as she hurried, a woman with her eyes rivetted
on the lattice of the window, held it up with a hand,
the lustre of the jewels on it entering her navel;

61

while another woman, busy threading a jewelled belt,
rose in great haste though it was only half done,

and with each awkward step, the gems ill-knotted kept slipping off
until only the thread wound round her big toe remained.[17]

62

The faces of women vibrant with curiosity,
eyes tremulous as bees, mouths infolding the fragrance of wine,
covered the lattices so completely the windows appeared
to be decorated with thousand petalled lotuses.

63

Meantime, the Moon-Crested Lord was riding on the Royal Highway
with its array of high arches and waving pennons
where He made the palace turrets twice as splendid
setting them awash with moonlight even in the day.

64

Drinking Him in with their eyes, who was the sole object
of all seeing, the women became oblivious
of other things, propelling with their whole being
the functions of the other senses into their eyes.

65

'Is it so very surprising that she, the Lady With No Leaves,[18]
most delicate, should have practised such harsh penances for Him?
When she who serves Him even as a handmaid is most blessed,
how much more blessed is she who lies in His arms?

66

Supposing the Creator had not brought together
this pair endowed with the kind of beauty the whole world
most longs for, the effort that he had expended
forming them would have been fruitless indeed.

67

Surely, it cannot be that the body of the Flower-Armed god
was burnt to ashes by Śiva's mounting anger.
Having seen the Luminous Lord, the god of love,
gave his body up, I think, out of shame, of his own free will.

68

Now that the King of Mountains through great good fortune has formed
this kinship with the Lord which he had wanted with all his heart,
he is sure to hold his head already so lofty
from his holding up of this Earth even higher, my friend!'

69

Listening to such comments of the elegant women
of Oṣadhiprastha, so sweet to His ears, the Three-Eyed Lord
arrived at Himālaya's palace where welcoming showers
of parched rice shivered to powder against jewelled armlets.

70

Like the brilliant sun stepping out of an autumnal cloud
Śiva descended from His bull, taking Viṣṇu's proffered arm,
and with Lotus-Seated Brahmā leading the way,
He entered the inner halls of the Mountain-Lord's palace.

71

Behind Him came the Immortals headed by Indra followed
by the highest sages preceded by the Seven Sages;
with the gaṇas bringing up the rear, they entered the mountain abode
like superb ends after an auspicious beginning.

72

Taking a seat, the Lord accepted the gifts offered
by Himālaya with the appropriate mantras; gifts befitting
a bridegroom: water with gems, milk and curds
blended with honey and a pair of new silk cloths.

73

Dressed in silks, He was led to His bride by attendants,
of the Inner Palace[19], well-trained and deferential,
as the Ocean with its fringe of gathering foam is led
to the shore by the soft rays of the new-risen moon.

74

In conjunction with that young girl whose radiant lotus face
grew more beautiful, Śiva's lotus-petalled eyes opened wide,
the waters of His consciousness shone calm and pellucid;
He appeared like the world transfigured by autumn's glow.

75

Their eyes yearning for each other met by chance,
and startled, then somehow steadied a little,
retreated that very moment shrinking
before the compelling force of shyness.

76

Offered by her mountain father, The Lord of Eight Forms[20] received
Umā's hand, its fingers rose-red, the colour of burnished copper,[21]
the first tender sprout of the form of the Lord of Memories
hidden within her body for fear of Śiva.

77

The hairs on Umā's limbs bristling; the fingers
of the Bull-Bannered Lord moist with sweat from
the meeting of hands;
it seemed the Mind-Born appeared to divide
his attentions equally between bride and groom.

78

When hands join in wedlock, any bride and groom
become vested in radiance quite out of the ordinary.
What words can be found to describe the splendour born
of the nearness to each other of this bridal couple!

79

Joined in wedlock the bridal pair stepping sunwise[22]
round the Holy Fire blazing high, shone like Day and Night
following each other closely
as they circle the edges of Mount Meru.

80

Having guided the bridal pair thrice round the Fire
while they kept their eyes shut from the touch of their hands,
the family priest instructed the bride
to offer rice into the blazing Fire.

81

Obedient to the priest's instructions, Umā held her face to the smoke
rising fragrant from the rice she had offered with reverence;
the crest of the smoke curling against her cheek seemed
for a moment a blue lotus adorning her ear.

82

The prescribed ritual of inhalation of smoke
caused the bride's cheeks to become a little flushed and moist;
the glossy collyrium ran all around her eyes;
the barley sprout at her ears wilted.

83

The priest addressed the bride: 'This Holy Fire, my child,
is the ancient witness to your marriage. Therefore,
lead with your lord, a life in accordance with the Law,
putting away all doubts and disagreements.'

84

Śiva's consort drank deeply of these words of the priest,
straining her ears almost to the corners of her eyes,
as the Earth parched by summer's punishing heat
drinks greedily of the first rains sent by great Indra.

85

Prompted by her husband, change-less, pleasing to the eye,
to look up and view the unchanging Pole Star,
Umā raised her face and in low tones overcome by shyness,
managed somehow to say: 'I have seen it'.

86

When the wedding ceremony performed with flawless care
by the Royal Priest expertly accomplished in ritual
was completed, the Parents of Living Beings bowed
in reverence to the Grandfather on his lotus throne.

87

The Creator blessed the bride with the words:
'Lady blessed with good fortune, be the mother of heroes!'
But though he was himself the Lord of Speech, he was speechless,
at a loss for words to bless the Lord of Eight Forms.

88

Then the married couple came to the four-sided altar
on which were arranged the ceremonial articles;
as they sat on thrones of gold, grains of moist rice were placed
on their foreheads according to custom and desired by all.

89

Lakṣmī, goddess of Wealth and Beauty held over them
by its long, slender stem, a lotus umbrella,
the web of drops of water clinging to its petals
beautiful as a net of lustrous pearls.

90

Sarasvatī, the Muse, praised the bridal couple
with a composition using two separate styles[23]:
a style faultless and pure for the groom most adorable,
and for the bride one easily grasped.

91

For a while they watched a play, in its first performance,
presented by the apsaras in graceful mime,
in which different dramatic styles were clearly displayed
at the several stages of the play,
and various moods captured in musical modes.

92

At its conclusion, the Immortals lifting their joined palms
to touch their diadems, fell at Śiva's feet who now had a wife,
pleading that the five-arrowed god be released from his curse,
regain his form and have his service accepted.

93

All anger spent, the Glorious Lord then consented
that the god of love's arrows might do their worst even on Himself.
Success is certain when those who know how things are done,
approach their masters at the right time with their request.

94

Having dismissed the celestial host,
the Moon-Crested Lord holding the hand
of the Earth-Bearer's daughter retired
to the bridal chamber where stood
a couch beautifully decorated,
and brimming jars of gold were placed;
and flowers besides, and weapons infused
with the power to ward off evil spirits.

95[24]

Bashfulness lent the newly-wed Gaurī
an added charm as she turned her face way
when Śiva drew her towards Him;
while she could barely say a few words
even to her friends who used to sleep beside her,
by directing His impish attendants,
to make funny faces, the lord
made her laugh secretly to herself.

Thus ends Canto seven entitled *Umāpariṇayam (Umā's Bridal),* in the long poem *Kumārasaṃbhavam* by the illustrious Kālidāsa.

Canto 8

1

After the completion of the wedding rites, that feeling
of love mixed with trepidation towards her husband
that seized the daughter of the Mountain King, heightened
the deep longing for her surging in Śiva.

2

Although she gave no reply when He addressed her,
and tried to leave when He caught hold of her garment;
and though she lay on the bed with her face turned away,
Umā was sheer delight for Śiva even as she was.

3

When He lay pretending to be asleep, Pārvatī turned
her gaze upon her husband's face. But no sooner
did He open His eyes smiling up at her
than she shut hers tight as if by lightning struck.

4

Trembling, she removed Śiva's hand
placed in the region of her navel.
But her silken garment parted all on its own
as the knot that held it in place loosened all the way.

5

Close to her husband, face to face with Him,
bewildered, she forgot the advice her friends had given her:
'Dear friend, when alone with Śiva, this is how you should act;
laying aside your fears, give yourself in love to Him.'

6

When the Lord who had once chastised the Bodiless God
plied her with questions, albeit on matters of no moment,
simply to engage her in a conversation with Him,
Pārvatī responded with a mere glance or nod of the head.

7

As she was being disrobed in the secrecy of their chamber,
Umā covered both eyes of the Spear-Armed Lord with her palms.
But seeing the eye on His forehead still gazing on her,
she was downcast seeing how vain her efforts were.

8

In kissing her, He could not grasp her lower lip between His lips;
His caresses were gentle, He embraced her tenderly;
yet, Śiva experienced intense pleasure in the loveplay,
despite His bride's shy reserve and lack of passionate response.

9

Pārvatī could bear only this much and nothing more:
kissing of the mouth without the lower lip bitten hard;
the play of nails on her limbs without drawing blood;
a tender way of lovemaking by her husband.

10

Her friends showered her with questions in the morning,
eager to find out all that had happened in the night.
But even if her heart trilled with excitement to tell all,
modesty held her back from satisfying their curiosity.

11

Even as she looked in the mirror at the marks of pleasure
lovemaking had left, Pārvatī saw her lover
seated behind her; His image behind her image. And then,
to what lengths did she not go to hide her embarrassment!

12

The mother, Menā, breathed easily as she observed
how much the Blue-Throated Lord was enjoying her daughter's youth.
A bride who confidently possesses her husband's love entire,
lifts the burden of care off the mother's heart.

13

Several days passed as Śiva, The Immutable,
managed to make love to His bride as best as He could;
until, having learned the taste of love's pleasures,
in time she rid herself of her distressing aversion to it.

14

And then, when Śiva held her close to His chest, she embraced Him;
she did not turn her face away when He pleaded to kiss her;
when His hand, trembling with passion crept towards her jewelled belt,
she made the feeblest attempts to restrain it.

15

In a matter of days, their love grew in secret, firm,
strong, grounded in each other; expressed in their gestures,
with never an unkind word or thought.
A moment's separation, and they felt forlorn!

16

The bride was enamoured of a bridegroom worthy
of her; and the bridegroom felt the same way for her,
just as Gaṅgā never departs from the Ocean
who makes the sweetness of her mouth his chief delight.

17

Skills in the art of lovemaking befitting young women
learnt from Śiva, her instructor, in secret,
were now offered by Umā to Him in the same form
as the gift for instruction duly given to a guru.

18

Her tender hands fluttering in pain
as her lower lip was bitten hard and released,
Pārvatī held it to the coolness of the crescent moon
on Śiva's forehead to ease its burning pain.

19

And if the sandalwood dust clinging to her fringe of curls
were to fall into Śiva's third eye while He was kissing her,
and make it smart, He would hold it against her mouth
whose breath held the fragrance of a full-blown lotus to blow it off.

20

In this manner, the Bull-Bannered Lord spent a whole month
in the palace of the Mountain King with Umā,
following the path of the pleasures of the senses,
restoring the god of love to favour and make him live again.

21

Taking leave of Himālaya who was saddened
by parting with his daughter, Śiva, the Self-Born,
mounted on the bull that went with measureless speed,
diverted Himself roaming in many different places.

22

Reaching Mount Meru on His bull swift as wind,
honoured by the gift of Pārvatī's breasts, the expert lover
enjoyed Himself on a bed of broken leaves of gold
that could bear the vigorous acts of passionate lovemaking.

23

A bee on the lotus of Pārvatī's mouth,
He resided on the slopes of Mandara[1]
where the stones marked by the imprint of Viṣṇu's footsteps[2]
had received drops of the Primal amṛta.

24

The Parent of the Universe then enjoyed the soft
autumnal moonlight on Kailāsa, Kubera's peak,
who possessed golden treasures, while Pārvatī alarmed
by Rāvaṇa's roars,[3] wound her arms tightly round His neck.

25

Once when Śiva was loving His beloved in the Malaya mountain
the southern breeze that had been rustling through sandalwood groves
and blowing through orchards of cloves came wafting their pollen
and like a sweet-spoken lover removed her tiredness.

26

Sporting in the restless waves of the celestial river,
striking her lover in play with a golden lotus,
closing her eyes as Śiva splashed her with water, Umā
needed no jewelled belt because the bright minnows swam glittering
round her.

27

Celestial women looked long with longing
at the Odd-Eyed Lord as He adorned Umā's hair
in the Nandana[4] groves with pārijāta blossoms[5]
that were used to dress the waving hair of Puloma's daughter.[6]

28

Then, Śiva, who had experienced the delights
of the earth and of paradise as well with His bride,
came one evening to the Gandhamādana[7] mountain
as the setting sun turned the sky crimson.

29

Reclining there on a rock of gold, His left arm around Umā,
the wedded wife who followed the path of dharma
with her husband, Śiva addressed her
as He faced the evening sun no longer eye-dazzling.

30

'Having transferred the glow of lotuses to your lovely eyes,
placing it at their rose-red corners, the Lord of Days
draws the day into himself just as the Lord of Creation
draws the world into himself at the hour of dissolution.

31

As the sun bends low in the sky and his rays
far distant no longer light up the spray
thrown upwards by your father's cascading streams,
they are now bereft of the rainbows encircling them.

32

The pair of cakravāka birds there on the lake,
parted, seeing the distance between them grow greater,
drop the half-bitten lotus filaments,
and forlorn, call to each other in mournful tones.

33

Leaving behind those grounds where they had foraged by day
for waters scented by broken sallaki branches,
where lotuses have shut with bees enclosed within them,
elephants drink their fill of water to last them till the next morning.

34

O, Lady of few words and fit! See how the sun
hanging low on the ridge of the western sky
seems to be laying a bridge of gold from shore to shore
as he casts his long reflection on the waters of the lake.

35

Wild boars, lords of herds, with long white tusks
that resemble curving lotus stalks being eaten,
now come up out of the shallow pools covered in thick mud
where they had spent the heat of day.

36

My love with magnificent thighs! Here on this tree top
sits a peacock, his circle of plumes fanning out,
and glowing like molten gold as if he were drinking up
the evening's golden light diminishing by the minute.

37

As the darkness advances there in the east,
the sky with the water of light drawn up
by the setting sun looks like a drying lake
with the dark mud at its bottom exposed.

38

How beautiful the hermitages now look:
deer enter the courtyards; cows that provide
the essentials of the sacrifices come home; young trees
glisten moist, freshly watered at the roots; fires are kindled.

39

Lotuses about to close keep slightly open
for a moment before folding their petals tight
like buds as if to offer lovingly
an entrance to bees that wish to sleep within them.

40

As the sun shimmers, its orange-gold rays so few and apart
they could be counted, the west glows like a young girl
adorned with the beauty mark of a bandhūka flower
on her forehead, flaunting its orange-gold filaments.

41

Thousands upon thousands of the sun's companions,[8] drinking
the rising vapours of his rays as he pours his lustre
into the Fire,[9] praise him with the śāma chants of eventide
whose tones enrapture the steeds that draw his chariot.

42

Having placed Day in trust with the mighty Ocean,
you see the sun now moving to the western mountain,
the necks of his steeds bent down, their manes curved by the yoke,
their eyes brushed by the tips of the plumes at their ears.

43

As the sun has set, the sky seems to be asleep.
Such is the way of a mighty Splendour.
What it illuminates as it rises,
it plunges into darkness as it falls.

44

And the twilight instantly follows the adored form of the sun
entrusted now to the western mountain. How could she not
follow him in his decline, when formerly she went
honoured, before him, at his rising in the east?

45

My love with waving hair! Do you see the edges
of those clouds gleaming crimson and gold and russet
as if the twilight has painted them with masterly strokes
of an artist's brush so that you might admire them.

46

See how the sun has now divided the evening light
and distributed it among the tangled manes of lions,
the tender new shoots of burgeoning trees,
and the rich ores on mountain peaks.

47

Daughter of the King of Mountains! These ascetics
well-versed in the prescribed modes of performing rituals,
sprinkle hallowed water with reverence from their cupped palms
as they silently recite the evening prayers to purify themselves.

48

Therefore, my sweet-spoken beloved, pray allow me
a little time to spend in performing the evening rite.
Your companions skilled in the ways and means to pass the time
will keep you entertained in the meantime.'

49

Treating her husband's words with supreme disdain,
the daughter of the King of Mountains, pouting,
turned to her friend, Vijayā, at her side
and carried on an aimless conversation with her.

50

Then the Lord having performed the evening rite
with the appropriate mantras accompanying it,
returned to Pārvatī where she sat in sullen silence;
and smiling at her, He addressed her again:

51

'Give up your anger, my love who has no cause for anger!
I went to pay my respects to the twilight; to no other.
Your true wedded husband, I follow the cakravāka's way
of fidelity to his mate; do you not know that?

52

Exquisite girl! Brahmā, the Self-Born,
once abandoned his body after forming the Fathers.
That body, Proud Lady, is this twilight, worshipped
at dusk and at dawn; her I feel proud to honour.

53

O, Daughter of the King of Mountains! See how the twilight
hemmed in on one side by the gathering darkness
appears at the moment like a flowing stream of molten ore
edged on one bank by a row of tamāla trees.

54

The western quarter bears a curving blood-red gash
slantwise of what remains of the gloaming,
like a battlefield where a blood-soaked scimitar
point down, has been planted aslant.

55

While the glow born of the meeting of day with night
has vanished behind Mount Sumeru,[10]
this blinding darkness spreads in all directions
unchecked, O, my love with long lovely eyes!

56

The eye has no way to go; neither above or below;
no way around, or before, or behind.
The world enveloped in the caul of darkness
lies within the womb of Night.

57

Pure or polluted; moving or unmoving;
straight or crooked; darkness makes all things equal.
Ah! What a shame it is, that dark forces have such power
to wipe out all distinctions.

58

Even so, the moon, Lord of Sacrificers, now rises
to chase away the shadows of Night. The face of the East,
appears dusted as it were with the pollen of ketaka flowers.
O, Lady with a face exquisite as a white lotus!

59

While the form of the hare-marked[12] moon is still hidden
behind Mount Mandara, Night with her stars looks like you
when you are surrounded by your loving friends;
and I, at your back, overhearing your talk.

60

Urged by Night, the East now spills out the moon's orb
held back from emerging till the close of day,
as if it were a secret, visible earlier
only as the faint glow of its moonlight smile.

61

See how the moon with his snow-cool rays
glowing in the sky like a ripe golden fruit
and mirrored in the waters of the lake, imitates
a pair of cakravākas far apart.

62

The rays of the moon, Lord of Plants, just emerging,
seem delicate as tender barley sprouts
that you could lightly snip with your finger-nails
to wear as your ear ornaments.

63

Boldly seizing Night's dark mass of hair
with his ray-fingers, the moon kisses
her face, the day-blooming lotuses
of her eyes shut tight as buds.

64

Pārvati, look how the vault of the sky swept clear
of dense darkness by the rays of the new-risen moon
is like Lake Mānasa becoming translucent again
after elephants revelling had muddied its waters.

65

Having shed the reddish tinge of his rising,
the orb of the moon now shines a pure brilliant white.
In the same way, changes wrought by Time
are not lasting in those pure by nature.

66

The moon's bright radiance settles in lofty heights;
Night's shadows seek the refuge of lowly depths.
It is clear, is it not, that the Creator
has allotted the right place for merits and for defects?

67

As drops of water drip from moonstones melting
under the touch of moonbeams, this mountain
strikes one as awakening at the wrong time
sleeping peacocks roosting in the trees girdling his slopes.

68

Look, my beautiful bride! The moon seems busy
threading with mounting excitement
the pearls of his lustrous beams into necklaces
on the tops of that Wish-Granting tree over there.

69

Because this mountain is contoured in heights and hollows,
the chequered pattern of moonlight and shadows,
makes it striking as an elephant in rut,
its frame painted with ashes in intricate designs.

70

All on a sudden, the moonlotus having drunk its fill
of the moonlight's brilliant essence, bursts open all the way
down to its calyx with the clamorous buzzing of bees
emerging from within, as if unable to hold anymore.

71

My angry darling! Do you see the dazzling-white
fine, silken robe hanging on that Wish-Granting Tree?
The brilliant moonlight casts doubts on what it truly is,
until it starts turning in the brisk-moving breeze.

72

How easy would it be to pick up with the fingers
these bright slivers of moonlight broken falling through leaves
and lying like delicate flower petals under the trees,
my love, and bind with them your curling tresses!

73

My love of endearing charm! The moon now conjunct
with the star of the day[13] looks like a bridegroom
uniting with a trembling bride fearful
of her first experience of love.

74

Watching you, your eyes rivetted on the orb of the moon,
your cheeks bright as the plumes of the blossoming sedge
with the translucent glow natural to them, it strikes me
that the moonlight springs from the orbs of your cheeks.

75

Who comes here? The guardian divinity herself
of the Gandhamādana Forests bearing wine
from the Wish-Granting Tree in a bowl formed
of the sunstone crystal[14] for you who are now here.[15]

76

Since your mouth holds the fragrance of bakula flowers
and the corners of your eyes are naturally rose-red,
what other grace, O, lady of sensuous graces
can a mouthful of wine impart to you?

77

On the other hand, honour your friend, the sylvan goddess,
by accepting her warm welcome; the wine will kindle
your passion for love: thus considerately speaking
Śiva offered Pārvatī the wine to drink.'

78

Once she had drunk that wine, a change came over Pārvatī,
making her even more enchanting as the common mango
is charmed by some indefinable power in Nature
into the special, fragrant sahakāra kind.

79

That very moment, the passion kindled in Pārvatī,
divesting her of all shyness, led her to the couch of love.
The lovely bride became then subject to the power
of Śiva's blazing passion and of her own desire.

80

As her eyes rolled and her speech faltered, while beads of sweat
gathered on Umā's face smiling for no reason
other than intoxication, the Lord drank deeply
of its beauty with His eyes, not His lips.

81

With her golden belt dangling loose, Śiva carried her
who was heavy from the fulness of her hips, and entered
a jewelled cave provided with all sumptuous comforts
created by the power of His meditation, to be alone.

82

There on a couch with a coverlet white as snow geese,
and delightful to the eyes as Gaṅgā's sands,
Śiva lay with His beloved and He looked like the moon,
Rohiṇī's lord resting on an autumnal cloud.

83

Vying with each other in pulling the hair roughly,
inappropriately scratching with the nails,
rubbing off the liquid sandal on the limbs,
the string of Pārvatī's jewelled belt snapping: and yet,
Śiva was not sated by His enjoyment of her.

84

Only out of sheer considerateness for His beloved
clasped close to His chest did Śiva deign to close
His eyes at last in sleep, as clusters of stars
were descending in the western horizon.

85

Accustomed to being eulogized[16] by the wise at dawn,
Śiva woke up along with the beds of golden lotuses,
to the well-modulated melodies of auspicious songs
sung by kinnaras playing lutes.[17]

86

As they relaxed their close embrace for a moment, the couple
were cooled by breezes from Gandhamādana Forests
that having rippled the waters of Lake Mānasa
brought news of the unfolding of its lotuses.

87

At that very moment, Śiva having caught sight
of a row of nail marks at the base of her thigh,
stopped His beloved from tying her lower garment
coming undone and slipping down.

88

Looking at the beloved's face, eyes dull, discoloured,
from lack of sleep, the lower lip bruised by His teeth,
the beauty mark on the forehead rubbed off, hair dishevelled,
the passionate lover made love to His bride once again.

89

The night had ended; it was broad daylight; the coverlet crumpled,
marked by red stains from her painted feet; lying in the middle
in a heap, her jewelled belt, its strings broken;
but the impassioned lover would still not leave the couch.

90

Eager to taste day and night the nectar
of His beloved's lips that produced such exhilaration,
with Vijayā at the door, Śiva became inaccessible
to those desirous of seeing Him.

91

Day and night were the same to Śiva
immersed in love's pleasures,
a hundred and more seasons passing
as if it were a single night;
His thirst for the raptures of love
knew no end; it did not abate;
It was like the Fire[18] in the Ocean's depths,
unquenched by its multitudinous waters.

Thus ends Canto eight entitled *Umāsuratavarnanah (The Description of Umā's Pleasures)*, in the long poem *Kumārasaṃbhavam* by the illustrious Kālidāsa.

Canto 9

1

And the Lord, the bee sipping the honey
of the beloved's face, tasting love's sensuous delights
as described before, now saw a dove come
flying into the Palace of Pleasures.

2

Darting its red eyes this way and that, stretching up
its curving neck, again and again bobbing
its tail feathers so pretty, cooing sweetly
like a woman dearly loved during passion's fevered pitch,

3

stepping daintily in circles on curving claws
in gay abandon, that bird ever free, never fettered,
lightly fluttered its pair of wings flashing gleams
of the moon's pale silver.

4

For a moment the Moon Crested Lord watched with delight
the bird that appeared like the foam rising
the instant the God of Love plunges
into a pool of nectar with Rati.

5

But seeing as its form was of something divine,
The Luminous Lord who dwells within all beings,
reflected: divining it to be the Divine Fire, Agni,
disguised, He grew furious, his brows bent and twisting.

6

Trembling in extreme terror, Agni, resuming his form,
folded his hands in reverence;
he spoke these words of truth, transparent,
shaking greatly all the while, to Kāma's bitter foe.

7

'You are the sole lord, supreme, of the universe.
You destroy all evils befalling the Dwellers in Light.
Therefore do the Immortals led by their lord, Indra,
seek Your help, lord, being harassed by the Titans.

8

A hundred seasons have passed while You stayed withdrawn
alone, in secret, enthralled by love for your beloved,
loving her; and at Your door, Indra and the Immortals,
have stood desolated, deprived of the seeing of You.

9

Pleaded with by the Immortals through Indra,
awaiting the opportune hour to attend on You,
I have come to seek Your presence, O Seer,
in the guise befitting the occasion, of a bird.

10

Mindful of our need, Lord, pray forgive us
our transgression; and consider for Yourself
how long the misery of these suppliants
can endure the long passage of time.

11

Be gracious, Lord; send forth Your Son soon.
Gaining him as commander of the celestial forces,
let Indra regain the sovereignty of Svarga;[1]
and, through Your grace be Protector of the Triple-World.'

12

Having heard Agni's plea spoken
so eloquently, Śaṅkara was pleased.
Those who have the gift of words humour their masters
with pleasing words, do they not?

13

With a mind clear, unperturbed, the foe of the God of Love
now turned His thoughts somewhat to the birth of the Son,
a conquering hero and Tāraka's foe,
leading to victory the forces of Indra.

14

He who held his seed aloft, unspilled, now cast it
spurting from interrupted coitus; insupportable,
fiery as World-Devouring-Fire at the end of Time,
into golden-seeded Agni so that it was not shed in vain.

15

As the mirror's bright face becomes blurred
by burning breath blown on it, Agni's pure form
became discoloured by the profuse surge of seed
of Śiva, Destroyer of Fortresses.

16

Cheated of love's pleasure the Daughter of the Mountain,
filled with fury cursed Agni with these words :
"Be Eater of all things! Be Doer of terrible deeds!
Let leprosy strike you and your belly fill with smoke!"

17

Like the moon wasted by Dakṣa's curse,
like a lotus bud burnt black by frost;
Agni was forced to leave the Pleasure Palace blasted
by the profusion of the fierce seed of the Lord squirting.

18

Śiva restored Pārvatī whose face had turned ugly
with fury at the sight of Agni, to a happy frame of mind,
with sweet words full of love and made it glow, smiling,
as she looked down with charming coyness.

19

Tenderly he wiped off with one end of the scarf
on his shoulders the dark collyrium running
out of the eyes and spreading over the spotless moon
of his best-beloved's face drenched with drops of sweat.

20

Gently wiping her lotus face
with his own perspiring fingers
Śiva dried the sweat off Pārvatī's face,
fanning it with playful tenderness.

21

With a wealth of Pārijāta blossoms, the Moon-Crested Lord
wreathed her splendid mane of hair where it lay loose
clinging to her shoulders, its knot undone
as they made passionate love; and all the flowers in it slipping down.

22

Having painted the cheeks of the lovely lady
in bright pigments with leaf-and-petal designs,
as if he were writing rows of letters to form charms
to bewitch the world of Love, the Magician;

23

the Lord whose face was brilliant as the moon, then placed in her ears
twin jewelled ear-tops, wheel-shaped, for the chariot of her face
which the God of the Flower Bow was sure to mount
as he set out on his World-Conquering triumphal progress.

24

Round her neck He placed a twining vine
of lustrous pearls that just hid the tips
of her breasts; and it wore the beauty
of Gaṅgā's twin streams poised on Meru's twin peaks.

25

The foe of the Lord of Memories wound round her ample loins
that appeared enchanting with the line of nail-wounds,
the exquisite, jewelled belt, a rope the mind-born god
had made to bind fast the bounding deer of His mind.

26

Warming the collyrium in the lamp of the eye
set in the middle of His forehead, He applied it expertly
to the newly-opened lotus-petals of her eyes,
wiping His finger clean on His own blue-black neck pulsing with delight.

27

Having tinted the tips of the lotus-petal-eyed lady's
lotus feet with rich red lac juice, the Moon-Crested Lord
washed the red stain off His hands in the waters of Gaṅgā
seated like a crest jewel on His head.

28

Polishing the mirror's surface bright, rubbing it
on His own ash-dusted body, Siva held it up
playfully for His dearest love to scrutinize
the splendour of her adornment in it.

29

Seeing the signs of love's enjoyment on her body
in the jewelled mirror held up by her lover,
Pārvatī, overcome by shyness, revealed the deep love
she bore Him by her tingling skin and hair standing on end.

30

Smiling, she saw in the mirror how her beloved lord
had succeeded in adorning her so beautifully;
brushing aside all former feelings of pique, she now
regarded herself the best among women blessed in life.

31

Presently Jayā and Vijayā, her two dear friends entered
to begin her toilette using the wealth of decorations
that Art could devise, as she sat enclosed in the arms
of the Lord Who Wore The Crescent Moon for his Crest.

32

Outside, bards sang in high, clear voices
auspicious songs of the wondrous deeds of the Lord
while a host of Gandharvas awakened Pinākī
with the sound of conches for His delight.

33

Then Nandī bending low with hands respectfully folded,
entered at the door to announce the host
of Celestials who had come at their proper hour
of service, eager to have a sight of the Lord.

34

And the mighty lord came nochalantly
out of the pleasure chamber holding by the hand
the Daughter of the Mountain of Snows—
the queen-swan gliding on the pool of His consciousness.

35

With great Indra at their head, the Celestials
raising their folded hands to their diademed heads
bowed in turn to the Supreme and to the Mother of the three worlds,
the Daughter of the overlord of Mountains of Ice.

36

Having bestowed lavish honours on the Celestials,
and giving them leave to depart in the order of their arrival,
the Bull-Bannered Lord took Nandī's arm
and mounted on His bull with the Mountain's daughter,

37

set out on His path through the skies on the bull
that raced swifter than thought; the Lord of the Mountain
was greeted with folded hands by Celestials roaming
without a care in their aerial chariots.

38

The Mountain-Lord and the Mountain's daughter enjoyed
the breezes cool from playing on the celestial river's waters,
fragrant from blowing through groves of blossoming Pārijāta trees,
and bringing welcome relief to women fatigued by love's passionate play.

39

Arriving on Kailāsa, lordly mountain of crystal,
mantled in space, beautiful with wondrous hooded serpents,
wearing the crescent moon on its peak, it seemed
The Bearer of the pināka had reached His very own Self.

40

Where, siddha women seeing their own reflections
in its crystal walls, labouring under the illusion
they were their rivals in love, turned resentfully away
from their loving husbands falling at their feet, pleading;

41

Where, the sparkling brilliance of the moon's rays got lost
in the crystalline brightness of the peak, and merely the dark spot
on the moon remained as if with the elegant charm of a beauty mark
of musk made by the Bright Goddess out of sheer pleasure;

42

Where lordly tuskers mistaking their own forms reflected
on the crystal mountain-side, for rivals in rut
begin to butt them, infuriated, only to feel
severe pain in their formidable tusks;

43

Where at night in crystal palaces
the wives of siddhas confusedly fancy
clusters of stars reflected on the crystal floors
to be large pearls fallen from neclaces during passionate lovemaking;

44

Where the moon, nectar's bowl, stands on Kailāsa's peak,
mirror for flying vidyādharīs; crest jewel,
priceless of Himālaya the Lord of Mountains;
the abode of Śiva with many sacred temples;

45

Where Immortals nagged by aching love, embrace in secret
the women they dearly love and satisfy their passion;
and see their bodies reflected many times over,
becoming multiple forms though they are single.

46

And the Moon-Crested Lord passed the days
with the Bright Goddess in amorous sport as He wished
for a long time, uninterrupted,
His heart enthralled by sweetest pleasure.

47

And Pārvatī glorying in her exquisite grace,
clasping Śiva's hand, The God of Love's Destroyer,
walked along, with languorous gait, Nandī
going before her holding his staff of office.

48

Ordered by the slight raising of Śaṅkara's eyebrow,
bhṛṅgī of projecting foreteeth and white pointed tusk,
danced to please Pārvatī, contorting his limbs
in grotesque movements, his tuft of hair slapping back and forth.

49

Of awesome face with protruding foreteeth,
a garland of skulls round her neck,
directed lovingly by the Lord, Kālī
lanced for the pleasure of Śiva's beloved.

50

Watching that fearsome duo, Kālī and Bhṛṅgī,
dancing frantically, the young girl
shaking with terror fell on her own into the arms
of Kāma's foe clinging close to Him in a passionate embrace.

51

Passionately embraced by Pārvatī,
feeling her full, high breasts pressed suddenly against Him,
as the Lord of Memories made thrills of pleasure
course through His limbs, Śiva was maddened by passion.

52

Enjoying the pleasures of love
with the Daughter of the Mountain
in many different ways, The Lord
Whose Crest-Jewel was the nectar-rayed moon
made Kailāsa, Lord of Mountains,
His abode to dwell in happiness,
and surrounded by the gaṇas
His obedient attendants, rejoiced.

Thus ends Canto nine entitled *Arrival at Kailāsa*, in the long poem *Kumārasaṃbhavam* by the illustrious Kālidāsa.

Canto 10

1

Burning with the fiery energy
of the three-Eyed lord, Agni
appeared in the Immortal's
Assembly before Lord Indra.

2

Indra looked at him with concern
out of his thousand eyes and saw him
deformed, blasted, a piteous sight,
all enveloped in smoke.

3

Seeing Agni in such a state
Indra's mind was in turmoil; he thought
long whether this had something to do
with the fury of Kāma's foe.

4

Watched every moment by the Immortals
Agni accepted the seat
Indra offered him with respect.

5

"Bearer of oblations! How come
you are in such a sorry plight?"
Thus asked by the Lord of Immortals,
Agni sighed deeply and then spoke:

6-7

"O Leader of the Immortals!
At your inviolable command
I approached the Great Lord Śiva
in the guise of a dove where He lay
in passionate union with Gaurī;
seeing Him seeming Death itself,
trembling in utter terror of Him,
Kāma's foe, I resumed my own form."

8

'Ah! Destroyer of Demons! That Seer
seeing me in the guise of a bird,
knew me; in anger He was about to offer me
into the fire in His forehead;

9

When I Began praising Him with words
sweet and eloquent; The Luminous One
was gratified; for whom does praise not please?

10

The Refuge, The All-Protector,
Śaṅkara, saved me from the fear
of ending up a morsel in the Fire
of His anger, inescapable."

11

The Lord desisted out of shame
from reaching love's rapturous heights
giving up the delicious pleasure
of Pārvatī's passionate embrace.

12

The potent energy spurting free
from their loving interrupted,
He cast that very instant into me
lest it burn the three worlds entire.

13

That blazing energy within
I bear in cruel agony.
No longer can I bear this body
singed and burning beyond all endurance.

14

As saviour of my life, Indra,
be renowned in ages to come.
For I am consumed by the blazing
potency of Rudra's fiery seed.'

15

Having heard Agni's words, Indra
racked his brain to find a way
of allaying the terrible agony
of Agni's Divine Fire.

16

Gently stroking the limbs of the god
born from wood, and burnt by Śiva's
fiery seed, the Lord of Immortals
spoke soothingly to Agni, thus:

17

'Pleased with the oblations offered
with due invocations: svāha, svadhā, hantā;
You Yourself please all: Gods, Fathers, Mortals.
Though You are One, You are the mouth of all of these.

18

Sacrificers sacrifice to You,
with oblations, and purged of dross
enjoy the World of Eternal Light.
You are the sole means of gaining that World of Light.

19

Eater of Oblations! Sages
pouring oblations into You
reap the reward of their penance.
You are the Lord of Penances.

20

You offer the Sun what is offered to You;
as the Rain-God he showers earth with rain;
from rain grows food; from food creatures are born;
therefore are You the Parent of the World.

21

You abide within all beings;
from You are they all born;
You are the Breath of Life;
You give life to the World.

22

Of this entire universe,
You are the sole benefactor;
so who can better help
in the accomplishment of all aims?

23

You are the sole means of accomplishing
the purpose of this assembly of Immortals.
Even the misfortunes of those bent
on helping others deserve praise.

24

The celestial river Bhāgīrathī
was formerly propitiated by us;
immerse Yourself in her waters,
Your burning heat will be allayed.

25

So go to her, do not tarry,
Bearer of Oblations! Approach Gaṅgā.
In matters of importance success
attends those who take speedy action.

26

That goddess, the celestial river
is the watery form of Śiva;
She will take over from you, the seed
so difficult to bear, of Kāma's foe, and bear it herself.'

27

Having said this, Indra fell silent.
Agni given leave to depart
set out on the path leading towards
the celestial streams of Gaṅgā.

28

Going along on his way
Golden-seeded Agni came to Gaṅgā
destroyer of all pain without a trace
flowing with swelling waves through svarga.[2]

29

Ladder to ascend to svarga,
divinity presiding over the path
to mokṣa[3], Dispeller of calamities,
the raft to cross life's perilous seas;

30

dwelling in the tangled topknot
of the Great Lord; Destroyer of sins,
Uplifter of Sagara's lineage,
Support and Upholder of dharma;

31

springing from the water that washed Viṣṇu's feet,
descending from the world of Brahmā,
tirelessly purifying
the Triple-World with her Triple Streams;

32

wearing an aspect most tranquil,
she greeted the Divine Fire approaching her
with her wave-hands raised high, eager
to make his coming a success.

33

Through the sweet, indistinct tones of wild geese
calling intoxicated in unison,
she seemed to say: "I shall give you
happiness and destroy your sorrows."

34

Her waves leaped up and came gambolling
to lap against the nearer shore
as if the celestial river
was coming joyously to meet Agni.

35

Then, the Divine Fire tormented
by Śiva's burning seed approached
the river and plunged into her waters.
How can one stricken by adversity wait?

36

Immersed in Gaṅgā's waters, restful,
salubrious, bestowing merit,
helping mortals to cross Life's Ocean,
Agni was relieved of his burning torment.

37

As Śiva's fiery energy passed
from the Eater of Oblations
into Gaṅgā, the burning pain deep inside her
surged, quivering upwards in billowing waves.

38

And, as the river with reverence
accepted the Divine Archer's
blazing energy, Agni emerged
from the waters filled with unalloyed bliss.

39

Agni having bathed in those waters
that seemed ambrosia distilled,
then went on his way elated,
with a feeling of supreme relief.

40

The celestial Gaṅgā flowing in the skies
having received the potent seed
of Kāma's foe that she was unable
to bear, quivered in intense pain.

41

Aquatic creatures burned by her waters
as if by the hundred flames emerging
from the Fire at the end of Time
came out panting from their watery home.

42

With immeasurable fortitude Gaṅgā
bore the waters boiling, bubbling fiercely
from the blazing fire of Śiva's seed,
tumultuously overflowing her banks.

43

In the month of Māgha, the krittikas,
the six Pleiades, came to the celestial river
at the moment the Eye of the World,
the hot-rayed Sun was about to rise.

44

With hundreds of her uplifted cloud-grazing white billows,
Gaṅgā seemed to be pouring out her woes
to the Dwellers in Light looking at her,
as they bathed and performed their rituals in her waters.

45

The white sands on her banks were spread
with flowers and dūrva shoots and grains of rice
befitting the customary offerings made
by the Seven Sages after their ritual baths.

46

She was frequented by the Holy Sages
with hooded serpents wound round their torsos
absorbed in profound meditation in the lotus-pose,

47

on the Supreme, the mind withdrawn from the world,
centred deep within in the Self; standing
on the tips of their big toes and reciting
mantras to the supreme Reality, Brahma,
with their gaze fixed steadfastly on the Sun.

48

Now the krittikas, seeing the goddess Gaṅgā,
divine river, greatly rejoiced;
who in the world would not rejoice
at the sight of her, The Bearer of Ambrosia ?

49

With devotion they meditated
in their hearts on her who was borne
on His head by the Luminous Lord, Moon-Crested,
whose very sight brought merit to the seer.

50

Bending their heads low in reverence, the krittikas
worshipped the Luminous One, the celestial river
who rises at Viṣṇu's foot, washes away impurities,
and provides the means of salvation.

51

With devout prayers, they who put their trust in her
who stood surety for salvation, gratified
The Pure One who flows through the worlds of Eternal Light,
she who was easy of access to those blessed with good fortune.

52

Cleansing themselves of impurities by bathing
ritually in Gaṅgā's translucent waters,
the krittikas rose after their baths
glowing with ascetic splendour.

53

Having bathed in that river, a happiness
granted by their good fortune now standing
at its height, the krittikas joyfully esteemed themselves
highly for having achieved their purpose in life.

54

As they immersed themselves in Gaṅgā's waters,
the splendour that was Śiva's powerful seed,
unfailing in its potency, was at once
transferred from the waters into their bodies.

55

Bearing within them that energy
which was of the essence of Fire, that was
in the nature of an ordeal to bear, their anguish
was such as if they were drowning in seas of poison.

56

Unable to contain that energy,
which was beyond their power to bear,
they came out of the waters with the sensation
of blazing fires burning inside them.

57

Śiva's potent seed with splendour glowing,
ripe and ready to bring forth fruit,
now lodged within their wombs,
was into an embryo growing.

58

Knowing that it was beyond their power to hold
and bring to full term this fiery conception,
the wise krittikas filled with shame and fear as well
of their husbands became desperate.

59

Out of the fear of incurring a curse,
and out of shame, they abandoned
what came out of their wombs
in a thicket of reeds, and went home.

60

The embryo placed in the reeds by them
glowed softly like a tender digit
of the nectar-rayed moon new-born in the sky:
with countless splendours shooting upwards
rivalling the splendour of a hundred suns,
it was born with six faces, as if it wished to surpass
four-faced Brahmā, Parent of Kāma's foe Himself.

Thus ends Canto ten entitled *The Birth of Kumāra,* in the long poem *Kumārasaṃbhavam* by the illustrious Kālidāsa.

Canto 11

1

Humbly beseeched by the host of Immortals
led by Indra, the celestial river
quickly assumed visible form and gave her own breast
filled with purest nectar to the infant god.

2

Drinking the nectar of Gaṅgā's breasts,
tended by the six krittikas, the infant god
grew great by the minute, gaining mighty strength.
Ah! What a form! Wondrous indeed, he acquired.

3

And O, what a clamour then arose, as the Divine Fire,
Agni, and the Divine river, Bhāgīrathī,
and the krittikas, their eyes misting with tears of joy,
all vied with each other to lift and hold
that luminous child who gladdened all hearts.

4

Meantime, Śiva and the daughter of the Mountain-King,
rolling along in the skies in an aerial car
that raced faster than thought, as their fancy prompted,
arrived at that spot where the uproar was raging.

5

The mountain-born goddess, Girijā, and Girīśa,
Lord of the mountain, were filled with overflowing joy
from parental love the moment they saw their son six-faced,
barely six days old; and their eyes welled with tears.

6

The goddess then spoke to the Crescent-Crested Lord:
'Who might this child be lying before us there, glowing with such brilliance?
Who might his father be most fortunate?
Who his mother most blessed among women blest?'

7

'For what reason are these, Gaṅgā and Agni
and the six krittikas, quarrelling among themselves,
each crying out aloud: "This is my son; he is not yours."
Why are they hotly disputing in this vain, unmannerly manner?

8

Whose child among these is he, my lord, glowing
as the beauty mark on the forehead of the Triple-World?
Or, whose else? Of Immortals or of Titans?
Of gandharvas, or of siddhas, or of the Great Snakes?'

9

To these words of his beloved eager to know,
the Crescent-Crested Lord, a radiant smile playing on his face,
spoke such words as glow with the happiness
that surges forth from the rising tide of intense joy.

10.

'Gracious lady! This hero, Gladdener of the Triple-World,
Bearer of good fortune to the Immortals,
is the son of the mother of surpassing heroes, yourself.
From whom else could such an offspring spring up?

11

Luminous One! Of this child who is the theme
of the joyous singing of the whole universe,
you are the origin ultimate; and consider this yourself.
Is not a lustrous gem born only
of the ocean-depths, the storehouse of all lustrous gems?

12

Now pay attention and listen to what truly happened;
my seed that I cast into divine Agni
entered Gaṅgā's waters; and from there passed
into the six krittikas who plunged into them to bathe;

13

that potent conception they then placed with care
in a clump of reeds. There was this being born;
a superb blossoming as never seen before
of this universe animate and inanimate.'

14

'You who are the delight of the eyes of all the worlds
have now through this child become the best of mothers
most blessed. Delay no longer, princess, mountain-born,
take your son in your arms and place him on your lap.'

15-16

As the Moon-Crested Lord was speaking thus,
the Daughter of the Mountain King and Supporter
of the entire world of things moving and unmoving,
Pārvatī, of beautiful limbs, aching in her heart
for her son, then dismounted at once
from the aerial chariot even as the whole host
of the Dwellers of the World of Light stood
in the empyrean adoring her with hands folded
and raised to the brim of their diadems.

17

Pārvatī went towards her son; in her eagerness
she passed by Gaṅgā, Agni, the krittikas and all the others
bending low before her in adoration; and did not heed them.
Who is not intoxicated with joy at a son's coming?

18

Her eyes misted with tears; for a moment
she could barely see him though he lay right before her.
The mere touch of him with the bud of her hand was enough
to fill her with happiness she had not known before.

19

No sooner did the child come into view than her eyes
opened wide with wonder and delight;
and filled with trembling tears; her heart overflowed
with the rising emotion of tenderness for him.

20

For a while she gazed upon him, wishing
she had a thousand eyes all unwinking.
Whose heart is satisfied even looking each moment
at things that bring happiness to the beholder?

21

With Immortals and Titans leading the way,
the Bright Goddess went to that child lovely as the new-risen moon,
and lifting him up with her hands beautiful
as lotuses placed him on her lap.

22

When she whose face held the moon's loveliness, set that child,
the one, unrivalled hero of the universe on her lap
that was the store of ambrosia, she became
the foremost of mothers most worthy of adoration.

23

The Sole Mother of the World was bathed
in a flood of tenderness for the only son
seated on her lap; her heart brimmed over
with excess of joy ambrosial; her breasts dripped milk.

24

As the Child of Six Mothers sucked the nectar
of her breasts, the divine river, Gaṅgā,
and the krittikas watched, looking time and again
with longing at the Mother of all the Worlds.

25

The consort of the Moon-Crested Lord, her face drenched
with tears of joy then kissed in turn with her lotus mouth,
each of the six faces of the child glowing with the glory
of a cluster of lotuses springing from the selfsame stem.

26

Like a vine on the golden mountain bearing golden fruit,
like the celestial Gaṅgā with a blossoming lotus
floating on it, like the east shining with the new risen-moon
did Pārvatī appear holding that child in her arms.

27

With the supporting arm of the Moon-Diademed Lord,
all lit within with happiness Pārvatī
mounted the sky-kissing aerial chariot with utmost caution
holding the infant securely clasped to her bosom.

28

The Great Lord, Śiva, also thrilling with joy took the boy
from the lap of the Mountain-Lord's beloved daughter,
on his own. Out of deep love for the child
the pair held the child by turn closely in their arms.

29

Clasped lovingly by the Daughter of the Mountain
holding their son, pure, the sole source of delight
ambrosial to their eyes, the Crescent-Diademed Lord returned
to his abode carried by the swiftly-racing aerial chariot.

30

Holding court in his gorgeous mansion on Kailāsa' lofty
crystal peak, Śiva commanded his host of gaṇas'
led by the pre-eminent pramathas
to arrange for a great celebration.

31

The entire host of gaṇas endowed with great qualities and skills
who attended the Lord whose vehicle was the Bull, now assembled
and in great jubilation started the preparations
for the celebration of the birth of Pārvatī's son.

32

In the halls of crystal, the gaṇas hung
festoons of leaves of Santānaka,
the tree of paradise, strung with threads of gold
that flashed filling the sky with glittering gleams.

33

Others beat deep-throated drums that resounded rolling
through space in all directions as if they were sounded
by celestials and guardian-lords of the quarters
announcing the great celebrations to the middle world.

34

In that great festival were gathered beautiful women,
of celestial gandharva and vidyādhara races,
who were welcomed into her palace by the Mountain's daughter
and duly honoured; and they sang auspicious songs.

35

The Seven Holy Mothers approached Pārvatī's son
with auspicious gifts in their hands; each in turn placed
sacred dūrva grass with coloured rice-grains on his head,
taking him into her arms like a mother.

36

As the horns, ankhya, āliṅgya and ūrdhvārka, all three,
sounded mellow and sonorous, apsaras danced
with beauty and grace to the accompaniment
of songs well-phrased, full of deep feeling.

37

Pleasant blew the breezes; all directions of space were clear;
smokeless burned the Sacred Fire; waters flowed pure;
and pellucid; the skies glowed translucent
for the festivities of Kumāra's birth.

38

War-drums in the Lord's mansions sounded high
blended with the mellow tones of conches.
Dwellers in the Light in aerial chariots
flew past showering flower petals.

39

In this fashion, the celebration of the birth of the son
of the Great Lord and Himālaya's daughter
filled the entire world, moving and fixed, with intoxicating joy;
only Tāraka's Royal Glory[4] trembled in fear.

40

And then, Kumāra captivated the hearts
of Śiva and Gaurī with delight
by his various, first playful acts of childhood.
Whose heart is not happy at the sight of a child playing?

41

The Great Lord and the Daughter of the Mountain
greedily printed long, deep kisses on his toothless mouths
so enchanting, one after the other,
repeatedly in joyous rapture.

42

The child's first attempts to move with grace,
slipping, stumbling in places, straight and steady in others,
wavering sometimes, firm and smooth at other times,
only increased the delight of the parents.

43

Climbing on to their laps all dusty from playing
in the courtyard, looking up at them and laughing
for no reason, prattling words that made no sense,
Kumāra made his parent's hearts dance with joy.

44

Seizing Śiva's mount by the horns,
stroking Umā's lion in total nonchalance,
pulling at the tip of Bhṛṅgī's thin tuft of hair,
Kumāra was the joy of his parents.

45

Seated on his father's lap, the Great Lord's son
in childish waywardness began counting
the fangs of the serpents wound round Śiva's neck,
sounding the words: one, two, five, seven, nine, ten.

46

Mistaking them to be pearls, Kumāra
put his finger into the crevices
of the skulls that hung in a garland
round Śiva's neck, to pull their teeth by force.

47

Plunging his lotus-hand into Gaṅgā's waves
rippling in Śiva's matted locks to feel their coolness,
he withdrew his hand as it turned numb with cold
to warm it at the fire of the eye in Śiva's forehead.

48

His baby neck wobbling a little, the child
reached up to the crescent of the moon set
like a diadem on Śiva's matted locks,
and out of curiosity felt it for long.

49

Girijā and Girīśa were so absorbed
all the time in their son's little tricks and whims
that totally captivated their hearts and minds
that they could not tell day and night apart.

50

Going through the many varied activities
of childhood so charming that gave his parents
ineffable happiness, delighting them each moment,
Kumāra reached the first flush of youth on the sixth day.
Indeed, the mighty god became master of all knowledge,
and gained complete mastery of all weapons.

Thus ends Canto eleven entitled *Kumārotpatti (The Birth of Kumāra),* in the long poem *Kumārasaṃbhavam* by the illustrious Kālidāsa.

Canto 12

1

Now Indra, beloved of Puloma's daughter,
with the whole host of Immortals writhing under the yoke
of the cruel Titan, came to Śiva, foe of Andhaka,
as the thirst-tormented cātaka comes to the rain-filled cloud.

2

Devastated by his fear of the arrogant Titan,
Indra, shame-faced descended with much hesitation
from the path of the rain clouds where they raced and gambolled,
towards the peak hallowed by the feet of Girijā and Girīśa.

3

Supported by the arm of his charioteer, Mātali,
Indra, The Roarer, then dismounted from his cloud-chariot,
and like a man in summer, thirst-ridden, walks towards water,
went towards the Pināka-Bearer's abode.

4

Walking on the surface of Kailāsa,
the Mountain of Crystal, Indra saw his single self
reflected becoming many selves; and then
he reached the abode of the Glorious Lord.

5

Indra came to the entrance to the courtyard
of the palace of Kāma's Destroyer, where Nandī
stood guard holding his golden staff of office, awesome
and glittering with multicoloured precious gems.

6

Leaning the golden staff in a corner of the courtyard,
Nandī at once went towards the Lord of Immortals;
welcoming him with great respect, putting his mind at ease,
Nandī went into the Lord's presence and announced Indra's arrival himself.

7

Granted permission by the Lord of the Universe
by the mere raising of an eyebrow, Nandī
walking ahead, ushered Indra together
with all the Immortals into the splendid Audience-Hall.

8

There, in that Audience Hall inlaid with presious gems,
Thousand-Eyed Indra looked upon Śiva
attended by many mighty gaṇas assuming
various forms, with Caṇḍī and Bhṛṅgī the foremost among them.

9

Tied by mighty serpent-lords whose hoods glittered with the lustre
of gems they bore on their heads, Śiva's topknot
of matted hair piled high, wore the semblance
of Sumeru's peak encrusted with rich gleaming ores;

10

wreathed with garlands of waves swirling high at the edges
of the topknot, Gaṅgā with her masses of foam
white as autumn clouds seemed to be laughing in derision
at Gaurī seated on Śiva's lap,

11

He bore on His head the nectar-rayed moon
that reflected in Gaṅgā's waves became multiple moons,
white as frost, sparkling bright from tremulous rays of light
glancing off them, making them appear luminous as snow.

12

The eye in his forehead growing in brilliance, blazing
like the world-dissolving fire at the end of an aeon,
that had once burned the dolphin-bannered god of love,
overshadowed the two eyes, the sun and the moon;

13

the sun and moon it seemed were adoring him, adorning
his ears under the pretence of being golden earrings studded
with priceless gems that spread all around circles of light—
glittering splendour immeasurable;

14

He gleamed resplendent, his blue neck scintillating
with brilliant sparkles of electric light as if Gaurī
prompted by fancy had placed round it a superb choker
all of deep blue sapphires shooting forth lustrous rays of light;

15

mantled in a huge elephant hide, his body whitened,
dusted with ashes from pyres of Immortals and Titans
mowed down by awesome Time, Śiva shone with the glory
of the Mountain of Snows with a mighty rain cloud resting on it;

16

waited upon by Viṣṇu himself who dwells in Vaikuṇṭha;
holding in his hands Brahmā's skull and the fierce trident,
weapon of death to foes in battle, lifted high;
adorned by ornaments of pieces of human bone;

17

wearing round his neck a garland of ancient skulls
of Brāḥmaṇas who, revived by streams of ambrosia
flowing down from the moon set in his diadem,
lived and breathed once more, chanting the Vedas;

18

resplendent like an autumnal cloud lit by sudden,
fitful gleams of branched lightning rapidly quivering,
Śiva glowed as well from the lustre of Himālaya's daughter
seated with exquisite grace on his lap, a slender vine of new-molten gold;

19

holding in his hand pināka, the bow of Time
that none else could lift and hold, Śiva who had taken
proud Andhaka's life and widowed the wives of mighty Titans;
to whom annihilating the Lord of Memories, Kāma was child's play,

20

Śiva sat gracing a gorgeous throne, auspicious, that was set
with priceless rubies in a variegated pattern,
and had a golden footstool, and fanned by the gaṇas,
his attendants with chowries bright as moonbeams.

21

His gaze was rivetted in boundless hapiness on Kumāra,
wholly absorbed in the study and practice of weapons and missiles,
watched with admiration by astonished gaṇas come to see him,
while the Crystal Mountain with its sparkling facets
waving lights before him, seemed to be honouring the boy.

22

Looking upon him the consort of Himālaya's daughter,
seated there in such dazzling splendour, Indra was for a moment
profoundly shaken. For who indeed is not affected
to the depths of his being seeing The Ineffable Effulgence!

23

Beholding Śiva with his thousand eyes that seemed a pool
of fullblown lotuses blowing in glory, svarga's Ruler
thrilling in awed wonder, all the hairs on his skin standing on end,
shone like a mango tree covered with clusters of blossoms.

24

Looking upon The Great Lord with all his thousand eyes, Great Indra
felt fulfilled and greatly blest; then, he realized
how disfiguring was the host of eyes covering
all his limbs, and rousing the anger of his consort.

25

Seeing Kumāra endowed with the strength and substance
of the Golden Mountain, Sumeru, and armed with weapons
and missiles, standing close to his father, Indra felt rising,
within his heart the hope of victory against his foe.

26-27

Then Nandī left his golden staff of office
in a corner and placing his palms together in reverence
spoke thus to the Destroyer of the Cities:
"O, illustrious Blue-Throated Lord! The Lord of Heaven
stands before you waiting to pay his respects.
Be pleased, O, Triple-Eyed Lord to favour
with your gracious glance the Thousand-Eyed Lord
standing in your presence waiting for your blessing."

28

Then, the Slayer of the Lord of Three Cities,
the Adored of the Three Worlds, graciously honoured
Indra adored by all the Immortals, with a glance
streaming with the essence of ambrosia.

29

The Luminous Lord, the one lord adored in svarga,
now bowed his head low before the Lord of Lords
adored by the whole world, clusters of pārijāta flowers
falling down from the points of his crown.

30

Having worshipped with devotion the Great Lord,
the One Lord worthy of adoration by all the worlds,
that Lord of Immortals, Indra, feeling immensely blessed,
became the vessel of ineffable purity.

31

Filled with devotion, the host of Immortals
stood in due order at the edge of the Lord's footstool
in front of the gaṇas, their heads bent low,
and bowed in adoration to the Foe of the Titans.

32

Indra accepted a splendid golden seat
offered by a gaṇa at the Lord's command;
seated in Śiva's presence he was filled with joy;
for who is not happy if favoured by his master?

33

All the other Immortals duly honoured
by the Lord in turn with a smile and a glance
sat down in full view of the Lord,
feeling happy that they had been singularly honoured.

34

Then the Luminous Power looking at the host of Immortals
headed by Indra standing in humble obeisance before him,
their faces drawn and pale, their glory eclipsed, overpowered
by the Titan, was moved by compassion and spoke to them thus:

35

'Ah! Dwellers in Light' You who possess weapons worthy
of great heroes, who are capable of performing
countless deeds of valour, why do you stand with faces
miserable as lotuses wilted, struck by cruel frost?

36

Dwellers in the Worlds of Light! Have you fallen from your world,
even as the count of your merit still stands high?
Do not throw away that mark of your sovereignty
that you have worn as your insignia for so long a time.

37

Dwellers in Light! Why have you left your glorious homes
to dwell on the same common level as mortal beings?
You who are great beings possessed of lofty pride,
what causes you to roam now on this earth?

38

How is it that you have lost that home so beautiful
that you earned the right to so long ago, gained
by exceptional success; by what act of transgression
did you happen to let your merit slip through your fingers?

39

You Dwellers in the Light, O nobles ones,
how did that dauntless courage of yours evaporate,
like the waters of an unfathomable lake
under the punishing heat of summer?

40

For what reasons does the great Tāraka,
conqueror of the three worlds, harbour
this bitter enmity against you Immortals
that you come here in great distress led by Indra your lord?

41

I alone have the power to challenge
the humiliation the great Titan has visited on you.
What other than a mighty raincloud
can extinguish a terrible forest fire?'

42

At these words spoken by Kāma's Destroyer,
Indra and the Immortals at once took comfort;
tears of boundless joy like waves rippled
over their faces that now regained their lost glory.

43

As Śiva had finished speaking, Indra seeing
it was the right occasion, prepared to speak.
Words spoken at the right time are bound
to bear fruit and lead to prosperity.

44

'Through the imperishable light of wisdom
that shines for ever and dispels the darkness
of ignorance, O, Lord, to you who knows all,
the past and present and the future are plainly in view.

45

Do you not know, my Lord, that Tāraka,
Destroyer of the Devas has through the might
irresistible, of his arm, gained
the sovereignty of heaven, and expelled us from there?

46

Having got an infallible boon from the Creator,
that haughty conqueror of the triple-world, invincible
through the dreaded might of his arm, regards the devas[5]
of whom I stand foremost, as worthless bits of grass.

47

Long ago, adored by us with praise songs,
the Grandparent of the Universe declared :
"The son of Kāma's Destroyer, as chief of your forces
will one day slay this Titan in battle."

48

Ah! Lord! Since that day we have borne the bitterness
of that humiliation insufferable,
even though we are divinities, luminous; and his commands as well
that wound us, alas, like arrow-heads embedded in our hearts.

49

Pray command your beloved son here, standing before you,
the joy of your heart to be the leader of our forces;
to be like the fresh raincloud that brings relief
to the herbs parched dry by summer's scorching heat.

50

Being in the vanguard of our forces, leading us
in battle, he is the one to remove our distress
by uprooting with his whole clan that mighty Titan
who is the sole barb in the heart of the Triple-World.

51

Let the ten cardinal points in space reverberate
with the lamentations of the wives of mighty Titans
whose heads severed by the sharp weapons of your son,
Great Lord, roll in the bitter battle-field.

52

There, when the mighty Titan, Tāraka, is offered up
as the sacrificial beast in the bloody battle
by Kumāra, let your son then loosen the single braids
of the lovely celestial women lying bound in captivity.

53

When Indra had thus spoken, the Enemy
of the Lord of Memories was filled with wrath
against Tāraka for his evil deeds. Taking pity
on the devas[6] the Lord of Beings spoke once more, thus:

54

'Listen, Indra and all of you, Luminous Beings,
listen to the words I speak now; this Luminous One,
Śaṅkara, will always be ready, he himself
and his son and others to accomplish your purposes.

55

Long ago, I, though I was a self-restrained ascetic,
did marry the daughter of Himālaya,
for the sole reason that the heroic son
born of her would doubtless slay The Enemy.

56

That purpose of yours is now at hand. Appoint my son,
Kumāra, to the supreme command of your forces;
destroy your enemy; may the Luminous Beings
with Indra at their head rule once more in svarga.'

57

Having spoken these words, the Glorious Lord said to his son,
eagerly thirsting to be in that bloody fray
that would be the supreme festival for him :
"Go! Slay the Foe of the devas in battle!"

58

Kumāra bending his head low in devout obeisance,
accepted the command of the Lord of Beings.
This is indeed ever the natural duty
of those prompted by filial piety.
That the Lord of Beings who is the Lord of Lords had spoken
thus to his son regarding the war with the Titans
made Pārvatī's heart swell with exultant joy; for who indeed
among mothers of heroes does not rejoice in the valorous deeds of her son?

60

Indra, Ruler of the devas having gained
the great and powerful warrior son of Umā's Lord,
who was certain to wipe off the collyrium from the eyes
of Tāraka's wives, the bane of the Immortals;
who was sure to grant freedom from fear to the universe,
at once became jubilant. Can one doubt that people
become exultant with joy when their heart's desires are fulfilled?

Thus ends Canto twelve entitled *Kumāra becomes Commander of the Celestial Armies*, in the long poem *Kumārasaṃbhavam* by the illustrious Kālidāsa.

Canto 13

1

Then Kumāra splendidly accoutred for battle,
and with the whole host of Immortals going behind him,
bowed with reverence at the feet
of the Parent of the Triple World.

2

Joyously the Lord blessed his son bowing low, and kissed
the top of his head, saying: "Slay the foe, my beloved son,
great warrior, on the battle-field and establish
firmly the Lord of Immortals in his sovereignty."

3

Bending his head low in all humility,
Kumāra then worshipped his mother's feet;
her tears of joy streaming in profusion served
as the water to consecrate him a warrior.

4

Taking him into her arms Himālaya's daughter
clasped him tightly with a mother's deep, tender love;
kissing him on the top of his head, she said: "Be victorious
over the enemy and make me the most blest mother of heroes."

5

Kumāra who had taken the vow dedicated
to the celebration that is war; who was death in person
to the Lord of Titans, Tāraka, respectfully requested permission
of Girijā and Girīśa to leave, and then set out for svarga.

6

And all the Dwellers in Light headed by Indra,
bowed to the Great Lord and the Luminous Goddess,
circumambulated the Divine Pair and followed Kumāra.

7

As the Luminous Ones without exception passed by,
their flashing aureoles scintillating, the skies blazed all around

as if a host of stars of tremendous effulgence
was shedding its brilliance even during the day.

8

And, in their midst, Kumāra shone brilliant,
with a brilliance even greater, like the splendour,
of the moon, the Night's lover, within the circle
of the constellations, the stars and the planets.

9

Indra and all his retinue of luminous divinities,
together with the son of Giriśa and Gaurī,
traversing the path of the stars, in a moment
reached their own abode glorious befiting their status.

10

Having lived under fear of the Great Titan,
the devas lingered hesitant outside svarga,
their celestial home they were seeing after so long a time;
and it was hard for them to enter straightaway.

11

With fear still haunting their minds, they began
quarrelling among themselves that very moment
over entering svarga, crying : "You'd better go first;
I will not; you enter first; I'll not lead the way."

12

Their eyes lit up with a bright smile from eagerness
to see their celestial abode once again;
but their glances fear-filled from awe of their foe
were rivetted expectantly on Kumāra's lotus-face.

13

Then Kumāra, valorous hero, looking forward
to do battle with Tāraka, and eager to go first,
spoke to the devas with a brilliant smile
playing on his face lovely as the moon.

14

'Dwellers in Light! enter svarga, now, at once;
have no fear. Let this foe of yours, Tāraka,

the Great Titan whom you have already seen,
now come right here in full view of me.

15

These shafts of mine, will here and now, drink
at once the blood of that caitiff who dares
stretch the circle of his arrogant arms out to seize
and drag by her hair, the Royal Glory of svarga.

16

And this my missile, irresistible, imbued
with supernatural power, far-sweeping in its effect,
will remove the distress of svarga's Royal Glory
and bring you joy by lopping off the enemy's head.'

17

Hearing the words of the son of Andhaka's Slayer,
whose mind was thirsting for war eager to slay the Titan,
the whole host of celestials rejoiced greatly,
their lotus-faces lit up by brilliant smiles.

18

Thousand-Eyed Indra thrilled all over with intense delight;
the hairs on his body stood erect;
he made the charming gesture of affection
of exchanging upper garments with Kumāra.

19

What a marvel indeed that the Ancient One,
the Primal Creator, his eyes overflowing
with tears of ineffable joy, kissed the tops
of Kumāra's six heads with his own four mouths.

20

Groups of gandharvas, vidyādharas and siddhas
made the son of the Destroyer of the Three Cities
exultant, praising him loudly on all sides
with joyous cries of "Victory to you, Great hero!"

21

The Luminous Sages, Nārada and others,
extolled him who was to conquer the enemy;
they expressed their deep affection with the exchange
of their bark garments with his upper garment of cloth of gold.

22

Like a herd of elephants led a by powerful tusker, the devas
casting aside all fear, feeling secure in Kumāra's power
who possessed the potent missile, were emboldened to enter svarga.

23

The Immortals at that time stood behind Girijā's son
eager for the killing of Indra's foe,
as did the pramathas who came out to stand around
Kāma's Destroyer resolved to burn the Triple City.

24

They reached the celestial stream flowing ahead,
whose waters were ever coloured red and gold
by unguents from the limbs of celestial women
throwing water around as they engaged in their water-sports.

25

The river was overflowing lapping at the base of the trees
growing on her banks to form a line of basins for their roots,
as tremendous waves arose from celestial elephants
sporting in the waters hitting them with their trunks with great force.

26

Her banks were studded with high altars of golden sands
heaped up with rubies hidden within them
by the daughters of Immortals
imbued solely with the spirit of play.

27

Pale gold were Gaṅgā's waters tinged by pollen
drifting down from golden lotuses blossoming;
murmurous with the music of bees hovering

coveting the fragrance of the lotuses;
and tremulous with the flash of wings of flights
of golden swans dipping and skimming playfully over them.

28

By offering reflections in her serried waves
of lovely celestial women standing
on the banks, drawn by eagerness to admire her beauty
the river gave joy to all passers-by.

29

Indra rejoiced greatly the moment he saw
the celestial stream that he had not set eyes upon
for a long time; then, going ahead he pointed her out
with veneration to the son of Śiva and Pārvatī.

30

Surrounded by all the Immortals, Kārtikeya[7],
looking upon that celestial river
that he had never seen before, marvelled;
his eyes were lit up by the radiance of an opening flower.

31

Coming closer to the river now extolled
by the whole host of Immortals, Kumāra
reverently raised his folded hands to the brim of his crown
and exultantly sang her praises.

32

Standing by the river, he enjoyed the breeze
fragrant from touching the blossoming lotuses,
and cool from playing with her swirling waters,
that gently fanned his cheeks to dry the sweat of fatigue.

33

Going a little further, Kumāra now saw
Indra's pleasure-garden named Nandana;
the trees in the sala-grove were all
broken and uprooted.

34

Seeing the demon-slayer Indra's garden laid waste
by the enemies of the devas, its glory vanished,
and reflecting on this, he was filled with wrath; his face
with twisted brows became terrible to look upon.

35

Kumāra then saw before him, Amarāvatī,
city of the devas, quintessence of the universe,
its pleasure-gardens ravaged, its bright mansions torn down,
and the paths of the aerial cars unfit to travel on.

36

Viewing that city conquered by a powerful foe,
shorn of her beauty, standing in a state pitiable
in the extreme like a woman whose husband
is impotent, his heart was flooded with intense pity.

37

Furious at the misdeeds of Tāraka, foe of the devas,
not downcast, but fired by the zeal to fight,
Kumāra witnessing the miserable condition
that Indra's kingdom lay in, entered it.

38

Seeing the interiors of crystal palaces smashed
by tusks of serried elephants of Titans butting them;
noting how discarded skins of mighty serpents formed networks
on lattices, Kumāra at once became dejected.

39-40

He had to bear the burden of misery intense, seeing
the pathetic sight within—lovely pools in pleasure-pavilions
where golden swans no longer came skimming lightly, gracefully,
lying soiled by the rut of the Titan's tuskers
that had overpowered the guardian-elephants of space;
clusters of golden lotuses lying around uprooted;
splendid seats all of sapphire lying shattered,
fresh grass growing in cracks and crevices.

41

Going before Kumāra, Indra led him
into his royal palace, Vaijayantī
whose golden walls were dented by the sharp tusks
of Tāraka's elephants; where the lovely webs of rubies
curtaining the halls were covered by fine cobwebs.

42

With all the devas coming behind him, and Indra
leading the way, Kumāra entered the palace
by a stairway once inlaid with many-coloured gems
prized up by the enemy and taken away.

43

Coming to that palace festooned with leaves and flowers
of the pārijāta tree, where the trees of paradise
formed a natural archway, where celestial beauties
had already entered, Kumāra was welcomed
by the great sages, luminous, with benedictions.

44

Kumāra bowed low with all his six heads
at the feet of the ancient sage, Kaśyapa,
primal ancestor of deva and daitya,
circumambulating him in reverence with palms placed together.

45

The son of The Mountain's Daughter bowed
with due reverence at the feet of Aditi,
consort of the sage, mother of the devas,
and sole object of adoration of the World.

46

The two, Kaśyapa and the mother of the devas
enhanced Kumāra's glory with such benediction
as would lend him power to overthrow in battle
Tāraka of blazing valour who aimed to conquer not one but all three worlds.

47

After that Kumāra bowed deeply at the feet
of the blessed goddesses who attended on Aditi
and who had come to see him; the chaste goddesses
one and all, blessed Kumāra extolling his might.

48

Kumāra now paid deep obeisance to Śacī,
daughter of Puloma and Indra's queen;
and she honoured him who was the son of Kāma's enemy,
and pronounced her benediction upon him.

49

Then Aditi in the company of Kaśyapa's other wives
and the Seven Holy mothers, all of one mind
filled with overflowing happiness, approached Śiva's son,
greeting him with utmost devotion, bestowing on him their blessings.

50

Indra and the leading devas, rejoicing greatly,
ineffable joy welling in their hearts, assembled;
together they consecrated Kumāra
as the supreme commander of the Celestial Army.

51

The entire world of devas now cast
all sorrow aside; they let arise
the hope of victory over the enemy;
seeing the chance of war near at hand.
Śiva's son, of infinite prowess
in possession of the splendid glory
of supreme command of the mighty
devasena, shone effulgent.

Thus ends Canto thirteen entitled *The Consecration of Kumāra,* in the long poem *Kumārasaṃbhavam* by the illustrious Kālidāsa.

Canto 14

1

Encouraged by Kumāra driven by the lust for battle,
the devas prepared themselves to attack
their enemy Tāraka, and kill him by their combined force.

2

Armed and ready with his bow and missile,[8]
Kumāra mounted the great war-chariot
Vijitvara,[9] faster than thought,
invincible, sure promise of victory.

3

Held over his head was the beautiful umbrella
of gold that would remove misfortunes besetting
the Glory of svarga, destroy the enemy's good fortune
and shatter adversaries to pieces.

4

Kinnaras and siddhas singing rousing songs of praise,
and waving beautiful chowries bright as autumnal moonbeams,
went before Kumāra wildly excited
by the impending war extolling him.

5

Behind him, riding the celestial elephant,
Airāvata, spotless white as the crystal mountains,
came Heaven's lord, Indra, dressed to march forth, wielding
his adamantine bolt that had severed the wings of mountains.

6

Following him, flame-haired Agni came, blazing in excess
with wrath rising from enmity with Tāraka;
wielding a flaming weapon and mounted
on a rutting goat huge as a mountain peak.

7

Then the stern judge, the son of the Sun, riding
a fierce buffalo, huge, dark-blue as the Sapphire Mountain,
appearing as if it had split mighty rainclouds
with its horns and thrown them down, joyously followed Kumāra.

8

Then a terrible demon, Nairṛta, blown with arrogance,
more terrible to look at from his hatred
of the great Titan, followed the son of Andhaka's foe,
thirsting for the bloody battle, mounted on a fierce goblin.

9

Terrifying in appearance as the fresh, dark rain cloud
came Varuṇa, mighty in battle, mounted
on a huge alligator and swinging his irresistible noose,
following behind the son of the Destroyer of Tripura.

10

Raring to play in the deadly game of war, Vāyu,
the Wind-God riding a deer fleet of foot, of swiftness
impetuous, able to cover space in seconds
unhindered, quickly followed the son of Maheśa.

11

Bearing a mace of enormous power that thirsted to drink the blood
of enemies, Kubera, Lord of Riches, mounted on a man
and eager and girt to plunge deep into the ocean
of the Great War, followed the Lord's dearly loved son forging ahead.

12

The Rudras came behind Kumāra, armed with pināka bows,
their matted topknots bound by the coils of mighty serpents,
riding great bulls resembling the Mountain of Snows,
holding flaming tridents of tremendous striking power.

13

Other Immortals, their lotus-faces glowing,
with radiant smiles lit by the zest
for the Great War impending, girding themselves,
mounted their mighty vehicles and brought up the rear.

14-15

And the son of the pināka-wielder rode thus to war
leading the mighty army of the Dwellers in Light:
a forest of flags fluttering on tall golden standards;
splendid royal umbrellas gleaming in variegated colours;
the tremendous sound of chariots racing like thundering clouds;
the clamorous ringing of chains of bells slung around
the necks of war-elephants; their earsplitting trumpeting;
glitter of weapons scintillating multi-hued,
circles of light that illuminated the many spheres of space.

16

The tumult raised by the mighty celestial army
on the move with their multitude of flags, made
the great circles of sky and earth and space itself stand
breathless dissolving all distinctions existing among them.

17

War drums beaten, reverberating prodigiously
in the circle of the zodiac, and magnified even more
in the hollows of space, spread the deep limitless sound
till Tāraka's Royal Glory quailed in fear.

18

With the tremendous booming of drums echoing and re-echoing
that brought about the miscarriage of the wives of Titans,
and that far surpassed the agonized roaring of the Ocean
when it was churned in the past, the skies enveloped
in clouds of dust, appeared to loudly lament.

19

Golden dust flying off Sumeru pounded,
pulverized by the tread of heavy chariot wheels,
and thundering hooves of horses, spread around
by the large, flapping ears of lordly elephants,
tossed up by fluttering flags, blown about by winds,
rose up gradually into the high vault of the sky.

20

Dust of the golden edges of the mountain, pounded
by the hooves of chariot horses was carried
to the farthest limits of space by sounding winds,
and there, they took on a beauty rare and ineffable.

21

The golden dust whirled around above and below,
in front of and behind the moving army
by the wind in many directions and high up,
surpassed the splendour of the rising sun.

22

The dust raised by that army rising from that golden ground
hung in the vault of the sky to its far reaches;
and it glowed like formations of dense clouds painted
by some twilight out of time, in hues of red and gold.

23

Each time they saw their own forms reflected on the mountain's
golden surface, great tuskers mistook them for elephants
risen out of the depths of the earth and kept
butting the reflected forms with the strong poles of their tusks.

24

But the elephants of the celestial army moving
majestically, seeing as they were dusted all over
with fine gold dust, saw no reflections of themselves
on the smooth surfaces of the golden mountain.

25

By degrees, the army of Indra, Lord of Immortals,
possessed by the craving to play in the ocean of war,
descended quickly from the golden mountain,
the resounding thunder of their descent setting up tremors in the caves.

26

Even though the mighty army rolled by with thunder
of war-chariots, the trumpeting of elephants,
the clamorous clinking of bells hanging round their necks,
lions resting deep within caves did not give up dreams of blissful sleep.

27

Lions truly deserve the appellation 'Lord of Beasts'
for they remained most unperturbed by the sound of the drums
booming deep, terrifying, magnified by reverberations

rolling within great caverns in the mountain,
and the tremendous rumblings of enormous chariot wheels.

28

As the sound that arose from the colossal army
of the devas marching was so immense as to crack
the edges of Mount Sumeru, lions became puffed up
with pride in the glory of their own prowess vested
in the undisputed lordship of the wild kingdom.

29

Deer ran far, far away, frightened of the life-threatening tumult
created by the celestial army while lions,
Lords of the Wild came playfully out of lairs deep within
caves to stand with utmost boldness free from fear.

30

The citizens of Amarāvatī and their wives
stood eager and excited watching from a great distance
the troops of the celestial army descend the slopes
of Sumeru and spread across its foothills.

31

It was easy indeed to create the illusion
of a city of gandharvas in the sky
extensively covered by the dust flying around
of minerals embedded in the outcrop of Sumeru,
the celestial mountain, of various colours,
yellow and black, white and copper.

32

The tremendous sound arising from the pounding army
and spreading to beat in the hollows of the ear
and fill the hollows of the world, agitated the ocean
and made immense billows swirl up high into space.

33

The sound of war drums was muffled
by awesome trumpeting of elephants,
the loud and harsh neighing of horses
and fierce rattling of heavy-wheeled chariots of war.

34

In an instant the dust raised by the celestial army
settled on the hair and lashes and the round orbs of the breasts
of noble ladies in the palaces of great Titans;
and on their flags, chariots, elephants and horses.

35

Wild geese looking at the sky overcast, covered with dust
of an army on the move, and seeing the sun's disc obscured,
began their flight to Lake Mānasa; and peacocks
imagining rain clouds gathering started their dance.

36

As dense clouds of dust raised by the army
were massed like thick banks of rain clouds in the skies,
the multitude of tall golden flags gleamed
like tremulous flashes of lightning.

37

Looking at the thick ceiling of dust
stretched across the vast space between sky and earth,
people started wondering if the dust
had come down from above or floated up from below.

38

The huge masses of dust clouds raised by the army spread
such a thick pall it could be pierced by the point of a needle;
no living being could see above or below,
in front or behind or at the sides.

39

The skies reverberated mightily with the unending sound
of many musical instruments augmented
by deafening echoes circling in the inner spaces
of aerial chariots; the flowing rut of the elephant corps
was dried up by the fearful commotion set afoot.

40

The mammoth army having covered the whole surface of the earth,
finding no room left anywhere was forced into the vast vault

of the sky; crowded together even there because of its great numbers,
it became uncertain what next to do.

41

From the excited trumpeting of the massive corps
of elephants flowing with excess of rut;
from the ear-splitting neighing of magnificent horses;
from the heavy, resounding tread of the wheels of chariots
majestic as dark rain clouds, the entire world
appeared to stand dazed in breathless excitement.

42

With the over powering roar of mighty tuskers,
the loud and brassy clanging of huge bells tied round their necks,
and the wild, exultant war cries of the warriors,
space in all directions became vividly articulate.

43

Rivers were flooded with waves of rut exuded
by the lordly tuskers; thundering hooves of horses pounded
the ground to dust that streamed into the water to form a film
of thick mud which the rolling chariots flattened out into level land.

44

Galloping horses beating down with their hooves,
great tuskers with their heavy, lumbering tread, chariots of war
rumbling along, all together made the land level
and flat, raising the lower and lowering the higher places.

45

The universe entire was in turmoil: the din of martial instruments
making sport of the ocean, agitating its billows,
cracking and rending outlying ridges of great mountains,
filling the sky to its farthest reaches
with terrifying reverberations.

46

Myriads of silken banners edged with tinkling golden bells
moving this way and that tossed about by the wind, stretching
across space so closely leaving no interstices

that it was hard to move around, became
lost in the skies in oceans of dust.

47

The sound of the drums was quite lost in the overwhelming din;
elephants in heat, maddened, fiercely trumpeting,
striking terror into all hearts; the furious clanging
endless of their bells spreading unease everywhere.

48

Seeing space in all directions covered in dust, the sky lost,
speaking in hideous tones through wide gaping mouths that echoed
the din raised by the army, the Lord of Day enveloped
in unfathomable, blinding darkness of dust, disappeared somewhere.

49

Witnessing the goddess who presides over the directions
violently assaulted already by the celestial warriors
and covered with dust, the vault of the sky, outraged, thundered
its wrath through the terrible reverberations of the boom of drums.

50

The array of elephants like mountains thrown up
by strong, impetuous winds plunged into the skies;
chariots wheeled on earth like massed rain clouds;
an alteration in the state of nature, it was.

51

With kings flooding into the firmament
in huge numbers, the celestial army
in full strength, raising a horrendous din,
grew still more formidable,
like turbulent oceans, boundless, that flood
the universe during that long time
at the end of an aeon, as it wound
its way to the worlds of the Titans.

Thus ends Canto fourteen entitled *The March of the Celestial Army,* in the long poem *Kumārasaṃbhavam* by the illustrious Kālidāsa.

Canto 15

1

Rumours that Indra, foe of Bala, the great Titan
having appointed Śiva's son to the command
of the celestial armies was now approaching
came to the ears of the Titans, and their hearts trembled.

2

Hearing that Kumāra, son of the Destroyer of
Kāma, World-Conqueror was leading the armies
attended by Victory herself and marching to conquer,
agitated the minds of the Titans for a very long time.

3

Assembling in Tāraka's capital, the Titan warriors
approached their great ruler bending low in obeisance,
to inform him that Indra with the son of Kāma's foe,
thirsting for victory was on his way.

4

'How many times has Śacī's lord won in battle
against me, the Enslaver of the Triple-World entire?
And is he now about to win once again with the strength
of Śiva's son' And with these words, Tāraka laughed derisively.

5

Tāraka's lower lip throbbed with anger; seized
by the itch to play again the game of winning the three worlds,
Tāraka commanded his generals puffed up with pride
in the strength of their arms, to get ready for war.

6

At once the commanders of Tāraka's great armies
took up their weapons and in a state of readiness stood
all around in the great courtyard of his palace,
thronged by a host of submissive vassal kings.

7

The emperor Tāraka saw bowing low in his presence,
his many generals all fully armed ready
to stir up into violent motion the ocean of bloody war,
each one announced by name by the warder at the gates.

8

The mighty warrior Tāraka then mounted a chariot
most awe-inspiring whose power mowed down Indra's forces;
whose sound forced into silence the trumpeting guardian elephants
of the quarters; whose progress no mountain or ocean could stop.

9

As he rode forth, his armies followed with the roar of seas
billowing turbulent at the end of an aeon;
a multitude of waving banners kept the sun's heat at bay;
the dust raised swallowed the ends of space and glittering rays of light.

10

Dust raised by the armies of the great Titans marching
against the Immortals settled on the long white tusks
of the elephants that guarded the quarters of space
covering their temples drenched in profuse rut with a muddy film.

11

The deep booming sounds of drums of his armies cracking the caverns
in the mountains stirred up the vast oceans so that the swelling tides
swept beyond their shores; the river flowing through the sky
suddenly rose to flood her banks.

12

With the tumultuous sounds of the mighty armies
of the great Titan cascading into her waters,
the celestial river overflowed till her waters
swirling up in multitudinous waves and carrying
the lotuses growing in them laved the rows
of celestial mansions.

13

A series of portents now appeared in front
of the great armies of the enemy of the devas

marching ahead, signalling his imminent fall
into the fathomless ocean of calamity.

14

Flights of grisly birds of ill-omen looking forward
eagerly to a delectable meal of Titans,
circled repeatedly over the armies of the foe
of the Immortals, flying high in the sky
without warding off the sun's hot rays.

15

A violent tempest gusting frequently shattered
the banners that provided protection from the sun;
whirling dust from earth up into the sky, blowing
it around and into the eyes, the multitudes
of horses, elephants, chariots could not be seen.

16

Suddenly mighty serpents appeared, enormous,
of terrifying aspect, lustrous as fresh-ground collyrium
frequently crossing the path of the Titan armies,
scattering before them fiery venom as they glided along.

17

The Lord of Day, as if incited by intense anger
and hatred of the great Titan, assumed a halo terrible,
terrible as coiling circles of several serpents,
awesome, prodigious that portended Tāraka's end.

18

A pack of vixens running ahead of the sun's orb
howled hideously in their excitement to drink
savagely and without delay the life-blood
of the foe of the celestials flowing on the battlefield.

19

Witnessing the rapid fall all around the armies
of Tāraka, of quivering stars, even during the day,
the world wondered if the end of the enemy
of the celestials was not near at hand.

20

And from cloudless skies, a blazing thunderbolt
spreading its scintillating flames of light
in all the directions of space, fell,
with a sound so dreadful that the hearts of onlookers cracked.

21

The sky rained burning cinders with blood
and bits of bone; the cardinal points in space
emitted through their gaping mouths,
dust-laden smoke charcoal-grey as an ass's neck.

22

The voice of the whirlwind thundering like the roar
of irate Time, The Destroyer, cleft the mountain peaks;
its tremendous volume filled the sky's hollows;
penetrating within, it split the ear-drums.

23

Through the quaking of the earth, through the swelling ocean
crashing mountains cracking them, the enemy's armies
fell into complete disarray; horses falling,
elephants stumbling, foot-soldiers falling into each other's arms.

24

Dogs all assembling bayed aloud lifting up their heads,
fixing their gaze on the sun. Tormented beyond
endurance by the ear-splitting sounds they howled piteously
in unison as they slunk past the armies of Tāraka.

25

Even though fully aware of this grim series of omens
foreboding; even though dogged by signs of disaster
impending; facing the direst of consequences,
Tāraka would not turn back, but in anger pursued his set course.

26

Though apprehending the dire consequences that would come
in the wake of these ill-omened events; though wise elders
did their best to dissuade him from his course, he still marched forth.
Wise counsel is always lost on those blinded by capricious resolve.

27

Tāraka's golden umbrella that shielded him from the sun
was flung down by an adverse gust of wind and lay
on the earth shining like a large golden dish
set out ready for Death to have its meal.

28

His royal crown seemingly possessed of intelligence,
knowing that soon Tāraka's head would fall severed,
wept bitterly, dropping one after the other
in quick succession, its tears of tremulous pearls.

29

Vultures circled repeatedly round him
though constantly driven off and swooped down on his head
as if eager to seize and devour him, sending
in this manner messages of his imminent death.

30

The world looking on saw all at once a huge cobra
on his banner, glossy black as fresh-ground collyrium,
the jewel on its expanded hoods gleaming encircled
by flaming rays of light; and it was hissing, shooting forth
firebrands pregnant with deadly poison.

31

Then a huge blazing fire broke out in the axle pin
of Tāraka's massive chariot of war, and in no time,
burnt the hair of the horses, the bright nodding plumes
at their ears and his quiver full of arrows.

32

When the great Titan blinded by arrogance, obstructed
time and again by such menacing happenings
that clearly conveyed dire warnings of coming disaster,
still would not retreat, an incorporeal voice rang out
from the skies, crying :

33

'O, Titan blinded by conceit! Proceed no further,
driven by overweening confidence in the prowess
of those powerful arms of yours to battle with the son

of the Destroyer of Kāma, riding all girt for victory,
and surrounded on all sides by Indra and other Immortals.

34

Guha, son of Śiva, born but six days back will not brook
an encounter in the battlefield with the dark Titan forces,
just as the blazing sun will not permit the darkness of night
to face him. Why then this enmity of yours against him?'

35

Why think of fighting with him who with his arrow
cleft and formed a pass in the Krauñca Mountain
encircled by a hundred sky-kissing peaks,
and hidden by the circles of the quarters of space?

36-37

Jamadagni's son, the all-devouring dark night
at the end of Time to kṣatriya clans, having learnt
the archer's art from Śiva, calmed down only after
he had quenched the fire of his fury in battle,
sprinkling himself ritually thrice-seven times
with rich, streaming blood of kings;
even he would not dare to face in battle
this leader of armies, a warrior unrivalled
in the three worlds. So where is the space for you
to stand and fight him?

38

'You fool, misled by overweening presumption,
give up your pride at once. Go not within the range
of the son of Kāma's Destroyer. Throw yourself on the mercy
of this greatest warrior in the world so that you may live long.'

39

Hearing these grave, warning words spoken in the sky,
the great Titan, full of himself and arrogant,
who had made the three worlds tremble, now trembled himself;
in anger he vehemently addressed the skies:

40

'You wretched sky-rangers! What kind of words are these?
Mighty celestials, are you now taking the side
of the son of Kāma's enemy? Have you forgotten
all the pain of the wounds made by my arrows?

41

Dwellers in the sky, why are you all raving shrilly
like mad dogs barking at midnight in the month of Kārtika?
Or like wild beasts howling confusedly in the woods?
And all because of the power of a child barely six days old!

42

Like an innocent man falling in with thieves,
this wretched child, miserable right from its birth,
will certainly meet its death from being in your company.
I shall kill you first and then this child.'

43

When the great Titan had thus spoken in anger
the devas fled to a great distance in abject terror
hitting one another with their knees as they ran.

44

Watching them, Tāraka, seated in his magnificent chariot,
laughed long and loud in great derision; drawing his wondrous sword
out of its scabbard he said to his charioteer:
"Drive the chariot quickly, Sir, to where Indra stands."

45

Riding in his chariot swifter than thought,
the great Titan soon came along the ocean
of celestial armies marshalled before him
in all its terrifying aspect.

46

Looking at that mammoth army of the Immortals
drawn up before him, the warrior, eager for battle,

felt a rush of thrills of pleasure coursing
through his strong arms stout as sturdy staves.

47

Then, the pick of Indra's warriors advanced to the front
faster than thought, seized by the boundless zest
for playing the game of war. Who would delay
when he is possessed by the tremendous desire to fight?

48

The fiercest warriors in Tāraka's armies
then approached the ocean of Indra's forces facing them,
and raising their arms high into the air,
loudly announced their specific names to their foes.

49

The great chieftains among the devas seeing the vast ocean
of enemy forces before them were trembling, agitated.
But Śiva's son measured the opposing armies
with a casual glance out of the corner of one eye
which showed sheer contempt for the war.

50

Seeing that the celestial armies were shaking in terror
at the sight of the enemy forces, Śiva's beloved son
threw an ambrosial glance in their direction
to reassure them and encourage them to fight their great war.

51

Encouraged by Kumāra's glance, the devas,
eaters of sacrificial offerings, led by Indra,
were cheered up, each saying 'I shall fight to win'
Who is not inspired to do their best when in the company of the best?

52

The warriors on Indra's side and Tāraka's as well,
raised aloft their weapons as the heralds on both sides
called out their names in loud, shrill voices
and advanced towards each other to fight and win.

53

The two armies of deva and daitya
fought to annihilate each other,
breaking all rules, transgressing
all accepted bounds.
Stretching over space to its ends,
they raised a commotion that could easily
rend and crack the sides of mountains
covered by lofty cedars and fill
the hollows within the World-Egg.
They enjoyed to the full
Death's bountiful hospitality.

Thus ends Canto fifteen entitled *The Clash of The Armies of Deva and Daitya*, in the long poem *Kumārasaṃbhavam* by the illustrious Kālidāsa.

Canto 16

1

Between the two armies, deva and daitya
a great battle then took place;
they hurled at each other clusters
of deadly arrows and deadlier missiles.

2

Foot soldiers against foot soldiers;
cavalry-man against cavalry-man;
elephant-borne against the elephant-borne;
chariot-riding warrior against the chariot-borne.

3

As warriors darted here and there
to attack enemy warriors,
bards, skilled of their kind, moved around
proclaiming each name to give each due praise.

4

As bards chanted a string of lauds celebrating
their mighty deeds, the warriors paused
a moment giving ear to the praises,
and inspirited then started fighting again.

5

As the opposing warriors met head-on,
thrills of excitement and the joy
of the battle growing great, their bodies
expanded, their coats of mail split open.

6

As coats of majl were pierced and torn to shreds,
mercilessly, out flew the stuffing;
bits of cotton that caused the sky
to turn grey as with white hair.

7

Swords glistened, streaked with blood,
flashing around with glittering lustre,
like the ray-fingers of fiery suns;
they wore the glory of lightning gleams.

8

Discharged by skilled warriors driven
by furious rage, the shafts vomiting
flaming meteors like huge awesome snakes,
filled entire space with fire.

9

Arrows shot by archers at each other
tore into bodies and then came out
tipped with blood to enter
deep into the earth.

10

In that great festival of war, arrows
shot by the best warriors, in exultation,
struck elephants, piercing and felling them first
to the ground, then falling down themselves.

11

As volleys of arrows with flaming heads
flew thick and fast filling space
leaving no space in between, celestials
in their aerial cars high in the skies, fled far.

12

The sky riddled by the archers' cruel arrows
moaned aloud it seemed, conveying
the pain of its wounds in the guise
of echoes of the raucous cries of hawks.

13

Shafts released from bows drawn right back
to the ear, flew great distances,
leaping forward as it were, greedy
to taste the blood of warriors.

14

Row upon row of swords leaping out
of their sheath and held in the hands of warriors,
seemed to be laughing with boundless joy,
weaving webs of light-rays on the battlefield.

15

Dancing gaily in valorous hands,
swords drunk with blood, glittered
with boundless glory of lightning flashes
in that dust-laden battlefield, endless.

16

The lances of warriors glittered passionately
like so many tongues of Yama,
God of Death, hanging out drooling
in the courtyard of war.

17

Whirling in the battlefield of the sky
flashing circles of radiance, scattering
splendour like the splendour of the angry sun
were wheels of stupendous chariots of war.

18

Some warriors were knocked off their mounts
by the thundering roars of warriors charging furiously,
others dizzied again and again,
fell senseless out of their vehicles.

19

A certain warrior mightily exhilarated
seeing some warrior or other approaching
intent on killing him was deeply
disappointed to see him slink away in fear.

20

Heroes, bold and daring, having fought
many warriors in battle, turned around
to fight with those they had already
encountered in battles before.

21

Warriors with the hairs on their brawny arms
standing erect because of the battle-lust
consuming them rejoiced to see all around them
battle-hardened heroes approaching to fight them.

22

Pearls fallen from globed temples of elephants,
broken open by missiles, fell
on the battle-ground to sprout
as if they were seeds of glory.

23

Elephants terrified by wild cries
of soldiers, disregarding the wounding control
of sharp goads ran trumpeting
to far horizons in distant space.

24

Great tuskers riddled with showers of arrows,
wandering riderless on the plains of war,
dived into rivers flowing with blood.

25

Warriors riding chariots which though
high off the ground were immersed deep
in rivers of blood, infuriated, bellowing,
continued to shoot arrows from within.

26

Warriors mounted on chargers,
dismembered their enemies with their swords,
even as their own heads were severed,
before falling off their mounts.

27

With fierce aspect, biting the lower lip,
severed heads of great warriors
leapt forward to pursue the enemy even
even as they fell to the ground.

28

Holding the heads of warriors severed clean
by crescent-headed arrows, falcons
flew filling the skies.

29

Infuriated foot soldiers and mounted horsemen,
clambered up the tusks of elephants
to skewer their riders with their lances.

30

Elephants whose riders had been mown down
by arrows, wandered here and there
looking like mountains uprooted
by whirlwinds bearing down at the end of the world.

31

Mercenaries mounted on elephants
charging elephants, attacked
with reckless courage to take
each other's life with powerful weapons.

32

From the violent clash of tusks of elephants
charging furiously at one another, arose
all on a sudden a fire that burnt the bodies
of warriors whose lives were already forfeit to missiles.

33

Soldiers who were picked up bodily
by elephants with their trunks and thrown with force,
yet managed to kill them with sharp strokes
of their swords before the eyes of their masters.

34

Warriors who had been hurled a long way up
into the skies by elephants attained
the world of eternal light;
their bodies fell to earth.

35

Soldiers lopped off the trunks of tuskers
with their bright-edged swords and felled them
to the ground laying them flat on the earth;
yet they were not satisfied.

36

Soldiers who were snatched up and flung up
into the air by the curling trunks of elephants,
having reached the World of Light were soon
sought after eagerly by love-smitten celestial women.

37

Bowmen mounted on horses waited
for warriors riding elephants who had fainted
from bleeding arrow-wounds to revive and rise up
so that they could fight them again.

38

A soldier lusting after the tusk
of an irate elephant, severed it
with his sword and clambered up
its pestle of a tusk to take it.

39

Having penetrated the enemies' ranks,
a soldier severed the twin tusks
of a lordly elephant, only
to retreat quickly and flee.

40

Seized with great strength by an irate tusker,
a warrior on a horse quickly despatched it,
himself remaining unhurt.

41

Another warrior, a mounted lancer,
pierced an enemy lancer in the chest
with his lance, barely realizing as he fell
that he himself was pierced through the heart.

42

A certain warrior killed by the lance of his foe
still holding high his powerful lance sat firmly
on his seat while his horse galloped all over the plain;
and he seemed as if he were still alive.

43

With tears rolling down from his eyes,
a majestic horse still stood and would not abandon
his rider lying dead on the bare earth,
waiting for him to rise up again.

44

Dismembered by the razor's edge of his enemy's
crescent-headed spear, a certain warrior
did not fall into a faint though he fell
off his horse; but enraged he yearned to kill his foe.

45

Struck by spears, knocked off their horses,
warriors in a fury fought with each other
on foot, with their daggers; while others
fought with bare hands violently pulling each other's hair.

46

Warriors fighting from chariots who killed their enemies
riding in chariots, seeing them still firmly seated
only their grip on the bows loosening
mistakenly took them to be still alive.

47

No warrior in a chariot would ever strike
another in a chariot reeling under a blow and fainting,
but eager to fight him once again,
he would wait for his enemy to revive.

48

Warriors fighting with choicest weapons,
having killed one another entered paradise;
and there they continued to fight
over the possession of the selfsame apsara.

49

Warriors riding in chariots after decapitating
their enemies with crescent-headed javelins,
ranging the skies blazing with glory, looked down
to see their headless torsos dancing on earth.

50

As trumpets blared and a ghoulish company
of corpse-eating female goblins sang, a long line
of headless bodies grasping weapons in their hands danced
in the strangest manner on the slimy, blood-soaked battle field.

51

While the armies of Immortals and Titans
fought each other in the war described above,
and on the battle plains an array
of war-elephants were sunk deep in mud
on the banks of rivers of blood,
Tāraka, his eyes red with boundless rage,
his beetling eyebrows twisting menacingly,
advanced that very moment, raring to fight,
towards the dikpālas, the presiding guardians of the quarters of space.

Thus ends Canto sixteen entitled *The Description of the War of Immortals and Titans*, in the long poem *Kumārasaṃbhavam* by the illustrious Kālidāsa.

Canto 17

1

Seeing the Supreme Lord of Titans at close quarters
facing them, the dikpālas brimming with boundless joy
born of the zest to play the game of war,
now proudly joined forces in the vault of the sky
darkened by flights of arrows, planning to fight Tāraka.

2

Like some huge, diluvial raincloud letting loose
unremitting, heavy downpours on colossal mountains,
the Chief of Foes of the devas burst out
in thunderous laughter showering the Immortals
with a rapid succession of deadly arrows.

3

Like a gathering of sun-bright falcons ripping straight
into an assemblage of snakes, the sharp arrows shot at once
by Indra and the other dikpālas shredded in no time
the rain of shafts discharged by the dānava Lord.

4

As Fire leaping across the skies in all directions would burn
to cinders bundles of grass that might cover the intervals
of space between cardinal points, so did the Foe of the Immortals
the shafts of the celestial armies with his own massive flood
of terrible arrows tipped with flaming points and marked with his name.

5

The flight of winged arrows that the daitya Lord blazing with the anger
making him appear exceptionally awesome let loose
with an easy-going air of contempt for the battle, were now
transformed into hissing serpents of horrible aspect
that firmly bound Indra and other leading deva chiefs.

6

The dikpālas chief of whom was Indra, Demon-Slayer,
tightly bound by the Great Titan's serpent-cords turned tail

and fled the battle-field. Choking for breath they rushed
to the presence of the son of Śiva, Kāma's Foe,
their sole refuge and the means to end their misery.

7

Freed by the power of a mere glance of Kumāra,
son of the Destroyer of the Cities, from the torment
of being bound tight in serpent nooses, the dikpālas
came bodily before the indomitable hero to extol him.

8-9

The ire of Indra's Foe that burned inexorably like Fire
now kindled, Tāraka with arms of indomitable power,
spoke at once to his charioteer : 'With what violent force
did I not bind the Indra-led devas; yet, a mere glance of a child,
the son of Him Who Wears a Great Matted Topknot, has freed their bonds.'

10

Then, Tāraka's chariot of war, expertly-driven, formidable,
rushed forward instantly with the rolling thunderous sound
of turbulent rain-packed clouds, crashing through mangled bodies
of Indra's armies, its wheels becoming besmeared
with the slime of pulped flesh, blood and bones.

11

The celestial armies shivered in terror watching
the chariot, racing swiftly, advancing upon them,
resembling Himālaya shaking buffeted by winds
of the World's Dissolution. As the chariot hurtled
through Indra's forces breaking their ranks, destroying them,
scattering them, it was even more awe-inspiring from the tumult
of terrible shrieks and wails that rose from the celestial armies.

12

Seeing the armies of the devas gripped by terror, the great Titan
fierce-looking, gripping hard his stout bow-staff in his powerful arm,
strode towards Kārtikeya, son of Śiva who stood raring
to engage in the sport of war, and spat out these words at him.

13

'Hey, you there, son of that hermit Śiva, come, come,
give up this pride in the strength of your twin arms.

Desist from your efforts to further Indra's cause.
What use are these weapons you brandish, so unbecoming
to your tender years, Sir; such a heavy burden to lay
on the delicate arms of a mere child.

14

Child! You are the only son of Gaurī and Girīśa.
Why such keenness to enter Death's kingdom, coming
within the range of my punishing arrows?
Leave the battlefield, and live. Go back at once;
crawl quickly into the arms of your parents and make them feel blest.

15

Son of Girīśa! Having considered well this point,
relinquish your hostility to me, Indra's foe.
Indra himself is drowning in impassable waters;
and like a boat made of stones, he'll draw you down with him.'

16

Hearing these words spoken on the battlefield by Tāraka,
the son of The Three-Eyed Lord filled with wrath, looked towards his bow;
in anger, his lower lip quivered, his eyes grew flaming red
as a fully-opened red lotus; mindful of his own strength,
Kumāra responded to Tāraka in kind.

17

'Supreme Lord of Titans, these words you have spoken
are indeed words you might be expected to speak.
I shall test the strength of those twin arms of your so celebrated.
So take up your bow; draw its string taut.'

18

To these words of Siva's son, the Titan replied
curling his lip in supreme disdain : 'You are swollen with pride
in the strength of your twin arms; now bear the onslaught
of my shafts that struck my enemies in their backs.'

19

Drawing taut the bowstring Tāraka awesome appeared unbearable
to his enemies like a lord of serpents roused to fury intense,

as he wielded his terrible longbow that instantly spat forth
volleys of sharp arrows thirsting for victory; they flew at Kumāra.

20

The bowstring stretched back to his ear, the fiery bow
delivered innumerable shafts all around, streaking
the courtyard of the sky with dazzling stripes of white light, it seemed
space in all directions was sprouting so many white hairs.

21

Unending lines of arrows with luminous tips discharged
by Tāraka's bow wove glittering webs of light-rays that struck
terror into the hearts of celestial warriors with their terrifying whizzing,
and blinded them with their effulgence so that they could not
see where Śiva's son stood.

22

Then Śiva's glorious son drew taut the string of his bow
stretching it up to his ear; and it delivered a volley
of sharp shafts that thirsting for victory at once shivered
to fragments the arrows pouring out of Tāraka's bow.

23

Once the pall of gloom cast by Tāraka's arrows
overhanging the skies to the extreme distress of sky-rangers lifted,
Śiva's son shone in unbearable dazzling splendour
like the Lord of Radiance released from thick, veiling clouds.

25

With his face discoloured by anger, contorted by outraged laughter,
the Titan lusting after world-dominion realized the futility
of fighting Kumāra with conventional weapons; and instantly fitted
on his bow with utmost unconcern a missile charged with
the power of the Wind-God.

26

The moment it was discharged, the missile zoomed ahead
with horrendous roar,
unimaginably terrifying, creating raging hurricanes : whirling clouds
of dust covered all space, veiling the hot-rayed sun;
all beings ran demented as if it were the day the world ended.

27

All the royal parasols bright as jasmines, held over
warriors in the celestial armies were blown away by the winds;
as they floated in the skies darkened by clouds of dust,
they looked like flights of splendid white swans coursing through the sky.

28

Banners of the armies of the devas glowing like fresh, bright jasmine-sprays,
were shredded by the whirlwinds and carried high up into the sky's vault
where they danced gaily like so many floating streamers displaying
the thousand graces of the mighty streams of the heavenly river, Gaṅgā.

29

The mighty elephants of the devas were tossed about and hurled
down to the earth; their howdahs and trappings were broken;
they seemed to be the great mountains that fell on earth
when their wings were clipped by an irate Indra.

30

Wild winds toppled the many serried rows of celestial chariots,
repeatedly battering them, sending the horses rapidly swirling
in the air, headlong down to earth; and the charioteers, skilled,
of renowned families, thrown off, tumbled into the sky.

31

Throwing away their weapons, the celestial cavalry
at the centre battered by the terrible winds,
fell off their magnificent steeds; so swift was their fall
that they remained untouched by arrows even as they fell.

32

Pounded hard by the winds, the infantrymen as well
of the celestial armies dropped their weapons, scoured
by excruciating agony, and lamenting bitterly;
hurled high up into the air by twisting tornadoes,
from the roof of the sky they fell to the surface of the earth.

33

Seeing the entire army of the devas paralyzed
by Tāraka's use of the wind-powered missile so potent,
and zealous in guarding well Indra's Royal Fortune,
the glorious lord, Kumāra put forth his divine powers.

34

Released thus from the baleful effects of the enemy's missile,
the celestial forces regained their strength and spirit
ready to fight once again. Seeing this, Tāraka burning with rage
released at once the flaming missile of the Fire-God.

35

Masses and masses of thick smoke glowing like dark-blue lotuses
gathered instantly on the horizon like dense, scurrying rain clouds
veiling the quarters of space in blinding darkness
until nothing was visible to the eye.

36

Seeing the clear, arching vault of the sky turn deep blue,
enveloped in smoke-swirls as if overcast
by a great mass of moist, rain-packed clouds, wild geese rejoiced,
filled at once with deep longing for high Mānasa Lake.

37

A fire beyond all compare, that seemed the very image of the fire
burning at the world's dissolution blazed on all sides
of the celestial forces turning the bright faces of the quarters,
and the entire sky tawny with a network of multitudinous flames.

38

As the marvellous flames unceasing of that rampant fire
blazing unhampered shot high up row upon fiery row,
swirling smoke-phalanxes billowed; it seemed massed rain clouds
shot through with brilliant flashes of lightning rolled through space.

39

Panic-stricken, the celestial luminaries lost
their bearings in space; the entire army of the devas
singed again and again by that unendurable blaze,
suffering agony beyond endurance came to Śiva's son.

40

Then Kumāra seeing the celestial forces wan, lustreless,
completely o'erpowered by that tremendous blaze,

with a smile playing on his lotus face, fixed on his bow
the terrible missile of Varuṇa, God of Waters.

41

Like dense smoke spewed forth by the World-Devouring Fire
at the end of Time, there arose in the sky a massive cloud
wearing the terrible shape of utter darkness, and rending
great mountain peaks with peal upon peal of rumbling thunder.

42

Forked lightning blindingly dazzling flashed forth
as if it were the hideous lolling tongue of Death itself
at the dissolution of the universe; it turned the horizons livid,
and roused dread amazement as deep awesome thunder rolled.

43

A bank of clouds, water gurgling in their throats,
streaked by fitful flashes of lightning leaping high
in the vault of the sky, glistened, illuminating the horizons
and veiling the sight, striking terror in hearts,
as if it were a long line of clouds of darkness
investing the fearful Night of Dissolution.

44

The roof of the sky was all overcast
with huge masses of clouds relentlessly pouring
steady torrents of rain, while unremitting
thunder made hearts quail in terror.

45

Clouds born of the Varuṇa missile thundered hideously,
spreading thick their layered darkness across the skies,
greatly tormenting the Titan's forces, and with their never-ending
downpours quenching the fire raging in the belly of the universe.

46

The great Titan, flaming with anger boundless,
bent his bow fully to let fly at Śiva's son
sharp arrows tipped with fine-honed razor blades,
so fierce that the celestial forces fled in terror.

47

As the yogi, sapless, drained of desires
from the practice of yoga breaks the potent bonds
tying him to the world of the senses,
by ascetic discipline, so did the glorious Kumāra
infused with enthusiasm for the sport of war
break into minute particles, Tāraka's bow and arrows.

48

The sovereign lord of the Titans looking fierce,
his face distorted by exploding fury, dismounted
and brandishing his venomous, gleaming sword,
leapt forward to stand facing Śiva's son.

49

Seeing that supreme monarch of all Titans, the power of whose arm
made the celestial forces tremble, rushing upon him,
Śiva's son, his lotus face radiant with joy, released a missile
that was like the Fire that consumed the universe at the end of Time.

50

That spinning missile illuminating all space
with scintillating circles of light, went straight to the heart
of the great Titan; great was the joy of the devas,
and bitter the burning tears of sorrow the dānavas let fall.

51

Seeing the Lord of Titans fatally struck by the missile
fall on the ground like a mountain peak hit
by world-destroying storms at the end of Time,
the devas led by Indra were jubilant.

52

Where he fell heavily, that mighty Titan monarch,
son of Danu, falling like a lordly peak,
the earth sank; Śeṣa, Lord of Serpents holding the Earth
on his expanded hoods felt the shock in an agony of pain.

53

A shower of blossoms of the trees of paradise, cooled by the spray
of the celestial river, Gaṅgā and circled by swarms of honeybees
drawn by the exquisite fragrance, fell from the skies
from all sides, over Kumāra, Foe of the Immortals' Foe.

54

Headed by Indra, the entire host of devas rejoiced,
swelling with such happiness as to burst the seams of their armour;
with faces radiant with lustre lent by boundless delight,
they came to Kumāra with high praise for the might of his arm.

55

Thus it was :
Once the mighty dānava Tāraka,
the thorn in the side of the Triple World
was laid low in battle by Kumāra,
the victorious son of Śiva; Indra gained once more
the sovereignty of the World of Light; his toes
were touched by gems set in the diadems of devas.

Thus ends Canto seventeen entitled *Tārakāsura Vadha (The Slaying of Tāraka)*, in the long poem *Kumārasaṃbhavam* by the illustrious Kālidāsa.

Meghadūtam

(The Cloud Messenger)

Meghadūtam

1

A certain yakṣa[1] unmindful of his appointed duties
and cursed by his lord to endure
a year's grievous separation from his beloved
dwelt exiled, his lustre dimmed, on Rama's hill[2]
in hermitages thick with shade-trees and waters
hallowed by the touch of Janaka's daughter.

2

The impassioned lover having passed some months
on that hill, parted from her unsupported
—the golden armlet slipping down
to lay bare his wasted fore-arm—
saw on āṣāḍha's[3] most auspicious day
a cloud embracing the crest of the hill,
strikingly-shaped[4] like a sportive elephant
bent down to butt a river bank.

3

Gazing on that which stirs the ketaka to bloom
the vassal lord of the King of kings
brooded long,
with effort restraining his tears.
The sight of rain clouds makes even happy hearts
stir with restlessness;
what then of one far from her who longs
to hold him in close embrace.

4

With the month of rains approaching,
desiring to sustain his beloved's life,[5]
hoping to send glad tidings of his well-being
through the life-giving cloud, he made with reverence
an offering of fresh blossoms of wild jasmine,
prefacing it with words of affection,
and joyously welcomed the cloud.

5

Blended of mists and light, winds and water
can a mere cloud bear messages
that only the living with keen senses
and intelligence can convey?
Unmindful of this the yakṣa entreated it,
overwhelmed by unreasoning eagerness;
indeed, the love-sick, their minds clouded,
confuse the insentient with the sentient.

6

Born in the lofty lineage of swirling diluvial clouds,
I know you are the god of thunder's minister
assuming what shape you will; so, banished
from wife and kinsmen by divine decree, I entreat you;
for it is nobler to address barren pleas
to the virtuous than fruitful to the vile.

7

You are the refuge, O Rain-Giver
for all who burn with anguish;[6] so bear
a message from me parted from my love
by the wrath of the Lord of Treasures;
go then to Alakā,[6a] abode of the yakṣa Lord,
her palaces washed by moonlight
streaming from Śiva's brow
where He is seated in her outer groves.

8

Women whose husbands travel to far lands,
pushing back their straggling hair
will eagerly look up to see you
riding high on the path of the wind,
and draw comfort; for when you arrive
all clad and girt for action,
who can ignore his lonely wife distraught
unless subject like me to an alien will?

9

While a friendly breeze impels you gently
as you loiter along, and here on your left
the cātaka in its pride sings sweetly,
hen-cranes will know the time ripe for mating
and rejoice when they note in the sky
your eye-delighting presence; rest assured
they will attend on you in patterned flight.

10

Arriving there unimpeded you are certain
to see that constant lady,
your brother's wife,[7] still living
engrossed only in counting the days;
Hope's slender thread serves to hold
the flower-hearts of women
tender and prone to droop too soon
under the burden of separation.

11

And, hearing your thunder—a sound sweet to their ears—
that can make Earth unfurl her mushroom parasols,
regal swans longing for Mānasa-lake,[8]
gathering tender lotus-shoots for the way
will be your companions in the sky
even up to Mount Kailāsa's peak.

12

Embrace and bid farewell to your loving friend,
this lofty mountain[8a] girdled by slopes marked
by the holy feet of the Lord of Raghus[9]
adored by the world.
Time and again, reuniting with you,
it displays its affection, breathing out,
burning sighs born of long separation.

13

Listen first, while I describe the way
fitting for your journey which you will follow
resting your foot on mountains when weary,
refreshed when wasted by the clear water of streams:
then you shall hear my message, O Rain-Giver,
drinking it in eagerly with your ears.

14

While simple siddha[10] maidens with upturned faces,
watching your impetuous power tremble in alarm
and cry: 'Is the wind carrying off the mountain's peak?'
soar high up into the sky facing north,
far above this thicket of sap-filled nicula,[11]
shunning on your path the proud sweep of the heavy trunks
of the elephants[11a] that guard the sky's quarters.

15

Here before you, a fragment of Indra's bow[12]
springs spectacular from the hill top, gleaming
as if blended of the lustre of brilliant gems.
Shot through by its sheen, your dark-blue body
shines resplendent like Viṣṇu's in his cowherd guise,
lit up by iridescent peacock-plumes.

16

While rustic women unversed in eyebrow play[12a]
drink you in with eyes moist with happiness

knowing the harvest to depend on you,
mount at once the upland fragrant from fresh furrowing;
veering slightly to the back, then once again
with a light step head straight north.

17

As you approach the noble mountain Citrakūṭa,[12b]
he will greet you, O travel-weary Rain-Giver,
and bear you on his head held high: you too
with sharp showers will quench summer's cruel fires.
The tenderness of true feeling in the great
bears fruit in no time, returning kindness for kindness.

18

With his forest fires fully quenched by your sharp showers,
Āmrakūṭa[13] will bear you gratefully
on his crown, travel-weary as you are;
even the meanest remembering former favours
will not turn his face away from a friend
who seeks shelter; what then of one so lofty!

19

Its slopes all aglow with the ripened fruit
of wild mangoes, and you on its peak set
like a coil of dark glossy hair, the mountain
—seeming Earth's breast, dark-blue centre
encircled by pale-gold expansive curves—
will appear entrancing to celestial lovers.

20

Resting awhile on that mountain
in whose bowers the brides of foresters sport,
and lightened by your waters' outpouring
you'll speedily cross the road beyond
and see Revā's[14] streams spreading dishevelled
at Vindhya's holy feet rugged, rock-strewn,
inlaying them like ashen streaks[14a]
decorating an elephant's body.

21

Your rain disgorged, draw up that river's water
whose flow impeded by rose-apple brakes
is pungent with the scent of wild elephants in rut,
and journey on; gaining inner strength
the wind cannot make light of you, O Rain-Cloud;
for hollowness makes things light; fullness bestows weight.

22

Seeing the green-gold Nīpa flowers
with their stamens half-emerging
and the Kandalīs showing their early buds
along the edge of every pool,
savouring the rich fragrance of the earth
in the forests burnt by fire,
antelopes will chart your path as you pass
shedding fresh rain drops.

23

Siddhas watching cātakas
skilled catching falling rain drops
and pointing out to egrets in flight
counting them on their fingers,
will pay you their grateful respect,
suddenly obtaining a flurry of unexpected embraces
from their beloved wives clinging to them in alarm
trembling at the sound of your thunder.

24

Even though you would wish to proceed with speed
for the sake of my happiness, my friend,
I foresee delay while you loiter
on peak after peak fragrant with wild jasmine;
though peacocks, their eyes moist with joy may greet you
with welcoming cries, I pray you, try to hasten onward.

25

The Daśārṇas[15] will put on a new beauty
at your approach:
woodlands ringed round by ketakas
with needle-pointed buds newly-opened
will glow a pale gold:
birds starting to nest will throng
the sacred peepuls in the village squares:[15a]
rose-apple groves will darken[15b]
with the sheen of ripening blue-black fruit;
and wild geese settle for a few days.

26

When you reach that royal city, Vidiśā[16] by name
widely renowned, you shall at once obtain
the unalloyed fulfilment of a lover's desire,
tasting Vetravatī's[17] sweet waters as a lover his beloved's lips,
with sonorous thunder passing along her banks
as she flows with knitted brows of tremulous wavelets.

27

There you shall alight seeking rest on Nicaī hill[18]
thrilling with delight at your touch
as kadaṃbas burst into sudden bloom;
the hill loudly proclaims through grottoes
exhaling fragrances of pleasure,
passions unrestrained of the city's youth
dallying there in love-sports with courtesans.

28

Having rested, go on, sprinkling with fresh rain drops
clusters of jasmine-buds in gardens by woodland streams,
enjoying a fleeting together-ness
as your gift of shade touches
the faces of flower-gathering maidens, who
each time they wipe the sweat off their cheeks, bruise
the wilting lotuses hung at their ears.

29

As your course points due north to Alakā,
the way to Ujjayinī[19] is a detour no doubt,
but do not therefore turn away from a visit to her palace-terraces.
Indeed you would have lived in vain if you do not dally there
with the tremulous eyes of the city's beautiful women
that dart in alarm at the branched lightning's flashes.

30

On your path, when you meet Nirvindhyā[20]
wearing a girdle strung of chiming bells
—a row of water-birds plashing on her undulating waves—
weaving her sinuous course with charming unsteady gait
to reveal eddies forming her navel
—such coy gestures are women's first statements of love—
be sure to be filled with love's fine flavour.

31

Crossing that river, O fortunate lover,
yours will be the happy task to induce Sindhu[21]
visibly grieving at your absence,
her waters shrunk to a thin braid and pale
with the paleness of dry leaves
fallen from trees rooted on her banks,
to cast off the sorrow withering her.

32

Reaching Avanti whose village-elders
are well-versed in the Udayana-tales,[22]
go towards that city already spoken of;
to Ujjayinī glowing in splendour
like a brilliant piece of Paradise
come down to earth with traces of merits
of dwellers in Paradise returning,
the fruit of their good deeds almost spent.

33

At day-break in Ujjayinī, Śiprā's[23] cool breeze
scented with the fragrance of lotuses comes
prolonging the piercing cries of love-maddened sarus-cranes.
Refreshing to the tired limbs of women
after passion's ecstatic play, it removes
their languor like an artful lover
plying his love with amorous entreaties.

34 & 35

Smoke drifting through lattice-screens
from aromatic gums[23a] that perfume women's hair
enhances your beautiful form;
palace-peacocks out of fellow-feeling
present you their gift-offering of dance;
worn out with travel, having passed the night
in her flower-fragrant mansions marked with red lac
from the feet of lovely ladies, approach
the holy shrine of Caṇḍeśvara,[24] Preceptor of the Triple-World,
watched with awe by the Lord's attendants,
because your hue is the blue of His throat,[24a]
its gardens stirred by Gandhavatī's[25] breezes
scented with the pollen of blue-lotuses
and fragrances wafted from unguents
used by young women sporting in her waters.

36

If by chance you reach Mahākāla[26] at a time other than sunset,
stay on till the sun disappears from sight;
by performing the exalted office of the temple-drum
in the evening-rituals offered to the Spear-Armed Lord[26a]
you will enjoy the full fruit, O Rain-Bearer,
of the deep-throated rumblings of your thunder.

37

With jewelled belts tinkling as they move with measured steps,
temple-dancers whose hands tire gracefully waving

chowries with glittering gem-studded handles,
will taste from the first rain-drops you shed,
pleasure as from a lover's nail-marks and shower on you
sidelong glances streaming like a line of honey-bees.

38

Then bathed in evening's glow red as fresh china-rose flowers
when the Lord of Beings commences His Cosmic Dance,[27]
encircling, merging into the forest of His uplifted arms,
dispel His desire to wear the blood-moist elephant-hide,[28]
your devotion observed by Bhavānī[29]
with steady eyes, her terror now calmed.

39

Young women going to their lover's dwelling at night
set out on the royal highway mantled
in sight-obscuring darkness you could pierce with a pin;
light their path with streaked lightning
glittering like gold-rays on a touchstone,
but do not startle them with thunder and pelting rain,
for they are easily alarmed.

40

On the top most terrace of some turreted mansion
where ring-doves sleep,
pass the night with your lightning-wife
much-fatigued by continual play. But pray
resume your journey the moment the sun rises;
surely, those who undertake to help a friend
do not linger over providing that help.

41

Philandering husbands come home at sunrise
called on to comfort their anguished wives
by drying the welling tears of betrayal;
therefore move quickly out of the sun's path;

he too returns at dawn to the lotus-pool
to dry the dew-tears on her lotus-face;
he would be not a little incensed
that you obstruct his bright ray-fingers.

42

Your self intrinsically beautiful
even in its shadow-form will enter Gambhīra's[30] clear waters
as into a tranquil pool of consciousness;
do not therefore cavalierly dismiss
her welcoming glances—those dazzling upward leaps
of glittering white fishes bright as water-lilies.

43

Her dark-blue waters like a garment
slipping off the sloping bank of her hips,
still cling to the reed-branches
as if lightly held up by one hand;
drawing it away as you bend over her, my friend,
will it not be hard for you to depart?
For who can bear to leave a woman, her loins bared,
once having tasted her body's sweetness?

44

Fragrant with the scent of the earth freshened by your showers,
a cool wind that ripens the fruit on wild fig-trees
is inhaled with delight by elephants
through their water-sprout-trunks;
it will waft you gently to Devagiri
that you seek to approach.

45

Skanda[31] has made that hill his fixed abode;
transform yourself into a flower-cloud[32]
and shower him with blossoms moist with vyomagaṅgā's waters;
for he is the blazing energy, sun-surpassing,
that the wearer of the crescent-moon[32a] placed
in the Divine Fire's[33] mouth to protect Indra's hosts.

46

Then, let your thunder magnified by the echoing mountain
spur the peacock[34] the fire-born god rides, to dance,
its eyes brightened by the radiance of Śiva's moon;
Bhavānī out of affection for her son
places its fallen plume
gleaming with iridescent circlets on her ear
in place of the lotus-petal she wears.

47

Having thus worshipped
the god born in a thicket of reeds[35]
and travelling some distance
as siddha-couples bearing lutes
leave your path free, from fear of water-drops,
bend low to honour Rantideva's glory[35a] sprung
from the sacrifice of Surabhī's[35b] daughters
and flowing on earth changed into a river.

48

Stealing the colour of the god who draws the horn-bow[36]
as you bend down to drink its waters,
sky-rangers looking down will indeed see with wonder
that river from the far distance
as a thin line, broad though she is,
as if Earth wore a single strand of pearls
set with a large sapphire at the centre.

49

Crossing that river go onwards making
yourself the target for the eager eyes
of Daśapura's[37] women accomplished
in the graceful play of curving eye-brows,
their eyes with upturned lashes flashing
with the beauty of gazelles leaping up
and far surpassing the grace of honey-bees
on white jasmines swaying.

50

Ranging with your shadow through the land
of Brahmāvarta[38] stretching below Kuru's field,
do not fail to visit the battleground
that marks the great war of the barons,
where the wielder of the Gāṇḍīva-bow[39]
showered hundreds of sharp arrows on princely faces
as you shoot driving downpours on lotuses.

51

The Plough-Bearer,[40] turning away from that war
out of affection for his kinsmen, renounced
the cherished wine reflecting Revatī's eyes[41]
and worshipped Sarasvatī's[42] waters; you too,
enjoying those waters, O gentle Sir,
will become pure within, dark only in form.

52

From there you should visit Jahnu's daughter[42a]
near Kanakhala's hill[42b] where she comes down
the slopes of the Lord of Mountains, making
a stairway for Sagara's[43] sons going up to Heaven.
She grasped Śiva's matted hair
clinging with wave-hands to His crest-jewel,[44] the moon,
foam-laughter[44a] mocking the frown on Gaurī's face.[45]

53

If you aim to drink her clear crystal waters slantwise,
hanging down by your hind-quarters in the sky
like some elephant out of Paradise,
as your shadow glides along her stream
she would appear beautiful at once as though
she and Yamunā flowed together at that spot.[46]

54

Reaching that river's true birth-place, the mountain
white with snows, its rocks scented by musk deer lying there;

and reclining on its peak to remove
the long journey's weariness, you will wear
a beauty comparable to the stain on the horn
of the Triple-Eyed Lord's white bull rooting in the mud.[47]

55

If a forest-fire born of cedar branches
clashing in the blowing wind
should assail the mountain, and its fiery sparks
scorch the bushy tails of yaks,
pray quench it fully with a thousand sharp showers.
The riches of the great are best employed
to ease the miseries of the distressed.

56

Unable to bear the thunder hurled down,
śarabhas[48] on the mountain, puffed up with pride
will suddenly spring up in fury towards you
who are beyond reach, only to shatter their own limbs;
scatter them with your tumultuous laughter of hail.
Who indeed that undertakes vain-glorious acts
would not become the butt of ridicule!

57

Bending low in adoration, go round
the rock bearing the foot-print of the moon-crested Lord
perpetually worshipped with offerings by siddhas;
looking upon it, the body abandoned
and sins shaken off, the faithful gain
the Eternal Station of the Lord's attendants.

58

The wind breathing through hollow bamboos makes sweet music;
woodland nymphs sing with passion-filled voices
of the victory over The Triple-City;[49]
if your thunder rumbles in the glens like a drum
would not the ensemble then be complete
for the Dance-Drama of the Lord of Beings?[50]

59

Passing over many marvels on Himālaya's slopes,
you should go north through the narrow krauñca-pass[50a]
—gateway for wild geese and path to glory
for the Bhṛgu Chief[51]—lengthened out cross-wise,
beautiful like Viṣṇu's dark-blue foot
stretched out to curb Bali's pride.[51a]

60

And going on be Kailāsa's guest
—mirror for goddesses—his ridges' joints
cracked by ten-faced Rāvaṇa's[52] straining arms:[53]
filling all space, the loftiness of his peaks
luminous as moonlotuses, seems
the tumultuous laughter piling up each day,
of the Parent of the Triple-World.[53a]

61

When glistening like smooth-ground collyrium, you lean
dark on its slopes white as ivory freshly cut,
that mountain, I imagine would, like the Plough-Bearer
with a dark-blue mantle slung o'er his shoulder,
attain to a grace so arresting
as to hold the gaze entranced.

62

And if Gaurī should stroll on that mountain
created for play, holding Śiva's hand
divested of its snake-bracelet,
hardening your mass of waters within
form yourself into wave-like steps
and go before her as she climbs the jewelled slopes.

63

When struck by swarms of sparks off Indra's thunderbolt[54]
your water-jets shoot out, celestial maidens there

will surely use you for their bath;
having found you in summer's heat, my friend,
if these girls eager for play will not let you go,
you should scare them with harsh-sounding roars.

64

Sipping Mānasa waters where golden lotuses grow;
joyfully giving Airāvata[55]
the fleeting pleasure of your veiling shade;
fluttering with rain-drenched breezes
the fine silk garments of tender leaves
the Tree of Paradise wears,[56]
amuse yourself on that majestic mountain
whose jewelled slopes glitter in chequered light and shade.

65

Once seen, O wanderer-at-will, you cannot but recognize
Alakā on its upper slope seated as on her lover's lap
—Gaṅgā, her fine garment, falling down—
High over her many-storied mansions
like a woman with her hair piled up
and bound in a net of pearls, she bears
masses of clouds shedding water in the rainy season.

66

Where palaces with their cloud-kissing tops
equal you in loftiness,
and their gem-paved floors rival the glitter
of your glistening rain drops;
where paintings on the walls vie
with your rainbow hues;
and graceful movements of lovely women
rival the lightning's play;
where drums beaten to the sound of music
resemble your thunder, mellow, deep-throated;
And in each particular more than compare with you.

67

Where women toy with a lotus held in the hand,
twine fresh jasmines in their hair;
the beauty of their faces glows pale gold
dusted with the pollen of lodhra flowers;
fresh amaranth-blooms encircle the hair-knot,
a delicate śirīṣa[57] nestles at the ear;
and on the hair-parting lie kadaṃba blossoms
born at your coming.

68

Where yakṣas accompanied by highborn ladies
resort to their palace-terraces
paved with precious gems star-flower-mirroring[58]
to partake of passion-kindling flower wines
pressed from the Tree of Paradise
while drumheads softly struck
throb deep-throated tones like yours.

69

Where at sunrise the path followed at night
by amorous women hastening to midnight trysts
with faltering steps, is marked by telltale signs—
Mandāra[59] flowers fallen from playful curls
and petals of golden lotuses worn at the ears,
dislodged, lie strewn on the ground, with pearls
scattered loose as the threads snapped
of bodices of pearls that closely held their breasts.

70

Where lovers undoing the knot at the waist,
hands trembling with passion,
toss aside silken garments loosening,
yakṣa women with lips like biṃba fruit,
overcome by shy confusion
aim handfuls of aromatic powder
at glittering gems serving as lamps.
Ah! What fruitless throws even though they hit their mark.

71

Where, led to terraces of lofty mansions
by their guide the ever-moving wind
rain clouds like you stain the paintings
with droplets of water;
then, seeming fearful flee at once
fragmented through lattices
assuming with practised skill
the shapes of smoke streaming out.

72

Where at midnight moonstones
hanging from networks of threads,
touched by the moon's feet
resplendent as you move away
shed clear drops of coolness
to dispel the languor born
of oft-enjoyed loveplay in women
just released from a loved husband's close embrace.

73

Where, knowing the Supreme One[60] to dwell incarnate,
friend to the Lord of Treasures,[61]
the God of Love out of fear refrains from drawing
his bow strung with honeybees,
his work accomplished by lovely women
displaying their alluring charms, who bend
the bow of their eyebrows to shoot bright glances
unerringly at Love's targets.

74

There, to the north of the palaces
of the Lord of Treasures stands our home
recognizable from afar by its arched gateway
beautiful as the rainbow.

Close by grows a young Mandāra tree
nurtured by my love like a son and now bending
with clusters of blossoms
within reach of her hand.

75

A flight of steps, all emerald slabs—
a pool patterned over
by full-blown lotuses on glossy beryl stems—
Wild geese haunt its waters, freed from restless longing,
no longer resorting to nearby Mānasa-lake
even after they see you coming.

76

By its edge is a miniature hill, wondrous,
with sapphire-inlaid crest, exquisitely blue
and ringed round by golden plantain-trees.
Watching you glitter at the edges with lightning-gleams
my heart trembles struck by the memory of that hill, my friend,
remembering how dear it was to my beloved wife.

77

On it by a fragrant jasmine bower
encircled by a hedge of amaranth
stands a red aśoka fluttering its tender leaves,
and the dearly-loved kesara too.
One craves the touch of your friend's lovely foot,
the other longs for the wine of her mouth,
pretending it is blossom-time.[62]

78

And between them a golden rod rising
from a pedestal of jade whose sheen
rivals that of bamboos newly-sprouted
supports a crystal tablet;

your blue-throated friend.[63]
settles on it at close of day
after my love clapping her hands has made him dance
to the sweet tinkling of her bracelets.

79

By these tokens of recognition
treasured in your heart, O wise one!
And noting the beautifully-drawn forms
of lotus and conch[64] on the sides of the door,
you will know the mansion, its lustre dimmed
no doubt by my absence: when the sun has set
the lotus does not show forth in all its glory.

80

At once becoming small as an elephant cub
for a speedy descent, seated on the charming crest
of that pleasure-hill I described before,
you may easily dart into the mansion
faint lightning-glances twinkling
like a glittering line of fireflies.

81

There you will see her, in the springtime of youth, slender,
her teeth jasmine-buds, her lips ripe bimba-fruit,
slim-waisted, with deep navel
and the tremulous eyes of a startled doe,
moving languidly from the weight of her hips,
her body bowed down a little by her breasts
—Ah! The Creator's master-work among women.

82

Know her to be my second life,
alone, speaking little,
mourning like a cakravākī[65]
her companion far away.

With the passing of these long days, racked
by intense longing, the young girl
would appear so changed I think,
like a lotus-plant struck by the chilling hoar-frost.

83

Weeping passionately, her eyes would be swollen
and her lips withered by burning sighs;
my beloved's face cupped in the palm of her hand,
only glimpsed through loose tresses flowing down
would surely appear like the miserable moon
stricken pale when shadowed by you.

84

She will come into your view absorbed
in the day's rites of worship or drawing my likeness
imagined wasted by separation,
or, asking the melodious songster in the cage,
'sweet one, do you remember our lord?
You were a favourite with him.'

85

Or, clad in a drab garment she may place
the lute on her lap, wishing to sing a melody
set to words signifying my name;
succeeding somehow in tuning the strings
wet with her tears, O gentle friend, she forgets
again and again the sequence of notes
even though she composed it herself.

86

Or, beginning with the day of our parting
she may count the months remaining,
laying out in order on the floor,
flowers placed at the threshold;[66]

or, savouring imagined pleasures of love
treasured in her heart:
—such are the only diversions of women
sorrowing in the absence of their husbands.

87

Occupied by day, the pangs of loneliness
would not distress your friend too keenly,
but I fear the nights devoid of diversions
would pass heavy with grief;
therefore, I pray, meet the faithful girl
at midnight with my messages,
standing at the window close to where she lies
wakeful on the ground, and comfort her.

88

Wasted by anguish
she would be lying on her bed of loneliness
drawing herself together on one side,
seeming like the last sliver
of the waning moon on the eastern horizon.
By my side her nights flew by
on winged moments in rapture's fullness;
now they drag on, heavy with her burning tears.

89

With a burning sigh that withers her lips
tender as leaf-buds, you will see her
toss aside those curling tresses
rough with frequent ritual-baths,
that stray down her cheeks uncared for.
Longing for sleep, hoping in dreams at least
she would be one with me in love,
a sudden torrent of tears might wash away those hopes.

90

On that first day of parting, her tresses
with their wreath of flowers stripped off were twisted

and plaited into one single braid[67]
which I shall unwind when the curse is ended
and all my sorrows melted away:
you will see her with untrimmed nails pushing
that tangled braid, rough and painful to the touch,
repeatedly off the curve of her cheek.

91

Remembering past delights her eyes would turn
towards the moonbeams, cool, ambrosial,
streaming in through the lattices,
and turn away at once in sorrow.
Veiling her eyes with lashes heavy-laden with tears
she will seem to be hovering uncertain
between waking and dreaming
—a day-lily on a cloudy day neither open nor shut.

92

Casting aside all adornments,
keeping alive her fragile body in measureless sorrow,
desolate, my love would try in vain
time and again to throw herself on her bed;
the sight I am sure will make you shed some freshwater tears;
for tender hearts ever melt in compassion.

93

I know well you friend's heart is filled with love for me,
hence I believe her brought to this pitiable state
in this our very first parting.
It is not vain self-esteem that makes a braggart of me;
all I have said, my brother,
you will soon see before your very eyes.

94

Lack-lustre without glossy collyrium,
the sidelong glance blocked by straying hair,
the eyebrow's graceful play forgotten
through abstaining from wine,

the doe-eyed lady's left eye
would throb at your coming, I guess,
and match the charm of blue lotuses
quivering as fishes dart among them.

95

And her left thigh—bare of my nail marks,
unadorned by the network of pearls of the long-worn zone
she cast aside struck by the turn of fate,
so used to the gentle stroking of my hands
after love's enjoyment—
pale as a tender plantain's stem will start quivering.

96

If at that time, O Rain-Giver,
she has found happiness, pray wait near her
just one watch of the night withholding your thunder;
having striven hard to find me, her beloved,
in a dream of love, let not her arms
twined like tender vines round my neck in close embrace,
suddenly fall away from their hold.

97

Awakening her with a breeze
cooled by your fine spray, when revived
along with the fragrant jasmine's
fresh clusters of buds, she gazes intensely
at the casement graced by your presence,
begin to address the noble lady
in vibrant tones courteous,
with your lightning-gleams hidden deep within you.

98

O unwidowed lady! Know me,
your husband's dear friend, a rain cloud
come to tender to you
his messages treasured in my heart.

With deep but gentle tones
I speed weary travellers yearning[68]
to unknot the tangled braids of their grieving wives,
on their way home from distant lands.

99

Thus addressed, like Mithilā's princess[69]
lifting her face up to the Son of the Wind,[70]
she will gaze on you, her heart opening
like a flower from eager expectation:
welcoming you at once, with deep respect
she'll listen with rapt attention, gentle friend;
for news of husbands brought by a friend
are to women the closest thing to reunion.

100

O long-lived one! In response to my plea
and to honour yourself, speak to her thus:
your consort lives,
haunting Rāmagiri's hermitages—
parted from you he asks
if all is well with you, tender lady!
Such soothing words should be addressed first
to living beings who fall prey to calamity.

101

Far off, his way barred by adverse decree,
in his imaginings
his body becomes one with your body;
thin with thin,
anguished with intensely anguished,
tear-drowned with tear-drenched
yearning with endlessly yearning,
your hotly-sighing body
with his racked by long drawn-out sighs.

102

Who, before your companions
loved to whisper in your ear
what could well be said aloud indeed,
for he longed to touch your face,
he, gone beyond range of your hearing,
not seen by your eyes, speaks
through my mouth to you, these words
shaped by his intense yearning.

103

In the śyāma-vines I see your body,
your glance in the gazelle's startled eye,
the cool radiance of your face in the moon,
your tresses in the peacock's luxuriant train,
your eyebrow's graceful curve in the stream's small waves;
but alas! O cruel one, I see not
your whole likeness anywhere in any one thing.

104

Scent of warm earth rain-sprinkled, rising, fresh,
O my darling, as the fragrance of your mouth, and
the God of Love, five-arrowed, wastes my frame
already wasted, grieving, far from you.
For pity's sake, think how my days pass
now at summer's close, as massed rain clouds
rending the sunshine, scatter the pieces
and cling enamoured to the sky in all directions.

105

With bright ores, I draw you on a rock
feigning anger, but when I wish
to draw myself fallen at your feet,
at once my eyes are dimmed by ever-welling tears.
Ha! How cruel is fate that even here
it will not suffer our reunion.

106

Striving hard I find you in a waking dream,
I stretch my arms out into the empty air
to fold you in a passionate embrace.
Those large pearl-drops clustering on tender leaf-shoots
are surely—are they not—the tears
the tree-goddesses shed watching my grief?

107

Sudden, Himālayan breezes split open
the tightly-shut leaf-buds on deodars,[71]
and redolent of their oozing resin
blow south; I embrace those breezes
fondly imagining they have of late
touched your limbs, O perfect one!

108

If only the long-drawn-out night
could be squeezed into a single moment;
if only the hot summer's day
would glow at all times with a gentle warmth;
my heart, breathing these unattainable prayers
is left a defence-less prey,
O lady with bright-glancing eyes!
To the fierce pangs of separation from you.

109

But no more of me; reflecting deeply
I bear up, drawing on my own inner strength;
you too, lady most blessed,
should resist falling into utter dejection.
Whom does happiness always attend
or misery always befall?
Man's state on earth like the rim of a wheel
goes down and comes up again.

110

With Viṣṇu[72] risen from His serpent couch
my curse shall be ended; closing your eyes
make the four remaining months go by;
then on autumnal nights bright with moonlight
we two shall taste together every desire
eagerly imagined when we were apart.

111

And further he said this: once in bed
asleep, still clinging to my neck
you woke up on a sudden, weeping a little,
and when I asked why again and again,
laughing to yourself you said,
—ah, you cheat, I saw you in my dream
playing with another woman.

112

By this token of recognition
know that I am well; and do not doubt me
O dark-eyed one, believing idle reports
that say for no good reason
that absence destroys the affections.
Ah no! The lack of pleasure makes
the craving intense for what is desired,
piling it up into love's great hoard.

113

I trust, noble friend, you are resolved
to do this kindly service for me?
I cannot think your grave look forbodes refusal;
without a sound you offer cātakas
the water they crave; the answer
noble ones make is to do the thing wished for.

114

Having granted this wish so dear to my heart,
strange as it may seem,
for friendship's sake or out of pity for me, desolated,
wander, O Cloud, in all the lands you choose,
gathering greater glory in the rains;
may you never be parted from the lightning
even for an instant.

Notes and References

Notes and References

CHAPTER: INTRODUCTION

1. The *Vāgsūktam* or hymn of the *Word* is one of the great poems of *Origins* in the Vedas; in it *Vāc* or *Vāk*, the creative Word (also meaning speech, voice), announces herself (the word is in the feminine) and speaks in images that combine power and beauty, of bringing the universe into being and establishing communion between human and divine. *Vāc* is the *Śakti* or inherent power of the creator as envisaged in the *Ṛgveda*.
2. Anon: The Sanskrit word for the ring finger is *a-nāmikā* (the nameless).
3. Bāṇabhaṭṭa, lived and wrote in the seventh century AD.
4. Kumārila Bhaṭṭa, the philosopher, AD 590–650, quotes two lines from *Śakuntalā*: I:20 in his Tantra-vārtika; cited in Nandargikar's ed. of *Meghadūtam*, 1893, intro. p. 31.
5. The Aihole inscription AD 634 of Pulikesena II, the powerful Chalukyan monarch who ruled over what is now Maharashtra; the poet is here mentioned by name.
6. *AV*. 19:53, 54
7. Śiva is the silence, quot. from Śaiva sacred texts; see Radhakrishnan I.P, vol. II, p. 727.
8. *Vāc* is later personified as Sarasvatī (flowing waters), goddess of wisdom and eloquence and the patron deity of the arts. In the Vedas, the *waters* are the infinitude of potentialities which is the origin of the universe; the space-ocean that forms the waters of creation.
9. 'The seers with wisdom searching within/discovered the bond of being in non-being.' *RV* 10:129:4.
10. 'Let us in well-wrought songs proclaim the origin of the gods that may be seen when chanted in the ages to come', op. cit., 10:72:1.
11. 'I reveal the Father at the World's highest peak', op. cit., 10:125:7.
12. *Kalpanā*, the poetic imagination, is the reflection of *Māyā*, the cosmic imagination; *māyā* derived from the root *mā*, 'to form, measure, display', is the shaping power of the Supreme.
13. The caves in the low hills near Bhilsa (Vidiśā) and on the way to Sanchi contain ancient rock-paintings and sculptured reliefs.
14. The Gaṅgā was an important waterway with fleets of barges carrying merchandise up to Indraprastha (Delhi) which was the last ford.
15. *Rām:* Sundara Kāṇḍam: canto 7.
16. *Harṣacaritam:* ch. 6. See p. 192 of trans. by Cowell and Thomas.
17. Veda is lit. wisdom; the Vedic texts are regarded as revelation.
18. *RV*. 10:108.
19. *RV*. 10:95.
20. Op. cit., 10:125
21. Op. cit., 7:86.

22. Op. cit. 10:100: the refrain is: 'For our boon we ask for felicity full and boundless', and in 10:134: The blessed Mother gave you birth.
    The glorious Mother gave you birth.
23. D.D. Kosāmbi. *The Culture and Civilization of Ancient India*, p. 199.
24. A.B. Keith. *The Sanskrit Drama*, pp. 36–7.
25. *NS*. 1:44.
26. Op. cit., 4:9, 10
27. Op. cit., 4:13, 14
28. Sūta in Sanskrit
29. Kuśī-lavas are bards, singers, actors.
30. These recitations have continued right to this day, performed in temples and village squares; the Sanskrit texts are explained in the vernaculars and the message expounded in simple language, and often accompanied by music and dance; such recitals are called Harikathā or Kathākālakṣepa. In Madhya Pradesh, the Pandavani is a re-telling by one or more persons with musical and drum accompaniments, of episodes from the Pāṇḍava story in the epic *Mbh*.
31. Indus Valley Civilization, circa 3,000. BC; the figures are housed in the National Museum, Delhi.
32. Matthew Arnold writes in 'The Function of Criticism', p. 4. (Everyman's): '. . . for the creation of a master-work of literature, two powers must concur, the power of the man and the power of the moment.'
33. *Bharata-Nāṭya-Mañjarī*. G.K. Bhat, Intro., pp. liii–liv and *NS*. 21: 76–80.
34. The Woman-tree motif has a continuous history in Indian art and literature; beginning with the Indus Valley goddess amid the leaves of a tree, through the art of Bharhut, Sanci, Mathura and the recently excavated Sanghol sculptures down to the dreaming Gyaraspur Vṛkṣikā (Gwalior Museum).
35. Rātri Sūkta: *RV*. 10:127.
36. Aranyānī Sūkta, op. cit., 10:146.
37. *RV*. 10:85
38. Pṛthivī Sūkta, *AV*. 12:1.
39. It is difficult to sustain an argument that nothing in the way of long poems was composed after the epic period, until we get to Aśvaghoṣa and Kālidāsa, but nothing has survived. A few stanzas from Pāṇiṇi's Jāmbavati-Vijaya and solitary stanzas from the works of other poets have survived, chiefly as quotations in other works.
40. He, covering the Earth on all sides
    dwells within, in ten fingers' space;
    Puruṣa alone is all this:
    What has been and what is to come,
    The Lord of Immortality
    and of that here which grows by food. (*RV*: 10:90:2)
    (Puruṣa is the Primal Being)
41. Corresponds to the present Holi Festival, though the dates are slightly different.
42. Mahākāla—Great Time or Sacred Time or Time projected onto a cosmic plane.
43. Umā (mother), Devī (shining one), Pārvatī (mountain-born), are all epithets given to Śakti, Śiva's inherent shaping power.
44. Ānandavardhana: *Dhvanyāloka*, I:8.
45. Guṇāḍhya's *Bṛhatkathā*, the Great Story, is the earliest to be mentioned, but only late adaptations of it, of the ninth–tenth centuries survive, like the *Kathāsaritsāgara*. The

story-cycles narrate the life and exploits of Udayana's son; perhaps the *Bṛhatkathā* also contained the tales of King Udayana of Kauśambi referred to in *Meghadūtam* (32). These are probably part of the lost body of popular tales.

46. *Ś.B.*:13:5:4:15.
47. Puṣpadanta, a *gaṇa*, or attendant of Śiva, is cursed and banished to earth as a mortal, because he overheard the lord telling Pārvatī a story never told before, and never heard before and recounted it to his own wife, who in turn repeated it to her mistress, Pārvatī as a brand-new story. Pārvatī was angry and cursed Puṣpadanta for overhearing a private conversation between herself and Śiva and for repeating it. She also cursed another *gaṇa* who interceded. Śiva out of pity set a period and a condition for the release of the two *gaṇas* and their return to Śivaloka (Śiva's world), which was for Puṣpadanta to tell the same tale that he had overheard to a *yakṣa* cursed by Kubera to be born on earth as a goblin (*piśāca*). At the end of the tale, Puṣpadanta would be released from the curse and return to Śiva's heaven and the *yakṣa* by telling the tale to the second cursed *gaṇa* would be also released from the curse and return to his celestial home. The third person in the frame-story (the second *gaṇa*) would be released from his curse when he published the tale to the whole world for every one to listen to. The tale told by all three, is the *Bṛhatkathā* and the author of it. Guṇāḍhya, is the second *gaṇa*, the last to find release. *Gaṇas* are divine beings like *yakṣas*, Gandharvas and Apsaras (*Kathāsaritsāgara*, ch. 1).
48. Intro. translation of *Śakuntalā* by Laurence Binyon.
49. De and Dasgupta, *History of Sanskrit Literature*, p. 144.
50. Urvaśī, 3:19.
51. *Raghuvaṃśam*, 8:32–95.
52. J.B. Chaudhuri, mentions hundreds of *Dūtakāvyas* as still existing; p. 12 of intro. to his edition of *Meghadūtam* with Bharata Mallika's commentary.
53. *Nāṭyaśāstra*, KS: 25:10–11.
54. *RV.* 10:108.
55. *Mbh.* 3:70:18–31.
56. Rām, Sundara Kāṇḍam, Hanumān shows Rāma's signet ring to Sītā in canto 36.
57. As theriomorphic forms of divine effluence; e.g. Śiva's Bull, Nandī; Skanda's peacock. Such forms are believed to have the power of mediating between human and divine.
58. A conversation poem has an auditor who is silent but has a clear identity and fully characterized personality.
59. *Kṛṣṇa Yajur Veda, Maitrāyani Saṃhita*, 1:10:13.
60. The *Purāṇas* in the form we have them now might be later than Kālidāsa, but the material contained in them is of great antiquity; earlier versions have been edited and written over.
61. Sandhyā (the meeting point), the points in time when day and night meet.
62. 'His form is everywhere: all-pervading is His Śiva Śakti.
    Chidambaram is everywhere: everywhere His dance. . . .
    . . . He dances with Water, Fire, Wind and Ether.'
    (Tirumūlar—The vision of the Divine Dance)
63. The *NS* lists eight *nāyikas* (heroines); they represent the state of a woman and the attitudes she adopts to her lover (husband): angry, scornful, jealous and quarrelsome, feeling betrayed and bitter, secure in her husband's affections, waiting for her husband all dressed to kill.

64. Certain words in the text indicate this: Śyāma is a young woman who has not yet given birth to a child; *bālā* is a young girl sixteen years of age (82) *prathama-viraha* (93) is the very first parting.

64a. *Mbh.* 3.83:88

65. Wilson, ed. of the Cloud Messenger, 18.

66. Ten stages in the emotional state of grief caused by separation from the loved one are described in the *NS* (24:160–2) the last being death.

67. Keats—*Hyperion*: 1:35–6.

68 & 69. The enumeration of the later stages in the MS is confusing, occurring as it does in a passage that is repetitive and obviously corrupt. They are: longing or craving, thinking or dwelling upon the beloved, recollection, enumeration of his virtues, anguish, lamentation, being distraught, sickness, stupor (withdrawal) and death. (KS 24:160 ff and MNG 24:168 ff). The *NS* text characterizes these stages as the *manner* in which a maiden, inexperienced, expresses her emotional state—i.e. it treats of the stages of *first falling in love* if it remains *unfulfilled*. But two things have to be kept in mind:

(1) there are interpolations in the *NS* texts and some verses may have been put in, Modelled on descriptions of persons in love and *portrayed* in literature—the *NS* description as already noted, applies to a maiden falling in love and not of a woman grieving separated from her husband.

(2) Bharata (the author of *NS*), has placed these descriptions in the chapter where he deals with histrionic representation of emotions—it is part of his aim to instruct actors *how* to portray emotional states. We should not view the enumeration of these ten states as describing how a woman ought to feel in a state of *love-in-separation* or of *unfulfilled* love.

70. *Poetics* as a formal discipline came later in the history of Sanskrit literary criticism. Drama was the form first to be treated.

71. Harisvāmin.

72. Reading between the lines of the *SB* text, the story was probably recited during the sacrifices but the *SB* being mainly a ritualistic text has just this cryptic indication; the story itself of Śakuntalā, the Apsarā who married the king of the lunar dynasty of Puru would have been part of the literary inheritance of Kālidāsa but unfortunately it is lost to us in its original form. We have only a very earthy version of it as one of the epic tales.

73. The Queen in *Mālavikā*.

74. The Queen in *Urvaśī*.

75. The Queens in *Raghuvaṃśam.*

76. The four *āśramas* or stages in a Hindu's life are: *Brahmacarya*, the student's when a young man gets instruction and is trained and equipped for a profession (and perhaps also apprenticed to some trade in other cases) *Gṛhastha*, the householder's, when the man gets married, manages his career and gets children; *Vānaprastha*, retirement to the forest, a kind of retreat from an active life in the world; *sannyāsa,* total abandonment of the world. The second *āśrama* or stage of life, the householder's, is considered the most meritorious, because the person is in the world, doing good, helping others and generally sustaining society and the state.

ṚTUSAMHĀRAM

1. An important item in the ancient Indian woman's personal adornments and still used on festive occasions. Like a belt it kept the lower garment, knotted at the waist in position, but it was also ornamental. They were made of gold or silver of filigree work, or they were gem-studded often fringed by rows of little bells; an essential part of a dancer's costume now-a-days usually in loops and these bells made a sweet tinkling sound as the woman moved around.
2. This is one of the brilliant conceits in the poem, beautifully controlled and hinged on a single word, 'pales' (*pāṇḍutā* in Sanskrit is paleness). All night the moon 'stares' at lovely women sleeping on terraces, like some peeping tom and at the first light of dawn it grows pale as if struck with guilty shame at being caught staring secretly at other men's wives.
3. *Mṛgatṛṣṇā*—a mirage, literally the antelope's parching thirst. The poet frames a whole stanza based on the etymology of this word without in the least looking pedantic.
4. Sarus cranes (*saras* are pools of water, ponds, lakes) stand five feet tall, have a bluish-grey plumage; the head and under feathers are a shining red. They inhabit pools, marshy places and frequent rice fields. They have a trumpet-like call.
5. Identified as the trumpet tree, a variety of Bignonia. The pale pink blossoms are trumpet-shaped and have a delicate fragrance.
6. Identified as the crested cuckoo. It is believed to subsist only on raindrops. As it disdains to drink any other water, it has become a symbol in literature for pride and self-respect. *Cātakas* are always associated with clouds and rain. To see a *cātaka* on one's left is a good omen (see *Megh.* 9).
7. *Kandalī* is a plant that appears with a profusion of tiny white or purple flowers during the rainy season.
8. *Kadamba* also known as *nīpa* is a large tree that blooms in the rains. The composite flowers made up of tiny tubular golden florets look like yellow balls, the styles of the florets protruding give the flower the look of a pin cushion.
9. *Sarja,* a variety of teak.
10. *Ketakī*, is the screw pine, *Pandanus Odaratissimus*; the outer leaves, a dark green. are long and tough with sharp serrated edges, like needle points. The inner leaves, softer, a pale gold, sheathe the creamy efflorescence, both carrying a heady perfume. Women wear these fragrant leaves stuck into their chignons or plait them into their braids. An essence made of the tender young inner leaves and the efflorescence is used as a perfume and also to scent drinking water, sweets and deserts. In Tamil the plant is known as *tazhambu* and in Hindi *kevda*.
11. Also known in Sanskrit as *kakubha*; *Terminalia Arjuna*, a tall tree that blooms at the beginning of the year, bearing creamy spikes of flowers.
12. Also known as *bakula;* a large tree with small brownish flowers that always look a bit dry so that wreaths and garlands made of these flowers can be kept for a long time and used and look none the worse for its age. The flowers are very fragrant which keep for a long time. See *Śakuntalā* 4:6.+ 7. Water spewed out of the mouth of a beautifully dressed, lovely, young woman is believed to make this tree bloom; see *Megh*. 77.
13. A variety of jasmine; all varieties of the jasmine are night blooming and very fragrant.

14. *Yuthikā*, is also a variety of jasmine, a creeper with leaves and slender needle-shaped buds; known as *jooyi* in Hindi. It is one of the most fragrant of jasmines.
15. A variety of tall feathered grass growing by pools and streams, seen mostly in autumn, bearing long, silky plumes of pale silver. The fluff floats free like bits of fine cotton wool, carrying the tiny seeds. Baskets are woven of the grass.
16. Fly whisks and fans made of the soft hair of a certain kind of deer, or the yak, bound and set in jewelled silver or gold handles were used ceremonially to fan deity and royalty; part of royal insignia.
17. *Jungle geranium, Ixora Coccinea*, a small shrub that blooms all the year round, but specially luxuriantly during the rains; the tubular flowers form thick heads, a brilliant orange in colour.
18. Mountain Ebony, Bauhinia; they come in several varieties, a lovely fragrant white and a deep rose or purple, also fragrant. The buds are cooked as a vegetable; *Kachnar* is the Hindi name. Parrots are fond of these buds and also the flowers which open out in large, showy single blooms on the twigs. The trees bloom at the beginning of the year and a tree in full bloom is a gorgeous sight. The leaves are kidney-shaped.
19. A beautiful and highly effective image functioning at several levels. Night grows imperceptibly longer day by day in autumn like a young girl gradually growing into womanhood. The first three lines are descriptive of both the young girl, *bālā* (a girl just turned sixteen, sweet sixteen in English poetry) and the autumn night, which it is not possible to render precisely in a translation because each of the three compound words that form an adjective to both Night and the young girl has to be split and separated differently to give the respective meanings that apply to the two subjects. Night and the girl, are related to each other by a simile. To explain: the moon is Night's face and freed of obscuring clouds, Night wears the shining robe of the moon's radiance—the moonlight. The young girl whose face is like the moon free of clouds wears a silvery, robe, bright as moonlight. The star-clusters adorning Night are compared to the girl's jewels and flower-ornaments; star-patterns are common in Indian jewellery. In both the cases of the girl and the night, beauties concealed within unfold slowly and gradually. The word describing the girl, *pramadā*, signifies a woman, no longer a girl, exulting. in her awareness of her own youth and beauty that gives her the power to *enchant* men, a word that appropriately describes the beauty of enchanting nights.
20. A tree that bears white, star-shaped, five-petalled flowers.
21. An evergreen blooming in Spring; the compact clusters of blossoms varying in colour from pale orange to scarlet, depending on their age, cover the tree completely; the flowers have a delicate fragrance. The *Aśoka* (*a-śoka*) meaning 'sorrow-less' is a tree celebrated in myth and legend. The flower is one of the five flower-arrows of Kāma, god of love; Sītā, the heroine of the epic *Rāmāyaṇa* who was abducted by Rāvaṇa, the demon-king of Lankā, spent a year in his *Aśoka*-grove, waiting in sorrow for Rāma to come and rescue her. The tree was believed to bloom at the touch of the richly-jewelled left foot of a lovely young woman.
22. 'Seven-Leaved'; the leaves grow in groups of seven; small pale clusters of flowers spring from the base of the leaf-whorls.
23. A tree that bears small, white, six-petalled flowers with coral stems and centres that bloom late in the evening and fall on the ground in the morning. They are fragrant and strung into garlands to be worn round chignons. It is called *Harsingār* in Hindi.
24. The word has three meanings: (i) a slender vine also known as *Priyangu*, (ii) a young

woman who has borne no children, (iii) a young woman with a glowing, pale gold complexion.

25. A brilliant word-picture brings sky and water together in an image drawn from a keen observation of nature. Fine emeralds when set, glow a very deep bluish-green. The waters of the pool reflect the deep, deep blue of clear autumn skies; but the dark blue is tinged with the dark green of the foliage at the water's edge, and the exact shade of a fine emerald is caught. The spotless white swan floating on the waters like the moon floating in space completes this exquisite picture. Kālidāsa sees nature and woman with the eye of a painter and sets down what he sees with the skill of a great poet whose language is musical. He was probably a painter and musician. Those days, poets as well as rich and cultivated young men and women were accomplished in many arts. *Rāja-haṃsa*, in Sanskrit, Regal Swans as I have rendered the term literally King of Swans. It is variously identified as the flamingo, the bar-head goose and the Chinese swan; the last is the most beautiful species of swans, a pure white, with vermilion beak, orange legs and black claws; a splendid looking bird in short, deserving the title of *King of Swans.* It is a rare species.
26. *Lodhra*—It blooms in winter. The flower-petals were used to perfume wine; crushed and powdered it became face-powder for the beauties of the ancient word; it is an important specific employed in Ayurveda.
27. *Priyaṅgu* is a vine with slender, dark blue stems. The flowers are fragrant; yellow in colour. The vine tends to grow into a thick bush.
28. Lover, invariably refers to the husband. Kālidāsa does not treat of illicit relationships. *Ṛtusaṃhāram* is a celebration of married love.
29. Fumigation to get rid of tiny pests like mosquitoes and the like.
30. The golden *campa,* has large, showy, flowers with slender petals that twist and curve back; a delicate fragrance.
31. Kāma, the god of Love; puffed up with pride, Kāma had the temerity to assail the Great Yogi, Śiva, seated on Mt. Kailāsa in meditation, to break the Lord's single-minded contemplation. A spark from Śiva's third eye—the inner eye of wisdom-burnt Kāma to ashes. This myth is beautifully developed in the third canto of *Kumārasaṃbhavam* by Kālidāsa.
32. This stanza is a good example of a distinctive feature of Kālidāsa's style—the multi-layered image. A number of elements go into building this image; it is also an example of the interweaving of human emotion with nature's beauty. Coral is usually shaded; so are the *aśoka's* cluster of blossoms, ranging from pale orange to scarlet depending on the age of the flower. The blossoms completely cover the branches and twigs to suggest branching coral—a forest of coral. The *aśoka* grove wears the mysterious beauty of a coral reef. Kālidāsa was a much-travelled poet; in *Raghuvaṃśam,* he describes the pearl and coral fisheries of the deep south. The word used for coral here is *vi-druma; druma* is tree. Sanskrit is rich in synonyms and Kālidāsa's choice of words is always dictated by the needs of the imagery, not by the exigencies of the metrical pattern. To give the latter as a reason for the choice of one word rather than another is to betray a lack of close reading of the text.

    Both the trees in the *aśoka* grove and the girls watching their beauty, are *budding* into youth; the delicate beauty of the leaf-shoots—*pallava*—suggests the fresh and delicate charm of young girls just stepping into womanhood. Poetic convention perceives the *aśoka* blossom as one of the five flower-arrows of Kāma, god of love; and the girls are filled with vague stirrings of emotion. But the poet uses the convention in a fresh manner. The girls are filled with a gentle sadness. The internal rhyme of *a-śoka* (free from sadness) which is the name of the flower and *sa-śoka* (filled with sadness) of the human emotion links the two words and sets them off against each other. The 'tree of no sorrow'—*aśoka*—induces not a real sorrow but the make-believe sadness of adolescence—*nava-yauvana.*

The compound word, *vidruma-rāga-tāmram,* is made up of three colour-words: coral-red-rich copper. *Rāga,* in addition, has the double meaning of redness of colour and of passion. The flowers are 'impassioned' and transmit their emotion to the nubile girls. Further it is the colour of the red *aśoka* blossoms that attracts the bees, leading to pollination and fruiting. The flower-bee relationship symbolizes love and union.

33. A variety of fragrant jasmine; the petals are sparkling white; the tubes and underside of two of the petals are a pale purple, clearly noticeable in the buds; probably what is commonly known as *Cameli.*
34. The Flame-of-the-Forest; a magnificent flowering tree; the scarlet blossoms form spikes; each flower has a curved petal forming a keel which makes it look like a parrot's beak. The word *kimśuka,* means 'what-a-parrot' or 'what? a parrot?; *Kim*—what? and *śuka*—parrot. Also known as Palāśa.

KUMĀRASAMBHAVAM

Canto 1

1. The north is the region of light and life because the sun is in the north in India in the bright half of the year, viz. Spring and Summer; therefore it is holy. The south is the region of darkness and death when the sun travels south in the dark half of the year, viz. Autumn and Winter.
2. The poem begins with the auspicious word *asti,* the present tense, singular, third person of the verb *as* 'to be', which indicates the eternal present. In Sanskrit Poetics, a literary work has to begin with a prayer, or benediction, or introduce the subject of the poem as in this case, where Himālaya, personified and divinized is the subject.
3. Literally, 'the Abode of Snow'.
4. The term *devatātma* conveys the idea that divinity (and life, because life is divine) animates the mountain. The Himālaya is thereby viewed as *living* and sacred, as befits its parentage of the Great Goddess, *Umā,* also referred to as *Pārvatī* (born of the mountain), *Gaurī* (The bright Goddess), and so on. The goddess, Mother of the Universe is (in metaphysical terms) *Śakti,* the creative, cosmic energy of *Śiva,* The Absolute Being. In mythic and poetic terms, the goddess is seen as the consort of *Śiva.* The two together are treated in mythology and in Kālidāsa's writings as the Primal Parents. The Himālaya is also holy because Mt. Kailāsa, the temporal abode of Śiva, The Absolute, is one of its lofty peaks.
5. As the calf, Himālaya is the son of the earth and essential to the sustaining and nourishing maternal aspect of the earth, as a calf is in stimulating the flow of milk in a cow.
6. The mythical mountain that in Indian cosmology, is the cosmic centre, and the terrestrial north pole. Meru is described in the Purāṇas as formed all of gold (the metal of enduring purity), studded with gems, 84,000 *yojanas* (leagues) in height of which 16,000 are embedded deep inside the earth. It is further described as shaped like the seed box of a lotus—the lotus is the symbol of the blossoming universe—from which the many islands (modern continents) radiate like the petals of the lotus flower. All the planets revolve round it. It is the home of the *devas*, divinities, The Immortals; its summit is the abode of Brahmā the creator and the meeting place of The Immortals. Presumably canto two of the poem is placed here in this location, the centre of the universe.
7. A mythical king who was chosen to be ruler of the whole earth; he gave his name to the earth—*Pṛthivī*—lit. 'that which belongs to *Pṛthu*'. *Pṛthu* was of divine birth.
8. A reference to the healthful and life-giving plants such as the *sanjīvanī,* the herb that restored the dead to life; *Som*a, the sacred plant extolled in poem after poem of The *Ṛgveda*, whose juice was offered to the divinities in the great vedic sacrifices, and other medicinal herbs that still abound in the Himālayan regions. (*Soma* stands for the sap of life itself).
9. In Sanskrit, the moon is masculine.
10. Lit. 'Born of The Waters'; that is, the 'waters' of the space-ocean, from which all life arose. In the cosmogonic myth. The Churning of the Ocean, many beautiful and wondrous things arose from the waters, among them the *apsaras*, who became the celestial dancers. *Apsaras* are guardians of sacred pools and fords (see Appendix II: Myths: The Churning of the Ocean).

11. Lit. 'perfected ones'; mortals who through severe penances acquired suprahuman powers known as the eight *siddhis:* viz. the power to become minute or enormous, light and aery or gross and heavy; to go where they pleased, to assume any shape at will, to be totally free and unbound, to have dominion over others.
12. The regions above the clouds.
13. Mountain tribes, hunters and gatherers.
14. Huge, full grown tuskers are believed to have pearls embedded in their frontal globes, the temples (cf. the European belief of toads wearing gems on their heads). The temples of elephants are vulnerable spots and lions often leap onto the heads of the animals and split them open.
15. Red spots are said to appear on elephants fifty years and over; the age of the animals could be determined by the number of spots on their bodies.
16. Fans, fly-whisks made of the soft, white, bushy tails of yaks. These fans, and the white umbrella are part of royal insignia together with the crown, sceptre and rod and the lion-throne.
17. One of the many names of the river Gaṅgā. In fact, *Bhāgīrathī* and *Alakanandā* are twin rivers rising in and flowing through the Garhwal Himālaya to join and become the Gaṅgā before the river rushes through the gorge at Hardwar to descend into the northern plains of India. The *Bhāgīrathī* gets its name from a pious king, *Bhagīratha,* whose severe penances brought the celestial river down the earth. See Appendix II. Myths: Descent of the holy river.
18. The primal sages, born of the mind of the Primal being, *Brahmā;* they were the first to have the right and power to perform the rite of sacrifice, *yajña*. Astronomically they were represented as the seven stars of the Great Bear, Ursa Major; that is, they were apotheosized.
19. The most sacred of the plants growing in the Himālayas, such as *Soma,* used in sacrifices, the holiest of sacrificial materials; *Soma*, *Palāśa* sticks, the Khadira tree and other items of worship employed in the sacrifice are all part of the Himālayan ecology.
20. All the divinities (*devas*) have a share in the *yajña;* the sacrifice and oblations are offered to them by name into the holy fire. Himālaya. already described as a divinity, also gets a share of the oblations.
21. The *Pitṛs* (Father or Patriarchs), are divine beings with the power to create offspring by an effort of the mind, that is, through yogic contemplation. In the Veda, *Pitṛs* are Primal Parents, viz. *Varuṇa* (the sky), *Bṛhaspati* (The Holy Word), *Prajāpati* (Creator). This use of the word *Pitṛs* should not be confused with the same word used to signify the Manes or departed ancestors.
22. Lit. 'Born of Menakā'; *Menakā* is a variant form of *Menā;* the mountain Maināka is variously placed geographically, in central India, at the tip of peninsular India or in the straits between India and Śrī Laṅkā.
23. Corresponding to a mermaid in European folklore; a fairy creature with a woman's body and serpent's tail. *Nāgas-Nāginīs* are semi-divine beings of uncommon beauty living in the oceans in an underwater kingdom of splendour and beauty whose capital is a jewelled city, *Bhogavatī.*
24. *Vrtra* is the demon, drought, represented as a huge serpent that confined the rays of light and the waters within the dense, dark rain clouds of monsoon. *Indra* as god of rain, storms, thunder and lightning cleft the serpent with his thunderbolt, releasing the pent-up rain. The movements of massed clouds looking like mountains and

creeping through the skies like a huge serpent (or dragon) lie behind the imagery of the myths in the context (see n. 59 of the introduction).

24b. A reference to an ancient Vedic myth of mountains that had wings and wandered at will through space, posing hazards to all aerial traffic. *Indra* who had to protect the world, severed their wings and fixed them firmly in the earth.

25. *Satī* is an example of a word signifying a metaphysical concept being personified and becoming anthropomorphized. The term is the feminine of '*sat*', meaning both 'existent' and 'virtuous', that is, the Real and the Good. As such it is employed as one of the many epithets for the feminine, maternal aspect of creative energy, and therefore, of the Mother Goddess. *Satī* means literally, 'one who *is*' and *Bhavānī* (another name for the goddess) 'one who is Becoming, coming into existence'. (See p. 22 of introduction, for the meaning of epithets in Indian metaphysics).

26. One of the Patriarchs (*Pitṛs*) from whom all forms of beings in creation were born. *Satī* was his daughter, one of several. See Appendix II: Myths: Dakṣa's Sacrifice.

27. Ascetics (*tapasvī*) and *Yogis* have the power to abandon their bodies at will by withdrawing their senses and physical motions, and willing the cessation of life through yogic power (*tapas*). *Yoga* is intense and single minded contemplation when the consciousness or the innermost core of being is on fire and absorbs all externals into itself and consumes them. The Veda talks of creation as arising from this sort of inner activity, *tapas* (*RV*. 10.129).

28. *Satī,* the Mother Goddess, reborn as *Umā*.

29. The personal energy or valour of a ruler, one of the three factors that makes him powerful, the other two being material resources and good counsel.

30. Hills where sapphires or lapis lazuli were mined; it is possible that the gem, cat's eye may be referred to here.

31. The word *lāvaṇya* has the literal meaning of 'saltiness'; but the literary meaning conveys a quality of beauty, especially of complexion that has 'the tremulous lustre of pearls'; a translucent iridescence that fine ocean-pearls possess and which probably is related to the salt water in which the oysters live and grow.

32. Reference to the many rivers and streams that rise in the Himālayas.

33. The three worlds, celestial, terrestrial and nether regions known as *pātāla;* the nether regions in Indian mythology/cosmography is neither the underworld of the dead and ghosts (as in Greek mythology), or hell as in Christian mythology (see also no. 23).

34. The river Gaṅgā; it is regarded in mythology as flowing through the three worlds explained in n. 33. See Appendix II: Myths: Descent of the holy river.

35. Gaṅgā; the word means flowing gently, softly.

36. *Kāma* or Eros has five arrows made of flowers; the *aśoka* flower, the mango blossom, the blue lotus, spring jasmine; sometimes the delicate *Śirīṣa* flower is substituted for the jasmine.

36a. *Sthalakamala* is identified with several flowers; *Hibiscus Mutabilis* of the mallow family like *japa* (China rose or rose of Sharon); the red day lily, *Gloriosa Superba*, a flower very sensitive to the sun's rays, opening at the first touch of the sunbeams at dawn and closing at sundown; and to several others.

37. The slender shoulders bend forward slightly from the fullness of the breasts; a slender body, slender shoulders, full breasts and hips and an hourglass waist are considered marks of feminine beauty.

38. See *Ṛtu* n. 5.

39. The calls of the swans are resonant like bell tones, high and clear; cf. 'The bell-beat

of their wings above my head'. W.B. Yeats, The Wild Swans at Coole, 3:5.

40. That is, neither too long or short.
41. An elephant's trunk, rounded and tapering, the stems of plantain trees, slender, rounded and smooth are common similes employed in Sanskrit poetry and prose, to characterize the thighs of lovely women.
42. An ornamental belt worn on the hips.
43. A deep, perfectly circular, sunken navel is a mark of beauty; a protruding belly-button is not.
44. *Acacia Sirissa.*
45. *Kāma*, the god of love, has many names or epithets descriptive of his form, functions and events related to the happenings in his personified presence in the lives of mortals and gods: *Manoja* and *Manobhava*, born in the mind; *Madana*, the god or power that maddens, intoxicates all beings; Manmatha, the Mind-Churner; *Kandarpa*, ah! So arrogant! *Puṣpabāṇa*, Flower-Arrowed, *Smara*, Remembrance, lord of memories (Memories of love recollected) and so on.
46. A kind of mountain deer; or possibly the yak; see n. 16.
47. For the special qualities in each object that provide the norms for beauty; e.g. the cool brilliance of the moon, the bright redness of coral and so on.
48. A great sage, foot-loose and fancy-free who made everyone's business his own and went around informing, interfering, counselling and starting quarrels as well as bringing people together.

48a. Appendix: Myths, Dakṣa's Sacrifice.

49. See *Megh.* n. 33.
50. A tree growing in the Himālayan submontane regions. It flowers during the rains. The flowers are a pale cream with a heady perfume, growing in tassel-like clusters with the stamens conspicuous forming brilliant orange circles.
51. Attendants of *Śiva* and *Pārvatī,* headed by *Gaṇeśa,* the elephant-headed divinity. The *Kālikāpurāṇa* describes them as adorned with various, beautiful jewels, wearing crest jewels in the shape of half-moons on their matted hair; flying in the air with *Śiva;* worshipping *Śiva;* singing with sweet voices, playing instruments and drums; and dancing before their lord, *Śiva.*
52. *Nandī,* the white, humped bull, *Śiva's* mount and the doorkeeper standing guard at the entrance, as huge stone bulls do at the entrance to the sanctum of *Śiva* temples. It is interesting to note that a humped bull with prominent dewlap as Sindhi bulls display, is engraved on seals of the Harappa-Mohenjadaro civilization of the 3rd millennium BC. Zimmer writing about the art objects of this civilization, says that the bull 'is the animal representation of the god's divine nature' (p. 23). The Art of Indian Asia. Heinrich Zimmer; Bollingen Series xxxix. Princeton, University Press, 1960). For further information on this point, see Zimmer.
53. *Ākāśa* (ether), Air, Fire, Water, Earth, the Sacrificer or Priest, the Sun and Moon; the first five are the primal elements, *pañcabhūta,* the basic building blocks of the universe; the Sun is the source of all life, its sustainer and the centre of our universe; the Moon, one of whose names is *Soma* (life-sap), nourishes all life.
54. The Sacred Fire is kindled by rubbing two pieces of wood, one from the sacred fig. tree, *Aśvattha* (*Ficus Religiosa*), and the other from the *Śami* tree, a softer wood.
55. The *Devas*, lit. The Luminous Entities or Shining Ones from the verb *div,* 'to shine, to illuminate'; they are beings who belong to the world of eternal light.
56. The absolute and transcendental nature of *Śiva* is underlined by the Sanskrit word in the text—*anarghyam.*

57. An offering to a divinity or a guest consists of eight items: water, milk, curds, tips of the sacred *Kuśa* grass, melted and clarified butter, grains of rice and barley and white mustard seeds.
58. As *Śiva* had chosen a peak in the Himālaya to perform His penance and meditations, He is the mountain's guest, to be honoured and offered the hospitality due to a guest. It was the practice, particularly in royal and in great families to depute the daughter of the house to attend on a guest and see that all his needs are met.

Canto 2

This canto is in the *Anuṣṭubh* or *Śloka* metre consisting of two lines of verse, or four quarters each of 8 syllables. It is the epic metre commonly used for narrative.

1. A celebrated titan; see Appendix II: Myths; Tāraka the great Titan.
2. Brahmā, the creator; in metaphysical terms, the demi-urge, the artificer of the universe. Brahmā in the masculine and Brahma in the neuter have to be distinguished from each other. The former is the creative power manifest in Time and Space, present in the creation; the latter often written as Brahman is the Absolute Being, the unmanifest creative power behind the universe and transcendent being outside Time and Space.
3. Lord of the *devas* or Immortals. Indra is less a name than a title. The post of Indra, the Indra-ship is the office and station of the protector of the universe (see v. 23). It could be held by anyone found worthy of the office; by one who has performed severe penances, been disciplined and just and also performed a hundred sacrifices'; in Sanskrit, *śatakratu.* In mythology, Indra is the god of rain and thunder who fructifies the earth by causing the rain to fall in time (see canto 1. n. 24).

   The root meaning of the word *Indra* is 'that beyond human ken', which, is the intangible spirit.

   In this verse (1) Indra is referred to as *turāsāha,* 'one who subdues the mighty' or 'one who comes to help immediately'.
4. The sun.
5. The Waters of the cosmic or space-ocean. In ancient Indian astronomy, space is viewed as filled with an almost intangible substance, named *ākāśa,* a subtle, ethereal fluid that forms a vast, reservoir of undifferentiated potentialities for life and all the possible forms of creation with as yet no distinct form. *Ākāśa* also has the property of conducting sound (*śabda*). All creation rises out of this potential mass, this sea of undifferentiated materiality at the beginning of time, and goes back into it at the end of time when the entire creation is dissolved.
6. Indra; see canto 1; n. 24.
7. Lord of Waters; regent of the western quarter. In the earliest phase of Indian religious thought as seen in the Vedas, *Varuṇa* is the Lord of Lords, the Supreme Power, All-Encompassing, just ruler of the universe. The noose stands for his functions as judge and chastiser of wrongdoing and transgression of his immutable Law (*Ṛtā*) which binds even himself and the other luminous powers that are in charge of the universe. Varuṇa loses his sovereignty in later phases of religious thought and is relegated to a subordinate position, that of lord of the earthly waters, the oceans.
8. Lord of Riches; regent of the northern quarter; overlord of *yakṣas* whose opulent and splendid kingdoms lay in the Himālayan-trans-Himālayan region. Kubera and the *yakṣas* were very ancient pre-vedic divinities of the land, worshipped by the very first peoples of India (see Megh. n. 1 under *yakṣa*) and later relegated to subordinate

positions and minor functions in the economy of the universe. Kubera attained his high position by practising humility.

9. Lord of the world of the dead; regent of the southern quarter (see n. 1 of canto 1). *Yama* is very much a vedic divinity where he is the first person to have accepted death voluntarily and passed on to the other shore. This action of his brought death into the world. In the other world, on the other shore, *Yama* sits as the supreme judge of the thoughts and actions of all living beings.
10. The mother of the *devas* who are also known as *Ādityas* (children of Aditi), and as The Immortals who dwell in eternal light. *Aditi* means infinitude; what cannot be cut or divided. *Aditi* signifies the infinity of space, stretching boundless.
11. Lit. 'The Howlers' or 'The Roarers.' The god of tempests and lord of the *Rudras,* eleven in number, and of the *Maruts,* the storm gods. In the Vedas, *Rudra* is *Agni* (Fire), the most important and most celebrated of divinities; and he is also *Kāla* or Time, the all-consuming. The eleven *Rudras* are the eleven flames of *Agni.* Later, both *Kāla* and *Rudra* are identified with *Śiva* and the eleven *Rudras* are viewed as emanations of *Śiva.*

    Rudra, the world itself, is also derived by some from the root 'to redden' and explained as meaning reddish, glowing, brilliant, which is indeed a very appropriate epithet for Fire, *Agni,* in the Vedas.
12. The Lord of Prayer; Prayer personified; the deity that mediates between the human and the divine and consequently is priestlike; He is the priest and preceptor of the Immortals. In astronomy, the planet Jupiter. Also the name of an author of a lawbook.
13. A titan; originally the word meant a living entity, or spirit, from *asu* meaning breath, life. In the Vedas, *Asura* was a title given to the luminous deities. to mainly Varuṇa, the Supreme Spirit. The word is employed later for the powerful forces of darkness, as opposed to the *devas* who are the forces of light.
14. The ocean.
15. The delightful pleasure garden in *Indra's* paradise where jewelled trees grew and trees such as the *pārijāta* whose fragrant flowers never faded.
16. The cosmic mountain; centre of the universe; see n. 6. canto 1.
17. The river Gaṅgā; lit. the river 'that flows softly'; the Gaṅgā in its upper reaches.
18. Yellow, lotiform flowers found growing in certain high regions of the Himālaya. The real lotus is an aquatic plant.
19. The implication is that *Tāraka* has set himself up as a divinity, as the supreme divinity entitled to all the oblations offered in the sacrifices.
20. The spotless, white horse; one of the many wondrous objects that rose from the waves when the ocean was churned to obtain the drink of immortality, *Amṛta* (see Appendix II: Myths: The Churning of the Ocean). In Sanskrit Literature, glory is represented as spotlessly white.
21. The spotless, white elephant that rose out of the waves together with the horse (n. 20) and other wondrous objects. See Appendix II: Myths: op. cit. It is Indra's mount.
22. These special classes of clouds are described as 'possessing deep resonant voices and the power to assume various shapes at will'; that is, as we actually see when a thick bank of rain clouds form in the sky. They are also described 'as brimful of water, raining beneficial rains'. Further they act as agents of destruction at time of the dissolution of the universe. See also reference to them in *Megh.* v. 6.
23. The chain of cause and effect of actions that binds people to the wheel of birth-death-rebirth.

24. *Tāraka: Diti* and *Aditi* were twin goddesses and wives of Kaśyapa, the Primal Parent.
25. *Śiva;* see *Megh.* n. 24a.
26. *Ātmā*, the word used in the text means the self or the essence; *ātmajā* and *ātmaja*, 'born of the self', signify the son and daughter of a man; they are born of his self or essence.
27. Women who were separated from their husbands took no thought of their bodies. They did not dress in fine clothes or dress their hair or wear flowers and jewellery, but simply washed their hair and bound it into a knot or wore it as a single braid. To oil and comb and let the hair flow loose and adorn it with flowers was done only when their separation was ended; therefore the phrase symbolizes reunion with the husband.
28. The *devas.*
29. *Brahmā.*
30. The God of Love; the Greek Eros. The god has many names or epithets; *Kāma, Kandarpa* (used here in the text), *Madana, Manmatha. Smara, Manoja, Manobhava.* The epithets are descriptive of the role of the god; e.g. *Madana*, The Inflamer of Passion; *Manmatha*, Churner of the heart and so on.
31. Pleasure, the consort of Love.
32. *Kāma;* Love's arrows are flowers. they are five: the *Aśoka*, the mango, the *Śirīṣa* or the Jasmine, the blue lotus.
33. *Indra*; by performing a hundred sacrifices he attained Indraship (see n. 3).

Canto 3

1. *Indra,* here referred to as *maghona,* 'Giver of Gifts'.
2. Personifications of cosmic and elemental forces; the twelve *Ādityas* who are the suns of the twelve months; the eight *Vasus,* chief of whom is *Indra,* or according to the *Viṣṇupurāṇa* water, air, fire, dawn, light, the pole star, *Dhara, Soma* (*Vasus* are the 'bright ones'); the eleven *Rudras,* that are eleven flames of *Agni* (Fire); the twin *Asvins* (or the sky and earth), making up thirty-three. *Vasu* in the plural *(Vasus)* signify riches.
3. *Indra*; the epithet employed in this verse is *vāsava* foremost of the *vasus* (see n. 2).
4. Or the distinctive merit and/or talent of a person; his special capability.
5. The many different worlds in the universe.
6. A reference to the idea that the position of the Lord of *Svarga* or the world of light, i.e. Indra-ship, was attainable by performing exceptional austerities (see also n. 3 of canto 2).
7. Release from the existential condition, is known as *mokṣa* or *mukti.*
8. *Nīti,* a special word in Sanskrit, almost untranslatable by a single, equivalent English word. *Nīti* is a life lived wisely and well, in which the claims of the moral, spiritual and material imperatives are balanced; where the head and the heart work together; where body, mind and spirit do not pull in contrary directions.
9. Writer of a *Nītiśāstra,* a text dealing with Right and the righteous conduct of life, the Śukranīti. Śukra is another name for the sage Usanas. He was the preceptor of the Titans in the mythology.
10. One of the epithets of *Śiva; Hara* is The Remover' of ignorance, evil and so on.
11. The bow that strikes at ignorance and evil; applies also to *Śiva's* three-pronged spear, the trident. The *pināka* is also regarded as symbolizing Time.

12. *Ākhaṇḍala,* the epithet used for Indra at this point means 'The Fragmentor'. As the rain god armed with the gleaming thunderbolt, Indra crushes the demon drought and breaks the clouds.
13. The literal meaning is 'The Remainder'.
14. *Viṣṇu,* the creative principle rests on the endless coils of *Śeṣa,* floating on the waters of the cosmic, space-ocean and sleeps the sleep of quiescence *yoganidrā* until the moment creation has to begin once more.
15. *Śiva.*
16. The *devas*, the luminous ones to whom mortals offer sacrifices.
17. *Bhava* means The Origin, The Source; one of the many epithets for *Śiva.* The feminine formed from this word is *Bhavānī*, meaning becoming.
18. Brahma in the neuter and Brahmā in the masculine have different meanings; the former signifies holy creative power and the latter, the creator in whom this power is vested. In the Vedas Brahma is primarily the creative power, though it also has the meanings of prayers, the sacred word as opposed to *vāc*, the words of man, and the Vedas themselves and the spiritual knowledge in the Vedas. Later, especially in Vedantic thought, Brahma came to mean the One, Absolute, the essence and source of all, from which all creation emerged and to which it returned. All the meanings of this richly resonant word ought to be kept in mind in interpreting this verse. The last quarter of this verse *brahmāṅgabhūḥ brahmaṇi yojitātmā,* can be translated in a number of ways depending on how the compound word *brahmāṅgabhūḥ* made up of three separate words, *brahma* + *aṅga* + *bhūḥ*—essence or reality, limbs + born—may be combined; and taking into consideration both meanings of Brahma, as the divine essence or Reality, the One and the creator, Brahmā as well.
    (a) He (Śiva) who has yoked his self *(ātmā)* born of Brahma (the divine essence and ultimate reality), in the ultimate reality (*brahmaṇi*); the Cosmic Self contemplating itself in its true form.
    (b) He who is the source of the Vedas and its auxiliary texts (Brahma meaning the Vedas and *aṅga* the auxiliaries) born from Him (*bhūḥ*), yoking Himself or centring (*yojita*) His Self in Reality (Brahma).
    (c) He from whom Brahma (the divine essence or reality) arises (*bhūḥ*) as His own splendour which He contemplates (*yojitātmā*).
    (d) He from whom Brahmā, the Creator is born and who contemplates (*yojitātmā*) Himself in Brahma (the essence or reality) or in the alternative meaning of Brahma as the Vedas and spiritual knowledge, He who contemplates Himself in the Vedas and the transcendental knowledge they contain or express.

    One further reading of this highly ambivalent line is possible. Taking the myth that Śiva, as Rudra was born of Brahma, issuing from the latter's forehead in the form of anger. In this case, the reading would be as follows:
    (e) He (Śiva) who being born of Brahmā the Creator yoking His Self in the ultimate Reality, and contemplating His own Self.

    Further readings are possible if we take the meaning of Brahma as *mantras* as Mallinātha does in his commentary. Perhaps this interpretation is not quite so rich and resonant.

    It has also been suggested that the compound word *brahmāṅgabhūḥ,* refers to and qualifies *senāni* (commander-in-chief or leader of the armies) in the verse; and therefore the poet is really referring to Kumāra, the Son who is to come to the rescue of the Immortals and kills Tāraka. In this case, I would translate the verse (3:15) as: 'The *devas* wish for a general born of Bhava's (Being) seed to lead them into victory;

and he born of Brahma could emerge from the contemplation of the Self (Śiva) in contemplation.' And I would then interpret the verse to convey the sense of Śiva's emanation in the form of divine energy emerging to destroy evil.

19. Śiva the *yogi*, the ascetic in mediation.
20. *Śiva.* The epithet in the context is *Sthāṇu*—lit. 'motionless', 'immutable', 'stationary', 'Immovable', The Pillar that supports the universe.
21. Celestial dancers; lit. 'born of the waters' dancers in Indra's court; courtesans whom Indra used to seduce those sages and other saintly persons who seemed a threat to him and his power and sovereignty.
22. *Agni; Agni* is here named *hutāśana,* 'one who consumes ritual offerings', the oblations thrown into the fire.
23. A sign of great affection, like patting a person on the back.
24. The spotless, white elephant; see Appendix II: Myths: Churning of the Ocean.
25. Pleasure; delight.
26. *Śiva.*
27. Different orders of ascetics follow different disciplines. The poet here uses the word *muni,* hermits who observe silence.
28. *Kāma,* Love.
29. The northern quarter; *Kubera* is a close friend of *Śiva* whose temporal abode is Mt. Kailāsa, a Himālayan peak. Alakā, the capital city of *Kubera* is situated in its vicinity, where the holy river Gaṅgā descends from the celestial world. The poet describes this in *Meghadūtam* where he also refers to the friendship of *Śiva* and *Kubera* and the latter's devotion to the Lord (*Megh.* v. 65; 73). See also canto 2, n. 8 this verse implies that the action of this canto takes place in the cold season; Spring and the sun are violating 'the fixed order', *ṛta* (the immutable cosmic Law).
30. There is a play on the word *dakṣiṇā;* the word signifies the southern quarter as well as tender loving wife. The Sun is the lover/husband of 'the directions of space' moving from one quarter (or house) to another. *Sūrya,* the sun is masculine and *dik,* directions of space, is feminine in Sanskrit. The imagery in this verse foreshadows the parting of *Rati* from her husband, Kāma.
31. See note 19, *Ṛtu.*
32. Aśoka flowers cover the stems of the shrub completely.
33. The Aśoka is believed to bloom and bloom profusely if kicked by the jewelled foot of a lovely, young woman. A poetic convention.
34. Great warriors, heroes, had their names engraved on their arrow-shafts.
35. Kāma.
36. The golden *campa*; see *Ṛtu* n. 25.
37. Also known as *Kiṃśuka*, The Flame-of-the-Forest (see *Ṛtu.* n. 29).
38. Nail marks made at the height of passion during sexual union. This is a poetic convention.
39. A play on the word *tilaka,* which is the name of a tree, the Persian Lilac, and also the word for the beauty mark placed on the middle of the forehead. These can be very elaborate and decorative.
40. The tender mango shoots are a glowing rose-red. Tender mango sprouts have a pleasant taste, slightly tart and astringent.
41. The phrase *kaṣāya-kaṇṭhaḥ* can be translated three ways:
    (a) a throat clear on account of the astringency of the mango sprouts.
    (b) a throat stained a reddish brown by the juice of these sprouts.
    (c) tinged with passion, which I have taken.

42. *Kiṃpuruṣa-aṅgana*; *Kiṃpuruṣa* women; lit. the word *Kiṃpuruṣa* and *Kinnara* (*kim* + *puruṣa* and *kim* + *nara*) mean 'What a person'! 'What a man', said in admiration or deprecation. They refer to a class of semi-divine beings living in the Himālayan slopes and valleys and the trans-Himālayan regions, like the *yakṣas*. These two words correspond to dryads, nymphs, fauns, centaurs and similar words used in European folklore and fairy tales. Often they are described (especially *kinnara-kinnari*) to be part human and part animal in form. This might be a misperception of men and women seen riding ponies, mules etc., at a distance, by people unfamiliar with such animals. Ignorance, as we know, frequently results in wonder or contempt.
43. Ancient Indian women applied salves, probably made of bees-wax blended with medicinal infusions to protect their lips from being chapped in the cold season.
44. Leaf-and-petal designs painted on cheeks and breasts with liquid sandal paste and pigments of aloe, saffron, leaves, henna-leaves, etc.; a practice similar to tattooing except that it is painless and washable, not permanent; as a result beads of sweat would mar the patterns.
45. *Śiva*: here the epithet is *Sthāṇu*, see n. 20.
46. *Madana*, 'one who inflames the passion of love' (of sexual passion); one of the god of love's many epithets.
47. *Cakravāka*, *cakra* = wheel the birds resemble chariot wheels when they are floating on water.
48. *Kiṃpuruṣa*, which I have translated as 'faun'; see n. 42.
49. Is the perspiration caused by her exertions from dancing or from playing an instrument or the drums? Such actions are depicted time and again in the great stone-friezes of Sanchi and other places where monumental art is found.
50. Śiva.
51. See n. 52 of canto 1.
52. See n. 51 of canto 1.
53. A reference to the belief that certain planets and stars are inauspicious for certain projects (travel, laying a corner stone, etc.) and good for others.
54. The verb *saw* governs all the adjectival clauses descriptive of Śiva, the *yogi*, in v. 45–50.
55. *Śiva*: the epithet used here is *Tryambaka*, a word with several meanings: (a) Triple-Eyed; (b) Parent of The Triple-World, pervading the three worlds; (c) knowing the three Vedas; (d) uttering the triple-syllable; the sacred *Om* has three sounds, *a-u-m*; *Śiva* is known as *Omkāranātha*, He whose form is the sacred *Om*.
56. Lit. 'the sacred wood'; deodar, the Himālayan cedar, a timber tree widely used for furniture and in railroad tracks; in Vedic times it had sacrificial uses.
57. From very early times, a tiger skin was spread over a seat used for meditation; also over the coronation seat on which a ruler was seated when the rituals were performed; he ascended the throne at the completion of the rituals.
58. The *paryaṅka* or *vīrāsana* is a well known yogic pose; it is frequently depicted in Indian art, Hindu, Buddhist, Jaina, in stone friezes, in sculptures in the round and in frescoes and paintings. It is the typical meditation-pose. It is carved even in one of the Indus seals, that are examples of the earliest Indian art.

The six verses, 45–50 form a continuous whole, an extended passage of description consisting of several clauses formed of compound words, all governed by one verb, *dadarsa* (he saw) in v. 44 which should be taken together with these six verses.

59. The dry seeds of the tree, *Elaeocarpus Ganitrus* used to make rosaries. The seeds known as *Rudrākṣa* (Śiva-beads) are specially associated with *Rudra-Śiva.* The rosary, according to M.R. Kale (Notes, p. 288) in his edition of *Kumārasaṃbhavam,* was hung on one ear, the left ear.
60. See myth; Churning of the Ocean Appendix II. Śiva swallows the deadly poison Pārvatī closes her fingers tightly round his throat to prevent the poison from going down his throat and it clots his throat permanently.
61. Ancient Indian Medicine and psycho-philosophical treatises list five vital breaths, *prāṇas,* that circulate through the body, vitalize it and maintain bodily functions. The text uses the word *maruts* (winds).
62. A fissure on the top of the skull known as *brahma-randhram.* In treatises on *Yoga,* 'the potential all-consciousness of the state of sleep is represented in the form of a radiant serpent called *Kuṇḍalini* or *Vāgdevī*' (p. 76. *The Principal Upaniṣads*: Radhakrishnan). *Yoga* practices are designed to rouse the *Kuṇḍalini* (serpent-power) lying coiled in the loins up by the main channel in the body, the *Suṣumna,* running through the spinal column to the heart where it unites with *prāṇa,* the life-breath in the heart and rises to the top of the skull where a powerful psychic centre is located—the *sahasrāra* or the thousand-petalled lotus (symbolically figured), brilliant, with rays of splendour radiating, which is the spot where enlightenment occurs. The brilliance passes out through the opening at the top of the skull, the *brahma-randhra.* This opening in the microcosm corresponds to the opening in the cosmos formed by the sun in the vault of the sky. This is the mystical experience of enlightenment by which the human is integrated with the divine. The word *jyoti* in the text is the unimaginable brilliance of the life force, the *kuṇḍalini śakti* (serpent power).
63. Once, *Śiva* cut off one of the five heads of Brahmā, the creator, and was cursed to wear the skull on His head.
64. When the moon rose from the waves as the ocean was being churned for the Elixir of Life, Śiva took it and placed it on His top knot of matted hair as a crest jewel.
65. *Manas* signifies mind as well as heart; however it is more often than not used in the latter sense,because in ancient Indian medicine, the heart is viewed as the seat of consciousness.
66. *Samādhi* is profound, single-minded contemplation and the power it has; the state of self-consciousness—self here means the *ātmā* or the inner being.
67. The two ears, eyes, nostrils, the mouth, genitals and the anus. These open out to the external world and the self establishes its relations with the outside through these portals. In *samādhi,* however, these portals are closed, the self withdraws from the external world and turns inwards.
68. The state of Self-contemplation: the self is the *ātmā,* the divine spark within which is part of the Supreme, Brahman, see v. 58, 3–4 where Śiva is described as contemplating His own self.
69. The phrase in the text is *ayugma-netra,* 'one with an unpaired eye' referring to the third eye of *Śiva.*
70. *Smara,* signifying memory, recollection, is the epithet used for Love, Kāma in this verse. *Smara* is love-in-recollection, a possible allusion by Kālidāsa, to Śiva's great love for His wife, Satī, who burned herself.
71. The world of beings on earth is divided into those that stand still and those that move. Himālaya is supreme among the former and therefore the ruler of unmoving forms of life.

72. Verses 52–56 form a cluster, all five verses being governed by a single predicate, viz. 'she appeared' referring to the arrival of Umā at the entrance to Śiva's hermitage.
73. Umā's garment was the colour of pale gold sunshine in the early morning.
74. A contrast is drawn here between Love, armed with flowers pitting himself against the Lord armed with a trident.
75. The Light Eternal (*param jyotiḥ*) that shines within in the consciousness (*antaḥ*) at the moment of self-knowledge and which is the goal of intense contemplation.

    This verse and the series of verses 45–50, describe the *yogi*, *Śiva,* the ascetic, as the paradigm for *yogis*.
76. Śeṣa, the thousand-hooded, world-bearing Serpent.
77. Śiva.
78. *Ibid*.
79. *Ibid*.
80. *Ibid*
81. Bright or light-skinned goddess; i.e. Umā.
82. I use the phrase, 'burnished rose'; for the Sanskrit compound word *tāmraruc,* lit. 'the glow of copper'. Umā's hand, rose-coloured, glows.
83. The Gaṅgā.
84. The word *sammohana* means 'captivating wholly', 'fascinating', 'bewitching'.
85. The *kadaṁba* flowers golden in colour with their pin-cushion-like appearance is a common simile for the golden skin of lovely women thrilling with intense emotion as the hairs bristle and stand on end.
86. Kāma.
87. The bow string had been pulled to its farthest extent, right back to the right ear of the archer and gripped tightly.
88. One of the five positions or stances adopted by skilled archers, depending on the situation.
89. *Maruts* are storm winds; a very appropriate use of this particular word considering the ominousness of what was happening.
90. Kāma—the word employed here is Madana, the Maddener, i.e. one who inflames the passions and makes men mad.
91. Lofty trees.
92. *Bhūtapati,* the word in the text has the meaning of Lord of beings; but *bhūta* also means goblins, imps, ghosts; *Śiva* being associated with the burning grounds as the god of death (as well as life), He has as attendants, goblins, ghosts and other macabre figures.
93. The word *ucciras* has two meanings: one who is most noble and holds his head high conscious of his nobility and noble deeds and is therefore liable to feel disappointments and reversals of fortune even more keenly (see canto 1, verse 52); and, in a literal, physical sense, one who has high peaks.
94. *Śiva;* the epithet *Rudra* employed here for the Lord is appropriate, because *Śiva* (an epithet meaning beneficent, auspicious) is at this point flaming with anger—*Rudra* is a word suggesting flames, fury. In the Vedas Rudras are the storm winds, Maruts, literally the Howlers; and also the many flames of Agni that roar and are red. See n. 11 of canto 2.

Canto 4

1. Note the irony; Rati is pleasure; therefore she has to be instructed to feel pain.
2. The husband is the whole world to a faithful wife, a *pativratā*.
3. *Smara*. It is ironic that Kāma whose other name is the Lord of Memories should forget names. There is also wordplay here on *smara*, a noun and *smarasi*, the second person singular of the verb *smṛ*, 'to remember'.
4. Cf. *Megh.* v. 39.
5. The astringent juice of mango blossoms are believed to clear the throats of the *koels* so that their notes become clearer and more melodious from sipping on them.
6. The song of the *koel* rouses the passion of love in young women and makes them yield to their lovers; sweet talks them into compliance.
7. The funeral decorations.
8. Looking knowingly at Rati, that is.
9. Śiva who wields the bow that destroys evil and ignorance; the *Pināka* is also regarded as Time.
10. Spring or more correctly the Spirit of Spring.
11. Veiled by sorrow as the bright wick is dulled by the swirling smoke when it is put out.
12. Spirit of Spring.
13. Brahmā, the Creator who felt an incestuous passion for his daughter. There are several variants of this basic myth. In some he is punished by Śiva.
14. A variant reading of this verse has the term *dharmacāriṇī* for *dharma*, the Holy Law. *Dharmacāriṇī* is the wife, literally she who follows the path of *dharma* with her husband. According to a purāṇic myth, Sarasvatī, the goddess of wisdom and speech and the Muse, and consort of Brahmā, the creator, interceded with him on behalf of Kāma. But in the reading that is followed here, *Dharma* interceded for his son *Kāma*, Desire.

Canto 5

1. *Samādhi* is a word with many meanings conveying several ideas and in this poem Kālidāsa rings the many changes on this term to express different ideas. The most common sense in which this term is employed is that of singleminded contemplation or deep meditation as here and in 1.59; 3.40. But the word also signifies discipline, that is the basis not only for the undertaking and performance of penance but also for leading a life of piety, as in I.22. This other meaning is also present in the use of the term here. In verses 6 and 18 in this canto, *samādhi* signifies the techniques and disciplinary practices necessary to undertake penance (*tapas*). In 3.50 where Śiva's *yoga* is described in some detail, *samādhi* signifies yogic techniques specially.
2. Refers to Nārada's prophecy in 1.50. But it suggests something more which is stated clearly in 1:37 and 7.28, that Umā would appropriate half of Śiva's body. This is the articulation of the concept of the two-in-one godhead of Śiva-Śakti in mythology. Metaphysically this mythic event articulates the concept of oneness of Being (Śiva) and Becoming (Śakti) through a conjoint image—Śiva-Śakti, *Vāk-Artha* (*Raghuvaṃśam.* 1.1) Silence-Voice as in *Śaiva Siddhanta* thought. Iconographically, the concept is concretized in the image of *ardhanārīśvara*—the figure that is half man and half woman.

3. Śiva and Pārvatī are both associated with the great mountains, the Himālaya and the Vindhya ranges. Pārvatī means mountain-born. Śiva is Girīśa, Lord of the Mountain.
4. Gaurī is literally the Bright One as distinct from Kālī, the Dark One, both aspects of the mother goddess, the benign and horrific aspects of the one goddess.
5. The matted hair piled into a topknot, the bark garment or *valkala*, the belt to hold it made of *muñja* grass (10) form the typical dress of ascetics. The *muñja* is a species of rush and grows ten feet tall in marshy places, swamps, and by the side of streams and rivers. The tall stems are used to make mats and baskets.
6. Two variant readings are known: *kanduka*, meaning ball and *kañcuka*, meaning bodice. Both unfortunately are not very happy images. Sometimes Kālidāsa also nods.
7. Same as *rudrākṣa*; see n. 59, canto 3.
8. The first two quarters translated literally would run:

   Keeping strict vows she pledged
   two with two, to be reclaimed later.

9. Guha, is one of the many epithets of Śiva's emanation, metaphysically speaking, who is regarded in mythology as Śiva's son, so called because he was reared in secret in a cave. Other names of this godhead are: Kumāra, the young god or prince which is part of the title of the poem; Kārtikeya, son of the Kṛttikas, the Pleiades who nursed the young god; Skanda, Subrahmaṇya, Ṣaṇmukha and so on.
10. The coldest month in the year, December 15th to January 15th; it is named after the star or lunar mansion of Puṣya, when the full moon is in conjunction with that star.
11. The tree *Butea Frondosa* or the Flame of the Forest, also known as *Kiṃśuka*; see *Ṛtu*. n. 34.

    A *Brahmacāri* carries a staff made of *palāśa* wood. The reference in this verse is to the first of the four *aśramas* or 'stations' in the life of an individual: *brahmacarya*, the life of a student in which celibacy is strictly enjoined; *gārhasthya*, the householder's life entailing the pursuit of a profession or trade, marriage and bringing up a family; *vānaprastha*, which marks retirement and retreat into the forest; *sannyāsa*, which is the complete abnegation of all worldly ties.
12. The *puruṣārthas: Dharma, Artha, Kāma. Dharma* is righteousness, the performance of good works, following the Holy Law as it is laid out in all its detail; *Artha* signifies the economy, material resources and their management; *Kāma* is Desire and Will in the broadest sense of these terms. The three terms embrace the whole of an individual's life: the ethical and social, the material and economic, and the emotional dimensions. To have an integrated personality, all three aims have to be balanced; that would be the good life.
13. The term in the text is *saptapadīnām;* the word signifies seven steps as well as seven words (*pada* signifies both a step and a word). Seven steps are taken by a bridegroom and his bride round the sacred fire to complete the marriage ceremony. This makes the couple man and wife. This suggestion ought to be noted, noting also the use of the term *Sangatam*, meaning 'coming together', in friendship or in marriage.
14. *Svarga*, the domain of the Immortals, of divinities.
15. *Tripura*, the three cities of gold, silver and iron built for the Titans (*dānavas*) or anti-gods in the sky, in air and on earth, by their architect, Mayā. It was destroyed by the flames from Śiva's third eye at the request of the gods or Immortals. At the metaphysical level of meaning, the Triple City represents the three-fold darkness of human consciousness.

16. See *Megh.* n. 24a.
16a. See note on *Megh.* n. 24a.
17. Ashes symbolize the remainder of the universe after it has been burnt by fire and dissolved by torrential rains at the end of Time. Out of the ashes rises the new universe, pristine and uncorrupted. The sacrality of the ash that is always given to the devotees in temples especially of Śiva and Kumāra is based on this metaphysical and mythic concepts that are part of Śaiva thought and belief.

Canto 6

1. The last quarter of the verse, *sasmāra smaraśāsanaḥ,* in the translation is a fine example of assonance and word play reinforcing each other. *Smara*, literally the god of memories, an epithet for Eros or Kāma, derives from the root *smṛ*, to remember used in the past tense of the predicate, *sasmāra*. The phrase in the text is literally, 'The Chastiser of the god of memories remembered (called to mind)' the sages. The same assonance-word play is seen in 4:8.
2. Arundhatī, wife of Vasiṣṭha, one of the seven sages, is regarded as the model of chastity and wifely devotion. For the Seven Sages see Canto 1, n: 18. Arundhatī is the smallest star in the constellation *Saptarṣi* or Ursa Major, and this star is pointed out to brides after their wedding as a model to be followed.
3. See note for *Megh.* n. 59.
4. *Kalpavṛkṣa*, one of the five trees in Paradise, that bore strings of pearls and jewels and cloths of silk on its branches. (cf. *Megh.* 64: 5,6).
5. Viṣṇu in his third incarnation (*avatāra* or descent into space-time) took the form of an enormous wild boar to rescue Earth who had been hidden deep under the ocean by the Titan, *Hiraṇyākṣa* (Golden-Eye), and bring it up. There is a beautiful representation of this myth in the colossal rock sculpture in the Udayagiri Caves, Bhilsa, Madhya Pradesh (Gupta period?). However, here the poet appears to be referring to the dissolution of the world at the end of time (*pralaya*) when all creation is submerged in the Space-Ocean (the ocean of potentialities, according to Coomaraswamy), to re-emerge at the time of creation. The point made here is, that the Seven Sages are indestructible and the sub-textual allusion to the other myth only adds to the depths of meaning in the image, and to its richness.
6. The Sanskrit term *manoratha*, for wishes, desires, is a very colourful one, a kind of dead metaphor. To bring this out, I have translated the word by its literal meaning, 'the chariots of the mind'.
7. *Brahmayoneḥ*, literally, of the source of Brahmā, the Creator, or Brahma, Creative Power (a Vedic use of the word), or the Vedas.
8. The spheres relating to the great constellations are above those of the planets and their orbits. In the 'western' intellectual tradition of the past, it is known as the sphere of the 'fixed stars', the eighth sphere above the seven planetary spheres as for example, Milton's use of the idea in Paradise Lost.
9. The epithet *virūpākṣa* employed here for Śiva can be explained in a number of ways, as M.R. Kale points out in his note (p. 328). Since only one can be used for a translation of the word, I have taken the following: *vividhāni ravicandrāgnirūpāṇi akṣīṇī yasya,* and rendered the word as I have, treating the Sun, Moon, Fire and the rest as Splendours.
10. See canto 1. n. 53.

11. See *Ṛtu* n. 6.
12. The phrase *vilolavitapāṃśukaiḥ,* could also be understood as: 'with cloths of silk fluttering from their branches'. Similarly in *Megh.* 64:5.
13. *Antaḥpura*; the secluded inner chambers where queens, princesses and high born ladies resided; also known as *śuddhānta,* used in the context.
14. The three upper classes in Indian society, the Brahmins, Kṣatriyas, and Vaiśyas (Scholar-priests, warrior-administrators, merchants) had to undergo the ceremony of initiation, a second birth as it were, to make them full members of the social group.
15. *Rajas*, the passions; the personality is formed of three elements; *sattva-rajas-tamas*-purity-goodness, passion, darkness-ignorance; the last is referred to here.
16. One of the ten mindborn sons of Brahmā, the Creator, sometimes said to have emerged from Brahmā's mouth; also one of the great seers of the *Ṛgveda*, the author of many of the poems of its ninth *Maṇḍala* (Book 9). He is further believed to be the author of a Code of Law and also of a treatise on astronomy.
17. The term in the text is Viṣṇu, meaning All-Pervading, and signifying the sun, which is the manifest form and symbol of the Creative Cosmic Power.
18. See canto 3, n. 76.
19. *Parameṣṭhinaḥ*: a word that is employed to designate many godheads and creative principles. The literal meaning is 'that which stands at the head; principal, highest; and the word has been applied in sectarian ways for Brahmā, Viṣṇu, Śiva. In the Vedas however, as for example in the *Atharva* (*Kālasūktas*), the term signifies the first emanation, Brahma manifest, that is, the creative principle, not as an abstraction but as a visible force within the cosmos.
20. Hari, an epithet for Viṣṇu; in his *avatāra* or incarnation as the dwarf, Vāmana; Viṣṇu-Vāmana asked the noble and magnanimous Bali, king of the Titans for land that could be measured by three of his small paces. Assuming his cosmic form, Viṣṇu-Vāmana compassed the whole earth and the skies with his first two paces and then placed his foot on Bali's head to take the third, pushing the king who never refused a supplicant, into the nether regions. However, as Viṣṇu was originally the descriptive epithet for the All-Pervading, All-encompassing Sun, the three strides are the three phases of the sun travelling through space: dawn to noon to dusk.
21. *Aṣṭa-siddhi*; supernormal powers gained and possessed through austerities and yogic practices. They are: the ability to become minute as an atom; enormous as a mountain; light as air; heavy as rock; the ability to obtain all desires; to control everyone and everything; and be free and uncontrolled oneself; in short to be as a god.
22. The space within the heart which is the corresponding microcosmic form of the macrocosmic form of Space. It is known in metaphysical terminology as *daharākāsa*, the small space (*ākāsa* is space).
23. Another example of assonance and word-play, the verb *vṛṇute*, is derived from the root *vṛ*, to crave for, to ask in marriage, to ask for a boon; and the adjective *varada* meaning giver of boons also derives from the same root.
24. It means what it states, a lotus held in the hand like a toy to play with; to use as a form of non-verbal communication as well somewhat in the manner that a fan was used in western societies of the past by high born ladies in social gatherings.
25. This phrase 'chosen as alms' is interesting in many ways. Umā is not a gift, the term used in the marriage rites where 'giving away' the bride is called *kanyādānam*, gifting the girl. The word alms also suggests one aspect of Śiva, that of the ascetic who begs for alms, as well as the guise in which Śiva approaches Umā in the penance

grove, the guise and garb of a *Brahmacāri*, a celibate who is expected to beg for alms and live on it. The word alms lends a religious tone to Himālaya's response to the sages who are speaking on Śiva's behalf, Śiva the *bhikṣu*, the ascetic, the *yogi*; whereas the use of the word gift is something else, something materialistic.

26. Aṃbikā means mother; literally 'little mother'. Pārvatī is the Mother of the Universe; but not yet in the narrative of the poem.

Canto 7

1. *Jāmitra* (*Jāmi* + *tra*, protecting the bride), the seventh house in the natal chart, calculated from the first house which is that of the *lagna*, or natal sign, the sign rising on the horizon at the moment of birth. The seventh house governs marriage. The natal chart is drawn with twelve houses, each governing one or other aspect of a person's life.
2. One of the five trees of paradise bearing never-fading flowers.
3. This refers either to the hour after sunrise or the time at which the sun passes through the constellation Anurādhā (*Scorpionis*). The word for the sun in the text, is *mitra*, a friend.
4. A very auspicious constellation, forming the stars in Leonis.
5. Mallinātha explains that a bride who is lower in status to the groom is expected to hold an arrow.
6. *Suṣumna*, one of the seven rays of the sun; it supplies light to the moon. The moon's light is a reflected light.
7. Floral designs are painted on the forehead and cheeks of brides, with sandal paste, powdered aloes, orpiment (bile of the cow), and mineral ores such as red arsenic.
8. See Appendix, Myths: The Churning of the Ocean. The Milky Ocean is the Primal Ocean in space containing all the unindividuated seeds of creation, all potential forms in a mass. Churning the ocean is the metaphor for the separation of the different germs that grow into the diverse forms of life.
9. See 5: n. 2.

9a. The faces of the Mothers radiant, lit up by the brilliant arcs of light cut by the swinging ear-rings are likened to lotuses, with clusters of stamens tipped by golden anthers.

10. Brahmā.
11. *Puruṣa*, the Cosmic Person, or Cosmic Man hymned in the great creation poem of the *Ṛgveda* 10.90, out of whose vast body emerges the whole of creation; later identified with Viṣṇu, the middle term in the Trinity.
12. Vṛtra, the demon of drought figured as a huge snake or dragon who holds the rain confined within his belly. Indra, Lord of the *devas*, or Immortals, who is the god of rain and thunder, slays Vṛtra with his *vajra*, the thunderbolt and releases the rain.
13. The traditional greeting for divinity and royalty. *Jaya* means victory. It corresponds to the word 'Hail' in English.
14. See note for *Megh*. 58: 3.
15. An interesting play of ideas. The moon, a symbol of change, is worn by Śiva on His forehead, but He Himself is beyond all change.
16. In the myth of the war of the gods and titans (*devas* and *asuras*), Viṣṇu transforms himself into a rain cloud to bear Śiva into battle. The image therefore in this reading of this verse delineates the descent of Śiva from the region or sphere of the clouds down to the city; the relevant phrase is: *svavāhaciḥnāt avatīrya mārgat*. . . . In a

variant reading—*svabāṇacihnāt* . . . (*bāṇa* is an arrow) that might be translated as 'descended from the path marked out by His arrow'; the reference is to another myth. Śiva shot an arrow at Brahmā who was pursuing his own daughter, Ṣatarūpa inflamed by an incestuous passion for her. The arrow became the star Ārdrā, alpha Orionis, and Brahmā himself who had assumed the form of a deer became the constellation *mṛgaśiras* (deer's head) Orionis. There are other myths relating to Śiva's arrow and the constellations mentioned in this note.

17. Even now women thread flower garlands, tying one end of the thread round one big toe and holding it firmly while knotting each flower with the other end of the thread.
18. Aparṇā, see 5:28:4.
19. The secluded wing of palaces and mansions of the wealthy, reserved for queens, princesses and other high-born ladies.
20. See 1: n. 53.
21. See 3: n. 82.
22. In a clockwise direction, the prescribed mode of circumambulation, keeping the divinities, sun, fire and so on to the right.
23. In the first canto (30), the poet has characterized Umā as one to whom all learning and knowledge came spontaneously, reappeared as it were, because she retained the knowledge that she had gained in her earlier lives. However, here, Kālidāsa refers to two styles of composition, the perfected style for the benefit of Śiva and the other the style 'easily grasped' for Umā.

    Sanskrit drama does use two styles, one composed in Sanskrit, for the high characters in the play and the other in Prakrit, the spoken language for women children, the jester and other low characters. (see introduction, section III, p.13). This is obviously a reference to this dramatic practice. It is still rather surprising in the context of what has been said in the poem about Umā in cantos 3 and 5.

    There is always the possibility of explaining it away as an interpolation; there are a number of interpolated verse in *KS*, though such explanations ought to be avoided, if possible.
24. The final verse strikes the reader (at least this reader and critic), as inappropriate and unnecessary. The thought in the first three lines (first two quarters of the verse in the text) is repeated though in slightly different words, in the first two verses of canto 8. The third and fourth quarters of the verse, lines 6–8 of the translation contain an idea that is surprisingly inappropriate and inelegant, even indecent. To have the *pramathas*, the impish, goblin attendants of Śiva making faces to amuse Umā, to be actually there with the bridal couple in the privacy of their bed-chamber on their first night, is tasteless, grotesque. Did Kālidāsa write this and has the verse come down to us as it is in the recensions? Or, is it someone else's writing; perhaps that of the poet, whoever he was, who is generally believed to have composed cantos 9–17, or 8–17.

    I would suggest that it would be infinitely more satisfying, aesthetically and artistically, if the canto had ended with v. 94.

Canto 8

1. A sacred mountain on which divinities dwelt, which was used as the churning rod when the Immortals and the Titans (*devāsurāḥ*), churned the Milky Ocean to obtain *amṛta*, the elixir of immortality or the sap of life. (See Appendix II Myth of the Churning of the Ocean)

2. At the time of churning of the ocean mentioned above, Viṣṇu helped in keeping the mountain Mandara firm and steady.

   There are two readings of the first quarter of this, verse (23): *padmanābha caraṇāṅkitāśmasu.* and *padmanābhavalayāṅkitāśmasu* (*caraṇa* meaning feet and *valaya*, bracelets).

3. Rāvaṇa who was a devotee of Śiva once went to Mt. Kailāsa to uproot the peak with Śiva and Pārvatī on it, and take it to his own city of Laṅkā to his palace gardens. As the mountain shook violently while Rāvaṇa was trying to uproot it, Pārvatī in terror threw her arms round Śiva's neck. Śiva at once realizing what was going on pressed down on the mountain with his big toe and Rāvaṇa was crushed under the weight of Kailāsa. But, cutting off one of his ten heads, and making it into an instrument, Rāvaṇa began hymning Śiva, who finally lifted His toe off, releasing Rāvaṇa.
4. The pleasure garden of Indra in *svarga* (the world of eternal light).
5. The never-fading flowers of the Mandāra tree that grew in Nandana (see n. 4, above).
6. Śacī or Indrāṇi, the wife of Indra and queen of *svarga*. She was the daughter of the Titan Puloma, whom Indra destroyed, afraid of being cursed by Puloma for having abducted his daughter and married her.
7. Literally 'delighting or intoxicating with fragrances'. The Gandhamādana range is west of Meru, north of Hindukush and perpendicular to it. Water draining from its slopes forms the Oxus (Amu Darya) according to S.M. Ali (Geography of the Purāṇas).
8. A reference to the sages known as Vālakhilyas, 60,000 or 80,000 in number who accompany the sun across the sky guarding his chariot wheels. Foot soldiers, armed used to run beside the chariots of kings and warriors like bodyguards. These sages were tiny, no bigger than a joint of the thumb, and resplendent as sunbeams. I would therefore suggest that this is only a picturesque way of describing the myriads of motes that follow in the wake of the streaming rays of the sun that are more clearly seen when the sun is not dazzling bright.
9. The sun is believed to leave his light with *Agni* (Fire) when he sets. *Agni*, the Creative Fire (Cosmic Energy) has three forms: Fire, Sūrya, the Sun and the lightning.
10. The same as Meru (see canto 1, n.6). As the sun revolves round this mountain which is the centre of the universe, it is spoken of as being concealed behind the mountain when it sets in the evening.
11. *Ketaka/Ketakī* flowers are a brilliant white.
12. Like the man in the moon to describe the dark stain on the moon's surface, Indian myth has a hare in the moon. Hares are therefore closely associated with the moon, their protector. This motif is used cleverly in one of the *Pañcatantra* tales—tale 2. Book III (p. 284, *The Pañcatantra*, Rajan, Penguin Classics 1993). where a hare fools the Elephant King whose herd on their way to a lake called Moon Lake ravaged a community of hares.
13. The lunar month is 27 days and 8 hours approximately. The moon is in conjunction with one of the 27 (28) stars or lunar mansions each day.
14. A variety of feldspar with red and bright yellow iridescence.
15. Pārvatī is a guest on the Gandhamādana Mountains and the divinity of the place comes to offer her the hospitality due to a guest.
16. The morning praise songs known as *suprabhātam*; literally, wishing the god a good morning. Princes and kings are also wakened with music at dawn.
17. *Kinnaras* are celestial singers. The term Kaiśika is interpreted as (a) lute-playing

musicians; (b) a *rāga* or melody suited to dawn. The word also implies gracefulness of singing and of the music.

18. The submarine Fire known as *Aurva* or *Baḍavānala* that blazes deep in the ocean's waters. This is sometimes regarded as a fourth form of *Agni* (Fire), referred to in n. 9.

Canto 9–17

1. The World of light where the Devas, the Luminous ones, dwell.
2. See note 1
3. Final Release—salvation.
4. Lakṣmī
5. *Devas*—Literally, Shining Beings, Luminous Beings; they are the Dwellers in Light, in *Svarga*, Immortals.
6. See note 5
7. One of the names of Kumāra; literally it means 'born of the Krittikas'.
8. The Sanskrit term is Śakti, a special weapon activated by a *mantra.*
9. Victorious.

MEGHADŪTAM

1. *Yakṣas* are pre-Brahmanic divinities of the ancient people of the country, replaced by Vedic and Puranic gods and fitted into the pantheon in subordinate positions; originally forces of nature and indwelling spirits of trees and pools they were associated with fertility and plenitude. They were worshipped as givers of life and riches. Kubera was their overlord, lord of all the earth's treasures; later assigned the position of regent of the north. Śiva himself probably a pre-Vedic deity is invoked as 'the lord in a *yakṣa*-form'. The Purāṇas place Kubera's kingdom in the trans-Himālayan region; he is sovereign over many *yakṣa*-rulers whose cities were wealthy, possessing splendid mansions and beautiful gardens—a kind of Earthly Paradise. For further information on *yakṣas*, see Ānanda Coomaraswamy: *Yakṣas.*
2. Rāma's Hill; Rāma spent part of his exile in this region with his wife Sītā and brother Lakṣmaṇa; it is identified with Ramtek, a few rules north-east of Nagpur, a place of pilgrimage; a great fair is held here in December. Its other name is 'the hill of red rock', so called because the rocks when broken are a bright red in colour, a reference to this is seen in *Megh.*: 104.
3. *Āṣāḍha* the month of June fifteenth to July fifteenth marks the end of summer and the onset of rains. Some of the months in the Indian lunar calendar are named after the constellation in which the moon is present on the day of the full moon e.g. *Āṣāḍha*-Sagittarius. The word Kālidāsa employs in this stanza, viz. *prathama divase* (variant reading '*praśama divase*' meaning 'in the restful close of the season'), which can signify both the first day of *Āṣāḍha* or the auspicious day of the full moon. Four months after this date which might have been the summer solstice at that time would be Hari-Prabodhinī, The Awakening of Viṣṇu referred to in V. 110. This is a very auspicious and sacred day of the year; and this was the special day when the *yakṣa* deeply in love failed in his duties and was cursed to be parted from his beloved for a year.
4. *Prekṣaṇīyam* = *pra* + *īkṣaṇīyam*, to view with eagerness; to see intently: *pra* is a prefix that possesses the senses of 'going forth', as if the eye darts forward; and of intensity and excess. The word expresses the idea of seeing something striking or spectacular, it also suggests the *viewing* of a show, a spectacle or a play; *prekṣāgṛha* is a theatre. The speaker of the poem may therefore be seen presented as a spectator, viewing a canvas that unrolls or a play presented on a stage. This is an interesting way of looking at the poem. (st. 2).
5. The unseen lady of the poem is first referred to as *kāntā* (st. 1), the beloved, a word derived from the root *kam* 'to desire; to be enamoured of'—a sexual undertone is present. Here, another aspect of the lover-beloved, *yakṣa-yakṣī* relationship is indicated by the use of the word *dayitā,* from the root meaning 'to have sympathy, compassion'; companionship rather than a sexual relationship is conveyed.
6. *Santapta*—applies to the burning of the sun's heat and the burning anguish of love and passion. The cloud gives relief from both, by providing shade and by heralding the return of the menfolk to their grieving women. In ancient India men who had to travel on business of various kinds invariably returned home at the onset of the monsoon.

6a. Alakā, Kubera's capital on Mt. Kailāsa. Kubera, Yakṣa overlord is the god of riches, lord of all the earth's treasures and one of the *lokapālas*, regent of the north, a position he is believed to have obtained by practising humility.

7. A respectful way of referring to one's wife or any other lady; no relationship is intended. 'Bhābhī' (brother's wife) is used in Indian languages as a mark of respect for a lady.
8. Mānasa lake, see n. 53a.
8a. The Mekhala Hills, part of the Vindhya Ranges in Central India. *Mekhala* has the meaning of girdle or jewelled belt worn by women.
8b. *Mekhala*—girdle; it is also the name of range of hills in the eastern part of the Vindhya mountains—the Maikal Hills.
9. *Bhavataḥ*—genitive form of the pronoun 'you' or more correctly 'Your Honour', qualifies both *samyogam* (union) and *sneha-vyaktiḥ* (display of affection). A variant of the word in other recensions is *bhavatā,* the instrumental of the pronoun, meaning 'with you': this multivalence allows for more than one reading of the stanza; I give below the alternative rendering of lines 3, 4 of the stanza.

   kāle-kāle bhavati bhavataḥ yasya samyogam etya
   sneha-vyaktiḥ cira-virahajam muñcato bāspam usnam (12)

   Note the wordplay of *bhavati* (becomes) and *bhavataḥ* (Your Honour's).

   Embrace and bid farewell to your loving friend,
   this lofty peak in the Mekhalas, marked
   by the holy feet of the Lord of Raghus
   adored by the world: reuniting with whom
   time and again your affection is displayed
   by the fall of burning tears born of long separation.

   In one case what results from the meeting of cloud and hill, is a shower of warm rain; in the other, the mists and vapours exhaled by the hill during the rains. To the reader of the original Sanskrit text, both meanings are simultaneously present.
10. Literally the 'Perfected Ones'; humans who become semi-divine, through merit and austerities and yogic practices to gain psychic and superhuman powers, known as *Siddhis,* which are eight in number. These are the ability to become minute, airy and light, enormous and powerful; to attain all wishes, assume any shape at will, possess complete control over everone and everything in the universe, possess a completely free will and lordship over the world.
11. Grows in marshy places; a shady tree with long racemes of pink blossoms and bright red clusters of stamens. The petals fall quickly carpeting the ground at the tree base, but the stamens remain on the stems, making it a striking tree.
11a. The colossal elephants that guard the directions of space; the eight points of the compass.
12. Indra's Bow—the rainbow.
12a. The language of coquetry.
12b. The hill where Rāma spent part of his exile. It is in Bundelkhand, Madhya Pradesh.
13. Mango Peak; source of the river Revā or Narmadā, in the eastern Vindhyas; identified with Amarkantak.
14. River Narmadā, rises in the eastern Vindhya ranges and flows right across the peninsula to fall into the Arabian Sea. The ancient port of Bhṛgu-kaccha (Broach) through which most of the extensive trade between India and Rome via Alexandria passed, was situated near the river's mouth.
14a. Sacred ash or *vibhūti*: ashes are the residue of the universe when it is burnt and destroyed completely at the end of a great epoch *(mahākalpa)*, by wind, fire and water. A new universe comes out of the ashes after a long period of quiescence.

Ashes are therefore a symbol of dissolution and creation and is part of the myth and metaphysics of Śiva. In the temples sacred ash is given to the devotees as a symbol of the cosmic process of creation-dissolution-recreation. Temple elephants are decorated with lines of ash and other pigments, red, yellow, black. Seen from a height as in the Arjun Falls in Madhya Pradesh, the grey rocks of granite of the Vindhyas, streaked with silvery streams and branches of rivers that divide and go round the rocks, look like supine elephants basking in the sun.

15. Literally 'Ten Citadels'—the region round modern Bhopal.

15a. Village-shrines *Caityas*, simple shrines, sometimes with a small image within and a flag on its roof were built at the base of ancient trees, especially the sacred fig tree, on a raised platform round the base of the tree trunk. A few flowers, fruit were placed there as an offering to honour the tree-spirit. Passers-by stopped to offer flowers, fruit or a few incense sticks. It is part of the *yakṣa-yakṣī* cults of ancient India. Such shrines can still be seen in central and southern India.

15b. Rose-apple; *Jāmun* in Hindi. A sweet fruit with a big nut; like dark cherries, in size, appearance and taste. One of the seven great continents surrounding the cosmic mountain, Meru, is Jambūdvīpa, in which India is situated.

16. Like Ujjayinī, a great and wealthy city, capital of powerful kingdoms in ancient India; on the trade route from the Imperial capital of Pāṭliputra to the Arabian Sea ports. The Emperor Aśoka's chief queen was the beautiful daughter of a banker of Vidiśā.

17. Vetravatī, the 'River with reeds'; River Betwa near the modern town of Bhilsa not far from Bhopal.

18. The low hills—a long row of low hills lie in the vicinity of Vidiśā near Bhopal. There are caves in these hills. Some with rock-paintings dating from early neolithic times; and also carved reliefs of the Gupta period, fourth-fifth century CE, are present in these caves.

19. Ujjain in Madhya Pradesh; one of the greatest cities in ancient India; It is also one of the earliest human settlements in the country.

20. The Nevaj; rises in the Vindhyas and joins the Chambal.

21. The Kali Sindh, a river in Malwa.

22. A famous king of the sixth century BC, contemporary of the Buddha. He ruled over the Vatsa kingdom, one of the three powerful kingdoms (with Avanti and Magadha); Kosāmbi (Kosam, near Allahabad) was his capital. A cycle of stories gathered round his fame as a hero, celebrating his exploits in love and war. He was also an accomplished musician and his lute was equally famous.

23. The river on which Ujjain is situated, a tributary of the mighty Chambal (Carmaṇvatī) itself one of the large rivers that join the Gaṅgā-Yamunā river-system.

23a. Aromatic Gums. A fragrant and resinous rock that is powdered and burned in a brazier; the smoke dries and perfumes women's hair after it is washed.

24. Preceptor of the Triple World: Three aspects of Śiva are presented in these two lines—'the holy shrine . . . blue of his throat'; the wrathful, Caṇḍeśvara, to punish evil; the preceptor (*guru*) to teach and guide the three worlds out of darkness into light; the Protector of the Triple-World, i.e. the universe. The three worlds are: Earth; the world of light above, of *Devas* (Immortals) or Shining Ones; the world below or the underworld. Śiva transcends these and as pure Being is beyond Time. Caṇḍeśvara 'The Wrathful Lord' is one of the names given to Śiva. It denotes the destructive aspect of Time, for all things are born in Time and are destroyed by Time.

24a. The poison that Śiva swallowed to save the world stayed in his throat when Pārvatī held it tight to prevent it from going down. See myth of the Churning of the Ocean, Appendix II.

25. The Fragrant Stream—an arm of the Śipra on which the celebrated Mahākāla shrine was situated in the past. There is no sign of it at the present day.
26. The name of Śiva in the shrine at Ujjain. Kāla is time; Mahākāla is time projected on to the cosmic plane. It is one of the many epithets of Śiva. The shrine of Mahākāla at Ujjain is of great antiquity; it may have originally been a cave-shrine because at present steps lead down to it. A silver serpent, symbol of Time, circles the *linga.*

26a. Śiva, who holds the trident in his hand.

27. The dance of creation and destruction; the two acts are inseparable; nothing can be formed without something else being destroyed; all creative acts are acts of *transforming.* Everything is born and destroyed in and by Time (*Mahākāla*). The metaphor of the dance is used in Śaiva myth and metaphysics to figure the process of creation-dissolution in an ever-revolving cycle till the end of Time (*kāla*). Dance is movement in space, that is in the temporal order. It is a 'Becoming' in Space an. Time. The forest of uplifted arms in the next line represents the multiplicity of arms to represent the omnipotence and the all-embracing, protective nature of godhead. It can also be the iconic representation of many functions or elements that went into the evolution of a composite figure of divinity.
28. Elephant-hide—when illusion in the form of a fierce, demonic tusker (*gaja-asura*) attacked Śiva's devotees (and in one variant Śiva himself), Śiva ripped the demon's hide in one clean sweep from trunk to tail and flinging the blood-moist hide over his shoulders, danced in ecstasy. The Śiva concept of godhead is a composite one and complex. One of its constituting elements is of an ancient war-god. In myth, *asuras* or demons, represent brute power, energy running rampant, unguided and uncontrolled by any higher principle, which makes it evil and destructive.
29. Bhavāni: 'Becoming' as opposed to 'Being'; the feminine formed from 'Bhava' one of Śiva's epithets. It is one of the many names for Śakti, Śiva's inherent power, that brings the world into existence.
30. Gaṃbhīrā: 'Deep River'; an actual river in Malwa; but it is also a type of woman, a *nāyika,* one who is high-souled and noble, strong-minded, dignified, yet loving; the opposite of the flashy and shallow woman.
31. Skanda, an emanation of Śiva created to fight the forces of darkness and therefore imaged as the son of Śiva and Śakti. Śiva's energy was deposited among the reeds on the banks of the River Gaṅgā and when it assumed the form of a child, the six Pleiades nursed it; it grew in strength and size by the minute, soon assuming command of Indra's hosts, the forces of light to fight against the dark forces.
32. Flower-cloud—the reference is to the daily temple rituals; to lustrations with holy water and adornment of the deity with flowers as well as adoration using flower-offerings.

32a. Śiva: See myth of the Churning of the Ocean Appendix II; and n. 31.

33. Agni: See n. 31 above.
34. The peacock, the gorgeous bird is the mount of Skanda, Śiva's emanation and a war-god; the rainy season is the time of courtship for these beautiful birds and one can hear their shrill mating-calls; therefore peacocks and clouds are closely associated in literature. Peacocks and peacock-eyes are seen on Indus valley pottery, symbolizing the human soul; they are held as sacred in many parts of the country. A natural enmity exists between it and the cobra.

35. Rantideva: A pious monarch, sixth in descent from Bharata, son of Śakuntalā and Duṣyanta; he is said to have performed so many sacrifices that the blood of the victims flowed as a river—the Carmaṇvati or Chambal.
35a. Surabhi: The cow of plenty.
36. Kṛṣṇa, who is dark blue like the night sky; his bow Śārṅga, made of horn, perhaps rhinoceros horn (*śṛṅga*), or coated with poison from a plant called *śṛṅga*.
37. Daśa-pura—'Ten Cities'—modern Mandasor in western Madhya Pradesh; mentioned in the *Mahābhārata* as one of the sixteen great kingdoms—*Mahā-janapada*; it was probably a confederation originally, of ten city-states; at the close of the first millennium BC it was headed by a powerful dynasty of rulers.
38. Brahmāvarta—'The Holy Land': 'the land where the gods came down'; original home of the Vedic people; it lay between 'the divine rivers Sarasvatī and Dṛṣadvatī': the land west of the Jamuna and modern Delhi; in Vedic times the great sacrifices were performed here.
39. Gāṇḍīva—Arjuna's celebrated bow; the swords, clubs, bows, conches of epic heroes had special names; cf. King Arthur's sword, Excalibur.
40. Plough-bearer—Balarāma, elder brother of Kṛṣṇa; he is said to have *drawn* the river Yamuna with his plough; this implies some agricultural and irrigation activities. It refers probably to an ancient legend about a cult-hero who harnessed the river for irrigation, digging canals and nurturing agriculture, and who was later deified for benefiting his people. Balarāma and Kṛṣṇa are the light and dark aspects of godhead. Being associated with wine. Balarāma may also have cultivated the grape-vine.
41. Revatī is Balarāma's beloved wife. An analogy is drawn between the *yakṣa* drinking wine in the company of his beloved wife and Balarāma also enjoying both the wine and the company of Revatī.

hitvā hālām abhimatarasām Revatīlocanāṅkām

(Renouncing the cherished wine marked by (or reflecting) Revatī's eyes

The last word in the line, a compound word is an adjective to the wine and yields more than one meaning. Revati's eyes, amber or wine-coloured are reflected in the wine; the wine itself is amber and therefore the colour of her eyes; it induces the exhilaration that Revati's eyes do in Balarāma; therefore to give up the wine and Revati with it is a great deprivation to Balarāma. Similarly with the *yakṣa* who has had to renounce the company of his beloved and the joys he enjoyed in her company, including drinking wine.

42. Sarasvatī—'Flowing waters'. The river celebrated as most sacred in the Vedas. The Vedic tribes performed their great sacrifices on its banks. The river loses itself in the sands of the Rajasthan desert. Later the word signifies the Śakti or power of Brahmā, the Creator; the name also symbolizes learning, eloquence, wisdom. Sarasvatī becomes the muse of poetry and the patron-deity of the arts. An ancient civilization, the Sārasvata, is believed to have flourished in the Sarasvatī Valley.
42a. Jahnu's daughter: The river Gaṅgā; Jahnu was an angry old sage who drank up the waters of the river Gaṅgā brought down from heaven because the river's flow inundated his sacrificial grounds. Relenting, he released the river through his ear; the river is therefore considered as his offspring or daughter born of his body.
42b. *Kanakhala,* a place close to the gorge at Haradvar where the Gaṅgā rushes down foaming on to the plains.
43. A mythical king—see the Descent of Gaṅgā, Appendix II. Because of his piety and renown, the Ocean formed by the large concourse of water when Gaṅgā descended

on to the earth with all her enormous water power was named after him, as *sāgara*.

44. Crest-jewel: The moon is depicted in iconography as Śiva's crest jewel; it might symbolize the life-sap contained in the bowl of the moon or be a residual feature derived from the iconographical representation of an ancient horned god depicted on Indus seals (second and third millennium BCE) and identified with an early form of Śiva; the bull as Śiva's mount might also be linked to this old conception and representation of deity.

44a. Laughter is white in Sanskrit literature, a poetic convention.

45. Gaurī—'the bright goddess'—one of the names of the mother-goddess, born of the snows of the Himālayas and hence. 'Gaurī'; white, brilliant. Pārvatī is another name meaning 'mountain-born'.

46. Yamunā—river Jamna; one of the three great rivers of the northern Indian plains; it joins the Gaṅgā at Allahabad; the confluence is a very sacred spot, Delhi is situated on the banks of the Yamunā. The waters of the Yamuna are blue and those of the Gaṅgā, white.

47. Triple-eyed Lord—Śiva; the third eye is the eye of inner vision of wisdom. Nandī, the white bull referred to here is the mount of Śiva.

48. Śarabha—A fabulous creature with eight legs; probably a species of large locusts. Locusts breed in dry, desert areas and fly in swarms with the prevailing winds; it is likely that rain and thunder scatter and destroy the hordes.

49. Triple-city—The three cities of gold, silver and iron built for the Titans (anti-gods) in the sky, in the air and on earth; a spark from Śiva's third eye burnt all three to ashes. At a metaphysical level the triple-city represents the three-fold darkness of human consciousness.

50. Dance drama—same as the cosmic dance. *The Burning of the Triple-City* was the first drama said to have been composed by Brahmā, the Creator, and performed on Kailāsa before Śiva and Śakti by Bharata and his troupe.

50a. Niti Pass, migrating birds are said to fly through it in their annual journey between India and Central Asia. Krauñca is a curlew.

51. Bhṛgu-chief—Paraśurāma (Rāma, wielding the axe) decimated the Baronage. The legend implies some enmity of Brahmins and Kṣatriyas (warriors). Paraśurāma is believed to have thrown his battle-axe and made the cleft in the mountain.

51a. *Bali*—literally an 'offering'. He was an extraordinarily magnanimous king, who was taken advantage of by Viṣṇu. see Appendix II: Bali and Viṣṇu's Triple Stride.

52. Rāvaṇa—a ten-headed demon king in the epic *Rāmāyaṇa,* ruler of Laṅkā; he abducted Sītā, wife of Rāma and kept her in the Aśoka grove in his palace for a year until Rāma with his brother and a great army of monkeys and bears (obviously tribes of Central India that had monkey and bear totems) fought and killed him. Laṅkā is traditionally identified with the island of Ceylon (Śrī Laṅkā), but strong arguments have been adduced to prove that Rāvaṇa was the monarch of a large and powerful Gond kingdom in Central India (MP). Rāvaṇa was a great devotee of Śiva; he tried to uproot Mt. Kailāsa with Śiva and Pārvatī on it, and carry it away and fix it in his own gardens, so as to have the sacred presence always close to him and for him alone. When the peak shook from his efforts to uproot it, Pārvatī was frightened; the Lord pressed it down with one big toe to steady it, crushing the intruder who cried for mercy. Repenting, Rāvaṇa cut off one of his ten heads and, hymned the Supreme power, using the neck and head as a stringed instrument—a drone, in fact—to accompany his singing.

53. Śiva, here called *Tryambaka,* i.e. *tri-ambaka. Ambaka* has 3 meanings, therefore the word has 3 meanings: Triple-Eyed; Śiva's third eye is the inner eye of wisdom; Parent of the Triple world (*ambaka* = parent): the Lord who utters the triple sound of the primal word *Auṃ* (*Oṃ*), Śiva is called *Oṃkāranātha,* the Lord whose form is *Oṃ*. Literally Good, Beneficent, Auspicious. In Puranic mythology, Śiva is defined as one of the Trinity; its destructive aspect; but in Saivism or *Śiva-ism* which in its earliest form is perhaps the earliest of the religions in the country, Śiva is the Supreme Being, the Absolute One; and Śakti, its inherent power. It should be remembered that the many names given to the divine are attributes of the unitive godhead or descriptive of its myriad functions; they are not separate gods.

53a. Mānasa—'mind-born'; the sacred lake in the Kailāsa range; haunt of wild geese, swans and flamingos that have their breeding grounds in that region. Both Kailāsa and Mānasa being in Tibet are now in Chinese territory.

54. The term used here for lightning is Kuliśa meaning both Indra's bolt and a diamond both hard, sharp, bright. In the latter meaning we can read the line as saying that the sharp bright points of diamond bracelets worn by celestial maidens prick the cloud to make the water jet out—this is a little far fetched.

55. The celestial elephant, spotlessly white; Indra's mount. See myth of the Churning of the Ocean—Appendix II.

56. (Sanskrit: *Kalpavṛkṣa*) the wish-granting tree that grows in Paradise. In later myths; i.e. in the Puranic mythology five trees are described as growing in Nandana, Indra's special grove in Paradise; the bowl containing ambrosia (*Amṛta*), the drink of Immortality, was set at the base of the Tree of Paradise, on its roots; the *Kalpavṛkṣa* is the original of the Tree of Life; the bowl of *amṛta* was guarded by a serpent, while an archer sat hid in the branches of the tree with his arrow fixed to shoot at anyone trying to steal it. The sun in the form of a golden falcon, stole the bowl, brought it down to earth in a golden boat and placed it on Mūjavat, the twin peak of Kailāsa. Through a mythic labyrinth to which I have as yet not found the clue, the bowl in later literature becomes the moon which is also known as Soma; the ancients believed that the life-sap (*Soma*) dripped from the moon on plants at night and from there entered animals and man. But whereas in Paradise the gods who drank from this ever-replenished bowl were ever-young and immortal, once the ambrosia *fell,* that is descended, into the world, this was not so. The trees in Paradise had jewelled leaves, fruits and flowers.

57. *Śirīṣa:* One of the loveliest of Indian flowering trees; the composite flowers are made up of tiny tubular florets, pale cream or deep rose in colour and crested with fine, long, silky filaments, the effect of which is to make the delicate flowers look like miniature powder puffs.

58. *Jyotiśchāyākuśumaracanāni*—literally, star-reflection-flower-forms. This compound word gives us and suggests the following: star-shaped flowers are strewn as decorations on the terrace floors; star-shaped designs in brilliant gems decorate the terrace floors; flower-shaped stars are reflected on the gem-inlaid terrace floors which sparkle like stars because they are inlaid with gems.

59. Never-fading flowers; one of the five trees in paradise, identified with the rhododendron, native to the Himālayan valleys. The Himālayan and trans-Himālayan valleys are associated with celestial and semi-divine beings: *yakṣa, gandharva, kinnara* and others of that class.

60. Śiva.

61. Kubera, close friend of Śiva. Śiva is associated with *yakṣa* and other semi-divine beings listed in n. 59. He is often adored as the Lord in *yakṣa*-form, *yakṣa-svarūpa*.
62. In Sanskrit the term is *dohada*, the longings of a pregnant woman. Certain trees were believed to yearn for the touch of the jewelled foot of a lovely young woman, or the sprinkling of wine from her mouth; a poetic convention.
63. The peacock.
64. Two of Kubera's treasures (*nidhi*), believed to ward off evil and drawn as auspicious signs on the doors of mansions. The lotus is the symbol of the blossoming world, coming into view, whorl by whorl, petal by petal, of the many orders of creation. The conch is a symbol of sound.
65. The female of the sheldrake or ruddy goose. They mate for life and are a symbol of constancy and connubial love. They were cursed by a sage or by Rāma to be separated. Actually they forage on opposite sides of a stream, constantly calling to each other, as many birds do.
66. Flowers offered daily to household gods at the threshold. The threshold has sacral associations as it protects the home from the dark forces outside waiting to enter.
67. The hair, uncombed, undecorated and twisted into a single braid to signify a woman grieving, separated from her husband. (See also v. 8, 31).
68. In ancient India, men who had to travel on business of various kinds to other lands invariably returned home to their grieving wives at the onset of the rains, to untwist the tangled twisted single braids of the wives, who in joy would again dress their hair, put flowers on it and dress beautifully to welcome their husbands. The rain cloud is therefore a harbinger of hope for women waiting for the husbands to come home to them (see also v. 90).
69. Sītā, daughter of Janaka, king of Videha, whose capital was the city of Mithilā. She was abducted by Rāvaṇa when she lived in exile with her husband Rāma and carried off to Laṅkā, where she remained sorrowing in the Aśoka grove and waiting for Rāma to come and rescue her.
70. Hanumān, the monkey chief who brought Rāma's message of hope to Sītā with his signet ring.
71. The Himālayan cedar.
72. Viṣṇu: 'All-Pervader'; originally a sky god; therefore depicted as blue in colour. Viṣṇu, in the earliest conception is a solar deity, the sun that pervades the universe with light and heat and strides across the sky, 'the wide-stepping second stride'. Viṣṇu is believed to be immersed in sleep for four months (mid-August to mid-November).

Appendices

Appendix I: Kālidāsa's Dates

To date old texts and ancient writers always poses several problems and in the case of a writer as reticent about himself and his work as Kālidāsa it is not possible to provide accurate and definite dates with the scanty facts we possess at this time. To say that the upper limit might be placed at AD 473, the date of the Mandasor inscription by one Vatsabhaṭṭi which reveals some indebtedness to Kālidāsa's poem *Ṛtusaṃhāram* (The seasons) and the lower limit a few centuries lower than that date, is not very helpful.

To speak of a sense of the poet's writings in general as pointing to a particular period in Indian history, viz. the Gupta period, or to a particular king's reign. Chandra Gupta II (AD 375–414) is by no means proof of conclusive evidence. Franklin Edgerton[1] makes a very valid point about the subjectivity underlying such conclusions. We cannot say with any certainty that the opulence and splendour or the peace and prosperity of the Gupta period is reflected in Kālidāsa's work. The manner in which a writer's work relates itself to its age and times is complex. The ominous shadow of the French Revolution with its consequences writ large in history hardly falls on the pages of Jane Austen's novels. Kālidāsa's plays and poems move in many worlds—mythic, epic and historic. Do the descriptions of Alakā reflect the splendour of cities—Ujjayinī. Vidiśa, Pāṭalīputra—of the Gupta period, or of an earlier period? Are they in part allusive of epic descriptions of the splendours of Indraprastha, Ayodhya and Lanka? Raghu's 'conquest of the quarters' (*digvijaya*) may or may not be inspired by Samudra Gupta's similar conquest in the early fourth century AD, but the conquests of the Pāṇḍava brothers as detailed in the *Mahābhārata* are certainly part of the literary consciousness of the poet's epic, *Raghuvaṃśam (Raghu's Dynasty).*

Tradition holds that Kālidāsa was the court-poet of Vikramāditya who ruled at Ujjain; a king who was a great conqueror and hero, a munificent patron of the arts, learned, wise and accomplished; a king who embodied the ideal of kingship in himself; who drove the invading Śakas out of Malwa presumably and established the Vikrama or Samvat (still used) era, in 57 BC to commemorate his victory. Story-cycles have gathered round his name and fame: the *Vetālapancavimśati* (*Twenty-five Tales of the Goblin*). *Vikramāditya-Caritra* (*Life and Stories of Vikramaditya*). Such story-cycles centre round the name of many ancient kings such as the Emperor Aśoka and Udayana, King of the Vatsas, who ruled at Kauśāṃbi during the time of Gautama Buddha, in the sixth century BC. We find a reference to the Udayana-tales in *Meghadūtam* (32). None has been as popular and widespread in the country as the Vikramaditya stories. But historicity has been denied to this Vikramāditya by some scholars who relegate him to the realm of legend and romance.[2]

The name, Vikramāditya which appears to have been the personal name of an ancient king, legendary or historic, occurs frequently in history. Three kings of that name ruled at Ujjayinī at various times; one of the most famous was Yaśodharman of Malwa who defeated the Huns in the sixth century AD. Some rulers assumed the name Vikramāditya, meaning The Sun of Valour, as a title representative of their heroic exploits and achievements as rulers, the most celebrated of these in history being Chandra Gupta II. Other great rulers have been indentified with the Vikramāditya of tradition, such as Gautamīputra Śātakarṇī (first century AD) the greatest of the Śātavahana emperors, who is recorded to have been a very handsome man, a great conqueror and a just and compassionate ruler, the qualities attributed to the traditional Vikramāditya. But this identification has also been disputed. The question is to determine which of the many Vikramādityas that history parades was the patron of Kālidāsa. Who is the real Vikramāditya?

Western Sanskritists after Sir William Jones and beginning with A.B. Keith, favour the identification of the Gupta emperor, Chandra Gupta II, as the Vikramāditya, patron of Kālidāsa, and place the poet accordingly in the fourth-fifth century AD. But this is open to challenge.

Kālidāsa's patron is identified by some scholars[3] as King Vikramāditya, son of Mahendrāditya of the Parmara dynasty ruling at Ujjain in the first millennium BCE. This dynasty belonged to the Mālwas mentioned in history as one of the clans following a republican form of government. It has also been suggested that the description of the *asura* Tāraka and his evil forces in Kālidāsa's long poem *Kumārasaṃbhavam,* is a veiled reference[4] to the invading Śakas[5] who were then in occupation of Sind and were pushing into Mālwa. This would be at the close of the first millennium BC and accord with the first century BC date of 57 BC for the poet and of his association with the Vikramāditya who defeated the Śakas.

Another veiled reference in the epic, *Raghuvaṃśam* is seen as evidence of a first century BC date for the poet. Devabhūti, the last of the Śunga emperors, who was a weak and dissolute monarch, was assassinated in his bed in the dark by a slave girl dressed as his queen; he is taken as the model for Agnivarṇa the last of the rulers with whom Raghu's dynasty came to an ignoble end, who was also a weak, self-indulgent and dissolute monarch as Kālidāsa portrays him in the last canto of the epic; and he also seems to have died in suspicious circumstances though the epic itself speaks of a wasting disease as the cause of his death.[6] This dating places Kālidāsa at the close of the first millennium BC; Devabhūti ascended the throne in 82 BC and was assassinated in 73 BC on the orders of his minister Vasudeva[7] who proclaimed himself emperor establishing the Kaṇva dynasty.

One of the three dates put forward for Kālidāsa places the poet in the second century BC during the period of the Śunga Empire (182–73 BC) and makes him the court-poet of Agnimitra Śunga, son of Puṣyamitra Śunga, the emperor, ruling at Pāṭalīputra, the ancient capital of the northern empires of India. Agnimitra was his father's viceroy for the western part of the empire ruling with the title of Mahārāja at Ujjayinī which had been the second and western capital from Mauryan times. Kālidāsa's first play *Mālavikāgnimitram* is about this monarch and has for its theme the romance between him and Mālavikā, princess of Vidarbha (Berar). Certain historical events that are referred to in the play relate to the two main power struggles of the period: the conflict in the north-western region of the empire with the Bactrian Greeks and the struggle for control over the southern boundaries against the expanding power of the Śātavāhana empire in the south. In the last act of the play certain interesting facts are contained in a letter from the emperor to his son Agnimitra that might have some bearing on the problem of Kālidāsa's dates. Puṣyamitra refers to himself in the letter as Senāpati (Commander-in-chief) writing from 'within the sacred enclosure of the Horse-Sacrifice (*Rajasūya Yajña*), already consecrated for its performance' and invites his son and daughter-in-law to the ceremony requesting them to 'attend without delay' and 'setting aside all feelings of anger' (*vigata-roṣa-cetasaḥ*). Now, this is a curious phrase that indicates that relations were somewhat strained between the emperor and his son. We know form Śunga coins unearthed in this century, that the Śunga emperors used their hereditary title of Senāpati or Senāni even though Puṣyamitra had performed two Horse-Sacrifices to legitimize and signify his accession to the throne at Pāṭalīputra after he had assassinated the last Mauryan emperor in public. The Śungas had been hereditary Commanders-in-chief of the Imperial Mauryan armies. It is somewhat extraordinary that a poet who lived and wrote more than 500 years after the events referred to here, which would be the case if Kālidāsa were to be placed in the fourth-fifth century AD as many Western and some Indian Sanskritists do, should refer to the small details contained in the letter, particularly to the fact of the strained relations between Agnimitra and his father. As Indians of the past are alleged to be sadly lacking in the historical sense (in the Western sense of the term) this would be even more extraordinary. The letter itself is not structurally important in the play, *Mālavikāgnimitram;* it serves to glorify the future emperor, Vasumitra, 'the mighty bowman', son of Agnimitra who had defeated the Greek cavalry that had captured the sacred horse on the banks of the river Sindhu after bitter fighting and brought back that 'king of horses' to his grandfather. Vasumitra is glorified in the passage by a comparison to Aṃśumat, a mythic hero who had also released the sacrificial horse of his grandfather, Sagara, from captivity and brought it back to the sacrificial enclosure. A fallout of Vasumitra's bravery in his fierce encounter with invading Bactrian Greeks is that his mother, Queen Dhāriṇī, is assured of her position as Chief Queen, even though Mālavikā had taken the King's affections away from her. The introduction of the letter into the play therefore seems to suggest a reference to events that were either contemporaneous with the dramatist or within living memory.

Considering these facts, viz. the letter in the last act of the play, *Mālavikāgnimitram;* the striking resemblance between the events in the life and death of Agnivarṇa in the poet's epic poem and the last Śunga emperor, Devabhūti; and the veiled references to the Śakas that are perceived in canto 2 of *Kumārasaṃbhavam,* where the Immortals pray for deliverance from the atrocities of the *asura* Tāraka, it is plausible to argue that Kālidāsa lived and wrote either at the close of the second century BC or the middle of the first century BC.

Claims have been made that the feel and tone of Gupta art of the fourth-fifth century AD indicate that it was contemporaneous with the great poet and dramatist. A strong case can be equally made out that the flowering in stone of the art of the Śunga-Śātavāhana period (second century BC to second century AD) reflects the flowering in the verbal arts of Kālidāsa's poetry. The great friezes of Bharhut and Sanci and the carvings on the great gateways of the *stūpa* in the latter reveal that same juxtaposition of the natural and human worlds seen in Kālidāsa's poetry, rendered in loving detail and exactitude, but stylized (Sanci—north gate, lowest beam).[8] In Bharhut and Sanci and in the very recently unearthed Sanghol sculptures in red sandstone belonging to the Mathura School, are carved *yakṣis* and *vṛkṣikas* (tree-nymphs) standing under flowering trees and vines, embracing them, leaning against them, clasping flowering sprays, kicking a tree with the left foot[9] ornamented with anklets or holding a wine cup in one hand. We see a beautiful example of the former motif in the figure of the *yakṣi* (unfortunately mutilated) who adorns the East Gate bracket at Sanci; she seems to be swinging gracefully in space, kicking the tree (probably an *aśoka*) with her left foot loaded with anklets, and clasping a flowering spray with her left hand, while the right is turned around another blossoming branch hanging down.[10] This sculptured beauty reminds us of the beloved in *Meghadūtam* (74) standing next to the Mandāra tree she had nurtured and whose clusters of blossoms 'bend . . . within reach of her hand', like a son bowing in respect to a mother and offering her flowers as a gift. The latter motif referred to, of lovely women holding a wine cup in their hands, perhaps to sprinkle the *kesara* tree with the wine from their mouths to make it bloom (again the *dohada*-idea, also referred to in the poem, st. 77) is sculpted in the Sanghol figures. A flowering in stone depicting the teeming energies of nature delineated and placed side by side with curving voluptuous figures of women with swelling breasts—a symbol of the maternal—and a smile and inscrutable look on their faces that seem to convey their awareness of their own youth, beauty and power to enchant men, it can be perceived as parallelling the flowering in verse of that age. Kālidāsa often uses the word '*pramadā*' to convey this self-conscious feeling of young women exulting in their youth and beauty. The *yakṣis* and *devatās* of Bhārhut, the Mathura *yakśī*[11] and the Sanghol Figures[12] (also belonging to the Mathura school, though found near Chandigarh) are all *pramadās* with that same inscrutable smile and look as if all lit within with happiness (*Ṛtu.:* 3:20); lovely women aware of and exulting in their own youth and beauty. A close-up of one of these lovely *yakṣis,*[13] is that of Chulakoka. She displays intricate patterns drawn with sandal paste on her cheeks (cf. *Ṛtu:* 6:7). In the Sanghol group we also find a depiction of young women intent on looking at themselves in a mirror and adorning themselves (*Ṛtu:* 4: 13–16) and consciously exulting in their husbands' love for them. A *yakṣa-yakṣi* couple[14] seated in a rocky niche (she is seated on his lap) and a deer? on one side, are chiselled behind a pair of jugate peacocks, with a melting tenderness in their faces as if lost in love for each other. A definite feeling of kinship is seen here of the arts; needless to say, that conclusions of this nature can only be drawn tentatively; we have, as already noted, no definite proof of the poet's dates.

In the final analysis, Kālidāsa's 'dates' are perhaps not that important Fixing them might bring the satisfaction that solving a mathematical problem. which has teased one into deep thought does; but does it add at all to the understanding of the poet's consummate art or enhance in any way the appreciation of his poetry that we should vex our minds with this problem, when the time and thought spent on it could be more profitably used in exploring the complexities of his works? The poet himself has chosen not to reveal anything about his life and work. So we might as well leave it at that.

Names and dates in ancient Indian history can be bewildering; the following note and table should be of some help.

Of the sixteen great kingdoms (*mahā-janapadas*) mentioned in the epic, Magadha with its capital at Rājagṛha (very close to the later capital of Pāṭalīputra—Patna), emerged as the most powerful around 600 BC. The sixth century BC is very important in ancient history, politically and culturally, because it saw not only the rise of Magadha (Bihar) as a power well on its way to becoming an empire, but also the rise of Jainism and Buddhism founded by Mahāvīra and Gautama Buddha as rival religions and systems of thought to Vedic Brahmanism. The empire under Chandragupta Maurya (325–298 BC) and his grandson Aśoka the Great (273–236 BC) included almost all of India, excepting the deep south and extended into Afghanistan and up to Khotan. The capital of the northern empire was at Pāṭalīputra and later, at Ujjayinī; Chandra Gupta II is mentioned as having shifted his capital from Ujjayinī to Ayodhya which was more central. But there seemed to have always been four capitals to facilitate the administration of a far-flung empire with princes of the royal blood in charge and Ujjayinī had been the western capital from very early times.

In the south the Śātavāhana rulers who are believed to have originated in Maharashtra (some historians think that they belonged to Āndhra-deśa and that they are the Āndhras mentioned in late Vedic texts prior to 600 BC), with their capital at Pratiṣṭaṇa (near Aurangabad) gradually spread east consolidating their power in the peninsula, excepting the traditional Chola-country in the deep south. Their kingdom grew into an empire (third century BC–third century AD).

The two powers, as was inevitable, met and clashed along the River Narmada (Kālidāsa's Revā) and the encounter of their armies is referred to in Kālidāsa's *Mālavikāgnimitram* (Act 5).

We can see that the descriptive phrase that Kālidāsa uses with reference to his heroes, 'rulers of the earth' (the world known to the ancients) 'from sea to sea', i.e. the eastern and western oceans bounding India may apply equally to the Śunga, Śātavāhana and Gupta emperors. The mythic rulers in his plays, Purūravas and Duṣyanta actually ruled over a very small part of the country between the rivers Sindhu (Indus) and Sarasvatī-Dṛśadvatī, celebrated in the *Ṛgveda.* Hastinapura across the river from Delhi was founded by Hasti, the king descended from Bharata, son of Duḥṣanta. The line of descent in the lunar dynasty is as follows:

Soma (Moon)
|
Budha (Mercury)
|
Ila
|
Purūravas
|
Āyus
|
Yayāti m. Śarmiṣṭha
|
Puru
|
Duṣyanta m Śakuntala
|
Bharata

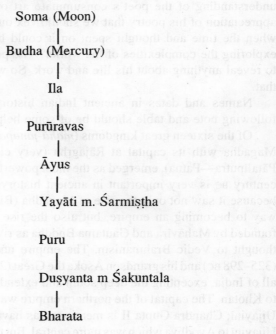

Dates of Imperial Dynasties, fourth century BC to third century AD (as having some bearing on Kālidāsa's dates).

Mauryan Empire—founded by Chandragupta Maurya contemporary of Alexander of Macedon

Chandragupta 324–321 BC

|

Bindusāra

|

Aśoka the Great

|

Bṛhadratha the last Mauryan emperor a weak ruler who could not stop Bactrian Greek incursions into the empire was assassinated in public at a review of the Imperial forces by Puṣyamitra Śuṅga, the commander-in-chief.

Śunga Empire

Puṣyamitra (187–149 BC)	Used the title of Senāni (commander-in-chief) and not of emperor.
Agnimitra (149–141 BC)	Viceroy at Ujjayinī, later succeeded his father; hero of Kālidāsa's play.
Vasumitra (133–128 BC)	Defeated the Greeks.
Devabhūti	The last Śuṅga emperor; assassinated in 72 BC.
Śātavāhana empire	3rd BC to 3rd AD.
Gautamīputra Śātakarṇi	70 BC.

Śaka Rule, followed by Śaiva kings, Bhara Śivas, Nāgas and Śātavāhana rulers in Malwa—'Kālidāsa country', succeeded by the Imperial Guptas 4th–6th centuries:

Imperial Guptas

Samudra Gupta	335–375 AD
Chandra Gupta II (Vikramāditya)	375–414 AD
Kumāra Gupta	415–455 AD

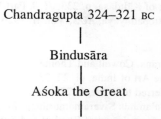

APPENDIX I

1. Intro. to the *Vikramādityacarita*, Harvard Oriental series.
2. D.C. Sircar, *Ancient Malwa and the Vikramāditya Tradition.*
3. Shembavanekar, Date of Kālidāsa, p. 233, *JUB*, Part VI, May 1933.
4. Ksetresachandra Chattopadhyaya, *AUS*, Vol. II, 1926.
5. Sakas or Scythians.
6. See intro. Section IV.
7. *Harṣacarita*, p. 193, trans. Cowell and Thomas.
8. Kramrisch, Stella, The Art of India, pl. 22, 23.
9. Known as *dohada* referred to in *Megh.* 77.
10. Mario Bussagli and Calambus Sivaramamurthi, p. 74. pl. 74; 5,000 Years of the Art of India. See also ch. 4. on the art of Bharhut and Sanchi.
11. Kramrisch, Stella, op. cit., pl. 39.
12. National Museum, New Delhi.
13. Bussagli and Sivaramamuthi, op. cit., pl. 67, p. 64.
14. Kramrisch, Stella, op. cit., pl. 21.

Appendix II: Myths

1. The Descent of the Holy River, Gaṅgā

Gaṅgā is a river goddess, one of the few female divinities celebrated in the *Ṛgveda*. The celestial river, celebrated under the name of Svargaṅgā (*Megh.* 45) flowed originally in space (*ākāśa*) in the form of what we now see and know as The Milky Way in our galaxy. She was brought down to earth by the severe penances of Bhagīratha, great-grandson of the mythic monarch Sagara.

Sagara wishing to attain the title of universal monarch arranged to perform a Horse-Sacrifice. Consecrating the right horse he loosed it to wander free all over the earth, guarded by his sixty thousand sons. The roaming of a sacrificial horse for a year symbolized the sovereignty of a monarch over all the lands the horse wandered unchallenged. Indra, Lord of Heaven, jealous of the power and glory that Sagara would gain by the successful completion of the sacrifice and afraid that the King might seek dominion in heaven itself, carried the horse away and left it to graze in the underworld near the hermitage of Kapila, a mighty sage who having adopted a vow of complete silence was performing austerities.

Searching high and low on earth and not finding the horse, the sixty thousand princes went down into the underworld and seeing Kapila asked if he had seen their father's sacrificial horse. When annoyed by the sage's silence they insulted him, Kapila opened his eyes in anger and burnt them all to ashes. After waiting for several years, the old king sent his eldest grandson Aṃśumat in search; Aṃśumat recovered the horse and brought back news that the ashes of his uncles were lying unconsecrated for want of the proper funeral rites and that only the holy waters of the heavenly river could purify them so that their souls would go to heaven. His son Bhagīratha undertook the task of bringing Gaṅgā to earth, performing hundreds of years of severe penance in the Himālaya mountains, until the goddess, pleased, agreed to come down, if someone could support her fall so that its force would not shatter the earth's surface and destroy all life. Nobody could be found fit to do this except Śiva, who, as the Lord of Beings, possessed the power to support Gaṅgā's descent. Bhagīratha went back to the mountains to perform more austerities, this time to please Śiva. Śiva agreed to bear the river on his head and let her flow down gently on to the earth. But Gaṅgā exulting in her own power fell on Śiva's head with such force that the god, infuriated, bound her up in his matted locks (*Megh.*: 52). Bhagīratha left his kingdom and once more began a series of penances to make Śiva relent, and succeeded. The great god unbound one of his locks to allow part of the river to flow down gently. Chastened, Gaṅgā followed Bhagīratha to where the unconsecrated ashes of his ancestors lay in the underworld in a pile. But that was not the end of Bhagīratha's trials and tribulations. On her way, the river inundated the sacrificial grounds of another irascible sage, Jahnu, who was performing sacrificial rites at that moment, and was swallowed up in one mouthful by him. It was yet another bout of hardship and penance for Bhagīratha. The sage, pleased with his dedication and loyalty to the family, relented and let the river out through one ear. Hence the river was reborn as it were, as the daughter of Jahnu (*Megh.*: 52). Her waters inundated and purified the ashes of Sagara's sixty thousand sons, who were then able to reach heaven (*Megh.*: 52). The huge concourse of waters formed the deep ocean and to honour Sagara, it was named, Sāgara, after him. And to honour that long-suffering and pious monarch, Bhagīratha, Gaṅgā was named, Bhāgīrathi. The name is still used for one of the three Himalayan rivers that join to form the great river Gaṅgā, before it comes bursting through the gorge at Hardvar (the gateway of Hara or Śiva). The other two rivers are known as Mandākini and Alakananda (*Megh.*: 65). Gaṅgā is described as triple-streamed (*Sak*: 7:6) because one stream still flows in heaven, one on earth and the third in the underworld. Mandākinī (softly-flowing) is sometimes the name given to the upper reaches of the river in the Garhwal Himalaya, and sometimes (as the poet perhaps employs it in the long poem *Kumārasaṃbhavam*), for the Svargaṅgā (celestial Gaṅgā) herself.

2. Bali and Viṣṇu's Triple-Stride

Aditi and Diti were sisters, daughters of Dakṣa, both married to Kaśyapa, the Primal Parent. Their sons were for ever fighting for supremacy over the universe. The sons of Aditi were the *devas* or gods, Immortals, with Indra as their overlord; the sons of Diti were *daityas*, Titans or anti-gods. Bali was a famous *daitya* king, who through devotion and penance had defeated Indra in battles, humbled the gods and extended his dominion over the Triple-World. He was virtuous, a just ruler and magnanimous to a fault; no one who came to him asking for alms went away empty-handed. The gods and Indra were disconsolate; Aditi, their mother wept in sorrow at their pitiable state and prayed to Viṣṇu, who out of compassion for her promised to be born as her son, Vāmana (dwarf) to humble Bali and restore their pristine glory to her sons (Śak. 7.27).

Bali once performed a great sacrifice on the banks of the river Narmada and gave wealth in crores, and lands and gifts to any one who came to him pleading need and distress. Vāmana arrived there and asked for some land just sufficient to cover three strides. Bali, though warned by his Preceptor, readily agreed. The dwarf put his foot out, grew in size and covered the whole earth in one stride. Growing enormously in size, he covered the whole of the heavens with a second stride, standing poised with uplifted foot to take the third and final stride. Bali, to keep his word meekly bent down and offered his head, saying 'This is all I have left, O All-Pervading Lord (Viṣṇu).' Viṣṇu-Vāmana put his foot on Bali's bowed head and pushed him down to Pātāla. In later mythological accounts, Pātāla signifies the nether world and Bali, therefore, became the King of the nether world. But, Pātāla was a big port in the estuary of the river Indus which together with Broach at the mouth of the Narmada handled the extensive trade between India and the Mediterranean lands—Alexandria, ·Rome and earlier with Greece. A war of two peoples seems to underlie this mythological tale of two peoples or two great confederations of tribes who fought for the land between the Himālayas and the river Narmada in the peninsula.

A solar myth is also involved in this tale. Viṣṇu—literally, All-Pervader—was originally the sun (*Ṛgveda*). The triple-stride represents the path of the sun across the sky with three clearly marked stations: dawn, noon, sunset. Vāmana, the dwarf, is the early morning sun that grows and waxes in power and pervades the whole universe, except the nether world (the antipodes), which then became Bali's realm or darkness. Obviously this myth belongs to the period in proto-history when the earth was conceived of as flat, prior to the round-earth theory (earth as a sphere) suggested in parts of the *Ṛgveda*.

3. The Churning of the Ocean

In the Beginning, *devas* and *asuras* (or *daityas*), gods and anti-gods strove to obtain *amṛta*, the elixir or immortality (the water of life). Viṣṇu advised them to throw in bits of all the great medicinal herbs into the Milky Ocean (Milky Way in the space-ocean) and churn it, using the cosmic mountain, Mandara as the stick, and Vāsukī, the serpent Time, as the rope. After great toil many wondrous things emerged out of the frothing ocean. First rose Surabhi, the cow of plenty, who granted all wishes to the good; then Varuni, Wine; third, the Tree of Paradise emerged, bearing innumerable, unfading flowers, whose fragrance perfumed the whole world; then rose the *apsaras* in all their beauty. The *apsaras* are twelve in number, but four of them, named *Rambhā, Urvaśī, Menakā, Tilottamā* were the main *apsaras* who figure in Sanskrit literature; who are constantly alluded to. *Apsara* means literally 'born of The Waters'.

The *apsaras* as soon as they rose from the waves were appropriated by Indra, Lord of The Immortals, the *devas*, as his own and became the dancers in his opulent court. They were often employed by Indra to seduce just rulers on earth and sages who performed severe austerities, as *Menakā* was—alluded to by Kālidāsa in his play *Śakuntalā* (Act I, 25–20 ff).

The *apsaras* were followed by the cool-rayed moon that Śiva claimed as his share and placed as a crest jewel on his topknot of matted hair.

Other fabulous objects then rose from the ocean's waves; the spotless white horse *Ucchaiśravas* and the spotless, white elephant, *Airāvata,* both of which Indra, as Chief of the *devas*, took for himself.

The Ocean then spewed out deadly poison that Śiva immediately swallowed to preserve the universe, retaining it in his throat which turned blue-black.

Beauty (*Śrī*) herself, seated on a lotus then rose in glory and was followed by the archetypal physician Dhanvantari holding the bowl containing the Water of Life (*amṛta*) in his hands.

The story continues with the fierce battle for the *amṛta* and the stratagem of Viṣṇu, by which only the *devas* (gods) got to taste the ambrosia and gained immortality, the *daityas* or *asuras* being defeated.

In this myth which is a very central myth in Indian metaphysics and art, *The Waters* are the waters, not of any earthly ocean but of the cosmic ocean in space. The image of the ocean is a metaphor for the sea of germs or seeds of creation that are contained in space which is viewed in ancient Indian cosmography as filled, pervaded, by an almost intangible substance, *ākāśa* (ether), a sort of gaseous substance which provides the building blocks for the creation of the universe with its various and varied forms of being, both moving and unmoving, sentient and insentient. This sea or cosmic ocean contains all the potentialities for form and life in an undifferentiated condition.

The lotus referred to above, supporting *Śrī*—Form, Beauty, Plenitude—is the symbol of the blossoming world that rose out of the still waters of the space-ocean. There are contradictions and inconsistencies in the many versions of the basic myths of origins, because they are layered, with different strands coming out of several ethnocultural sources that reflect the heterogeneity of the people and the cultures that made up India and her civilization in the past. They are all fitted together to form a rich mythological mosaic but the joints sometimes show.

4. *Dakṣa's Sacrifice*

As already noted, there are many versions of the central myths: of origins, and other perennial themes that have always exercised the human imagination. The myths, rising perhaps in different ethno-cultural contexts, crisscross in a bewildering web of interrelated stories, legends all woven round perennial themes, to form a fascinatingly rich fabric. All this material has been fitted over millennia into a pattern that reflects the true mosaic of India's many peoples with their diverse cults and cultures. India's civilization is a product of multiple streams of tradition, both the greater and the lesser traditions. And sometimes there appear some inconsistencies, even some contradictions.

Dakṣa is one of the central figures in mythology, being a primal creator, around whom several varying myths have gathered. I shall not rehearse all of them, but confine myself only to what is relevant in the context of the narrative structure of Kālidāsa's poems.

Dakṣa—'dexterous' was born of Brahmā, the Primal Creator, from his thumb. He is one of the fourteen Prajāpatis, Patriarchs (*Pitṛs*) Ancestors, from whom all forms of creation, human and non-human came into existence. Each of the Prajāpatis presided over a *Kalpa,* an Age of the Cosmos extending over an immeasurably long period of millions of years; each initiated the process of creation at that point in time. At the end of a *Kalpa*, when Time itself came to an end, the Cosmos was totally destroyed by the Great Deluge, *Pralaya* and dissolved into the Primal Waters to emerge again as a fresh world with a new Prajāpati to start creation after a period of quiescence lasting millions of years. In Śaiva mythology, the ashes of the destroyed cosmos remained and out of these the new universe emerged. We are believed to be living in the fourteenth *Kalpa,* initiated millions upon millions of years ago by the Prajāpati, Vaivasvata Manu, the son of the Sun.

Dakṣa had seven daughters, the youngest being Satī, given in marriage to Śiva. Once Dakṣa held a sacrifice, the Great Sacrifice, *Mahāyajña,* to which he invited all the divinities (or gods), to participate in the rite and receive their allotted share; all except one, Śiva, his own son-in-law.

Satī was all excited to attend the sacrifice though her father had not invited her. Though she was strongly dissuaded from attending the sacrifice by Śiva, she insisted on going to her parental home. Humiliated beyond measure because she was not welcomed and her husband, Śiva had been pointedly excluded, Satī abandoned her life through *Yoga-Samādhi.* Śiva's grief and wrath knew no bounds, so terrible was it that he destroyed Dakṣa's sacrifice, and demons that he created out of his anger rampaged and killed and committed general mayhem in the sacrificial hall.

In one variant myth, Dakṣa is killed. In another he is restored to life but given a goat's head instead of his own that had been severed by Śiva's arrow. In a further variant myth, the Sacrifice itself, assumed the form of a deer and flew up in terror into the sky to escape Śiva's arrow. A reference to this arrow and the deer is contained in the poem *Kumārasaṃbhavam* (*KS*. 7:51; and n. 16 explaining the reference).

Śiva wandered over the whole universe carrying Satī's corpse on his shoulders, until Viṣṇu dismembered it with his discus.

5. *Tārakāsura, the Great Titan*

Tāraka was the son of the *dānava*, Vajrāṅga (Adamantine-Limbs), one of the great Titans, son of Kaśyapa, the Patriarch and Primal Ancestor of all forms of being in creation, and his wife Danu.

Vajrāṅga who was extremely pious and virtuous once decided to perform severe austerities to rid himself of all the dark passions, the āsuric elements that exist as part of the personality in all beings. When he returned home after a thousand years, he could not find his wife, the beautiful Varāṅgi. Searching everywhere, he finally found her under a tree, weeping bitterly. And she told her husband how she had been harassed all the time, the thousand years that Vajrāṅga had been away performing penance, by the *devas*, the Immortals or Luminous Ones (gods as they are sometimes referred to), chiefly by the Lord of the Immortals, Indra himself, who had taken terrifying shapes to terrorize her, who had assaulted her and tried to violate her. Cut to the heart, the grieving Vajrāṅga, performed harsh penance once again to Brahmā, the Creator, the Grandfather. Brahmā, pleased with Vajrāṅga, appeared before him and offered him a boon. Vajrāṅga asked that a son be born to him who would surpass Indra and all the *devas*. After twelve months Tāraka was born to Vajrāṅga and his wife.

When he was very young, the brilliant Tāraka, decided to perform severe penance to Brahmā. He was granted a boon by the Grandfather that he would meet his death at the hands of none but a child seven days old. In a variant, Tāraka performed penance to propitiate Śiva who granted him the boon that none but a son of his own (Śiva's) would kill him.

Armed with the boons, Tāraka grew arrogant. He conquered the Triple-World and became master of the universe. Canto 2 of *Kumārasaṃbhavam* contains these details.

At the zenith of Tāraka's power, certain factors that worked in his favour were present in the universe. The *devas* were childless on account of Pārvatī's curse. Śiva was still lamenting the death of his beloved wife, Satī. He had turned away from the world, immersed in *yoga*; and Pārvatī herself, as we know from the poem *Kumārasaṃbhavam* (cantos 3, 5) was doing arduous penance to gain Śiva again as her consort.

The emanation of Śiva became manifest as Kumāra who waxed enormously from the moment of his birth in the clump of reeds by the banks of the river Gaṅgā to become a full-grown warrior on the seventh day after his birth and he fought Tāraka and killed him.

At this point, a brief note is needed to explain the term *asura*. In the *Ṛgveda*, the term *asura* is employed to designate the Supreme godhead; *Varuṇa;* it is also used for Indra, Agni and others as well. Asu + ra, splitting the word to make the meaning clear—*asu* meaning breath, life, existence; the spirit and *ra* being the possessive termination, the word denotes the 'divine', 'spiritual', incorporeal', basically the *living,* implying an entity that has power, life and goodness, a meaning it retains in the old Iranian religion and its sacred texts—e.g. *Ahura (Ahura Mazda* is the mighty divinity). Later its meaning was changed to its opposite and signified an evil spirit. *Asuras* then were ranged against the *devas* to become demonized. The *deva-asura* battle was drawn as the war of the forces of light and those of darkness. This might have some historical basis in a war of opposing tribes or peoples. In war and other confrontational situations, the enemy's gods are always demonized as his culture is denigrated.

Keeping this history of the word in mind, we might explain āsuric as demonic. The word demon itself has changed its meaning in English, from the Greek-derived *daemon* (*daimon*) meaning an attendant spirit or guardian spirit, to the current pejorative sense of the words, demon, demonic.

Appendix III: Interpolated Stanzas

The following verses, not included in the Bharata Mallika text of *Meghadūtam*, are found in Mallinātha's text:

1

Countless pearl-garlands
with lustrous gems flashing at the centres,
conches, mother-of-pearl and coral branches,
emeralds green as young grass
with fiery rays of light shooting up, lie
spread out for sale in Ujjayinī's marts.
Seeing, one wonders if the oceans lie
bereft of all its treasures save their waters.

2

Here, in this city,
the Vatsa-monarch carried off
King Pradyota's beloved daughter:
and here, in this very spot
stood that same king's grove
of golden palm-trees:
here too, his elephant, proud Nalagiri
crazed with frenzy
tore up
its strong tying-post
to run wild—
thus recounting old tales
skilful story-tellers entertain their visiting kin.

Mallinātha places these two stanzas after st. 33; the verses that follow are part of his *Uttaramegham*, the Alakā-section of the poem and he places them after st. 68. These six stanzas, part of the Alakā-section of *Meghadūtam* are not found in all recensions; some old commentators considered some or all of them, interpolations.

1

Where the hum of intoxicated honey-bees
fill the ever-blossoming trees;
Where rows of wild-geese like jewelled girdles stretch
across pools ever full of lotus-blooms;
where garden-peacocks whose trains ever gleam
resplendent, raise their necks up to call:
where evenings are beautiful, always bright
with moonlight keeping darkness at bay.

2

Where tears are shed only from an excess of joy,
and no other cause; where pain is caused
only by the God of Love's arrows of flowers,
easily assuaged by union with the beloved;
where parting comes only through lovers' little quarrels:
Indeed! Do the lords of wealth know
of no other time of life than youth?

3

Where maidens sought for as brides by gods
and waited upon by breezes cooled
by Mandākinī's waters, shaded from the heat
by Mandāra-trees growing on her banks,
play hide-and-seek with gems held tight in fists
thrust deep into her golden sands.

4

Where yakṣas with inexhaustible treasure-troves
enjoy banquets each day accompanied
by apsaras, choicest courtesans,
in the Gardens of Light in Alakā's outskirts,
while kinnaras sing of the glories of the Lord of Wealth
in high, sweet voices.

5

An array of richly-dyed cloths,
wine that expertly instructs lovely eyes in graceful play;

sprays of blossoms bursting out of tender shoots,
varied jewels, decorations,
glowing juices worthy of tinting red
the soles of lotus-feet; all things of adornment
for lovely women are brought forth
solely by the Tree of Paradise.

6

Where horses sleek, glossy, dark, as Palāśa-leaves
rival those that draw the chariot of the sun,
and elephants massive as mountains,
drip streams of rut that pour like your rain;
where the foremost warriors steadfastly face
ten-faced Rāvaṇa in battle fierce—
the scars of their wounds, his gleaming scimitar made
put to shame the lustre of jewels they wear.

A Select Bibliography

Sanskrit Texts and Translations

Atharva Veda. ed. Devichand. Munshiram Manoharlal, Delhi: 1982

Dhvanyāloka. Ānandavardhana. ed. K. Krishnamoorthy (with English translation, Motilal Banarsidass, Delhi: 1980

Harṣacaritam. Bāṇabhaṭṭa Translated Cowell. E.B. and Thomas. F.W.

Kṛṣṇayajurveda, Maitrāyani Saṃhita. ed. Devichand (with English translation) Munshiram Manoharlal, Delhi: 1980

Mahābhārata, The Critical Edition ed. by several scholars. *BORI*

Manu Smṛti, ed. Pt. Hargovinda Sastri with Kulluka Bhatta's comm. Chaukhambha, Varanasi:1982

Meghadūtam, ed. S.K. De. Sahitya Akademi, Delhi: 1957

——, ed. J.B. Chaudhuri with Bharata Mallika's comm. *Subodha Pracyavani series,* Calcutta: 1952

——, ed. Nandargikar, G.R. with Mallinātha's comm. 1893

——, ed. Wilson. H.H. (with a free metrical trans. into English) London: 1843

Nāṭyaśāstra of Bharata Muni, ed. M.M. Batuknath Sharma and M.M. Baldeva Upadhyaya, Chaukhambha, Varanasi: 1929 (*Kashi Sanskrit series*)

——, ed. Ghosh. M. (with English Trans.) chs I-XXVII only *Bibliotheca Indica* No. 272, Calcutta: 1950

Nītisāra of Kamandaki, ed. Rajendra Lala 1861; revised by Sisir Kumar Mitra (with English Trans.) The Asiatic Society, Calcutta: 1964

Rāmāyaṇa of Vālmīki, Critical ed. in several volumes *BORI*: 1966

Ṛgveda ed. Max Mueller *Kashi Sanskrit series* Chaukhamba reprinted Motilal Banarsidass in 2 vols. Delhi: 1965

Ṛtusaṃhāram of Kalidasa, Nirnaya Sagar Press with Maṇirama's comm. Bombay: 1952

——, ed. M.R. Kale with Sastri Venkatacarya Upadhya's comm. Motilal Banarsidass, 2nd ed. Delhi: 1967

Śatapatha Brāḥmaṇa with the commentaries of Sāyaṇa and Harisvāmin. Ganga Vishnu and Srikishandass. Bombay: 1940

The Complete Works of Kalidasa, ed. V.P. Joshi E.J. Brill, Leiden

Kumārasaṃbhavam of Kalidasa, ed. Vasudeva Laxman Sastri Pansikar.

Nirnaya Sagar Press with the commentaries of Mallinātha (cantos 1-8) and Sitaram (cantos 9-17), 12th edition, Bombay: 1935
——, ed. M.R. Kale
——, ed. Dr. Suryakanta. Sahitya Akademi

BOOKS REFERRED TO OR CONSULTED

Ali, S.M.: *The Geography of the Puranas*. Peoples Publishing House, Delhi: 1966

Bhat, G.K.: *Bharata-Nāṭya-Mañjari* (Extracts from the *Nāṭyaśāstra* with Eng. translation; has a long and detailed Introduction) *BORI:* 1975

Bhattacharya, P.K.: *Historical Geography of Madhya Pradesh* from early records. Motilal Banarsidass, Delhi: 1977

Chattopadhyaya, K.C.: *The Date of Kalidasa* (reprint) *AUS*

Coomaraswamy, A.K.: *Yaksas*. Washington: 1931

Cowen, D.V.: *Flowering Trees and Shrubs in India*. Thacker & Co. Bombay: 1950

Dave, K.N.: *Birds in Sanskrit Literature*. Motilal Banarsidass, *Delhi:* 1985

De. S.K. & Dasgupta, S.N.: *History of Classical Sanskrit Literature*. Univ. of Calcutta: 1977

Keith, A.B.: *Sanskrit Drama*. Oxford Univ. Press, 1924

——, : *A History of Sanskrit Literature*. Oxford: 1920

Kosambi, D.D.: *The Culture & Civilization of Ancient India in Historical Outline*

Kramrich, Stella: *The Art of India through the Ages*. Phaidon Press, London

Mario Bussagli: *5000 Years of the Art of India*, Harry N. Abrams, New York & Calambus Sivaramamurti

Mirashi, V.V.: *Sanskrit Studies*. vol I

Panikkar, K.M.: *A Survey of Indian History*. The National Information and Publications Ltd., Bombay: 1947

Radhakrishnan, S: *Indian Philosophy* 2 vols.

Shembavanekar, K.M.: *The Date of Kalidasa* (reprint) *JUB:* 1933

Sircar, D.C.: *Ancient Malwa and the Vikramāditya Tradition,* Munshiram Manoharlal, Delhi

Upadhyaya, B.S.: *India in Kalidasa*. Kitabistan, Allahabad: 1947

Zimmer, H.: *The Art of India and Asia*. (compiled and edited by Joseph Campbell) Bollingen

Suggested reading: Wendy O'Flaherty. *Hindu Myths*. Penguin.

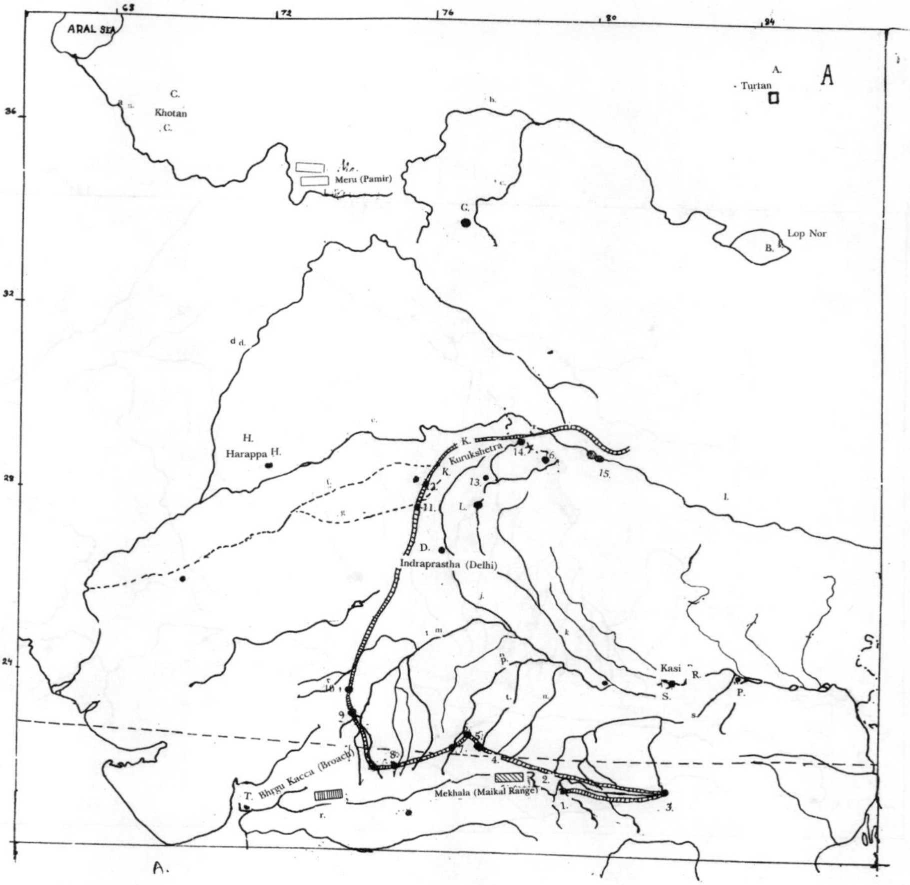

The cloud's route in Meghadūtam

A. Turfan
B. Lop Nor
C. Khotan
D. Indraprastha (Delhi)
K. Kurukshetra
H. Harappa
P. Pataliputra
R. Kasi
S. Prayag
T. Bhṛgu Kacca (Broach)
L. Hastinapura

a. Vankshu (Oxus, modern Amu Darya)
b. Sita (Yarkand)
c. Khotan
d. Sindhu (Indus)
e. Sutudri (Sutlej)
f. Sarasvati—Drshadvati—
dry beds of the rivers
j. Yamuna
k. Ganga
m. Charmanavati (Chambal)
n. Karnavati (Ken)
Vetravati (Betwa)
Reva (Narmada)
Hiranyavyaha (Son)
Lauhitya (Brahmaputra)
Dasarna (Dasan)

Map A Legend

Meru (Pamir)

Mekhala (Maikal Range)

Vindhyapada (Satpura Range)

.... dry bed of Sarasvati-Drshadvati

1. Ramagiri
2. Mekhala (Maikal Hills)
3. Amrakuta (Amarakantak)
4. Vindhyapada (Satpura Range)
5. Dasarna (valley of the R. Dasan)
6. Vidisa (Bhilsa)
7. Nicai (Udayagiri hill and caves)
8. Ujjayini (Ujjain)
9. Devagiri
10. Dasapura (Mandasor)
11. Brahmavarta
12. Kurukshetra
13. Kanakhala (Hardvar-Har ki paudi)
14. Kraunca randhra (Niti Pass)
15. Manasarovar (L. Manasa)
16. Alaka

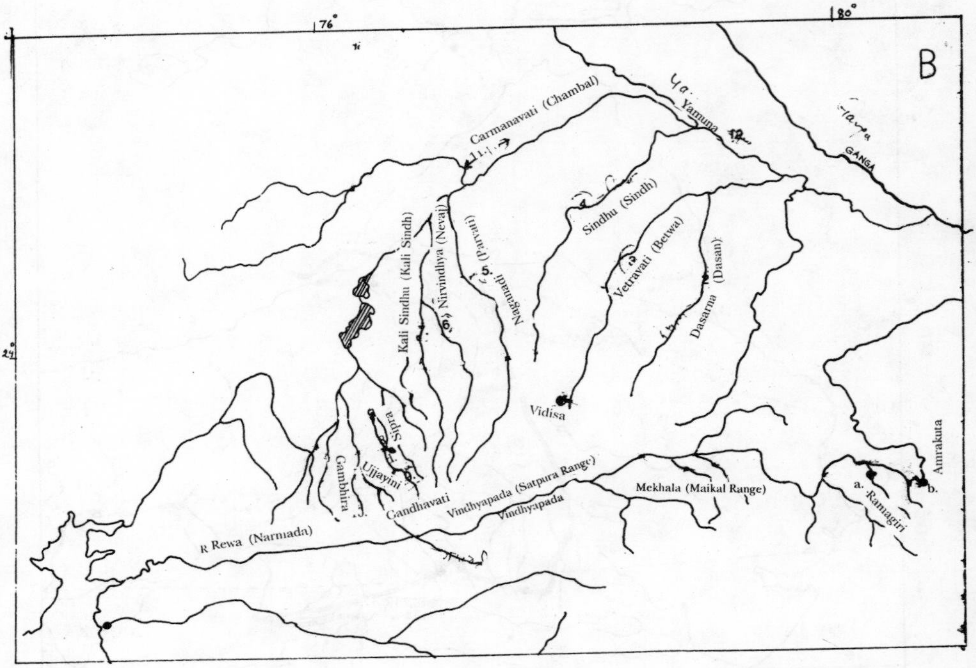

Map B.

Legend :

Rivers in Meghdutam

1. Rewa (Narmada)
2. Dasarna (Dasan)
3. Vetravati (Betwa)
4. Sindhu (Sindh)
5. Naganadi (Parvati)
6. Nirvindhya (Nevaj)
7. Kali Sindhu (Kali Sindh)
8. Sipra
9. Gandhavati
10. Gambhira
11. Carmanavati (Chambal)
12. Yamuna

Related Places :

a. Ramagiri
b. Amrakuta
c. Vidisa
d. Ujjayini

Afterword

A map is appended marking the many places mentioned in the poem, *Meghadūtam*. It charts the course of the raincloud, *Megha*, over a vast stretch of land, from the Maikal Hills (a part of the Vindhyas) in central India to the holy peak of Kailāsa in the Himālayas.

"Listen while I describe the way" (13) says the *yakṣa*, the speaker of the poem to the cloud (and the poet to us).

The poet relates each place of importance, mythic, literary, historical to the event that occurred there and places it in a topographical context, so that each myth and legend or event of historical importance is given a name and a "local habitation" in the geography of the land.

The poem functions at many levels: exploratory, both physical and psychical, the expiatory and redemptive, the celebratory. All these many levels of meaning are firmly grounded on the topography traced in the poem. And the map traces these in a concrete manner which would otherwise remain fuzzy spots in the landscape of the reader's mind.

The rivers of Madhya Pradesh that the poem describes in loving detail, giving each an exquisitely crafted verse (20-43), are *nāyikās*, each expressing one part, one mood of the *nāyikā*, the *yakṣa's* beloved: Revā, (Narmadā, v. 20) Pārvatī (28), Nirvindhyā (30), Sindhu (31), Śiprā (33), Gandhavatī (34-35), Gaṃbhīrā (42-43) all rivers flowing in Malwa and falling into the Carmanvatī (47), which itself joins the Yamunā which a little further down joins the Gaṅgā.

These rivers that rise in the Vindhya-Satpura (*Vindhya pādas*) Range and flow through Malwa are important in the structure of symbolism of the poem. For this reason they are marked separately in an inset.

Pārvatī, the second of the rivers listed (v. 28) is called *Naganadī* (mountain river) in a variant reading; other readings name it as *vananadī* (woodland river), and *navanadī* (the fresh river). *Naganadī* is perhaps the correct reading, because it is a specific name for the Pārvatī (the modern Parvati is a great river that flows into the Chambal in the Alwar district).

Sindhu is the Kali Sindh; Gandhavatī, an arm of the Śiprā (no longer exists); Gaṃbhīrā is a tributary of the Śiprā.

The identification of Rāmagiri needs some explanation. I have placed it in the Maikal Hills (Mekhalas, v, 12) by one of the smaller feeder streams west of Amarkantak. Ramtek with which Rāmagiri is usually identified is near Nagpur. As the cloud is first seen clinging to the east of the hill, as it is asked to bid farewell to this lofty mountain *girdled* by slopes. . ." (*mekhala* is the word for girdle) and further as it is directed to soar high above the "thicket of sap-filled *niculas*" (14) this location for Rāmagiri, situated between two thickly wooded arms of the river rising in the Maikal Hills, is perhaps a more correct identification. Another point of importance is contained in v 16. where the cloud is directed to veer (turn right) back track to Āmrakūṭa, Amarakantak which is definitely in the eastern Maikal Hills and then go north, the direction that the Rewa (Narmada) takes before it turns westward.

I have been unable to locate Devagiri (44-45) correctly. Names must have changed over the centuries.

Errata

Page	Line	For	Read
14	29	cannot 19	canto 19
14	34	lying	laying
43	29	st. 68-115	st. 66-114
49	34	no. 48 in brackets	49
57	1	lirerally	literally
59	26	world	word
70	23	Knowing	knowing
160	53.3.	pinaka-Armed	pinaka-armed
164	77.4	Wielder	wielder
219	34.1	nochalantly	nonchalantly
224	9.1	Began	began
225	15.4	Agni's Divine Fire	of Agni, Divine Fire
245	39.1	nobles	noble
315	93.1	you	your
328.n.68,69	10	Modelled	modelled
335.n.24		in brackets is for the following note	24b
335	25	p. 22	p. 2
335	38	Ṛtu n.5	Ṛtu n.25
336	49	Megh n.33	Megh n.28
341	31	note 19 Ṛtu	Ṛtu n.32
341	36	n.25	n.30
341	37	n.29 in brackets	Ṛtu n.34
344	89	Maruts are storm winds	Maruts, storm winds;
347	16a.	n.24a	n.28
349	14	Megh.58.3	Megh.n.49
353	n.2	Megh 104	Megh.105
370	6	section IV	section V